CW01086413

Death to Tyrants!

Death to Tyrants!

Ancient Greek Democracy and the Struggle against Tyranny

David A. Teegarden

PRINCETON UNIVERSITY PRESS
Princeton & Oxford

Copyright © 2014 by Princeton University Press

Published by Princeton University Press, 41 William Street, Princeton, New Jersey 08540

In the United Kingdom: Princeton University Press, 6 Oxford Street, Woodstock,
 Oxfordshire OX20 1TW

press.princeton.edu

Jacket Art: Attic stammos. Harmodios and Aristogeiton murder the tyrant Hipparchos.
 ca. 470 B.C., L 515 © Martin von Wagner Museum, University of Würzburg,
 Germany. Photo: P. Neckermann.

Library of Congress Cataloging-in-Publication Data

Teegarden, David Arlo, 1973–
 Death to tyrants! : ancient Greek democracy and the struggle against tyranny / David A.
 Teegarden.
  pages cm
 Includes bibliographical references and index.
 ISBN 978-0-691-15690-3 (hardcover : alk. paper)   1. Tyrannicide (Greek
 law)   2. Greece—History—Age of Tyrants, 7th–6th centuries.   I. Title.
 KL4372.T44 2014
 342.3808′54—dc23   2013015337

British Library Cataloging-in-Publication Data is available

This book has been composed in Minion Pro and Myriad Pro

Printed on acid-free paper ∞

Printed in the United States of America

10 9 8 7 6 5 4 3 2 1

For Paola

Contents

Illustrations

Figures

Tables

Twice in the past quarter century the world watched in amazement as popular uprisings in multiple countries suddenly overthrew seemingly stable authoritarian regimes. Enough time has now passed to conclude that the Eastern European revolutions of 1989 led to the establishment of genuine democracies in several states. The outcome of the (still ongoing) Arab Spring is yet to be determined. But the recent elections in Tunisia and Egypt provide democracy supporters some basis for cautious optimism. At the very least, authoritarianism is in retreat in that part of the world.

These uprisings provoked such widespread amazement because they are difficult to accomplish and thus surprising. This is somewhat ironic, of course: one would initially suppose that, if an overwhelming percentage of the population wanted to overthrow the ruling regime, they would do so. But that obviously is not the case. Authoritarian regimes know that, through intimidation and the control of publicly known information, they can prevent the people from acting together in numbers sufficient enough to pose any real threat. A few brave radicals might protest the regime; but the majority will stay silent out of fear, all the while hoping that their fellow citizens join in the protest. Thus despised regimes maintain their hold on power.

These modern-day examples from Europe and the Arab world suggest that the capacity to effect a large-scale popular uprising, although difficult, is virtually a necessary condition for combating tyranny and preserving democracy. If the majority cannot draw upon their collective strength and impose their will, elites will dominate the state with varying degrees of benevolence or (more likely) malevolence. If the masses learn to work together and take advantage of their numerical superiority, however, the tyrant is helpless. Thus all tyrannical regimes seek to hinder their citizens' efforts to coordinate, while genuinely democratic regimes do the opposite. And history tells us that most often the anti-democratic forces win. But there are two conspicuous exceptions: the modern world and the ancient Greek world.

In this book, I demonstrate that the ancient Athenians invented, and the citizens of many Greek poleis subsequently adopted, an institution that facilitated large-scale, pro-democracy uprisings: tyrant-killing law. This peculiar law type essentially harnessed the dynamics of bandwagoning. It encouraged brave individuals to strike the first public blow against a nondemocratic regime—to "kill a tyrant"—and convinced everybody else that, should he follow the tyrant killer's lead, other individuals would follow. Thus, in the event of a coup, somebody would likely commit a conspicuous act of political defiance and thereby precipitate an ever-growing pro-democracy cascade. It was a simple, yet profound invention. And I will argue that it contributed to the success of democracy in the ancient Greek world.

Democracy ultimately represents a victory of the nonelite masses over the elite and powerful few. But the victory is not "once and for all." I think it is safe to say that there always have been and always will be enemies of democracy: individuals and groups that seek to overthrow the people and hold the reigns of power themselves. The ancient Greeks learned how to combat those forces and thereby helped to ensure the success of democracy for several generations—the world's first democratic age. I suspect that the length and scope of our modern democratic age will likewise depend on how well pro-democrats learn to draw upon their collective strength and combat the modern "tyrannical" threats.

I received a lot of support during the years that I worked on this book. Josiah Ober's advice and encouragement has been crucial; he oversaw this project when it was in its dissertation phase (Princeton 2007) and has been very helpful ever since. The Loeb Classical Library Foundation awarded me a generous fellowship so that I could devote the entire academic year of 2010–11 to research and writing. The Department of History at Cornell University kindly provided me a home for that year as a visiting scholar. At Cornell, I learned a lot about Greek history from my many conversations with Barry Strauss. The University at Buffalo generously granted me a leave for the academic year of 2010–11. My colleagues in the Department of Classics at UB have been very supportive; I would like to thank Martha Malamud in particular. The two anonymous readers of both *Hesperia* (which published in article form what is now chapter 1) and Princeton University Press provided many helpful suggestions for improvement. And finally, my wife Paola. I could not have written this book without her support, good humor, and sage advice. I dedicate it to her.

*ARV*²	J. D. Beazley, *Attic Red-Figure Vase-Painters*, 2nd ed. (Oxford: Clarendon, 1963).
ATL	B. D. Meritt et al., *Documents on the Athenian Tribute Lists*, 4 vols. (Cambridge, Mass.: Harvard University Press, 1939–53).
Austin	M. M. Austin, *The Hellenistic World from Alexander to the Roman Conquest* (Cambridge: Cambridge University Press, 1981).
CIG	A. Boeckh, *Corpus Inscriptionum Graecarum*, 4 vols. (Berlin, 1828–77; repr., Hildesheim: Subsidia Epigraphica, 1977).
DK	H. Diels and W. Kranz, *Die Fragmente der Vorsokratiker*, 6th ed., 3 vols. (Berlin: Weidmann, 1952).
FGrH	F. Jacoby, *Die Fragmente der griechischen Historiker*, 15 vols. (Berlin: Weidmann and Brill, 1923–58).
HD	Phillip Harding, *From the End of the Peloponnesian War to the Battle of Ipsus* (Cambridge: Cambridge University Press, 1985).
I. Ephesos	H. Wankel et al., *Die Inschriften von Ephesos*, 8 vols. (Bonn: Habelt, 1979–84).
I. Erythrai	Helmut Engelmann and Reinhold Merkelbach, *Die Inschriften von Erythrai und Klazomenai*, 2 vols. (Bonn: Habelt, 1972–73).
I. Ilion	Peter Frisch, *Die Inschriften von Ilion*, (Bonn: Habelt, 1975).
I. Labraunda	J. Crampa, *Greek Inscriptions*, in *Labraunda: Swedish Excavations and Researches*, 2 vols. (Lund: Gleerup, 1969–72).
I. Priene	F. Hiller von Gaertringen, *Die Inschriften von Priene* (Berlin: Reimer, 1906).

*IEryth*McCabe	D. F. McCabe and J. V. Brownson, *Erythrai Inscriptions: Texts and Lists* (Princeton, N.J.: Institute for Advanced Study, 1986; online edition at http://epigraphy.packhum .org/inscriptions/.)
IG	*Inscriptiones Graecae* (Berlin: De Gruyter, 1873–).
IJG	R. Dareste, B. Haussoullier, and T. Reinach, *Recueil des inscriptions juridiques grecques: Texte, traduction, commentaire*, 2 vols. (Paris, 1894–1904; repr., Rome: Studia juridica 6, 1965).
IOSPE	B. Latyšev, *Inscriptiones Antiquae Orae Septentrionalis Ponti Euxini Graecae et Latinae*, 3 vols. (St. Petersburg: Petropoli, 1885–1901).
LSJ	*A Greek-English Lexicon*, compiled by Henry George Liddell and Robert Scott, revised and augmented by Sir Henry Stuart Jones, 9th ed., with supplement (Oxford: Clarendon, 1968).
ML	Russell Meiggs and David M. Lewis, *A Selection of Greek Historical Inscriptions to the End of the Fifth Century B.C.* (Oxford: Clarendon, 1988).
OGIS	W. Dittenberger, *Orientis Graeci Inscriptiones Selectae*, 2 vols. (Leipzig, 1903–5; repr., Chicago: Ares, 2001).
RC	C. B. Welles, *Royal Correspondence in the Hellenistic Period: A Study in Greek Epigraphy* (New Haven, 1934; repr., Chicago: Ares, 1974).
RO	P. J. Rhodes and Robin Osborne, *Greek Historical Inscriptions: 404–323 B.C.* (Oxford: Oxford University Press, 2003).
SdA	H. Bengtson and H. H. Schmitt, *Die Staatsverträge des Altertums*, 2 vols. (Munich: C. H. Beck, 1962–69).
SEG	*Supplementum Epigraphicum Graecum* (Leiden: Brill, 1923–).
*Syll.*³	W. Dittenberger, *Sylloge Inscriptionum Graecarum*, 4 vols., 3rd ed. (Leipzig, 1915–24; repr., Chicago: Ares, 1999).
TGR	P. C. Rossetto and G. P. Sartorio, *Teatri greci e romani: alle origini del linguaggio rappresentato* (Rome: Edizioni SEAT, 1994).
Tit. Calymnii	M. Segre, *Tituli Calymnii* (Bergamo: Instituto italiano d'Arti Grafiche, 1952).
Tod	M. N. Tod, *A Selection of Greek Historical Inscriptions*, 2 vols. (Oxford: Clarendon, 1933–48).

Death to Tyrants!

Introduction

A deciding factor for the survival of a democratic regime in an ancient Greek polis was the capability of its supporters to defeat their domestic opponents in an armed confrontation. If they had that capability, pro-democrats (the *dēmos*) would have the power (*kratos*) to impose their will. The polis would thus be governed by a *dēmokratia*. If pro-democrats did not have such capability, however, anti-democrats would take control of the polis and impose their will. The polis then would be governed by either an oligarchy or a tyranny.[1]

Whether or not the pro-democrats of a given polis could defeat their domestic opponents depended largely on the number of men who would mobilize on the pro-democrats' behalf. It is true that, on average, anti-democrats likely had important advantages, such as greater financial resources, superior weaponry and training, important interpersonal connections, and more free time to plot and to plan. Thus one pro-democrat did not necessarily "pack the same punch" as one anti-democrat. Nevertheless, the deciding factor in an armed confrontation almost certainly would come down to numbers: the pro-democrats' chances for victory increasing in more or less direct proportion to the extent of their numerical superiority over their anti-democrat opponents.

---

1 My factional and power-based understanding of the meaning of ancient Greek *dēmokratia* is based on two points. First, *kratos* connotes bodily strength and thus physical domination (see *LSJ* s.v. κράτος). Thucydides, for example, wrote (8.70.1–2) that the Four Hundred ruled *kata kratos*: they had citizens executed, imprisoned, and banished. Second, in addition to referring to the whole citizenry, *dēmos* refers more specifically to the subset of the population that believed that the very poorest citizen should have equal political standing with the very richest citizen. Thus *dēmokratia* was a regime type wherein those who believed that the very poorest citizens should have equal political standing with the very richest are able to physically impose their will on the polis. In support of this conception, note the "Old Oligarch's" direct statement (1.9) about nondemocratic regimes: if "the good" (*hoi chrēstoi*) controlled the city, "the *dēmos* would swiftly fall into slavery." Many of the incidents explored in this book also provide support. On the meaning of ancient Greek *dēmokratia*, see Ober (2006).

This logic is simple, but it could be quite challenging for pro-democrats to mobilize in response to a well-organized coup. The most crucial explanatory dynamic is straightforward: an individual pro-democrat who publicly defended his regime with insufficient support from his fellow pro-democrats would almost certainly be killed. In the event of a coup, therefore, individual pro-democrats likely would give no clear public indication of their actual political preference and would wait for a large number of people to join the fight *before* they thought it safe enough to join. As a result, an insufficient number of pro-democrats would fight in defense of their democracy and the anti-democratic regime would retain power. The pro-democrats would thus have had what I call a "revolutionary coordination problem."

Despite the apparent difficulty involved in mobilizing in defense of a given democracy, democratic regimes flourished in the ancient Greek world during the Classical and early Hellenistic periods. Data culled from Hansen and Nielsen's *Inventory of Archaic and Classical Poleis* supports two crucial points. First, with respect to those cites for which the *Inventory* provides information on regime type, the percentage of cities that experienced a democracy, however briefly, increased over time: 8 percent (6 out of 76 cities) experienced democracy at some point during the second half of the sixth century;[2] 18 percent (16 out of 89) did so in the first half of the fifth century; 40 percent (51 out of 126) did in the second half of the fifth century; 46 percent (54 out of 117) did in the first half of the fourth century; and 46 percent (52 out of 112 cities) did at some point in the second half of the fourth century. Second, the number of geographic regions that contained at least one polis that experienced democracy increased over time: during the second half of the sixth century, there is evidence for democratically governed poleis in five (out of thirty-nine) regions; during the first half of the fifth century the number rises to twelve; in the second half of the fifth century it is twenty-one regions; for the first half of the fourth century it is also twenty-one; and the number of regions rises to twenty-four in the second half of the fourth century. The data, admittedly, are noisy and often problematic. But the trend is clear: the ancient Greek world became increasingly more densely democratic during the Classical and early Hellenistic periods.[3]

In light of the preceding comments, it appears reasonable to suspect that democratic regimes flourished in the ancient Greek world in large part because their supporters developed methods or mechanisms to mobilize en masse in response to coup d'états—to solve the revolutionary coordination problem. That is, admittedly, a simple conclusion. But there would seem to be only three principal objections. And each may be countered.

---

2 Note that both Megara and Herakleia (Pontica) experienced democracy in the first half the sixth century. For democracy outside of Athens, see Robinson (1997 and 2011).

3 See the appendix for a presentation of the data and an explanation of the method.

The first objection is that most democratic regimes survived, in large part, because they did not have motivated domestic opposition. That there were anti-democrats in most cities is obvious—there can be very little doubt about it.[4] But it does not necessarily follow that the anti-democrats in the various cities were sufficiently motivated to overthrow democracies. They might have concluded, for example, that the democratic status quo—despite its injustice (in their minds)—was tolerable. Or perhaps they had been effectively socialized by pro-democracy ideology. They might actually think that democratic governance advances their interests.[5]

This "lack of credible domestic opposition" theory is not particularly persuasive. First, stasis was a common problem for most poleis from the Archaic through the early Hellenistic periods. Hansen and Nielsen's *Inventory* (index 19), for example, records 279 instances of stasis in 122 different poleis. And, as Hansen and Nielsen note (p. 125), those numbers—impressive as they are—do not capture the full extent of the phenomenon. It is thus reasonable to conclude that most regimes, be they democratic, oligarchic, or tyrannical, had motivated domestic opposition.[6] Second, literary passages clearly suggest that, generally speaking, oligarchs in most cities were eager to overthrow the governing democracy. The fifth-century author known as the Old Oligarch, for example, wrote (1.5) that "everywhere on earth the best element (*to beltiston*) is opposed to democracy." And according to Aristotle (*Pol.* 1310a8–12) the oligarchs in some poleis swore, "I will be hostile to the *dēmos* and will plan whatever evil I can against them."[7]

The second objection is that most democratic regimes survived, in large part, because they were propped up by an external power or powers. The logic of this objection is quite simple: (1) if anti-democrats staged a coup, they would be challenged militarily by the outside power that supported the *dēmos*; (2) the combined forces from the outside power and the *dēmos* would likely defeat the anti-democrats in an armed confrontation; (3) the anti-democrats would thus choose not to stage a coup in the first place.

This "external power theory" is intelligible, but its significance should not be overstated. Even the Athenians, a people most willing and able to prop up

---

4 The general presence of anti-democratic forces in democratically governed poleis is certainly implied by Aristotle (*Pol.* 1304b19–1305a36; 1309a15–1310a35). And it is tendentiously asserted by Demosthenes (10.4).

5 Note, for example, Aristotle's suggestion (*Pol.* 1310a5–8) that, in a democracy, political leaders should "pretend to be speaking on behalf of men that are well-to-do."

6 See Hansen and Nielsen (2004: 124–29). The presence of motivated opposition in most poleis is also strongly implied in Aeneas Tacticus's fourth-century work titled *How to Survive Under Siege*. That work focuses heavily on internal antiregime elements. See Whitehead (1990: 25–33).

7 Note too the description—provided by a scholion to Aischines, *Against Timarchos* (DK 88A13)—of the relief on Kritias's tombstone: personified Oligarchia setting fire to personified Dēmokratia. (Kritias was the leader of the so-called Thirty Tyrants who ruthlessly dominated Athens for several months after the Peloponnesian War.)

democracies, were by no means consistent in their interventions: the afore-mentioned Old Oligarch, for example, wrote (3.11) that, in the fifth century, they supported the upper classes in many cities; and we know that they even supported "tyrants" in the fourth century.[8] It would, in fact, stand to reason that, in general, an external power would prop up a given democracy only if it concluded that that democracy's domestic supporters would soon be able to maintain control of the polis by themselves. One might appeal here to the difficulties recently encountered by the United States in its attempt to prop up democracies in Iraq and Afghanistan. For the survival of a given democracy, internal factors are primary and external factors, although important, are generally secondary.

The third objection is that pro-democrats would have "naturally" over-come difficulties of mobilization in defense of their democracy. The best basis for that objection is that most Greek poleis were rather small. And if the citizen population of a given polis was small enough, each citizen might gain knowledge of both the nature and intensity of each of his fellow citizens' po-litical preferences simply from everyday interpersonal interactions. If he knew from such interactions that a majority of them are willing to fight to defend the democracy and that everybody knows that, he likely would as-sume greater risk in defending the democracy too: he would not wait for a large number of other individuals to act before he does because he would trust that a sufficient number of individuals would follow him.

This "natural solution" theory is reasonable, but its applicability should not be overstated. Malcolm Gladwell has suggested that members of a com-munity larger than about 150 active members cannot rely on interpersonal relationships to solve problems that affect the community as a whole.[9] Most poleis (even small ones), however, had several times that number of citi-zens.[10] And mobilizing in response to a coup attempt is particularly danger-ous: a person would not act unless he was fully confident that his fellow citi-zens would risk their lives in defense of the democracy too. One might thus conclude that something "artificial" (i.e., the use of some technology) would have to be created to instill and maintain that trust.

Since the preceding three objections do not fully persuade, it remains rea-sonable to suspect that democratic regimes persisted in the ancient Greek world in large part because their supporters devised means to mobilize en

---

8 Meiggs (1972: 54–55) notes that the Athenians did not always insist that their allies be democratically governed. Individual autocrats in Karia appear in the tribute lists: Meiggs cites *ATL* i. 297 f (Κᾶρες ὦν Τύμνες ἄρχει). For this question, see now Brock (2009) and Robinson (2011: 188–200). The Athenians supported several tyrants in Eretria during the fourth century. See chap-ter 2.

9 Gladwell (2000: chap. 5). Josiah Ober (2008: 84–90) addresses this issue and cites the im-portant literature (including Gladwell).

10 A so-called *Normalpolis* (Ruschenbusch 1985) had a few hundred to several thousand citi-zens and a territory of less than 100 square kilometers.

masse in response to a coup attempt. Some democratic regimes, it is true, might not have had motivated domestic opponents. Some might have been completely propped up by external powers. And the supporters of some democratic regimes might have been able to solve their coordination problems naturally. But, in general, the survival of a given democracy ultimately came down to the capability of domestic supporters to act in its defense. A fundamental question for historians of ancient Greek democracy thus should be, how did pro-democrats in the various democratically governed poleis ensure that they could mobilize in the event of a coup?

This book examines one peculiar, but apparently quite popular, means by which pro-democrats in ancient Greece facilitated large-scale mobilization in defense of their democracy: the promulgation of tyrant-killing legislation—the promulgation, that is, of laws and decrees that explicitly encouraged individuals to "kill a tyrant."

The Athenians promulgated the earliest known tyrant-killing law—called the decree of Demophantos—in June 410, immediately after the democracy, which had been overthrown in the coup of the Four Hundred, had been re-established.[11] That decree required all Athenians to swear an oath both to kill "whoever overthrows the democracy at Athens (ὃς ἂν καταλύσῃ τὴν δημοκρατίαν τὴν Ἀθήνησι) or holds any office while the democracy is overthrown" and to reward anybody who kills such a man. In crafting the language of that oath, however, Demophantos included language found in an old Athenian anti-tyranny law (*Ath. Pol.* 16.10)[12] and made specific reference to Harmodios and Aristogeiton, Athens's two famous tyrannicides. Thus, in addition to a general pledge to kill participants of an anti-democratic coup and to reward anyone who kills such a man, all Athenians pledged both to kill "anyone who aims to rule tyrannically or helps to set up the tyrant" (ἐάν τις τυραννεῖν ἐπαναστῇ ἢ τὸν τύραννον συγκαταστήσῃ) and to treat "just like Harmodios and Aristogeiton" (καθάπερ Ἁρμόδιόν τε καὶ Ἀριστογείτονα) anyone who might die attempting to kill a tyrant.[13]

---

11   There are no known tyrant-killing laws that were promulgated prior to the decree of Demophantos (for a full discussion of which, see chapter 1). The Athenians, as noted immediately below in the introduction, promulgated an anti tyranny law sometime in the Archaic period (*Ath. Pol.* 16.10). But it did not explicitly call for the killing of a tyrant (and, in any case, it was an Athenian law). Also antecedent to the decree of Demophantos is the well-known decree from mid-fifth-century Miletos (*ML* 43): it records the banishment of certain named individuals and explicitly incentives individuals to kill them. But that decree does not mention "tyrants," and the incentives were for the assassination of named individuals, not of potential future revolutionaries.

12   The law reads, ἐάν τινες τυραννεῖν ἐπανιστῶνται [ἐπὶ τυραννίδι] ἢ συγκαθιστῇ τὴν τυραννίδα, ἄτιμον εἶναι καὶ αὐτὸν καὶ γένος (If any persons rise in insurrection in order to govern tyrannically, or if any person assists in establishing the tyranny, he himself and his family shall be without rights).

13   Harmodios and Aristogeiton killed Hipparchos, the brother of the tyrant Hippias, in 514. See the "Oath of Demophantos" section in chapter 1.

Three tyrant-killing laws, promulgated in three different cities, were al-most certainly modeled off of the decree of Demophantos. The Eretrians rati-fied the earliest such law in 341, immediately after the Athenians overthrew a pro-Macedonian "tyranny" in that city and reestablished a democratic re-gime. The Athenians themselves passed another tyrant-killing law, called the law of Eukrates, in the spring of 336, nearly two years after Philip II defeated the Athenian-led coalition at the epoch-making battle of Chaironeia. And the third law comes from Ilion and dates to circa 280. It was likely promul-gated shortly after Seleukos I defeated Lysimachos at the Battle of Kouroupe-dion and consequently assumed control of much of Asia Minor. Each of these laws contains the generic language similar to that found in the decree of Demophantos: a reward is publicly offered to "whoever kills a tyrant" (ὃς δ᾽ ἂν ἀποκτείνηι τὸν τύραννον) and the primary concern articulated is the "overthrow of the democracy" (καταλύειν τὴν δημοκρατίαν).[14]

Inscribed tyrant-killing documents from two additional cities must be considered together with the aforementioned laws. From Eresos we have a dossier of inscribed texts concerning a trial, ordered by Alexander the Great, of two men who ruled Eresos as "tyrants" in 333. Significantly, the Eresians executed those tyrants and did so in accordance to their "law against tyrants" (ὁ νόμος ὁ κατὰ τῶν τυράννων). We do not have that law. But we know that they had one. And the dossier allows us to assess the significance of its ap-plication for the survival of the Eresian democracy. The second city is Eryth-rai, from which we have an inscribed decree of the *dēmos*, dating to the early Hellenistic period, that ordered the repairing and frequent crowning of their statue "of Philites the tyrant killer" (Φιλίτου τοῦ ἀποκτείναντος τὸν τύραννον); during an earlier oligarchy, the oligarchs had desecrated it. The document from Erythrai is not a law, but it publicly encourages tyrannicide and thus contains the defining element of an inscribed tyrant-killing law.[15]

The aforementioned tyrant-killing laws and decrees were thus promul-gated in three distinct periods, each of which was important in the history of ancient Greek democracy. The first period, to which belongs the decree of Demophantos, is late-fifth-century Athens, when the viability of the demo-cratic regime that governed that most important polis was severely threat-ened. Indeed, it is not unreasonable to conclude that the viability of Greek democracy in the post–Peloponnesian War period was largely dependent on the viability of Athens' democracy.[16] The law from Eretria and Athens' law of

14   A full discussion of the Eretrian, Athenian (Eukrates), and Ilian law is found, respectively, in chapters 2, 3, and 6.

15   A full discussion of the texts from Eresos and Erythrai is found, respectively, in chapters 4 and 5.

16   The combination of several factors supports that assertion. First, Sparta—the sole hege-monic power in the Greek world immediately after the Peloponnesian War—sought to establish an oligarchic order in Hellas. See, for example, Diod. Sic. 14.10, 14.13. Second, the Athenian *dunatoi*—

Eukrates, on the other hand, date to the end of the so-called Classical period, when the Athenians and their allies combated the attempts by Philip of Macedon and his supporters to subvert democratic regimes on the Greek mainland. And the final three texts—the dossier from Eresos, the "Philites stele" from Erythrai, and the Ilian tyrant-killing law—date to the early Hellenistic period, when, quite remarkably, Alexander and several of his successors encouraged the democratization of the Greek poleis in the eastern Aegean and western Asia Minor. There is reason to conclude that tyrant-killing legislation was much more popular than the six aforementioned texts might suggest. As we will see in chapter 4, Alexander the Great heavily promoted anti-tyranny and tyrannicide ideology during his conquest of western Asia Minor: he ordered the citizens of various cities to punish the leaders of their pro-Persian faction, whom he specifically referred to as "tyrants"; he issued an anti-tyranny proclamation to the Greek cities in 331, after the battle of Gaugamela; he publicly announced his intention to return to Athens the original statues of Harmodios and Aristogeiton that had been stolen by Xerxes's forces in 479.[17] And, as we will see in the conclusion to chapter 6, there is (often very fragmentary, to be sure) epigraphic evidence from several Asia Minor cities for anti-tyranny or tyrant-killing promulgations that date to the first several decades after Alexander's conquest. Important examples come from Kalymna, Ephesos, Mylasa, Priene, Olbia, and (perhaps) Nisyros. Thus, when one also takes into consideration the inscriptions from Eresos, Erythrai, and Ilion, there is reason to suspect that the use of tyrant-killing legislation was particularly widespread in western Asia Minor during the earlier years of the Hellenistic period.

Another reason to conclude that tyrant-killing legislation was much more popular than it might originally appear is the fact that the literary sources indicate that tyrant killing was praised throughout the Greek world.[18] Au-

---

those in power in Athens after the Spartans defeated the Athenians—also supported an oligarchic order in the Aegean. Note, admittedly with reference to 411, the actions by Athenian anti-democrats to overthrow the *dēmos* and establish oligarchy in various Aegean poleis: Thuc. 8.64.1, 65. Third, it is unlikely that another large polis would have championed democracy, being a model and defender: Syracuse was governed by the "tyrant" Dionysos I (ruled 406–367), and Argos was not a very influential polis at this time. Fourth, democracy had been discredited: Athens, the paradigmatic example of democratic government, (foolishly) invaded Sicily with tragic results, lost the war with oligarchic Sparta, and suffered through a brutal stasis. It is reasonable to suppose, then, that it would take some time before a sufficient number of individuals in a given polis could convince their (non-thetic) citizens to adopt that form of *politeia*.

17   See the conclusion to chapter 4.

18   I am unaware of any overt criticism or problematizing of tyrant killing in ancient Greece on general, theoretical grounds. Aeschylus's *Oresteia*, however, appears to come close: Orestes is clearly depicted as a tyrant killer (e.g., *Cho.* 973), yet he must stand trial and is barely acquitted (*Eum.* 752–753), and the furies, who drove Orestes to become a tyrant killer (i.e., to take the law into his own hands, as it were) are escorted beneath the earth (*Eum.* 1007, 1023) and largely ren-

thors as different as Aristotle (*Pol.* 1267a15–16), Xenophon (*Hier.* 4.5, cf. 6.11), Isokrates (8.143), and Polybios (2.56.15) state that general fact.[19] And there are several particular cases that support such generalities. Xenophon, for example, wrote (*Hell.* 6.4.32) that the assassins of Jason of Pherai were honored in cities specifically because he was a potential tyrant. And the same author wrote (*Hell.* 7.3.10) that, in trial, one of the men involved in the successful conspiracy to kill Euphron, the tyrant of Sikyon, said that he could expect to receive praise for his act of tyrannicide. In addition, the people of Sikyon erected a statue of Aratos (Plut. *Arat.* 14), the famous opponent of tyrants, and, after he died, performed sacrifices annually on the day that he deposed the tyrant Nikokles (Plut. *Arat.* 53). The Achaeans dedicated in Delphi a statue of Philopoimen that depicted him in the act of killing the tyrant Machanidas (Plut. *Phil.* 10.8; cf. *Syll.*[3] 625).[20] And the people of Syracuse buried Timoleon in their agora at public expense and held annual musical and athletic games "because he overthrew the tyrants" (Plut. *Tim.* 39).[21]

Scholars have published important work on each of the known tyrant-killing laws and decrees. The work by epigraphers is particularly helpful. Simply put, as a result of their efforts, historians can both read what is on the extant portions of the stones and be reasonably confident about what was written on the lost portions. Epigraphic work on the dossier from Eresos and the laws from Ilion and Eretria is particularly impressive. Progress also has been made on the historical front. Many of the most important dates have been established, a task much more difficult than it might seem. And analyses of the documents' historical contexts have provided a fine initial orientation for further, more extensive inquiries.

---

dered inoperable in the future. It is possible that the recent and no doubt politically motivated assassination of Ephialtes convinced Aeschylus that unreflective praise of tyrant killing could actually harm the community. In addition, there are examples of certain individuals finding fault with specific anti-tyranny acts. For example, Aratos, a prominent leader of the Achaean League during the second half of the third century, was apparently tried in absentia before the Mantineians and fined for plotting to depose Aristippos, the tyrant of Argos (Plut. *Arat.* 25). And according to Plutarch (*Tim.* 5), some men in Korinth—those who "could not bear to live in a democracy"—were outraged by the assassination of Timophanes, the tyrant of Korinth.

19 Aristotle: "accordingly high honors are awarded to one who kills a tyrant"; Xenophon: "cities heap honors on one who kills a tyrant"; Isokrates: "those who kill [tyrants] receive the highest rewards from their fellow citizens"; Polybios: "the killer of a traitor or tyrant everywhere receives honors and the front seat at festivals."

20 Plutarch writes (*Phil.* 21.5) that, after he died, the citizens of many cities erected statues of Philopoimen and gave him honors.

21 Another interesting indication of the widespread praise for tyrannicide: the people of Messana reportedly brought their children to a theater to witness the torture and execution of their tyrant Hippo (Plut. *Tim.* 34). One should also note that Aeneas Tacticus (10.16–17) apparently advised the public announcing of rewards that would be given to a tyrant killer. This can be taken as an indication of the popularity of tyrant-killing legislation. On the passage in Aeneas Tacticus, see Whitehead (1990: 125) and the note on pp. 58–59 of the Loeb edition.

As solid as the existing scholarship on tyrant-killing legislation is, it is still incomplete. For example, there is no comprehensive work that studies all of the relevant texts: most studies focus on a particular text, citing the others as parallels. The only attempt to study all tyrant-killing documents in a single monograph was published by Friedel in 1937. But two important inscriptions have been discovered since then (the Eretrian law and the law of Eukrates). And Friedel's analysis of the other texts is rather brief. Much more fundamentally, scholars have not yet explained how the promulgation of a tyrant-killing law might actually have helped pro-democrats defend their regime against a coup d'état in practice—the obvious purpose of such legislation. Such an explanation is essential, of course, simply to understand the nature of this peculiar type of legislation. And that understanding might, in turn, provide important insights into both the nature of ancient Greek democracy and the basis of its persistence within the larger Greek world.

As already noted, this book's overarching thesis is that pro-democrats promulgated tyrant-killing legislation in order to facilitate large-scale mobilization in response to an organized coup d'état. That is, it helped individuals work as a group and take advantage of their numerical superiority. I will fully explain the means by which the promulgation of such legislation achieved that end in chapter 1, when we examine the historical and sociopolitical context within which tyrant-killing law was invented in late-fifth-century Athens. But it will be helpful to anticipate the discussion here.

The promulgation of tyrant-killing law facilitated large-scale pro-democracy mobilization by accomplishing two complementary tasks. The first task was to widely publicize the pro-democrats' commitment to defend their democratic regime in the event of a coup d'état. That demonstration of commitment would convince moderately risk-averse individuals that, should they defend the democracy, a sufficient number of individuals would follow them. Those moderately risk-averse individuals would thus require fewer people to act in defense of the democracy *before* they do. Such commitments, however, since they concern actions that are so dangerous, almost certainly would not be fully credible to everybody. But an individual who, before the promulgation of the law, would have required roughly 35 percent of the population to act in defense of the democracy before he thought it safe enough to act, might now—that is, after its promulgation—require only 30 percent of the population to act before he acts. And an individual who would have required 30 percent of the population to act before he did might now require only 25 percent of the population to act first. Again, the reason is that they believe that others will follow them.

The second task was to widely publicize the rewards that would be given to an exceptionally brave individual who struck the first blow in defense of the democracy—to the individual, that is, who "killed a tyrant." Before the promulgation of the law, such an individual might have waited for "one person" to defend the democracy before he thought it safe enough to do so. But, after the law's ratification, he would conclude that the positive, selective incentives made it worth the risk to go first: like the moderately risk-averse individuals, he would believe that a sufficient number of people will follow him. And should such an individual "kill a tyrant," another individual who, after the promulgation of the tyrant-killing law, was waiting for only "one person" to act before he did, would join in the defense of the democracy. And then someone who was waiting for "two people" to act would act, and so on. The first person's act of "tyrannicide" would thus have initiated a pro-democratic revolutionary bandwagon; the pro-democrats would overwhelm their opponents.

The promulgation of tyrant-killing legislation thus, in theory, gave the pro-democrats a credible "second strike" capability. Anti-democrats might still conclude that they could stage a well-coordinated coup, perhaps killing prominent pro-democrats and quickly seizing control of the public space. But those anti-democrats also would have to factor into their calculus of decision the likelihood that pro-democrats, nonetheless, would be able to mobilize in defense of their democracy pursuant to a public act of tyrannicide. If the pro-democrats were able to mobilize (i.e., if the act of tyrannicide initiated a revolutionary bandwagon), the resulting conflict would be between two unequally sized factions: minority anti-democrats and majority democrats.[22] And since anti-democrats would likely lose that battle, they might choose not to defect in the first place. The result of such a successful "unilateral deterrence" scenario would be a stable democracy.[23]

Each of the following six chapters presents a historical and sociopolitical analysis of one tyrant-killing enactment. As would be expected, the chapters exhibit a great deal of variety. The text of the decree of Demophantos and its context, for example, are quite different from the remarkably long law from Hellenistic Ilion. There are, however, three elements that are common to them all.

One common element is the identification of the "tyrannical" threat. It perhaps goes without saying, but pro-democrats promulgated tyrant-killing legislation because they believed that anti-democrats might stage a coup. But why did they feel threatened? Or, perhaps better, what, in particular, were they afraid of? The quantity and quality of evidence available to answer such questions vary from case to case. But, in each instance, it is important to consider both internal and external factors.

---

22   That the number of potential pro-democrats (i.e., the poor) in a given city was greater than the potential number of anti-democrats (i.e., the rich) is asserted and discussed by Aristotle (*Pol.* 1279b11–1280a6).

23   For an extended analysis of unilateral deterrence, see Zagare and Kilgour (2000: 133–66).

Another common element is an explanation of how the promulgation of the law or decree would have addressed the tyrannical threat. Generally speaking, the answer is the same for them all: namely, by facilitating large-scale mobilization in the event of a coup. (And, again, the means by which that end was accomplished is fully described in chapter 1.) But each of the texts is different from the others. Thus the task is to explain how the unique elements or provisions contributed to the workings of the law as a whole. To put it in the form of a question, how would the various unique elements of the law—and thus the law as a whole—alter the behavior of individuals to the advantage of the democratic regime?

A final common element is an assessment of the law or decree's effectiveness. The operative question here is straightforward: Did the promulgation of the law or decree help the pro-democrats maintain control of their polis? That is, no doubt, a difficult question to answer: discerning cause is problematic in general, and there are no sources that assert that a particular tyrant-killing law or decree "worked." But, unless one concludes that the promulgation of tyrant-killing legislation could never contribute to the defense of a democracy, it is worthwhile looking at the evidence in order to determine what sort of circumstantial case can be made.

And, finally, a few minor matters. All three letter dates are BCE. Except when noted otherwise, translations of Greek authors are from the most recent volume of the Loeb Classical Library. And with respect to the English spelling of Greek words, I have not been doctrinaire, but the spelling of any particular word is consistent throughout the book.

The Invention
of Tyrant-Killing
Legislation

The Decree of Demophantos

Introduction

The history of democratic governance in Athens nearly ended in 404. In the spring of that year, the Athenians surrendered to the Spartans, thereby losing both the lengthy Peloponnesian War (431–404) and their naval empire. During the following several months, enterprising anti-democrats diligently worked within their network of conspiratorial clubs in order to overthrow the Athenian democracy and establish a *politeia* inspired by the Spartan system.[1] The conspiracy of the oligarchs culminated in late summer 404, during a notorious meeting of the Athenian assembly wherein the *dēmos*, under strong pressure from the Spartan admiral Lysander, ratified a decree establishing a board of thirty men to "draw up the ancestral laws according to which they would govern" (Xen. *Hell.* 2.3.2).[2] Those thirty men, known to history as the Thirty Tyrants, subsequently dominated the polis. With help from a Spartan garrison, they controlled the council and other magistrates and restricted citizenship to three thousand men; those excluded from citizenship—if not executed—were disarmed and scattered. Athens thus became an oligarchic, Spartan client state.

That democratic rule in Athens did not permanently end in 404 must be attributed in large part to the fact that individuals opposed to the rule of the Thirty Tyrants successfully mobilized to reinstate the recently overthrown democracy. The pro-democracy movement began in the winter of 404/3 when Thrasyboulos and perhaps as few as thirty men set out from Thebes and secured Phyle, a hill approximately twenty kilometers north of the Athenian acropolis.[3] Within a month or so, the rebels' numbers swelled to seven

---

1 The oligarchs' conspiracy: Lys. 12.43–44. The oligarchs' attempt to make Athens's *politeia* similar to Sparta's: Krentz (1982: 57–68).

2 The assembly was compelled to vote to change the *politeia*: *Ath. Pol.* 34.3; Lys. 12.75. Specifically, the assembly ratified the decree of Drakontides (Xen. *Hell.* 2.3.2, 2.3.11; Lys. 12.73; Diod. Sic. 14.3.5). There is some controversy over the content of that decree. But it almost certainly called for the selection of thirty men both to craft new laws and to act as a provisional government until a new, permanent constitution was established. On the decree of Drakontides, see Rhodes (1993: 434–35); Ostwald (1986: 476–78); Krentz (1982: 50).

3 The ancient sources do not agree on the number of men who accompanied Thrasyboulos on

hundred, then to a thousand, then to well over twelve hundred.[4] Eventually, Thrasyboulos had a sufficient number of men and the necessary confidence to march to the Piraeus, where he was joined by the "whole *dēmos*" (*Ath. Pol.* 38.3). The rebels fought two pitched battles in the Piraeus. In the first, the battle of Mounichia, they defeated the Thirty's forces, killing over seventy of their men, including Kritias, that regime's most prominent member (Xen. *Hell.* 2.4.11–22). They fought their second battle against a force led by Pausanias, a Spartan king. The fighting in that battle was particularly fierce, with Thrasyboulos's forces taking most of the casualties: 150 were killed (Xen. *Hell.* 2.4.30–35). Nevertheless, the rebel force's performance convinced the Spartans to withdraw their support from the Thirty and accept democratic rule in Athens: it simply would have been too costly to prop up an oligarchy in the face of an obviously coordinated and motivated majority who opposed it.

The successful mobilization in defense of Athens's democracy is so familiar to students of the city's history that it is easy to overlook just how surprising an accomplishment it actually was. Why, for example, did Thrasyboulos and his thirty-odd supporters think that it was worth taking the risk to launch a direct and conspicuous attack against the Thirty? And why did so many other individuals subsequently follow them? Everybody must have known that the Thirty and their allies would easily crush the rebellion, if the democratic forces remained small. What, then, convinced individuals that, should they join in the movement, a sufficient number of other individuals would follow them and that the rebellion might thus actually succeed? That is a very important question, the answer to which may provide insight into the sociopolitical basis of the remarkable refoundation of the Athenian democracy.

This chapter accounts for the successful mobilization in defense of Athens's democracy. I begin by exploring the collective response by citizens in Athens to the coup of the Four Hundred (411), an experience that taught the Athenians important lessons about mobilization in defense of their democracy. Two significant points emerge from that discussion. First, individuals in

---

his march from Thebes. Numbers range from "not more than 50" (Nep. *Thr.* 2.1) to 70 (Xen. *Hell.* 2.4.2). The other ancient sources (conveniently collected in Krentz [1982: 70–72n4]) are [Arist.] *Rhet. ad Al.* 8 (50 men); Aristid. *Or.* 1.254 Lenz-Behr (just over 50 men) and 43.556 Dindorf (70 men); Paus. 1.29.3 (60 men); Plut. *Mor.* 345d (70 men). Krentz believes that Thrasyboulos left Thebes with 30 men. For a detailed account of the life of Thrasyboulos and his role in Athenian politics, see Buck (1998).

4 The rebels' numbers increasing to 700 men: Xen. *Hell.* 2.4.5; to 1,000 men: Xen. *Hell.* 2.4.10; to well over 1,200 men: Diod. Sic. 14.33.1. The political status of the men at Phyle is a vexed question. For a cogent and persuasive discussion, see Taylor (2002b). Taylor argues that about 60 percent of the men besieged at Phyle were citizens and that about 90 percent of the men at Phyle at the time of the march to the Piraeus were citizens. She accepts important conclusions reached by Raubitschek (1941) and refutes Krentz's conclusion (1982: 83–84) that the vast majority of the men first at Phyle were not Athenian citizens.

Athens did not respond to the coup initially because they had what I call a "revolutionary coordination problem": many wanted to oppose the coup, but, because of the great risk that that involved, each individual waited for others to act before he did. Thus nobody acted. Second, the conspicuous assassination of Phrynichos, a prominent figure in the regime of the Four Hundred, set in motion a "revolutionary bandwagon": that public act of defiance encouraged others to oppose the regime, which, in turn, encouraged yet others to act.[5] As a result, the previously quiescent individuals were able to mobilize en masse against the regime of the Four Hundred.

The second part of this chapter examines the consequence of the fact that all Athenians swore the oath of Demophantos—an oath mandated by the very first decree promulgated by the *dēmos* after they regained control of the city in (probably) June 410. I argue that, by swearing the oath of Demophantos, the Athenians greatly increased the likelihood that, should the Athenian democracy be overthrown once again, pro-democrats would not be paralyzed by a revolutionary coordination problem; instead, somebody would commit a conspicuous act of defiance that would set in motion a revolutionary bandwagon and thus enable a large-scale mobilization in defense of the democracy. This interpretation thus strongly suggests that the Athenians did, in fact, learn about the dynamic of revolutionary action from their experience with the coup of the Four Hundred and thus prepared themselves for similar events in the future. And that leads to the chapter's third and final section wherein I demonstrate that the successful mobilization against the Thirty Tyrants should be attributed, in part, to the fact that all Athenians swore the oath of Demophantos.

The Coup of the Four Hundred

I begin with two questions about the collective response of individuals in Athens to the coup of the Four Hundred. First, why were the citizens then in Athens initially unable to work together in order to oppose the coup? Subsequent events demonstrate that the vast majority of those individuals wanted to do so. And if they all just did what they all wanted to do, they easily would have overwhelmed the Four Hundred. Yet they did nothing, and the oligarchs dominated Athens for four months (roughly June 411–September 411). Second, why were those formerly quiescent individuals eventually able to work together to overthrow the Four Hundred? Something must have radically altered the calculus of decision for each individual and thus the underlying operative macro-dynamic, for when the people rose up, they did so remarkably quickly and the Four Hundred surrendered immediately.

---

5 The concept of the revolutionary bandwagon (a term coined by Kuran [1991: 20]) is discussed in detail below, in the section titled "Mobilization."

In order to answer those two questions, I analyze Thucydides's account of the coup of the Four Hundred in light of a theory of revolutionary action developed by the social scientist Timur Kuran.[6] Thucydides himself offered important sociological analysis to account for the events he described: his emphasis on the paralyzing effect of fear compounded with ignorance, for example, is an important case in point. Kuran's theoretical insights, however, provide the historian even better insight into the underlying causes of significant group action and inaction during that coup. In particular, the theory explains how the behavior of one individual affects the behavior of other individuals and thus the behavior of an entire group. And that, in turn, will help account for the paradoxical acquiescence and sudden resistance to the Four Hundred by the citizens in Athens.[7]

COORDINATION PROBLEM

The movement that eventually overthrew the Athenian democracy originated in the late fall of 412 among influential Athenians stationed with the Athenian fleet on the island of Samos.[8] Thucydides, a primary source for the coup and its accompanying intrigue, wrote that those influential men received a message from Alcibiades, the infamous Athenian then in exile and likely residing with Tissaphernes (the Persian satrap of Sardeis): He desired to return to Athens, he apparently told them, but only if that city were governed by an oligarchy and not the "base democracy" that had exiled him three years earlier. He also hinted at the possibility of securing for Athens the friendship—and thus financial support—of Tissaphernes. The Athenian aristocrats at Samos, who were *already* set on overthrowing the Athenian democracy, then secretly traveled to meet with Alcibiades in person. In that meeting, Alcibiades apparently promised to secure Persian assistance (even that of the king himself) for the Athenian war against the Spartans, but, again, only if Athens was no longer governed democratically. The men, no doubt delighted with the news, then returned (without Alcibiades) to Samos

6   Kuran (1989 and 1991).

7   It is to be noted that the following analysis treats Thucydides's narrative of the coup of the Four Hundred as an acceptably accurate description of actual events. Such an approach might be defended on two complementary grounds: the events described are quite plausible (indeed, as discussed below, they support modern social scientific theory), and no extant source contradicts Thucydides's account. The author of the *Ath. Pol.*, which preserves the only other surviving narrative of the coup, complements Thucydides by focusing virtually exclusively on formal, constitutional arrangements. It is certainly possible, of course, that Thucydides took great historiographic liberty in his account of the coup. But the burden of proof must be on those who come to such a conclusion.

8   The Athenians began to station their naval forces on Samos in the summer of 412 (Thuc. 8.16.1). By winter, there were seventy-four Athenian ships stationed there (Thuc. 8.16.1, 30.2; see Gomme, Andrewes, and Dover [1981: 28–29, 73]). The Athenians stationed their navy on Samos in order to quash revolts in Chios, Miletos, Klazomenai, and Lesbos.

and formed a conspiracy to overthrow the Athenian democracy (Thuc. 8.47.2–48.2).

The members of the newly formed conspiracy, after successfully manipulating the Athenian naval rank and file stationed at Samos, sent Peisandros along with some other men to Athens to work for the recall of Alcibiades and the "overthrow of the *dēmos*" (Thuc. 8.49). After he arrived in the city, Peisandros addressed the Athenian assembly, presenting a logical, yet ultimately disingenuous argument. According to Thucydides (8.53), he asserted that the war against the Spartans threatened the very existence of the Athenian state, that the Athenians currently did not have enough resources to defend themselves, and that the Persian king would provide such resources, but only if the Athenians recalled Alcibiades and instituted a "different type of democracy." The logical consequence of the argument, of course, is that the Athenians should choose not to govern themselves democratically at all: the survival of the polis is prior to the form of its *politeia*. There were vocal skeptics, but Peisandros managed to persuade the assembly as a whole—at least to the extent that the *dēmos* decided to send him and ten other men to meet with Alcibiades and Tissaphernes in order to learn the details (Thuc. 8.54.2).[9]

Before he left Athens to meet with Alcibiades, Peisandros organized other oligarchic sympathizers residing in Athens into an underground network aimed at overthrowing the democracy. Specifically, Thucydides wrote (8.54.4) that he "visited all of the *xynomosiai* which chanced previously to exist in the city for the control of courts and officials and exhorted them to unite, and by taking common counsel to overthrow the democracy." Before Peisandros's initiative, the *xynomosiai* were secret clubs whose members swore to work together within the democratic system in order to accomplish various legal and political objectives. The members of one *xynomosia* apparently did not work in concert with the members of another. After Peisandros's initiative, however, the members of Athens's *xynomosiai* did work in concert and with the goal of overthrowing the democratic system.[10]

While Peisandros was in Asia Minor (likely Magnesia) meeting with Alcibiades, the members of the newly coordinated and revolutionized *xynomosiai* made important, preliminary moves of the coup d'état. As described by Thucydides, they implemented a two-pronged plan. The first part of the plan, carried out in secret, was to intimidate the population. That was accomplished, most notably, by the assassination of Androkles, "the foremost leader of the *dēmos*" and a man that rank-and-file democrats would have looked to for guidance in such uncertain times. He was not the conspirators' only vic-

9 As Gomme, Andrewes, and Dover argue (1981: 126), this embassy was not empowered to promise a constitutional change in Athens.

10 On the *xynomosiai*, see Gomme, Andrewes, and Dover (1981: 128–31); Rhodes (2007: 17–19).

tim, however: Thucydides wrote that they killed anyone deemed to be "inconvenient." The second part of the plan was to spread political propaganda. One of the goals of that propaganda, of course, was to remind citizens that, if a "different type" of democracy governed Athens, the Athenians would receive Persian financial support. But they also openly floated, perhaps in assembly speeches, a specific proposal: only those serving in the war should be paid by the state, and no more than five thousand men—those who could serve as hoplites and/or financial backers—should have control of the affairs of state (Thuc. 8.65).

According to Thucydides, the Athenians who were then in Athens and supported the democracy were unable to counter the campaign of intimidation and propaganda waged by the conspirators. His description of and explanation for their inability is very important for the present argument.

> And no one of the others any longer spoke against them, through fear and because it was seen that the conspiracy was widespread; and if any one did oppose, at once in some convenient way he was a dead man. And no search was made for those who did the deed, nor if they were suspected was any legal prosecution held; on the contrary, the populace kept quiet and were in such consternation that he who did not suffer any violence, even though he never said a word, counted that a gain. Imagining the conspiracy to be much more widespread than it actually was, they were cowed in mind, and owing to the size of the city and their lack of knowledge of one another they were unable to find out the facts. For the same reason it was also impossible for any man that was offended to pour out his grievances to another and thus plot to avenge himself, for he would discover any person to whom he might speak to be either a stranger or, if an acquaintance, faithless. (Thuc. 8.66)

Thucydides describes the "official" overthrow of the Athenian democracy immediately after the passage just quoted. There were two important contributing events. The first event occurred during a meeting of the assembly—held, notoriously, not in the Pnyx, but a few kilometers away in the deme of Kolonos—wherein the *dēmos* ratified a motion, made by Peisandros: there were to be all new magistrates who would work without pay; four hundred men would be chosen to rule as they saw fit; those four hundred would convene a council of five thousand when it seemed advisable. Thucydides, using words that recall the dynamic of silence and intimidation described earlier, wrote that those measures were adopted "with no one objecting." The second important event occurred soon after the meeting at Kolonos when the newly appointed Four Hundred, accompanied by 120 youths, burst into the Bouleuterion and ordered the *bouleutai* to leave their post. Thucydides, again stressing what is clearly a leitmotif of his narrative of the coup, wrote (8.70.1) that the *bouleutai* "quietly withdrew without making any objection" and that "the citizens at large raised no disturbance but kept quiet." Thus the Athenian democracy was overthrown for the first time in its history.[11]

Thucydides, particularly in the passage quoted above, strongly suggests that the individuals in Athens who supported the democracy were unable to respond to the coup d'état because they had a "revolutionary coordination problem." The term "coordination problem" refers to a situation in which individuals would like to participate in a particular group activity but do not do so because they are unsure whether or not other individuals will also participate: the cost of inaction or nonparticipation, that is, is lower than the cost of acting with an insufficient number of participants.[12] Such problems are very common. Something as commonplace as meeting a group of friends for coffee, for example, can become a coordination problem: if an individual is not sure that the other individuals will attend, he or she might not make the effort to go to the coffee shop.

Coordination problems in revolutionary situations, like that confronting the Athenians in 411, have special characteristics and thus require separate analysis. A modern case study by Timur Kuran elucidates the general operative dynamic of the revolutionary coordination problem. Kuran examined the dramatic fall of communism in Eastern Europe in 1989 after four decades of stable rule. He was particularly interested in both accounting for the failure of experts to predict the catastrophic collapse and explaining why that collapse nevertheless seemed so explicable after the fact. But his theoretical insights are also of great use for an analysis of revolutionary activity in late-fifth-century Athens: they clarify the social dynamic described by Thucydides in the passage quoted above and account for the emergence, persistence, and ultimate collapse of that dynamic.[13]

---

11 The sequence of events that led to and immediately followed the formal overthrow of the Athenian democracy is notoriously difficult to recreate, and the historicity of some events is uncertain. Thucydides and the *Ath. Pol.*, the two major sources, are difficult to reconcile; indeed, they are virtually impossible to reconcile on the existence (or nonexistence) of the Five Thousand during the rule of the Four Hundred. For the problems, see Rhodes (1993: 362–415) and Gomme, Andrewes, and Dover (1981: 184–256). For a detailed diachronic narrative with commentary, see Ostwald (1986: 337–411) and Shear (2011: 22–51).

12 On coordination problems in general, see Chwe (2001: 11–13 and passim) and Ober (2008: 168–210).

13 One might be skeptical initially about the applicability of a theory used to analyze modern nation-states to the study of democratic Athens. Athens was certainly a smaller and more traditional state, but while the Athenians may not have encountered the difficulties of information management that confront modern states, Thucydides (8.66.3) clearly concluded that they did have analogous problems ("owing to the size of the city and their lack of knowledge of one another"). It is thus reasonable to suspect—although it certainly must be demonstrated—that various Athenian institutions and practices may be analyzed profitably in light of modern theories that explore information exchange. Josiah Ober's most recent book (2008) demonstrates the potential benefits of such an approach.

Kuran's theoretical analysis rests on the fundamental distinction between an individual's "private preference" and his "public preference" about the regime in power. The former preference refers to how an individual *actually* feels about the regime and is, more or less, beyond his immediate control. The latter preference refers to how an individual *appears* to feel about the regime and is, to a considerable degree, under his immediate control. If an individual's private preference about the current regime is not the same as his public preference—that is, if he appears to support the regime but actually does not support it—he is engaging in what Kuran calls "preference falsification."[14]

Kuran suggests that every individual makes a simple cost-benefit analysis in order to determine the nature of his public preference concerning a regime that he does not actually support. Specifically, each person has two payoffs to consider. The first payoff is "external" and refers to what members of the ruling regime will do to him should he publicly oppose the political status quo. The value of that payoff is, under most circumstances, directly tied to the current extent of public opposition to that regime: the less opposition is publicly expressed, the more severely a regime will punish it, while the more opposition is expressed, the less severe the punishment will be.[15] The second payoff is "internal" and refers to the psychological toll one inflicts on one's self by preference falsification. The value of that payoff is directly tied to the extent to which one actually opposes the current regime: the more one dislikes it, the more "costly" the toll of acting like a supporter. If the actual internal cost of preference falsification is lower than the expected external cost of publicly opposing the current regime, an individual will falsify his preference and *appear* to support the regime. However, if the actual internal cost of preference falsification is greater than the expected external cost of public opposition, an individual will align his two preferences and publicly display his opposition. Kuran calls the tipping point at which that alignment occurs—that is, the point at which an individual will change his public preference to match his private preference—his "revolutionary threshold."[16]

Kuran developed a simple model, called a threshold sequence, in order to explain the relationship between the public preferences of particular individuals concerning the ruling regime and the stability of the state.[17] Here is an example of a threshold sequence.

---

14   Kuran (1991: 16–17).

15   Of course, not all unpopular regimes will necessarily follow this general rule. A regime might tolerate a small percentage of the population engaging in public dissent, for example, and clamp down only when that percentage increases beyond a certain threshold. But, generally speaking, the nature of a regime's response to public dissent is contingent on the strength of the dissent movement.

16   Kuran (1991: 17–19).

17   Kuran (1991: 19–25).

$$\{1, 1, 2, 3, 3, 4, 5, 6, 8, 10\}$$

Each of the 10 numbers in that sequence represents the revolutionary threshold of one person.[18] Thus the person represented on the far left with a revolutionary threshold of 1 will publicly display his opposition to the current regime only if one person has *already* done so; otherwise, he will continue to falsify his preference and appear to support the regime. Likewise, the person represented fourth from the left with a revolutionary threshold of 3 will publicly display his opposition to the current regime only if three people have already done so; and so on.[19]

The threshold sequence presented above describes a stable political status quo (i.e., one in equilibrium) despite the fact that many individuals either are greatly dissatisfied with the regime or, if supporters, are nevertheless willing to participate in the early stages of a revolution. The person represented on the far left of the sequence is willing to publicly oppose the regime if only one person (or 10 percent of the population) does so first. According to the model, however, that will not happen. Likewise, the person represented in the position third from the left is willing to act if only two people "go first." But, again, that will not happen. Thus the tragic irony of the revolutionary coordination problem is that many people want to depose the regime and, if they did act, likely would succeed. But they do not act, and the unpopular regime stays in power.

In the standard terminology of social scientists, the individuals represented in the threshold sequence who want to overthrow the current regime are handicapped by "pluralistic ignorance": they do not know the relevant political preferences of their fellow citizens.[20] Indeed, if the regime's policies are repressive, it would be very difficult for such information to become widely known: individual A would either not take the risk to find out what individual B thinks or, if somehow he did find out, he would not risk telling individual C. Even if each citizen suspected, or knew with certainty, that the vast majority of his fellow citizens were falsifying their preferences, he still would not know those citizens' revolutionary thresholds; that is, he would not know how many people would have to publicly oppose the regime before those citizens would also publicly display their opposition. It thus would be

18   Kuran uses units of ten in his thresholds. Thus Kuran would write the threshold sequence given above as $\{10, 10, 20, 30, 30, 40, 50, 60, 80, 100\}$. He does so because, at times, he considers each of the numbers as representing 10 percent of the population, while at other times as representing a single person in a state with a population of ten. The analysis is the same. But, for simplicity, I use single numerals.

19   Different individuals will have higher or lower thresholds depending on a variety of factors. But it ultimately comes down, one would think, to a combination of personality type and experience.

20   According to Kuran (1991: 20n34), the term "pluralistic ignorance" was first used in print by Richard Schanck (1932: 101).

rational (and safer) for every individual to suppose that other individuals—despite the fact that they are adamantly opposed to the regime—will engage in public dissent only if a rather large percentage of the population has already done so. As a result, nobody publicly opposes the regime, because each person thinks that an insufficient number of people will follow him. In other words, the expected external cost incurred by action is too high.

The concepts developed by Kuran make it relatively easy to account for the inability of the Athenians to respond to the coup d'état in 411, in spite of the fact that a significant majority of the population supported the democracy. As noted above, the oligarchs implemented a two-pronged plan of intimidation (including assassination) and propaganda (promising Persian assistance against the Spartans in return for a change of regime). An Athenian citizen therefore knew that, if he should demonstrate political dissent without sufficient support, he would suffer a very high external or physical cost. He also had some reason to believe that other individuals might actually support the change of regime and thus would not support his public protest: they might actually believe that the Athenians would receive Persian assistance should Athens be governed by an oligarchy. In such circumstances, concluding that the expected external/physical cost of public opposition is greater than the internal/psychological cost of preference falsification, individual A falsifies his preference and appears to support the regime, although he does not actually support it. Then individual B, following the same thought process and noticing that individual A appears to support the coup, falsifies his preference too. Individual C follow suit, as does individual D, and so on. Thus an "ignorance cascade" sweeps through the Athenian population, resulting in higher and higher revolutionary thresholds for successive individuals and, consequently, a high average number in the population's threshold sequence.

The supporters of Athens's democracy, in other words, had a revolutionary coordination problem: despite the fact that most individuals do not support the coup, nobody does anything to oppose it. As Thucydides wrote in his description of the ramifications of pluralistic ignorance, they were "powerless because of the size of the city and ignorance of each other."[21] The fact that

---

21 For a very different interpretation of the *dēmos*'s response to the coup of the Four Hundred, see Taylor (2002a). In that article, Taylor accuses the *dēmos* of cowardice and lack of commitment to the democracy, and of being more interested in money. In support of this view, she rather aggressively reads between the lines of Thucydides's account of the coup. Thucydides's direct statement (8.68.4), for example, that "it was difficult . . . to deprive of their liberty the Athenian people" rises, in Taylor's view (p. 108), "to the pitch of sarcasm." To validate her thesis on the *dēmos*'s complicity in the overthrow of the democracy, she analyzes five significant moments when Athenian democrats could have objected to the coup, but did not: at Samos, during Peisandros's address to the Athenian assembly, while the conspirators implemented their strategy of intimidation and disinformation (8.66), the assembly meeting at Kolonos, and the takeover of

the Athenian fleet, and with it a significant percentage of the reliably pro-democratic *thetes*, was at Samos certainly contributed to the coup's success.[22] Nevertheless, the important point here is that those individuals who were in Athens and did not want the Four Hundred to dominate the city were unable to strike back. They wanted to act in defense of their democracy, but, given the high stakes involved in action and the uncertainty about their fellow citizens' views, each person waited for others to act before acting himself.

I would like to suggest, if only for heuristic purposes, that the threshold sequence discussed above—{1, 1, 2, 3, 3, 4, 5, 6, 8, 10}—plausibly models the population in Athens at the time of the coup of the Four Hundred, when most of the *thetes* were with the fleet at Samos. This suggestion cannot be fully proven, of course, but three points argue in its favor. First, the sequence describes a population in which a slim majority of the population opposes the regime but does not take action: 60 percent of the population has a revolutionary threshold below 5 (the number at and above which generally indicates support for the status quo), while nobody has a revolutionary threshold of 0 (which indicates that an individual will oppose the status quo before anybody else does).[23] Second, that threshold sequence describes a population in which a large minority supports the regime: 40 percent of the population has a revolutionary threshold of 5 or above. Third, the sequence describes a population susceptible to the type of revolutionary action analyzed in the following section.

---

the *boulē*. At each of these moments, she concludes that the democrats were either complacent or cowardly.

Taylor's analysis, however, is debatable. First and most important, it does not take into account the (apparent) underlying operative dynamic in Athens at that time (i.e., how fear and disinformation affect behavior of individuals and thus of groups). Second, it ignores subsequent fervor for democracy described in Thucydides's text, including the uprising in the Piraeus (8.92) and the oath of the Athenian soldiers on Samos (8.75.2). Third, it ignores the decree of Demophantos and other texts that show strong support for democracy (e.g., *ML* 85, honoring the killers of Phrynichos and their accomplices).

22   On the demographic reality, see Munn (2000:138, 390n24). Munn suggests that 9,000–10,000 Athenians were killed or captured at Sicily and that two-thirds of that number were *thetes*. He also suggests that most of the remaining population of *thetes* was, after the disaster at Sicily, with the Ionian fleet and thus not in Athens. For Athenian demography between 431 and 395, see Strauss (1986: 70–86).

23   It should be noted that a revolutionary threshold above 5 does not necessarily indicate support for the regime. A person with a threshold of 6, for example, might oppose the regime, but nevertheless be quite timid and thus require a very large percentage (in this case, 60 percent) of the population to act in opposition before he does. And, on the other hand, a supporter of the regime could have a threshold lower than 5, if, for example, he is afraid that the regime is vulnerable, and would thus act with the opposition in the early stages of a revolt. Nevertheless, a person with a threshold above 5 would not act in opposition to the regime unless over half of the population has already done so. And such behavior is consistent with someone who supports the status quo—thus the general rule asserted (without argument) by Kuran (1991: 23).

MOBILIZATION

Thucydides strongly suggests (8.72.2) that fear felt by the leaders of the regime for the Athenian naval forces stationed at Samos was the ultimate cause for the collapse of the regime of the Four Hundred. They had reason to be afraid: when word of the coup came to Thrasyboulos—the soon-to-be general and future democratic hero—he had all the soldiers and sailors stationed at Samos swear an oath to (inter alia) support democracy and oppose the Four Hundred (Thuc. 8.75.2). They even threatened to kill ambassadors sent to them by the Four Hundred (8.86.2) because they "overthrew the democracy." When the members of the Four Hundred learned of that determination, a split within their leadership emerged. Some—the so-called moderates—wanted to empower five thousand men to govern Athens in fact, not only in name, as had been the case up to that point, arguing that by doing so they would placate many of the Athenians stationed at Samos and thereby allow Athens to continue fighting Sparta and maintain the Athenian Empire. Others—"the most influential men" (*hoi dunatōtatoi*), as Thucydides refers to them—wanted to make peace with Sparta quickly. They clearly concluded that, should they ally with the Spartans, they could defeat the forces at Samos and maintain control of Athens, thereby saving their own lives. The members of this latter group thus sent ambassadors to Sparta to negotiate an end to the war and fortified Eetionia in order to facilitate the entry of Spartan ships into the Piraeus (Thuc. 8.90–91).

As described by Thucydides (8.92.2), the immediate cause for the collapse of the Four Hundred was the assassination of Phrynichos, a leading member of the Four Hundred and a participant in the embassy to Sparta. He wrote that, before the return of Phrynichos from the diplomatic mission, conversations critical of the regime were conducted in secret and between only a few individuals—and this despite the fact that the hard-liners were fortifying Eetionia more energetically and thereby increasing the probability that their city would be subjected to Spartan rule. Thucydides continues,

> But finally, Phrynichos, after his return from his mission to Lacedaemon, was stabbed in the full agora as the result of a plot by a man of the frontier patrol, and before he had gone far from the council chamber suddenly died. The assassin escaped, while his accomplice, an Argive, was seized and tortured by the Four Hundred, but did not reveal the name of anyone who instigated the deed nor anything else, except that he knew that many used to assemble in the house of the commander of the frontier patrol and at other houses.[24]

Significantly, Thucydides causally connects the conspicuous assassination of Phrynichos with a large-scale uprising against the regime in the Piraeus. The

---

24 Thuc. 8.92.2. The translation is slightly modified from the Loeb.

uprising had three stages, each of which was defined by the status and number of its participants. Those who took part in the first stage were "moderate" regime members. Thucydides (8.92.2) clearly connects the commencement of this stage with the assassination of Phrynichos: "then [i.e., after the assassination], when no single action had been taken in consequence of this, Theramenes and Aristokrates and all the rest who were of the same way of thinking went to work more boldly." And in another marked phrase (8.92.3), which echoes and inverts an important leitmotif of his account of the coup, he asserts that Theramenes concluded that "it is not possible to keep quiet any longer." The moderates then acted in earnest.

The second stage of the uprising involved the hoplites who had been fortifying Eetionia. After Theramenes and his allies had broken their silence, those forces—men who had been working to advance the interests of the hard-line conspirators—arrested Alexikles, a general of the oligarchic regime and "very favorably inclined toward the members of the political clubs" (Thuc. 8.92.4). Significantly, Thucydides adds (8.92.5) that "most important of all, the mass of the hoplites were in sympathy with all this."

The final stage of the uprising drew in everybody else. After the arrest of Alexikles, chaos erupted both in the Piraeus and in the city. "Thereupon," Thucydides reports, "the hoplites and many of the people of Piraeus at once mounted the fortification [at Eetionia] and began to tear it down." The rioters shouted "whoever wants the Five Thousand to rule in place of the Four Hundred, let him set to work," but Thucydides explicitly states that what they really meant was "whoever wants the *dēmos* to rule" (8.92.6–11). Clearly nobody was "keeping quiet" anymore.

The next day, the Athenians who were dissatisfied with the political status quo mobilized to overthrow the regime of the Four Hundred. They first held an assembly in the theater of Dionysos near Mounichia. There is no word on what they discussed there, yet they obviously articulated a consensus and formulated a battle plan. They then marched on the city. The regime members, quickly realizing that they had no chance to defeat such a large number of coordinated men, offered to surrender and turn over control of the city to the Five Thousand. The mobilized hoplites, concerned for the safety of the state (a Spartan fleet was set to sail), agreed to meet in the theater of Dionysos on the south slope of the Acropolis to discuss the restoration of concord (Thuc. 8.93.3). And in a latter assembly meeting, held in the Pnyx, the Four Hundred were formally deposed and the Five Thousand installed (Thuc. 8.97.1).[25] Thus, wrote Thucydides (8.98.4), "the oligarchy and stasis came to an end."

---

25 The meeting in the Pnyx wherein the Four Hundred were officially deposed took place after a devastating Athenian defeat at Eretria (Thuc. 8.95). Thucydides wrote (8.96.1) that, after that defeat (and subsequent revolt throughout Euboia, except Oreos), "there was greater consternation than ever before."

Kuran's work helps to account for the remarkable series of events described by Thucydides. As noted above, the threshold sequence {1, 1, 2, 3, 3, 4, 5, 6, 8, 10}—a sequence that I have suggested might apply (very roughly) to the population in Athens at the time of the coup of the Four Hundred—describes a stable status quo in spite of fairly widespread dissatisfaction with the ruling regime. Suppose, however, that the person represented on the far left of the threshold sequence with the revolutionary threshold of 1 lowered his revolutionary threshold to 0. The cause for that change could be virtually anything: he witnessed a gross injustice carried out by the regime, for example. The population's threshold sequence would then look like this: {0, 1, 2, 3, 3, 4, 5, 6, 8, 10}. Now that person represented on the far left would not wait for somebody else to "go first" before he publicly displayed his opposition to the regime; he would, instead, act immediately. After he acts, the person represented second from the left will stop falsifying his preference and publicly express his opposition to the regime as well, because his revolutionary threshold has been met. The person represented third from the left will then act, and so on. Thus, using Kuran's terminology, the first person's action was a "spark" that ignited a "revolutionary bandwagon."[26]

It is reasonable to conclude that the assassination of Phrynichos was the spark that ignited the revolutionary bandwagon that ultimately brought down the regime of the Four Hundred. Before that act, opponents of the Four Hundred, despite the fact that they constituted a majority of the citizen population then in Athens, were handicapped by pluralistic ignorance and thus unable to rise up en masse against their oppressors. But the assassination radically altered the underlying strategic dynamic. Once individual B (with revolutionary threshold of 1) became aware of what individual A (with a revolutionary threshold of 0) had done, and thus knew what he thought, he too aligned his public and private preferences and publicly opposed the regime. Then individual C (with a revolutionary threshold of 2), seeing what individuals A and B did "no longer stays quiet," but instead joined in the uprising as well. Thus a "knowledge cascade" swept through the Piraeus: the greater the number of individuals who aligned their preferences and acted out publicly against the regime, the more the remaining individuals knew that, despite earlier appearances to the contrary, others opposed the regime and were willing to actively oppose it. In short, pluralistic ignorance was quickly replaced by common knowledge, and that knowledge allowed the

---

26 Kuran (1989: 60; 1991: 20). In Kuran's model, each person's action is as significant as the action of any other individual. In reality, of course, that is not the case: a prominent person's act, in most circumstances, is more influential than the action of an obscure one. That important nuance does not invalidate the operative dynamic of Kuran's model: one need only to suppose that, should an influential individual join in a protest, an ordinary individual would consider that act to be equivalent to, say, the actions of two ordinary people. Granovetter (1978: 1428) comes close to this observation when he discusses the significance of "the effects of friendship and influence."

supporters of democracy to coordinate their efforts to overthrow the Four Hundred.

This account of the collapse of the Four Hundred places great causal weight on the action of a single individual. The analysis is grounded in a seemingly plausible theory of collective action.[27] Nevertheless, one might ask whether or not the Athenians also considered the assassination of Phrynichos to have been such a significant event in the history of their democracy. Two pieces of evidence demonstrate that they did. First, as attested by an extant inscription dated to 409 (*ML* 85), the *dēmos*, at the very first Dionysia after the restoration of the democracy, publically honored Phrynichos's assassins and their accomplices.[28] (Significantly, that particular Dionysia is explicitly associated with the oath of Demophantos, discussed below, in which all Athenians swore to kill tyrants and reward tyrant killers.) Second, as is made clear by Lykourgos (*Leok.* 112–14), the assassination of Phrynichos was still remembered as an important event eighty years after the fall of the Four Hundred.[29]

27 The seminal early essay on threshold modeling is Granovetter (1978). Kuran (1989 and 1991), because his focus was high-stakes political revolution (whereas Granovetter's analysis was generic), introduced the important psychological element of preference falsification. That psychological element is important (inter alia) in accounting for the fact that people do not necessarily free ride in revolutionary situations (as would be expected, according to rational choice theory—see Olson [1965] for the classic formulation). Lohmann (1994) also employed threshold modeling in studying the fall of communism in East Germany. She criticizes Kuran's model as being "monotonic" (pp. 87–88): i.e., it suggests that the number of individuals engaged in anti-regime activity simply increases until it stops. Her analysis of the Monday Demonstrations in Leipzig (pp. 65–84), however, shows that the number of individuals protesting fluctuated: sometimes it was very high, sometimes significantly lower. Lohmann also downplays the role of radicals in protest movements, stressing instead the importance of "activist moderates." Those later individuals, she asserts, provide more information to the whole public concerning the amount and nature of support for the protest (pp. 53–54). It is important to recognize the difference, however, between demonstrations or protests against a modern government and an armed rebellion against an ancient regime. First, in the latter case, radicals are essential—and even in modern protests against oppressive governments, activist moderates would not join if radicals have not already acted. Second, individuals who join in the armed rebellion against an ancient regime on one day likely would not go home the next day (as in modern demonstrations). Lohmann's objections thus do not invalidate Kuran's theory as applied to the armed uprising in Athens. And it is to be noted that Lohmann sought to combine her theory with Kuran's (pp. 54–55). For further reading on threshold models, see Kuran and Sunstein (1999); Bikhchandani, Hirshleifer, and Welch (1992). For an overview on the modern study of revolutions, see Goldstone (2001). For a brief critique of the use of game theory to analyze collective behavior, see Granovetter (1978: 1433–35).

28 The restoration of the Dionysia in line 13 of the inscription is nearly universally accepted; see Wilson (2009: 1–16) for a discussion.

29 The sources on the identity of the assassins and their accomplices, as well as on other details, are difficult to reconcile: see *ML* 85; Lykourg. *Leok.* 112–14; Lys. 13.71; the comments in Gomme, Andrewes, and Dover (1981: 309–11); the comments in *ML* 85. Further (indirect) evidence for the conclusion that the Athenians considered the assassination of Phrynichos to have been an important moment in their political history is found in the verdict pronounced against

The Athenians must have considered themselves fortunate in that Phrynichos was assassinated before the conspirators surrendered the polis to the Spartans. It is impossible, of course, to know what would have happened if the Spartans had actually gained control of the polis in 411, but, according to Thucydides (8.76.7), the Athenian sailors stationed at Samos considered the possibility that they might be forced to abandon Athens and establish a new city. It is thus reasonable to suspect that Athenian democrats, after reclaiming control of the polis, sought to ensure that, if they should be overthrown again, history could be repeated: someone, that is, would "go first," initiate a revolutionary bandwagon, and thereby enable democrats to coordinate a mobilized response in defense of their democracy. The mechanism by which they hoped to achieve this was the oath of Demophantos.

The Oath of Demophantos

The earliest known piece of legislation promulgated (perhaps in June of 410) by the Athenian *dēmos* after they regained control of their polis following the coup of the Four Hundred is the decree of Demophantos. Unfortunately, the stone upon which that decree was inscribed has not been found.[30] An apparently verbatim quotation, however, is preserved in Andokides's speech *On the Mysteries*, which the orator delivered in 399.[31]

Ἔδοξε τῇ βουλῇ καὶ τῷ δήμῳ· Αἰαντὶς ἐπρυτάνευε, Κλειγένης ἐγραμμάτευε, Βοηθὸς ἐπεστάτει. τάδε Δημόφαντος συνέγραψεν. ἄρχει χρόνος τοῦδε τοῦ ψηφίσματος ἡ βουλὴ οἱ πεντακόσιοι λαχόντες τῷ κυάμῳ, οἷς Κλειγένης πρῶτος ἐγραμμάτευεν. ἐάν τις δημοκρατίαν καταλύῃ τὴν Ἀθήνησιν, ἢ ἀρχήν τινα ἄρχῃ καταλελυμένης τῆς δημοκρατίας, πολέμιος ἔστω Ἀθηναίων καὶ νηποινεὶ τεθνάτω, καὶ τὰ χρήματα αὐτοῦ δημόσια ἔστω, καὶ τῆς θεοῦ τὸ ἐπιδέκατον· ὁ δὲ ἀποκτείνας τὸν ταῦτα ποιήσαντα καὶ ὁ συμβουλεύσας ὅσιος ἔστω καὶ εὐαγής. ὀμόσαι δ᾽ Ἀθηναίους ἅπαντας καθ᾽ ἱερῶν τελείων κατὰ φυλὰς καὶ κατὰ δήμους, ἀποκτενεῖν τὸν ταῦτα ποιήσαντα. ὁ δὲ ὅρκος ἔστω ὅδε· "κτενῶ ⟨καὶ λόγῳ καὶ ἔργῳ καὶ ψήφῳ καὶ⟩ τῇ ἐμαυτοῦ χειρί, ἂν

Archeptolemos and Antiphon ([Plut.] *X orat.* 834b). The verdict was delivered after the fall of the Four Hundred and before the reinstatement of the democracy—that is, during the regime of the Five Thousand (411); it concludes, "This sentence shall be inscribed upon a pillar of bronze and set up in the same place as the decrees concerning Phrynichos."

30 The decree was certainly inscribed. Andokides, *Myst.* 95, wrote that the stele was placed "in front of the Bouleuterion." Lykourgos, *Leok.* 124, wrote that the stele was "in the Bouleuterion." Demosthenes (20.159) refers to "the stele of Demophantos," but not its location.

31 The text for the decree of Demophantos: Andok. *Myst.* 96–98. The date for the decree is based on information provided in *ML* 84, lines 1–3, where it is stated that Klegenes (Kleigenēs in Andokides's text) was secretary while Glaukippos was Archon (i.e., in 410–409) and that Aiantis, the tribe in prytany when the decree of Demophantos was promulgated, held the first prytany of that year.

δυνατὸς ὦ, ὃς ἂν καταλύσῃ τὴν δημοκρατίαν τὴν Ἀθήνησι, καὶ ἐάν τις ἄρξῃ
τιν᾿ ἀρχὴν καταλελυμένης τῆς δημοκρατίας τὸ λοιπόν, καὶ ἐάν τις τυραννεῖν
ἐπαναστῇ ἢ τὸν τύραννον συγκαταστήσῃ. καὶ ἐάν τις ἄλλος ἀποκτείνῃ,
ὅσιον αὐτὸν νομιῶ εἶναι καὶ πρὸς θεῶν καὶ δαιμόνων, ὡς πολέμιον κτείναντα
τὸν Ἀθηναίων, καὶ τὰ κτήματα τοῦ ἀποθανόντος πάντα ἀποδόμενος
ἀποδώσω τὰ ἡμίσεα τῷ ἀποκτείναντι [καὶ λόγῳ καὶ ἔργῳ καὶ ψήφῳ], καὶ
οὐκ ἀποστερήσω οὐδέν. ἐὰν δέ τις κτείνων τινὰ τούτων ἀποθάνῃ ἢ
ἐπιχειρῶν, εὖ ποιήσω αὐτόν τε καὶ τοὺς παῖδας τοὺς ἐκείνου, καθάπερ
Ἁρμόδιόν τε καὶ Ἀριστογείτονα καὶ τοὺς ἀπογόνους αὐτῶν. ὁπόσοι δὲ
ὅρκοι ὀμώμονται Ἀθήνησιν ἢ ἐν τῷ στρατοπέδῳ ἢ ἄλλοθί που ἐναντίοι τῷ
δήμῳ τῷ Ἀθηναίων, λύω καὶ ἀφίημι." ταῦτα δὲ ὀμοσάντων Ἀθηναῖοι πάντες
καθ᾿ ἱερῶν τελείων, τὸν νόμιμον ὅρκον, πρὸ Διονυσίων· καὶ ἐπεύχεσθαι
εὐορκοῦντι μὲν εἶναι πολλὰ καὶ ἀγαθά, ἐπιορκοῦντι δ᾿ ἐξώλη αὐτὸν εἶναι
καὶ γένος.

Resolution of the council and the *dēmos*. The Aiantis tribe were presidents,
Kleigenes was secretary, Boethos was chairman. Demophantos drew up the
following proposal. This decree dates from the council of five hundred appointed by lot, for whom Kleigenes was the first secretary. If anyone overthrows the democracy at Athens, or holds any office when the democracy
has been overthrown, he shall be an enemy of the Athenians and shall be
killed with impunity, and his property shall be confiscated and a tenth part
of it devoted to the goddess; and he who kills or helps to plan the killing of
such a man shall be pure and free from guilt. All Athenians shall swear over
perfect victims by tribes and by demes to kill such a man. The oath shall be
as follows: "I shall kill, by word and deed, by vote and by my own hand, if I
can, anyone who overthrows the democracy at Athens, and anyone who,
when the democracy has been overthrown, holds any office thereafter, and
anyone who aims to rule tyrannically or helps to set up the tyrant. And if
anyone else kills him, I shall consider that man to be pure in the sight of both
gods and spirits, because he has killed an enemy of the Athenians, and I will
sell all the property of the dead man and give half to the killer and not keep
any back. And if anyone dies while killing or attempting to kill any such
man, I shall care both for him and for his children, just as for Harmodios
and Aristogeiton and their descendants. And all oaths that have been sworn
against the people of Athens, at Athens or on campaigns or anywhere else, I
declare null and void." All Athenians shall swear this oath over perfect victims, in the customary manner, before the Dionysia, and they shall pray that
he who keeps his oath may have many blessings, but that for him who breaks
it destruction may befall himself and his family.[32]

32   Trans. MacDowell (1962: 134–35), slightly modified. For earlier scholarship on the decree
of Demophantos, see Droysen (1873); Günzler (1907); Friedel (1937: 56–58); Ostwald (1955; 1986:
414–18); McGlew (1993: 185–87); Shear (2007; 2011: 71–75, 96–106, 136–41, and passim). Mac-

There are two parts to this decree. The first part states that anyone who overthrows the democracy at Athens or holds any office while the democracy is overthrown shall be considered to be an enemy of the Athenians and thus may be killed with impunity. It further states that the assassinated person's property is to be confiscated and that not only the assassin but also anyone who might assist in the assassination shall be deemed pure and guiltless. The second part of the decree contains the text of a loyalty oath that all Athenians were required to swear before the next Dionysia. The oath echoes and amplifies the content of the first part of the decree and concludes with an annulment of all other oaths that individuals may have sworn against the democracy.

Two features of the oath of Demophantos are particularly important to the arguments presented in this section and thus require some discussion. First, the oath taker pledged to kill tyrants and reward tyrant killers. Athenian democrats believed that Harmodios and Aristogeiton, their paradigmatic tyrannicides, had killed a tyrant (Hipparchos) in broad daylight at the Panathenaia and that that assassination, despite the fact that Harmodios and Aristogeiton died, was the founding act of the Athenian democracy.[33] It is thus reasonable to suppose that, in the minds of those who swore the oath of Demophantos, an act of tyrannicide had two constituent elements. First, it must be a highly public first strike against a nondemocratic regime. Second, the act must be committed in order to usher in a democratic regime. Tyrannicide was the act of a committed democrat who was unwilling to wait for others to liberate his fellow citizens. A tyrant killer, on his own initiative, "goes first."[34]

In recognition of the inherent danger involved in tyrannicide, the oath of Demophantos states that a would-be tyrant killer will be rewarded substan-

---

Dowell (1962: 134–36) provides a brief commentary on the decree. Each of these works is an important contribution. But none of them explains either how the oath would help defend the Athenian democracy or whether or not the oath actually did facilitate the Athenians' attempt to do so.

33 See Thuc. 6.54–59 and *Ath. Pol.* 18–19 for a narrative of Harmodios and Aristogeiton's act. The democrats' version of that assassination—what happened, why it happened, and its consequence—was challenged in the fifth century by citizens of a less democratic persuasion. Thucydides (1.20.2–3; 6.54.1) and Herodotos (6.123.2) explicitly challenge the popular and thus democratic version. The debate over the true history of the tyrannicides continued into the later fourth century: the author of the *Ath. Pol.* (18.5) states that "democrats" had one version, while "some" had another. For Athenian democrats' views of Harmodios and Aristogeiton, see Taylor (1981); Raaflaub (2003: 63–70); Ober (2005c).

34 It might appear as though the reference to tyranny (and thus tyrannicide) in the oath of Demophantos is anachronistic. But, as is well known, later fifth-century Athenians considered any nondemocratic regime to be a "tyranny," and thus the assassination of any high-profile member of a nondemocratic regime would be an act of tyrannicide. Thucydides (6.60.1), for example, asserts that the Athenians were so frightened by the mutilation of the Herms (415) because "the whole thing seemed to them to have been done in connection with an oligarchic and tyrannical conspiracy." And Andokides (*Myst.* 75) referred to the period of the Four Hundred's domination as "during the time of the tyrants."

Figure 1.1. Roman copy of the Kritios and Nesiotes statue group. Photo by permission of the Deutsches Archäologisches Institut-Rom.

tially for his act of individual bravery. Should he survive, he would receive one-half the sale price of the victim's property. And since the "tyrant" would almost certainly be a member of the economic elite, the monetary reward could be considerable. Perhaps more importantly, he no doubt would be honored as a liberator in his lifetime, and if he should die, he and his children would be treated "just like Harmodios and Aristogeiton and their descendants." It is not entirely clear what that would have entailed. But, based on what is known about late-fifth-century practice, two things seem likely: a statue of the slain tyrant killer would be erected in the agora and he would be the object of a hero cult,[35] and his oldest living descendant would receive *sitēsis* in the Prytaneion in perpetuity.[36] It is also quite likely that, if he had young children, they, like war orphans, would be provided for by the state.[37] Whatever the exact contents of the "tyrannicide incentive package," it clearly represents a serious attempt to alter an individual's calculus of risk versus reward so as to benefit the democratic collective—in other words, to increase the likelihood that, should the democracy be overthrown, a brave individual would take the risk to go first and "kill a tyrant."

The second significant feature of the oath of Demophantos is the fact that "all Athenians" were required to swear it. It is well known that the Athenians relied heavily on oaths both in the performance of public, political acts (e.g., serving as archon, a council member, or jury member) and their private, personal interactions (e.g., contracts).[38] Andokides (*Myst.* 9) even went so far as

35 The earliest statues of Harmodios and Aristogeiton were sculptured by Antenor in, according to Pliny the Elder (*NH* 34.17), 509. Those statues were stolen by Xerxes's forces in 478 and returned to Athens by either Alexander the Great (Arr. *Anab.* 3.16.7–8 [referring to 331]; Arr. *Anab.* 7.19.2 [referring to 325/4]), or Antiochos I (Paus. 1.8.5), or Seleukos (Val. Max. 2.10, *ext.* 1). Very little can be said about them; see Taylor (1981: 34–37). A second pair of statues was made by Kritios and Nesiotes in 477/6 (*Marmor Parium*, A, ep. 54 [*FGrH* 239 A54, lines 70–71]); the earliest references to them are Ar. *Lys.* 631–35 and Ar. *Eccl.* 681–83. For this statue group, see esp. Brunnsåker (1971) and Taylor (1981: 33–50). See Figure 1 for a picture of a Roman copy of the Greek original. The earliest evidence for the Athenian tyrannicide cult is *Ath. Pol.* 58.1. The date for the foundation of this cult cannot be determined with any specificity beyond the obvious fact that it must antedate the composition of the *Ath. Pol.* But it is not unreasonable to suppose that the Athenians started the cult in the early to middle fifth century, perhaps soon after the foundation of the Kleisthenic democracy, perhaps after the erection of the Kritios and Nesiotes statue group, perhaps in the context of the promulgation of the "Prytaneion decree" (for which, see the next note).

36 *IG* I³ 131 (ca. 440–432). On this decree—the "Prytaneion decree"—and its substance, see Taylor (1981: 10–12) with literature cited in the notes.

37 This speculation is based on the decree of Theozotides (Stroud 1971). Promulgated after the fall either of the Four Hundred or (more likely) of the Thirty, the decree provides for the sons of those Athenians who, "during the oligarchy, died a violent death helping the democracy."

38 On the oath in Athenian political culture, see Cole (1996), Rhodes (2007), and the essays in Sommerstein and Fletcher (2007). The Athenians also used the oath as an instrument of imperial control. For the texts of such oaths, see Meiggs (1972: 579–82); for a discussion, see Bolmarcich (2007).

to assert that it was the oath that "alone holds the city together." The only known possible precedent for all citizens swearing the same oath, however, took place in the early sixth century, when, according to Herodotos, "the Athenians" swore to follow Solon's laws for ten years.[39] But that was nearly two centuries prior to the promulgation of the decree of Demophantos; and it is not entirely clear who would have sworn that oath at such an early date; perhaps only men above a certain property class participated in the ceremony. For all practical purposes, then, the decree of Demophantos appears to have mandated an unprecedented act: that all Athenians, organized according to the Kleisthenic (and therefore democratic) system of tribes and demes, swear the very same oath. The oath would thus have been a significant and highly memorable moment in late-fifth-century Athens.

The discussion of the oath that follows has three parts. In the first, I attempt to reconstruct the oath ritual to the extent possible. The second part draws on the insights of Michael Chwe to demonstrate that, as a result of having sworn the oath, the Athenians generated common knowledge of widespread credible commitment to kill tyrants and reward tyrant killers. In the third part, I argue that the Athenians would have been better able to solve a revolutionary coordination problem and thus mobilize en masse against a nondemocratic regime if such a commitment were in fact common knowledge.

RECONSTRUCTION OF THE OATH RITUAL

The ritual requirements articulated in the decree of Demophantos provide the primary information upon which must rest any reconstruction of the oath ceremony. Two of those requirements are more or less straightforward. First, the decree explicitly states that "all Athenians" (Ἀθηναῖοι πάντες) must

---

39 "Of themselves, the Athenians could not do so [sc., abrogate any of Solon's laws)] since they had bound themselves by great oaths that for ten years they would live under whatever laws Solon would enact" (Hdt. 1.29, trans. Grene, Chicago, 1987). Cf. *Ath. Pol.* 7.1: "they wrote up the laws on the *kyrbeis* and placed them in the Royal Stoa, and all swore to use them."

In two publications, P. J. Rhodes (1993: 135; 2007: 18–22) has identified several examples where all the citizens of a polis took the same oath: Thera, late seventh century (*ML* 5); Kyzikos, late sixth century (*Syll.*³ 4); Naupaktos, circa 500 (*ML* 20); Teos and its colony Abdera, circa 480–450 (*SEG* xxxi 985); Erythrai, circa 450 (*ML* 40); Chalkis, 446/5 (*ML* 52); Megara, 424 (Thuc. 4.74.2–3); Thasos, 407/6 (*SEG* xxxviii 851); Kyrene, 400 (Diod. Sic. 14.34.3–6); *sympoliteia* of Euaimon and Arkadian Orchomenos, 378 (*IG* V 2, 343; *SdA* 2, 297); Keos, 363/2 (*RO* 39); Xanthus, 337 (*RO* 78); Mytilene, 324 (*RO* 85); Tegea, 324 (*RO* 101); Tauric Chersonese, circa 300 (*Syll.*³ 360); Itanos in Crete, circa 300 (*Syll.*³ 526); Absorption of Magnesia-by-Sipylos into Smyrna, post-243 (*OGIS* 229); Kos and Kalymna, end of third century (*SdA* 3, no. 545). There are other instances of such mass public oaths not noted by Rhodes: Halieis, 424/3 (*IG* I³ 75); Selymbria, 407 (*ML* 87). It is also possible, though unlikely, that all Athenians swore a mass public oath pursuant to the decree of Patrokleides in 405 (Andok. *Myst.* 76) and their surrender to the Spartans in 404 (Andok. 3.22). The most celebrated example of all mass public oaths is the amnesty oath that the Athenians swore after the fall of the Thirty (Andok. *Myst.* 90), discussed below.

swear the oath. As fantastic as it might appear, this must be taken literally: it is stated twice in the decree, one time with the emphatic form of the adjective (ἅπαντας). Second, the oath had to be sworn "over perfect victims" (καθ' ἱερῶν τελείων), that is, over fully grown sacrificial animals.[40] The preposition κατά perhaps means that the participants performed some sort of downward motion during the ritual.[41]

Two other ritual requirements of the decree are ambiguous, but of considerable importance for the reconstruction of the oath ritual. The first is that the oath be taken "by tribes and by demes" (κατὰ φυλὰς καὶ κατὰ δήμους). This does not mean that all Athenians swore the oath twice, once with their tribe and once with their deme. Rather, the members of a given tribe were required to swear the oath together, deme by deme.[42] Thus, for example, when the members of tribe Pandionis swore the oath, it was sworn eleven times—once by the members of each of its eleven demes. The text of the decree does not make clear, however, whether or not the members of all ten tribes swore the oath together and at the same time.

The second ambiguous requirement is that the Athenians swear the oath "before the Dionysia" (πρὸ Διονυσίων). The City Dionysia was held annually in the month of Elaphebolion. The Athenian *dēmos* promulgated the decree of Demophantos in the month of Hekatombaion, eight months before the festival. The text does not make clear whether the oath had to be sworn more or less immediately before the festival or sometime within the eight-month period between the promulgation of the decree and the beginning of the festival.

It is tempting to suppose that all Athenians swore the oath at the same time, but that is very unlikely.[43] It simply would take too much time to do so. There were 139 demes in Athens. If one assumes that it took ten minutes for the members of a deme to make their way to a specified location, organize themselves, and swear the oath, the whole oath ritual, if run without interruptions, would take nearly twenty-four hours to complete. Other objections might also be raised. Even if "all Athenians" could have congregated in one place, for example, the resulting crowd would surely have been chaotic and

40 On τέλειος, meaning "fully grown," in the sense that the victim has a complete set of teeth, see Rosivach (1994: 91–93, 148–53).

41 Cole (1996: 230). See also Plescia (1970: 10) for movements that accompanied oath rituals.

42 Günzler (1907: 5) concluded that an individual swore the oath twice, once with his deme and once with his tribe. As Whitehead (1986: 109) notes, that is quite unlikely; he suggests that the oath was sworn at each tribe's tribal assembly.

43 Julia Shear (2007; 2011: 136–41) has argued that all Athenians, except for those away on campaign, swore the oath in the agora on 9 Elaphebolion, (probably) the day before the first day of the Dionysia. More recently, Wilson (2009) has argued that all Athenians swore the oath in the theater of Dionysos just before the tragic competitions and before the *dēmos* honored the assassins of Phrynichos.

distracting, and this might have called into question the seriousness of the oath and Athenians' commitment to it.

It is thus more reasonable to conclude that the members of each of the ten tribes organized their own, separate oath ceremony. Four simple points support that conclusion. First, under such circumstances, the oath ritual would not take too long to complete. Tribe Aigeis had the greatest number of demes at twenty-one. If we assume again that it took ten minutes for each deme to swear the oath, the entire tribe could have completed the ritual in three and a half hours. Second, the members of each tribe were accustomed to working together to achieve certain objectives and each had a sanctuary where the members met to conduct tribal business.[44] Third, such a decentralized oath ritual would make sense of the fact that the *dēmos* provided a text of the oath eight months before the Athenians had to swear it: such advance notice would be necessary if the members of each tribe were to figure out all the specifics (when, where, how) and complete the ritual before the beginning of the Dionysia. Fourth, a decentralized oath ritual would conform to the requirement that "all Athenians" had to swear the oath "by tribe and by deme."

In light of these considerations, I offer the following as a plausible, if somewhat schematic, depiction of the oath ceremony. The members of a given tribe gathered together at a specified location (probably a theater, perhaps the theater of Dionysos at Mounichia) at a time chosen beforehand.[45] The members of the first deme of that tribe—the order might also have been determined in earlier tribal meetings—proceeded as a group to some sort of stage. One or more of the deme members then struck a sacrificial victim and all the deme members, facing the audience and perhaps making some sort of downward motion, swore the oath of Demophantos in unison. Upon completing the oath, the members of the first deme returned as a group to the audience, while the members of the next deme came forward and followed the same steps. Thus the members of the tribe Pandionis, for example, saw and heard the oath sworn eleven times.

COMMON KNOWLEDGE

By swearing the oath of Demophantos, the Athenians generated common knowledge of a credible commitment to kill tyrants and reward tyrant killers. In the following discussion of this concept, I draw heavily on the work of the

---

44   Hansen (1999: 105). Josiah Ober has recently argued (2008: 205–8) that each tribe had at least one theater wherein the members of its constituent demes could meet to conduct tribal business. Such a structure would have been ideal for the oath ceremony. For local theaters in Attica, see now Paga (2010).

45   The theater of Dionysos at Mounichia would have been a suitable location, both practically and symbolically, for swearing the oath: it was within the long walls, and thus the participants would not have been at risk of an attack from the Spartans stationed at Dekeleia; and it was there that, after the assassination of Phrynichos, the Athenians had met in order to coordinate their attack on the regime of the Four Hundred.

modern social scientist Michael Chwe, and in particular on two ideas that are especially relevant to this study.

The first point is that the generation of common knowledge of credible commitment is virtually a necessary condition for solving coordination problems.[46] Contrary to what one might initially expect, common knowledge of fact x does not exist simply because everybody knows fact x. Nor does common knowledge of fact x exist if everybody knows that everybody knows fact x. Instead, common knowledge of fact x exists only if everybody knows that everybody knows that everybody knows fact x. Thus common knowledge of a widespread credible commitment to participate in an action exists only if everybody knows that everybody knows that everybody knows that many individuals are, in fact, set on participating in that action. Only given the existence of such complete metaknowledge (i.e., knowledge of other people's knowledge) can people coordinate.

A simple example effectively demonstrates the central importance of common knowledge for the solution to coordination problems. Imagine that two generals for the same army, A and B, would like to join forces in order to attack an enemy. Assume, too, that neither general has a sufficient number of soldiers to confront the enemy alone; if either general should bring his soldiers out of their defensive positions without the help of the other general's soldiers, his soldiers would be defeated by the enemy. Before ordering his troops to leave their current positions, general A needs to know three things: first, that general B is committed to the plan of a coordinated strike; second, that general B knows that general A is also committed to the plan; third, that general B knows that general A knows that general B is committed to the plan. If this last link is missing, A might reasonably conclude that B will assume that A thinks that general B is not committed to the plan and consequently that B will not act. Therefore A himself will not act; it would be too risky. Only when he possesses all three pieces on information can general A act with confidence, and obviously general B must have the same information vis-à-vis general A.

The second important point developed by Chwe is that the performance of public rituals generates common knowledge and thus may be helpful in solving various large-scale coordination problems. As one example, Chwe analyzes royal progresses (rituals wherein a king conspicuously and ceremoniously travels throughout his kingdom) conducted in sixteenth-century England, fourteenth-century Java, and eighteenth- and nineteenth-century Morocco.[47] Such rituals did not simply provide an opportunity for the king to

---

46   Chwe (2001: 13–16 and passim). Strictly speaking, Chwe notes only that common knowledge is required for individuals to coordinate. But his analysis certainly assumes that the substance of that common knowledge must be a credible commitment.

47   Chwe (2001: 20–22).

demonstrate his power to his subjects; they also were opportunities for each individual in the various crowds to see other individuals in the crowd witness the king's power and grandeur, and each witness also knew that other individuals at other points in the progress, although not directly observed, would see the same thing. It is easy to see how such progresses would help a king maintain control over his subjects: they generate common knowledge both of the king's great power and of the apparently widespread support for his rule.

Chwe's insights suggest that one might profitably interpret the oath of Demophantos as a "rational ritual" that, through the generation of common knowledge, would help Athenian democrats solve a large-scale revolutionary coordination problem. Three aspects of the oath ritual greatly facilitated the generation of common knowledge of widespread commitment to kill tyrants and reward tyrant killers. First each participant was in the presence of the other participants (his fellow tribesmen) and could see that the other participants actually were paying attention to the ceremony. Chwe points out that inward-facing, circular architecture, such as the kivas of New Mexico and the meeting chamber of the city hall in Fort Worth, Texas, helps large numbers of individuals quickly build common knowledge from eye contact.[48] We do not know where the Athenians swore the oath of Demophantos. But it is not unreasonable to suppose that they did so in a theater or similar structure; they certainly benefited from the use of such structures in other political activities. Such a setting would have maximized the number of people each individual participant could see. Second, the oath was repeated several times during each tribal ceremony. The importance of repetition for the generation of common knowledge is obvious enough: if a message is repeated several times, everybody knows that everybody else has heard it.[49] Third, the expression καθ᾽ ἱερῶν τελείων ("over perfect victims") suggests that the demesmen swore the oath while moving in unison, perhaps in some sort of downward motion. It is also possible that the men touched or held part of the sacrificial victim. Such synchronized movement, if conducted successfully, would demonstrate to both the participants and the rest of their fellow tribesmen that each individual was fully aware of what he and others were doing.[50]

There are also three reasons to conclude that the widespread commitment to kill tyrants and reward tyrant killers would have been considered largely credible. First, everybody would have known that the *dēmos* does, in fact, reward tyrant killers: statues of Harmodios and Aristogeiton were prominently placed in the agora; the oldest descendants of those two tyrannicides received *sitēsis* one hundred years after that famous act of tyrant killing; and honors were voted not only for the assassins of Phrynichos, but also for each

---

48   Chwe (2001: 30–33).
49   Chwe (2001: 27–29).
50   Chwe (2001: 29–30).

of their accomplices. Consequently, few Athenians would have doubted a pledge to reward future acts in the same way. Second, everybody knew that individual Athenians had in fact killed or conspired to kill subversive Athenians in the past and that they would presumably do so in the future. The assassination of Phrynichos is the single most conspicuous example, but after that act hundreds of other Athenians—the exact number is unknown—likewise armed themselves in order to kill the supporters of the Four Hundred, if necessary. It would thus be reasonable to believe their pledge to do so again. Third, everybody would have known that the vast majority of Athenians did not reluctantly swear the oath, but rather welcomed the opportunity to publicize their commitment to defend the democracy. After the fall of the Four Hundred, democrats certainly knew that pluralistic ignorance (or, in the words of Thucydides, "being powerless because of their lack of knowledge of one another") had prevented them from defending their democracy as quickly and effectively as they might otherwise have done. Thus most individuals would have been eager to let their fellow citizens know what they really thought.

Despite the fact that each Athenian probably swore the oath with the other members of his deme in the presence of his fellow tribesmen, and not before the entire citizen body, the cumulative effect of the many separate, tribally organized oath rituals would have been to generate common knowledge that every Athenian was publicly committed to killing tyrants and rewarding tyrant killers. The members of each tribe would have known that the members of the other nine tribes were required to swear the same oath, and likely in the same way. They would have learned that from a variety of sources: the decree of Demophantos, tribal meetings, deme meetings, and casual conversations with individual citizens. It is also important to note that, at the time the Athenians swore the oath of Demophantos, most citizens were living within the city walls because of the Spartan occupation of nearby Dekeleia. It thus would have been virtually impossible for a group activity involving over one thousand men, such as the kind of oath ceremony envisioned here, to pass unnoticed. Consequently, despite the fact that different groups of Athenians swore the oath on ten different occasions, the ultimate effect would have been the same as if all had done so together at the same time.

SOLUTION TO COORDINATION PROBLEM

I have suggested that the Athenians would have been better able to solve a revolutionary coordination problem if it had been common knowledge that a majority of the citizens were credibly committed to killing tyrants and rewarding tyrant killers. Two lines of reasoning support this conclusion.

First, in the postulated post-oath epistemic environment, a "non-bold" individual—one whose revolutionary threshold before the oath was greater than 1—would lower his personal revolutionary threshold and thus take the risk to defend the democracy earlier than would otherwise have been the case. He would do so, of course, because he would reasonably expect a sufficient number of other individuals to follow him, because he would believe that those other individuals believe that yet others will follow them. The psychological cost of preference falsification would thus overbalance the expected physical cost of public action, making it rational to vigorously defend the democracy. Since, however, nobody can ever be absolutely certain about what other individuals are thinking and thus what they will actually do, a typical democrat would not take the risk to defend the democracy in the earliest stages of an anti-democratic coup; that is, he would not lower his revolutionary threshold to 0. Instead, he might lower it from, say, 4 to 3, or 2 to 1. Other individuals would do likewise. Thus an initial threshold sequence of {1, 2, 3, 3, 4, 4, 5, 6, 8, 10} would, after the oath, become {1, 1, 2, 2, 3, 3, 4, 5, 7, 9}, and the conditions necessary for the emergence of a latent revolutionary bandwagon would be established.

Second, in the postulated post-oath epistemic environment, a "bold" individual—one who, before the oath, had a revolutionary threshold of 1—would lower his revolutionary threshold to 0. Such an individual would know that, if he should go first and "kill a tyrant," he would receive in return a considerable amount of money (one-half of the amount raised from the sale of the tyrant's assets), in addition to fame and honor. He would also know that, should he die attempting to kill the tyrant, he would become even more esteemed among his fellow citizens, who would likely honor him with a statue, and his children would be cared for by the state. Such positive, selective incentives, however, regardless of their credibility, might not be enough to entice such individuals to go first if they believed that the movement they were initiating might fail. But when those incentives are presented within an epistemic context of common knowledge of widespread credible commitment to defend the democracy, the bold individual can safely conclude that others will in fact follow him. It would be rational, therefore, to take the risk, in the confidence that such an action would spark a revolutionary bandwagon.[51]

It is thus reasonable to conclude that, as a result of the fact that all Athenians swore the oath of Demophantos, the democrats would in the future be more likely to overcome a potentially debilitating revolutionary coordination problem and mobilize en masse against a nondemocratic regime. Imagine a hypothetical situation in which oligarchs once again relied on intimidation and disinformation in order to overthrow the democracy and maintain control of the state. If no precaution had been taken, a revolutionary coordina-

---

51 The application of such a rationalistic calculus has limits, of course. An individual, for example, might decide irrationally to kill a tyrant, without careful reasoning of the sort described here. My point is simply that, under the circumstances created by the oath of Demophantos, such an act might also be arrived at rationally, by a balancing of costs and benefits.

tion problem might prevent the numerically superior democrats from responding. But now that the Athenians had sworn the oath of Demophantos, a bold individual who had recently lowered his revolutionary threshold from 1 to 0 would be much more likely to go first, in the expectation that other individuals would follow him. Someone who had recently lowered his revolutionary threshold from 2 to 1 would follow him, and so on. Thus the Athenians would be able to replicate (mutatis mutandis) the sequence of events that brought down the Four Hundred: a spark (the assassination of Phrynichos) setting in motion a bandwagon (the uprising in the Piraeus), followed by a large-scale coordinated action (the meeting in the theater of Dionysos at Mounichia and the subsequent march on the city).

The oath of Demophantos was not the first Athenian attempt to legislate against tyranny, and at this point one might ask why the protections in place before the coup of the Four Hundred failed. Several earlier measures against tyranny are known, all presumably intended to ensure quick action in defense of the democracy.[52]

- An old law of uncertain date against aiming at tyranny or assisting someone in an attempt to become tyrant (*Ath. Pol.* 16.10).[53]
- A prayer-cum-curse against individuals contemplating tyranny and anyone who might help them (Ar. *Thesm.* 335–39), possibly articulated at the beginning of sessions of both the *boulē* and the *ekklesia*.
- A traditional proclamation likely announced at the beginning of the Dionysia, which promised a talent for anyone who "kills a tyrant" (Ar. *Av.* 1072–75).[54]
- A provision in the heliastic oath (Dem. 24.149) against voting for tyranny or oligarchy.
- A possible provision in the bouleutic oath against voting for tyranny or oligarchy (Dem. 24.144).[55]

52 In addition to the general measures listed below, two acts of the Athenian state taken against specific tyrants should be noted. A stele commemorating the injustices of the Peisistratidai stood on the Acropolis (Thuc. 6.55.1); the members of the family were named and no doubt banned. A stele was also erected to record the banishment of the followers of Isagoras because they had ambitions at tyranny (Schol. Ar. *Lys.* 273).

53 ἐάν τινες τυραννεῖν ἐπανιστῶνται [ἐπὶ τυραννίδι] ἢ συγκαθιστῇ τὴν τυραννίδα, ἄτιμον εἶναι καὶ αὐτὸν καὶ γένος (If any persons rise in insurrection in order to govern tyrannically, or if any person assists in establishing the tyranny, he himself and his family shall be without rights). On this law, the language of which is explicitly echoed in the decree of Demophantos, see Ostwald (1955: 105–10); Gagarin (1981).

54 This proclamation probably originated during the very first years of the Athenian democracy, when Hippias was still alive and the Athenians were concerned about "friends of the tyrants" (*Ath. Pol.* 22.6). That conclusion—accepted by Dunbar (1995: 583–84)—would conform well with Connor's conclusion (1989) that the City Dionysia originated circa 501 as a celebration of the end of tyranny and the creation of the new democracy.

55 Rhodes (1985a: 36–37). Rhodes assumes this based on the fact that the procedures for the *boulē* and *ekklesia* were often parallel.

- The state-maintained hero cult for Harmodios and Aristogeiton should perhaps also be included here, since its clear purpose was to encourage others to act as tyrannicides.[56]

It is likely that that these measures were ineffective because they did not convince individuals that, should they act to defend the democracy, others would follow. That guarantee is a key element in the oath of Demophantos, by which every Athenian individual pledged to act, to kill "by word and deed, by vote and by my own hand whoever overthrows the democracy at Athens." None of the aforementioned mechanisms articulated that important commitment. The law against tyranny simply declared that a tyrant would be pronounced *atimos* (and thus could be killed with impunity). The prayer-cum-curse requests only that the gods punish a tyrant or an aspiring tyrant. The proclamation at the Dionysia just promises to give a tyrant killer a talent. An individual swearing the heliastic oath (and perhaps the bouleutic oath) simply pledged "not to vote for tyranny." The honors for Harmodios and Aristogeiton offered only the prospect of similar rewards to subsequent tyrannicides. None of these measures did anything explicit to convince a would-be tyrant killer that others would follow his lead. A bold individual would thus question whether or not he should take the all-important first step to protect the democracy.

Thucydides's explanation for the panic of the Athenians after the mutilation of the Herms (6.53.3) supports the interpretation offered here: "For the *dēmos*, knowing by tradition that the tyranny of Peisistratos . . . had been put down, not by themselves and Harmodios but by the Lakedaimonians, were in constant fear and regarded everything with suspicion." The Athenians were clearly afraid that they would be unable to protect their regime against a future coup. If that view was commonly held, as Thucydides suggest, it would have been reasonable to suppose that a typical person would not fight to defend the democracy unless many had already done so. Thus a bold individual, unsure whether or not his fellow citizens were committed to act, would choose not to go first: despite the many measures against tyranny, he would not believe that a sufficient number of people would follow him. As a result, nobody would attempt to start a revolutionary bandwagon.[57]

Mobilization Against the Thirty

In light of the analysis presented above, one might suspect that the oath of Demophantos helped facilitate the large-scale mobilization against the Thirty

---

56   See above in the section titled "The Oath of Demophantos."

57   There is another possible reason for the apparent failure of the measures against tyranny: it might have been a common perception that they were antiquated and thus irrelevant. Aristophanes certainly appears to suggest as much when he ridicules the traditional proclamation

Tyrants. The Athenians, after all, had sworn the oath of Demophantos for precisely this reason, and after the democracy was again overthrown in 404, Athenian democrats did in fact mobilize in defense of the democracy. That mobilization should not be taken for granted; it did not "just happen." The Thirty, like the Four Hundred before them (but on a much larger scale), used fear and disinformation to divide the population and prevent effective coordination; public dissent would have been very risky.[58] Thus the men of Phyle and their subsequent supporters would have required some clear reason to believe that, should they act to defend the democracy, others would follow them. The oath of Demophantos provided that reason.

Several lines of reasoning support the conclusion that the oath was in fact largely responsible for the successful mobilization against the Thirty. First, it is clear that Athenian democrats attributed the fall of the Thirty to an act of tyrannicide analogous to that performed by Harmodios and Aristogeiton. Lysias (12.35) provides an early indication that the Thirty were actually called "tyrants," and Xenophon also equates their rule with tyranny (*Hell.* 2.3.16, 2.4.1). Moreover, Plutarch (*Arat.* 16.3) calls the campaign led by Thrasyboulos an act of "tyrant killing" (τυραννοκτονία). And Philostratos (*VA* 7.4) reports that songs were sung at the Panathenaia celebrating both Harmodios and Aristogeiton, and the heroes of Phyle, who are explicitly said to have overthrown the "Thirty Tyrants" (τριάκοντα τυράννους).[59]

A renewed public interest in Harmodios and Aristogeiton at the end of the fifth century likewise suggests that the leaders of the opposition against the Thirty were associated by democrats with the original tyrannicides. Vase

---

announced at the Dionysia (Ar. *Av.* 1072–75): "On this particular day, you know, we hear it once again proclaimed that . . . whoever kills any of the long deceased tyrants shall get a talent."

58   The Thirty were supported by a Spartan garrison of 700 men and 3,000 fully armed citizens. The rest of the Athenian population was disarmed. The substance of the Thirty's propaganda is provided by Lysias (12.5): "the Thirty . . . declared that the city must be purged of unjust men and the rest of the citizens inclined to virtue and justice." Few would have disagreed with such generic objectives, and the Thirty did begin their rule somewhat moderately, executing only individuals whom many people thought should be eliminated. For sources for the so-called good period, see Ostwald (1986: 478n72).

59   These are admittedly late sources, but three points suggest that the tradition is genuine, and that the practice described by Philostratos began at the end of the fifth century, perhaps at the Panathenaia of 402. First, the most logical time to begin honoring the heroes of Phyle together with Harmodios and Aristogeiton would be immediately after the overthrow of the Thirty. Second, the deeds committed by the heroes of Phyle were analogous to the deeds attributed to the tyrannicides: the latter, according to the democratic version of events, founded the democracy by overthrowing a tyranny; the former refounded the democracy by overthrowing the Thirty Tyrants. Third, in the decree of Archinos (Aischin. 3.190), the Athenians, shortly after the fall of the Thirty, honored the heroes of Phyle both for being the first to resist the unjust regime and for risking their lives in doing so: "they first began (πρῶτοι . . . ἦρξαν) to depose those who ruled the polis with unjust ordinances, risking their lives [sc., for the cause]." These are precisely the reasons for which the Athenians honored the original tyrannicides.

painting provides the best evidence for this. Although three or four Athenian vases with representations of Harmodios and Aristogeiton survive from the period circa 470 to 450, no such decoration appears on extant vases or fragments for the next half century.[60] Intriguingly, however, the tyrannicides reappear on five vases that date to circa 400, shortly after the overthrow of the Thirty. Three of the five are Panathenaic prize amphoras, which likely date to the festival of 402.[61] Following the tradition of Panathenaic prize amphoras, each of the vases carries a picture of Athena depicted in the act of advancing upon an enemy: her left leg leads her right leg, in her left hand she holds a spear in the throwing position, and in her right hand she holds a shield. On the shield is painted an image of the statue group of Harmodios and Aristogeiton by Kritios and Nesiotes (see Figure 1.2). One interpretation of the image is that democratic Athens (symbolized by Athena) is protected (symbolized by the goddess's shield) by tyrant killers.[62] Given that the *dēmos* commissioned the amphoras and that the Panathenaia in question was likely the first to occur after the overthrow of the Thirty and restoration of the democracy—not to mention the fact that two other vase fragments carrying an image of the tyrannicides also date to circa 400—it seems certain that the figures of Harmodios and Aristogeiton were intended to allude to the recent overthrow of the Thirty, and to characterize their fall as an act of tyrannicide.

Another sign of renewed democratic interest in the original tyrannicides is the fact that, after the overthrow of the Thirty, the Athenians may well have granted new honors for the descendants of Harmodios and Aristogeiton. The only such honor securely attested in a fifth-century source is *sitēsis* (*IG* I³ 131, circa 440). The orator Isaios, however, in a speech delivered in 389 (5.47), mentions among their honors not only *sitēsis*, but also *proedria* and *ateleia*. We cannot be certain that the Athenians first granted the honors of *proedria* and *ateleia* years after the grant of *sitēsis*, and even if they did so, it does not

60   The early representations are a black-figure lekythos, 470–460 (Vienna, Österreichisches Museum 5247; Brunnsåker [1971: 102–4, fig. 15, plate 23]); a red-figure stamnos, 470–460 (Würzburg, Martin von Wagner Museum 515; Brunnsåker [1971: 108, fig. 16]); and a fragment of a red-figure skyphos, 460–450 (Rome, Museo Nazionale Etrusco di Villa Giulia 50321; Brunnsåker [1971: 108–9]; Neer [2002: 175, fig. 86]). A possible fourth example is a fragment of a red-figure glaux in Agrigento, ca. 470 (*ARV*² 559, no. 147; Brunnsåker [1971: 110, fig. 17]).

61   Hildesheim, Pelizäus-Museum 1253, 1254; London, British Museum B 605; Brunnsåker (1971: 104–5, plate 23). Two of the amphoras were painted by the same hand (Aristophanes); Beazley (1986: 89) accepts a date of 402 for all three. The other two vases dated circa 400 are both red-figure oinochoai, one (supposedly found in the grave of Dexileos) in Boston (Museum of Fine Arts 98.936; Brunnsåker [1971: 105–6, plate 24]), the other in Rome (Museo Nazionale Etrusco di Villa Giulia 44.205; Brunnsåker [1971: 106, plate 24]).

62   One is reminded here of the chorus's prayer to Athena in Aristophanes's *Thesmophoriazusae* (1136–59). Therein the chorus prays, "Pallas Athena . . . who alone safeguards our city . . . you who loathe tyrants."

Figure 1.2. Panathenaic prize amphora, circa 402. Photo © The Trustees of the British Museum.

necessarily follow that the additional honors were granted after the over-throw of the Thirty. Nevertheless, this remains a very reasonable reconstruction of events, both chronologically (because the honors are first attested soon after the fall of the Thirty) and contextually (because they would fit well with the heightened interest in the tyrannicides at the time). Assuming it is true, it would suggest an increased appreciation of the value of tyrant killing in preserving democracy, and further support the conclusion that Athenian democrats considered the Thirty to have fallen in an act of tyrannicide.

In order to facilitate their efforts to mobilize in defense of the democracy, Athenians swore an oath to kill tyrants and reward tyrant killers—in other words, to become tyrannicides, a point made explicit by their pledge to treat a fallen assassin "just like Harmodios and Aristogeiton."[63] After swearing the oath, many Athenians did in fact successfully mobilize against the Thirty and killed many of their supporters, in a movement characterized by democrats as a collective act of tyrannicide. The logical consequence is clear: Athenian democrats attributed the fall of the Thirty, at least in part, to the fact that all Athenians had sworn the oath of Demophantos.

A second indication that the oath of Demophantos was largely responsible for the success of the democratic response is that the Athenians, very soon after the mobilization against the Thirty, swore another mass public oath, the function of which was virtually identical to that of the oath of Demophantos. In this oath, known as the amnesty oath, they pledged "not to remember past wrongs" (μὴ μνησικακεῖν).[64] As I attempt to demonstrate, this oath too affected the revolutionary thresholds of the participants and thus the ability of democrats to mobilize en masse, but whereas the oath of Demophantos lowered thresholds in order to facilitate stasis, the amnesty oath raised thresholds in order to make stasis much less likely.

By swearing the amnesty oath, the Athenians generated common knowledge of a credible commitment "not to remember past wrongs." Andokides (*Myst.* 90) makes it clear that all Athenians participated, describing it as "the

---

63   It is interesting to compare the provision in the oath of Demophantos whereby the *dēmos* promised to treat a fallen tyrant killer "just like (καθάπερ) Harmodios and Aristogeiton" with the pledge found in the Athenian tyrannicide *skolia* (Ath. 15.695a–b): "I will carry my sword in a myrtle branch, just like (ὥσπερ) Harmodios and Aristogeiton when they killed the tyrant." The tyrannicides were, in the words of Ober (2005c: 219), models of "democratically correct" behavior. It is almost certainly the case, then, that the Athenians viewed the oath of Demophantos as a means to encourage individuals to emulate the famous models. (Ar. *Lys.* 630–35 humorously depicts a man's futile attempt to act like Harmodios.) One need not doubt, however, that the Athenians were also aware of the oath's epistemic value in generating mutually shared knowledge: compare Plato's comment (*Leg.* 738d–e) on the importance of public rituals: "The people may fraternize with one another at the sacrifices and gain knowledge (γνωρίζωσιν) and intimacy, since nothing is of more benefit to the state than this mutual acquaintance (οὗ μεῖζον οὐδὲν πόλει ἀγαθόν, ἢ γνωρίμους αὐτοὺς αὑτοῖς εἶναι)."

64   Andok. *Myst.* 90–91; Xen. *Hell.* 2.4.43.

oath in which the whole city joined, the oath which you swore one and all after the reconciliation: ' . . . and I will not remember the past wrongs (οὐ μνησικακήσω) of any citizen except for the Thirty, the Ten, and the Eleven.' . . ." We do not know how the Athenians actually swore the oath, but it is certainly conceivable that they did so "by tribe and by deme," as in the case of the oath of Demophantos, which provided the only real Athenian precedent for such a large-scale oath ritual. But even if the amnesty oath was sworn in a different manner, the important point remains that everybody knew that everybody knew that everybody knew that all Athenians had solemnly pledged "not to remember past wrongs."

This pledge was tantamount to a pledge not to engage in violent acts of vengeance against members of the oligarchic faction. Traditional interpretations of the phrase μὴ μνησικακεῖν stress its relevance to "partisan" activities directly involving the law courts: according to this interpretation, a citizen pledged not to bring anyone (with a few exceptions) to trial for crimes that he may have committed during the reign of the Thirty, and a juror pledged not to convict individuals for such crimes.[65] Three points, however, strongly suggest that the phrase "not to remember past wrongs" had a broader relevance, referring to violent acts of vengeance generally speaking, not just to those involving the law courts. First, if the Athenians had intended to refer only to actions involving the courts, they easily could have crafted a more specific law that explicitly forbade the indictment of individuals for actions they may have committed during the time of the Thirty. Second, the author of the Platonic *Seventh Letter* (336e) directly associated the verb μνησικακεῖν ("to *remember* past wrongs") with σφαγή (slaughter, butchery). The term σφαγή specifically refers to intentional killing and appears to have been associated with political violence.[66] In the decree of Patrokleides (Andok. *Myst.* 79), for example, σφαγή is paired with tyranny. And Xenophon (*Hell.* 4.4.2) called the bloody massacre in Korinth in 392 a σφαγή. Third, according to the author of the *Ath. Pol.* (40.2), Archinos, a leading democratic figure in the period immediately following the civil war, convinced the members of the *boulē* to execute an unnamed individual because he "began to remember past wrongs" (ἤρξατο μνησικακεῖν). The passage in no way suggests that the unnamed individual did so in the law courts.[67]

Thus, by swearing the amnesty oath, the Athenians generated common knowledge of (at least apparently) credible commitment not to engage in vio-

---

65 Thus, as Andokides attests (*Myst.* 90–91), the Athenians also included the pledge οὐ μνησικακήσω in the jury oath.

66 MacDowell (1962: 118).

67 For further discussion of the meaning of μὴ μνησικακεῖν, see Carawan (2002: 3–5) and Joyce (2008: 508–12). For a detailed examination of the reconciliation agreement, including the amnesty provision, see Loening (1987). On the paradoxical sociological complexities of collectively forgetting, see Loraux (2002) and Wolpert (2002).

lent acts of vengeance against members of the oligarchic faction. In order to understand what that has to do with the potential effectiveness of the oath of Demophantos, it is necessary to determine how an oath containing the pledge "not to remember past wrongs" might have helped prevent stasis and thus helped to defend the recently reestablished democracy. Let us posit that every Athenian has a "stasis threshold" that represents the number of individuals who must participate in stasis activity before he does. An individual with a stasis threshold of 2, for example, will participate only if two other individuals (out of a population of ten) have already done so. This individual wants neither to initiate stasis nor to join in its earliest stages, for he is afraid that an insufficient number of other individuals will follow him and thus he will be punished as a revolutionary. If 20 percent of the population has already joined in the stasis, however, he too will join, in order to protect himself or those with whom he is in sympathy, and because he now believes that others will follow.[68] An extreme radical on the other hand, an individual who wants to reignite the civil war and eliminate members of the rival faction, will have a stasis threshold of 0: he believes that, if he commits some conspicuous act of violence, others will follow and thus the polis will be engulfed in stasis.

The most important consequence of the fact that all Athenians swore the amnesty oath is that most individuals would have raised their individual stasis thresholds and thus participated in a stasis later than they otherwise would have. Most individuals, that is, would have waited until more people joined in the stasis before they themselves decided to join. The oath, by generating common knowledge of an apparently credible commitment not to engage in acts of stasis, would lead most individuals to think that, if they were to engage in such acts, others might not follow them, because those others would think that others might not follow them, and if an insufficient number of individuals should take part, those who had done so would be more easily punished as revolutionaries or agitators. Since credibility is never perfect, however, an individual Athenian might not raise his stasis threshold by much, but he would still probably raise it, say, by 1 (e.g., from 2 to 3).

It is easy to see how even a small increase in an individual's stasis threshold could prevent an initial act of stasis from initiating a "stasis bandwagon." Imagine the following stasis threshold sequence: {0, 1, 2, 3, 3, 3, 3, 4, 5, 7}. The person in the first position in the sequence, with a threshold of 0, is a radical who wants to provoke civil strife; perhaps he hopes to eliminate those citizens who sided with the oligarchs. He thus commits some conspicuous act of violence in the hope that other individuals will follow. And they will, for after

---

68 On the danger of neutrality during stasis in a Greek polis, see Thuc. 3.82.8: "Neutral citizens were continuously destroyed by members of both factions, either because they would not fight with them or because of jealously that they should survive."

he acts the person in the second position in the sequence, with a stasis threshold of 1, will join in, and his action will draw in the next person, with a threshold of 2, and so on. Very soon the entire population could find itself taking part in the stasis, even if a majority might not wish to do so.[69] If, however, after swearing the amnesty oath, all but the most radical individuals raised their stasis thresholds by 1, the threshold sequence would look very different: {0, 2, 3, 4, 4, 4, 4, 5, 6, 8}. In this scenario, the radical represented in the first position in the sequence would still act in the hope that others would follow him. Since there is no citizen with a stasis threshold of 1, however, nobody would follow him and his efforts to initiate a stasis bandwagon would fail.[70]

The amnesty oath was thus functionally similar to the oath of Demophantos. Both represent an attempt to control sparks and bandwagons in order to defend the democracy. The Athenians swore the oath of Demophantos in order to increase the likelihood that someone would go first and initiate a revolutionary bandwagon. They swore the amnesty oath in order to prevent someone from going first and initiating a stasis bandwagon. They are two sides of the same coin, both working to defend and preserve the democracy.

The similarity of both means and ends between the amnesty oath and the oath of Demophantos suggests that—in the minds of the Athenians, at any rate—the successful response against the Thirty should be attributed in part to the oath of Demophantos. After the fall of the regime in 403, the Athenians must have concluded that the oath of Demophantos had been shown to be an effective tool, and they decided to use the tool once again in the amnesty oath to achieve a very similar end. If the goal of the oath of Demophantos was to facilitate democratic efforts to mobilize in response to organized attempts to overthrow the democracy, the conclusion that the oath had actually worked must have been based on the conviction that it did, if fact, facilitate mobilization. Since the only such mobilization that postdated the oath of Demophantos and antedated the amnesty oath was that conducted against the Thirty, the conclusion is clear: Athenian democrats saw a causal connec-

69 A large-scale modern example of this dynamic followed the explosion of the golden dome of the Askariya mosque in Samarra, Iraq, on February 22, 2006. The mosque is a particularly sacred site for Shiite Muslims, and its destruction, especially given the political instability of Iraq at the time, predictably ignited widespread sectarian violence. It would be interesting to know whether most of the individuals who participated in the violence following that explosion actually wanted to do so, or if they concluded that they must participate because they believed that a significant number of other individuals would participate.

70 Archinos, who urged the *boulē* to execute a citizen because he "began to remember past wrongs" (*Ath. Pol.* 40.2), was perhaps worried that one person might set off such a stasis bandwagon. The fact that all Athenians had sworn the amnesty oath might have prevented such an outcome.

Table 1.1. The Law of Eukrates and the Decree of Demophantos

Eukrates		Demophantos	
7–8	ἐάν τις ἐπαναστῆι τῶι δήμωι ἐπὶ τυραννίδι|ἢ τὴν τυραννίδα συνκαταστήσηι	(b)	καὶ ἐάν τις τυραννεῖν ἐπαναστῆ ἢ τὸν τύραννον συγκαταστήσῃ
8–10	ἢ τὸν δῆμον τ|ὸν Ἀθηναίων ἢ τὴν δημοκρατίαν τὴν Ἀθήνῃσιν| καταλύσηι	(a)	ἐάν τις δημοκρατίαν καταλύῃ τὴν Ἀθήνησιν
		(b)	ὃς ἂν καταλυσῃ τὴν δημοκρατίαν τὴν Ἀθήνησιν
10–11	ὃς ἂν τὸν τούτων τι ποιήσαντα ἀπο|κ⟨τ⟩είνηι ὅσιος ἔστω	(a)	ὁ δὲ ἀποκτείνας τὸν ταῦτα ποιήσαντα καὶ ὁ συμβουλεύσας ὅσιος ἔστω καὶ εὐαγής
21–22	καὶ ἡ οὐσία δημοσία ἔστω αὐτοῦ|καὶ τῆς θεοῦ τὸ ἐπιδέκατον	(a)	καὶ τὰ χρήματα αὐτοῦ δημόσια ἔστω, καὶ τῆς θεοῦ τὸ ἐπιδέκατον

tion between the swearing of the oath of Demophantos and the mobilized response to the Thirty.

A final point in support of this view of the oath is that the next time the Athenians feared an attempt to overthrow the democracy they passed a law that virtually quoted the language concerning tyranny contained in the oath of Demophantos. This was the law of Eukrates, dating to the spring of 336, when democrats feared a pro-Macedonian domestic coup. I will provide a full analysis of that law in chapter 3. So all I demonstrate here is that it does, in fact, incorporate the important language found in the oath and decree of Demophantos.[71] Table 1.1, based on that crafted by Martin Ostwald in his classic article on Athenian anti-tyranny legislation, makes the case most efficiently.[72] In the right-hand column, (a) refers to language found in the rule proper, (b) refers to the oath.

The verbal echoes make it clear that the provisions concerning tyranny in the law of Eukrates should be interpreted as a reaffirmation or a reminder to potential revolutionaries of the decree and the oath of Demophantos. Such a reaffirmation was almost certainly predicated on the widespread consensus that the earlier oath had worked, and indeed there is other evidence (Dem. 20.159–162; Lykourg., *Leok.* 124–27) that fourth-century Athenians thought highly of its effectiveness in generating mass action in defense of the democ-

---

71   It is important to note here, however, that the Athenians, when they promulgated the law of Eukrates, were concerned that they would be unable to respond to a pro-Macedonian coup due to a revolutionary coordination problem. See the section in chapter 3 titled "The Tyrannical Threat."

72   Ostwald (1955: 121).

racy. Since, as noted above, the only such action that postdated the decree of Demophantos was that against the Thirty, one should again conclude that Athenian democrats causally connected the swearing of the oath with the success of the response to the Thirty.[73]

The natural conclusion of the arguments presented above is that the successful democratic response against the Thirty should be attributed, at least in part, to the fact that all Athenians swore the oath of Demophantos. I have shown, first, that the Athenian democrats attributed the fall of the Thirty to an act of tyrannicide; second, that very soon after the successful mobilization against the Thirty, they swore another public oath (the amnesty oath), the function of which was complementary to that of the oath of Demophantos; and third, that the next time the Athenians feared an oligarchic attempt to overthrow the democracy, they promulgated a law that virtually quoted the anti-tyranny language contained in the oath of Demophantos. These three points might not be conclusive individually, but their cumulative weight seems to validate the thesis.

Conclusion

The viability of democratic governance in a Greek polis during the Classical period depended on it supporters' ability to solve a revolutionary coordination problem. If the supporters were able to solve that problem, they could capitalize on their numerical superiority and respond to a successful coup or, better still, prevent a coup from succeeding in the first place. Should the democrats be unable to coordinate in defense of their regime, however, their superior numbers would be meaningless and the anti-democrats would quickly dominate the polis. A fundamental question for historians of ancient Greek democracy should thus be, how did the citizens of the various democratically governed poleis solve, or attempt to solve, the revolutionary coordination problem?

In this chapter, I have attempted to demonstrate that Athenian democrats in the late fifth century were able to solve the problem in large part because of the fact that all Athenians swore the oath of Demophantos. The public performance of that oath accomplished two ends. First, it generated common knowledge of credible commitment to defend the democracy. Individual democrats were thus willing to oppose an anti-democratic coup earlier than

---

73 Two further points are worth mentioning. First, Lykourgos (*Leok.* 124) states that the Athenians swore the oath of Demophantos after the fall of the Thirty. In this he is probably mistaken, but if he is correct, it might suggest that the Athenians swore the oath a second time precisely because they believed that it had contributed to their recent victory. Second, the following chapters will demonstrate that the citizens of other poleis promulgated tyrant-killing legislation that clearly echoed the decree of Demophantos. That borrowing suggests that, in the opinion of the citizens of those states, such legislation was effective.

otherwise would have been the case, for they believed that other democrats would follow them. Second, the oath gave an incentive to particularly brave individuals to take the all-important first step in defense of the democracy— to "kill a tyrant" and thus initiate a revolutionary bandwagon. The oath directly contributed to the successful mobilization against the Thirty: Thrasyboulos and his men were confident enough to go first, and other individuals were subsequently confident enough to follow them. As a result, the democrats were able to capitalize on their numerical superiority and reclaim control of the polis.

This analysis suggests that the remarkable stability of the fourth-century Athenian democracy should ultimately be attributed to the fact that all Athenians swore the oath of Demophantos, and to the successful mobilization against the Thirty Tyrants that followed. After those events, anti-democrats would have known that, should they stage a coup, democrats would in fact be able to mobilize en masse in defense of their *politeia*; and since the number who favored democracy was greater than the number who opposed it, the former would almost certainly prevail. Thus anti-democrats were deterred from staging further coups.[74] This strategic dynamic goes a long way toward accounting for the persistence of democracy in fourth-century Athens.[75]

---

74 Political scientists would say that the Athenian democracy became "self-enforcing." For self-enforcing constitutions and the important role of coordination therein, see Weingast (1997).

75 It is interesting to note, in this regard, Hypereides's comment about the Thirty (*Against Philippides*, 8): "You [Philippides] have concluded that one person will be immortal, yet you sentenced to death a city as old as ours, never realizing the simple fact that no tyrant has risen from the dead while many cities, though utterly destroyed, have come again to power. You and your party took no account of the history of the Thirty or of the city's triumph over her assailants from without and those within her walls who joined in the attack upon her." Hypereides delivered this speech between 338 and 336. Thus the fact that democrats successfully mobilized against the Thirty was still viewed as having deterrent value three generations later.

II

Tyrant-Killing Legislation in the Late Classical Period

2

The Eretrian Tyrant-Killing Law

Introduction

In the summer of 342, Philip of Macedon commenced large-scale military operations on the island of Euboia in order to support pro-Macedonian regimes in two prominent cities. He first sent Hipponikos with one thousand mercenaries to Eretria. That force crushed the exiled democrats' fort at Porthmos and secured in power Kleitarchos, Automedon, and Hipparchos, men who recently had overthrown the Eretrian democracy. Later—exactly how much later is unknown—Philip ordered two additional invasions into Eretria in order to assist that puppet regime's efforts to quash a serious insurgency. It is likely in conjunction with the final (i.e., the third) intervention in Eretria that Philip's mercenary forces, led this time by Parmenion, stormed the northern Euboian city of Oreos and secured in power five men (Philistides, Menippos, Sokrates, Thoas, and Agapaios) who had recently overthrown the democracy in their city. Thus, by the fall of 342, Philip's partisans controlled two of Euboia's four major cities.[1]

---

1 The Macedonian supported invasions of Eretria: Dem. 9.57–8. The Macedonian invasion of Oreos: Dem. 9.59–62. It should be noted that Cawkwell (1978b: 131–32) doubts that Philip was behind the invasions of Euboia. His reasoning: (1) Philip does not appear to have supported those regimes subsequently; (2) Demosthenes did not emphasize the Macedonian invasion in Euboia in his speech *On the Chersonese*, a speech likely delivered only a few weeks before his *Third Philippic* and wherein reference to the invasion of Euboia would have strengthened the case that Diopeithes should not be recalled—the argument advanced in that speech. Denis Knoepfler (1995: 347n144) understandably rejects Cawkwell's position as being too dismissive of Demosthenes's repeated assertions. The date of the invasion of the Macedonian sponsored invasion of Euboia is also debated. The chronology accepted above is that of Ellis (1976: 162–66). Sealey (1993: 260), however, argues that the first invasion of Eretria (led by Hipponikos) took place in 343 and before the trial of Aischines, which took place in autumn of 343. This disagreement of date is largely due to different interpretations of Demosthenes's repeated references in *De Falsa Legatione*—a speech delivered at the trial of Aischines—to Philip's action in Euboia (87, 204, 326, 334). Sealey (1993: 260) concludes that Demosthenes referred to Hipponikos's mission in that speech. Ellis (1976: 279n109), however, argues that Demosthenes simply amplified Philip's diplomatic (as opposed to militaristic) moves in Euboia. Ellis rests his case on the fact that that Hegesippos, in chapter 32 of *On Halonnesus* (a speech perhaps dating to early 342 and wrongly attributed to Demosthenes), does not mention an invasion of Eretria as one of Philip's misdeeds.

Philip's gains in Euboia directly threatened Athenian security. Demosthenes, in his speech *On the Chersonese* (delivered in early 341), concluded that Philip invaded that island in order to establish bases (*epiteichismata*) from which he would attack both Attika and the island of Skiathos (36). That was a reasonable concern: Eretria was less than five kilometers away from Attika; Skiathos, near Oreos, was an important base for Athenian military operations in the northern Aegean.[2] And, although Demosthenes did not articulate this concern in his aforementioned speech, Philip's gains in Euboia also put him in a position, potentially, to take the southern Euboian city of Karystos and thus disrupt Athens's important grain shipments.[3]

The Athenians, led by Demosthenes, responded decisively to Philip's aggressive move into Euboia. They first (late spring/early summer 341) formed an offensive and defensive alliance with Kallias, the strongman of the Euboian city of Chalkis (Aischin. 3.91; Philoch. Frag. 159). For years, that man sought to bring the cities of Euboia into a federal league (*koinon*) that would be heavily influenced by Chalkis. And in 348, the aggressive pursuit of that objective led him into military confrontation with the Athenians—much to the Athenians' dismay.[4] Later (perhaps by mid-343), however, he incurred the enmity of both Philip and Thebes while in the pursuit of those imperial ambitions. How he managed to anger those important powers is unknown. But it was serious: according to Aischines (3.89–91), Philip and the Thebans actively moved against him. It is thus not particularly surprising that he formed an alliance with his former enemy, the Athenians.

Soon after forming the alliance with Kallias, the Athenians invaded both Oreos and Eretria, expelled their pro-Macedonian regimes—regimes that Demosthenes repeatedly referred to as "tyrannies"—and reinstalled the *dēmos*. The tyrants in Oreos were overthrown (and killed) in early summer 341. In that operation, the Athenian general Kephisophon led forces from Athens, Chalkis, and Megara. The tyrants in Eretria were toppled (and killed), after a siege, a few weeks later in an operation led by the Athenian

2 On the importance of Skiathos, see Dem. 4.32. It is to be noted that the Athenians had troops there at least as late as 344/3 (*IG* II² 1443, 106–8). Demosthenes often wrote that Philip intervened in Euboia in order to secure a "base of operations" against Athens and Athenian interests: Dem. 8.36, 66; 10.8, 68; 18.71; 19.326 (*hormētēria*).

3 Karystos was important for Athens's grain supply due to the proximity of Cape Geraistos: Strabo 10 C444; cf. Dem. 4.34. Twice, in his *De Corona* (230, 241), Demosthenes wrote that, if the Athenians had not controlled Euboia in the war with Philip, pirates (*lēstai*) would have harassed Attika and disrupted shipping routes.

4 This unfortunate period in fourth-century Athenian history began when the Athenians invaded Eretria in order to support Ploutarchos (the pro-Athenian "tyrant") in his struggle against Kleitarchos (the man subsequently secured in power by the Macedonian-led invasions of 342). The Athenian invasion backfired in large part because Kallias and his brother Taurosthenes mobilized a pan-Euboian response. For this episode, see Parke (1929); Cawkwell (1962); Carter (1971); Picard (1979: 240–45). The primary ancient sources: Plut. *Phok.* 12–14; Aischin. 3.86–88.

general Phokion.[5] It is possible that the Athenians, in order to execute that siege, mounted catapults on their ships. If they did, the siege of Eretria marks a milestone in ancient Greek warfare.[6]

After successfully completing military operations in Eretria, the Athenians and the Eretrians forged a bilateral alliance. The inscription (*IG* II[2] 230) that likely carries the text of that alliance is very fragmentary.[7] But it is almost certain that the Eretrians pledged to assist the Athenians if they were attacked or if their democracy were overthrown. And it is quite reasonable to conclude that the Athenians reciprocated: the Athenians likely pledged, that is, to assist the Eretrians should they be attacked or should their democracy be overthrown. First of all, such reciprocal agreements appear to have been common practice in Athenian alliances in the mid-fourth century: such was the case, for example, with the Athenian alliance with the Thessalian *koinon* (*RO* 44) and their alliance with Arkadia, Achaea, Elis, and Phleious (*RO* 41).[8] Second, there is an exceptionally fragmentary inscription, found in Eretria, which contains the text of an oath to be sworn by Athenians wherein they pledge to militarily assist the Eretrians should the Eretrian democracy be overthrown. Knoepfler has demonstrated (1995: 362–64) that that inscription might date to 341. And he has suggested that it might be the Eretrian copy of the alliance made with the Athenians in 341. The Athenian-Eretrian alliance was thus not simply between two states, but between the sociopolitical factions (i.e., *dēmos*) that controlled those two states.[9]

5   The invasions were pursuant to a decree drafted by Demosthenes: Dem. 18.79. The date for the overthrow of the regime at Oreos: Philochoros, F 159 with Schol. Aischin. 3.85 (confirming the month Skirophorion, which must be restored in the Philochoros fragment). The date for the overthrow of the regime at Eretria cannot be pinpointed to a certain month within the year 341/0. But the entry in Philochoros (F 160) apparently cited the Athenian-led liberation of Eretria after the words ἐπὶ τούτου ("during that man's [sc., archonship]"—that man being Nikomachos, archon in 341/0). And it is widely held that citations immediately following that chronological marker (i.e., ἐπὶ τούτου) occurred early in the year. Additional sources for the liberation of Eretria: Diod. Sic. 16.74.1; Schol. Aischin. 3.103 (where it is explicitly stated that the tyrant was killed).

6   That the Athenians mounted catapults on ships during the siege of Eretria is inferred from Athenian naval inventories (*IG* II[2] 1627, B, lines 328–41 [year = 330/29]). Knoepfler (2002: 196n256) accepts the use of ship-mounted catapults during the siege. Marsden (1969: 57–58), however, does not; he suggests that the "frames of the catapults from Eretria" (πλαίσια καταπαλτῶν ἐξ Ἐρετρίας) were given to the Eretrians by Philip II in order to help defend Eretria against the Athenian-led invasion. According to that interpretation, the frames (πλαίσια) were subsequently brought home by the victorious Athenians as booty. It should be noted, however, that Alexander used ship-mounted machines during the siege of Tyre (Arr. *Anab.* 2.21.7). It is thus conceivable that the Athenians used ship-mounted catapults nine years earlier.

7   For this inscription, see Knoepfler (1995: 346–59).

8   Knoepfler (1995: 364) supports this general conclusion.

9   It should be noted that a few months after the Athenians and Eretrians made their alliance, Eretria and Oreos joined the Euboian League and thus no longer paid "contributions" (*syntaxeis*) to the Athenians—although they were still in a bilateral alliance with Athens (Knoepfler [1995: 355–59]). The joining of those two poleis (Eretria and Oreos) to the Chalkis-dominated Euboian

One obvious aim of the Athenian-Eretrian alliance was to deter Eretrian anti-democrats from staging a coup. Henceforth, those anti-democrats had to ask themselves whether or not they could defeat in battle their domestic opponents (i.e., the pro-democrats) *and* a force sent by the Athenians. If the answer was no—that is, if they concluded that they would be defeated in such a confrontation—they almost certainly would choose to cooperate with the new regime. Thus the Eretrian democrats would maintain control of their polis and the Athenians would maintain influence in a strategically important region.

Although by no means insignificant, the alliance between the Athenians and the Eretrians likely would not have been sufficient to deter Eretrian anti-democrats from staging a coup. On the one hand, anti-democrats might have doubted the Athenians' commitment to defend the Eretrian democracy. It would have been reasonable to conclude, for example, that the Athenians, then following Demosthenes's policy to "protect and assist all" Greek cities from the Macedonian threat (8.46; cf. 9.70–75), would be too occupied elsewhere to intervene in Eretrian affairs.[10] And some anti-democrats might have suspected that the Athenians would even support an Eretrian tyrant, if he appeared to be pro-Athenian: just a few years earlier (348), after all, the Athenians invaded Eretria in order to support the pro-Athenian Ploutarchos.[11] Philip, on the other hand, had already ordered three separate invasions of Eretria: his commitment to a nondemocratic regime in that city was credible. In short, the Athenians potentially had a credibility gap while Philip did not. Anti-democrats thus might very well have concluded that it would be worth the risk to stage a coup.

The Eretrian democrats thus needed to deter their anti-democratic opponents without recourse to an outside power. They needed to have a credi-

League was done pursuant to a successful decree of Demosthenes (Aischin. 3.85–105). Some scholars (e.g., Cawkwell [1978a], Sealey [1993]), however, believe that the Athenian assembly promulgated Demosthenes's decree in late 343/early 342—that is, before the liberation of Oreos and Eretria. Those scholars thus associate the decree with Athens's resistance to Philip's advance on Ambrakia. But the arguments for dating that decree to late 341/early 340—i.e., after the liberation of Oreos and Eretria—are stronger. See Brunt (1969) and Knoepfler (1995: 352–55). For a concise presentation of both cases, see Sealey (1993: 262–64).

10   One might note here the letter that Philip sent to "the Euboians" (Dem. 4.37–38). The letter—which dates to the late 350s—has been lost. But a scholiast wrote that Philip advised the Euboians "that they should not put hope in an alliance with the Athenians since they [the Athenians] are not able to help themselves." The scholiast's report is likely correct, since Demosthenes cited the letter while bemoaning the fact that the Athenians were unable to act in defense of their interests.

11   See above, note 4. Eretria's mistrust of the Athenians is also behind an interesting Athenian inscription (*RO* 69) that perhaps dates to 343. That inscription records a decree whereby the Athenians pledge to punish any Athenian (or any Athenian ally) who invades Eretria. As Knoepfler (1995: 338–46) argues, the Athenians likely promulgated that decree in order to assure the Eretrians that Athens would not intervene in Eretria's domestic affairs—that is, they would not support another pro-Athenian strongman like they did in 348.

ble threat of their own. And it was to achieve that objective that the Eretrians promulgated their tyrant-killing law.

Until quite recently scholars knew very little about the Eretrian tyrant-killing law. In 1854, Baumeister discovered a small fragment of an ancient stele in Aliveri, approximately twenty kilometers east of Eretria. He carefully drew what he could see on the stone and published that drawing in 1857.[12] By 1892, the stone fragment that he discovered had been lost. In 1905, however, Adolf Wilhelm published an article demonstrating that the stone that Baumeister discovered recorded the opening lines of an anti-tyranny law. Also in that article, Wilhelm published (with very limited restoration) his own text and suggested (based on historical and orthographic grounds) that the Eretrians promulgated the law immediately after the fall of the "tyrant" Kleitarchos.[13] Finally, in 1915, E. Ziebarth republished Wilhelm's text as *IG* XII, 9, 190. After that, scholars did not seriously engage with the law in any significant way for more than eighty years.[14]

Thanks to two lengthy articles written by Denis Knoepfler and published in *Bulletin de Correspondance Hellénique*, scholars now have a much longer text of the Eretrian anti-tyranny law.[15] Knoepfler's original project was to publish the editio princeps of an inscription, found near ancient Eretria in 1958, that contained anti-tyranny language. In the course of his study, however, Knoepfler (following a suspicion first articulated by V. Petrakos and then by many others) concluded that the newly discovered stone and the fragment discovered by Baumeister in 1854 were, in fact, part of the same stele.[16] Knoepfler then re-edited the old, lost fragment (with significant restorations) and published it along with the editio princeps of the new, much larger fragment. As a result, scholars now have much of the original law: only (perhaps) four or five lines are missing completely.

Here is Knoepfler's text of the Eretrian tyrant-killing law and an original English translation. "Old Fragment" refers to the stone fragment discovered by Baumeister in 1854. "New Fragment" refers to the stone fragment discov-

---

12 Baumeister's facsimile was actually published in Vischer (1857: 352).

13 Wilhelm (1905).

14 It is somewhat surprising that Friedel, in his 1937 book titled *Der Tyrannenmord in Gesetzgebung und Volksmeinung der Griechen*, did not even mention the law from Eretria. Martin Ostwald also chose not to mention the Eretrian tyrant-killing law in his classic article (published in 1955) titled "The Athenian Legislation Against Tyranny and Subversion."

15 Knoepfler (2001b and 2002).

16 Knoepfler's argument for joining the new fragment with the old: (2001b: 197–206). The argument is based on (1) find spot (the old fragment was found in Aliveri, 20 km east of Eretria; the new fragment was found right next to Aliveri [likely ancient Porthmos], at port Karavos); (2) orthography (letterforms are similar, spellings share features of dialect, and the old fragment—like the new fragment—was written in *stoichedon* [51 letters per line]); (3) content (the new fragment is not the beginning of a law, the old fragment is the beginning of a law, and the new fragment refers to information found in the old fragment).

ered in 1958. The vast majority of the Greek text of the old fragment and about one-third of the text of the new fragment have been restored by Knoepfler. The underlining in the following translation attempts to demonstrate what parts of the translation do *not* come from restored sections (i.e., the underlined parts are actually on the stone).[17]

ΣΤΟΙΧ. 51

(Old Fragment)

[θε]ο[ί].

[οἱ πρόβουλοι καὶ οἱ στρατηγοὶ εἶπον· τύ]χει ἀ[γα]θεῖ τοῦ δ[ήμου το]-
[ῦ Ἐρετριῶν· ὅπωρ ἂν καθιστῆται ἐν τεῖ πόλει ἡ] μ[ετὰ] ἀλλήλω[ν ὁμόν]-
[οια καὶ φιλίη, ἔδοξε τεῖ βουλεῖ καὶ τοῖ δήμοι· ἄτι]μον εἶναι τὸ[ν τ]-
5 [ύραννον καὶ γένος τὸ ἐξ αὐτοῦ καὶ ὃς ἂν] τυραννίδι ἐπι[θ]ῆται· ὃς [δ]-
[ὲ ἂν ἀποκτείνει τὸν τυραννίζοντα ἢ τὸ]ν τ[ύ]ραννον, ἄμ μὲν π[ο]λ[ίτη]-
[ς εἶ, δίδοσθαι αὐτοῖ ---- 10 ---- καὶ στῆσα]ι αὐτ[οῦ π]αρὰ [τὸν βωμὸ]-
[ν τὸν --------18------- εἰκόνα χαλκῆν] καὶ εἶ[ναι αὐτοῖ προε]-
[δρίην εἰς τοὺς ἀγῶνας οὓς ἡ πόλις τίθηριν] καὶ σίτηριν αὐτο[ῖ ἐμ]
10 [πρυτανείοι ἕως ἂν ζεῖ· ἐὰν δὲ ἀποθάνει ὁ ἀπ]οκτε[ίν]ας τὸν [τύρανν]-
[ον ἢ τὸν ἡγεμόνα τῆς ὀλιγαρχίας ?, ἐκείνου] τοῖς π[αι]ρὶ δ[ίδ]ο[σθαι,]
[ἄμ μὲν ἄρρενες ὦριν, ἑκάστοι τὴν δωρειὰν] τὴν γεγραμμέ[νην ὅταν]
[εἰς τὴν νομίμην ἡλικίην ἀφίκωνται· θυγ]ατέρες δὲ [ἂν ὦριν, λαμβά]-
[νειν ἑκάστην αὐτῶν εἰς ἔκδοσιν χιλίας ?] δραχμ[ὰς ὅταν τεττάρω]-
15 [ν καὶ δέκα ἐτέων γέγωνται ---- 12 ----]ΙΝΑ[------ 15 ------]

(New Fragment)

[----------------------- 33 ----------------------- εἰ δὲ] μή, ὅσ[οι] ἂν βούλων-
[ται------------------ 23 -------------- εἰς τὴν] βουλὴν ἢ εἰ[ς] τὰ ἱερὰ ἐν Τ̣-
[----------------------- 32 -----------------------]ΙΑΝ ἤ τι[ς] τῶν βουλευτέ-
[ων ἢ ἀρχόντων, καὶ(περ or τῆς) βουλῆς ἀπα]γορ[ευ]ούρης αὐτοῖ, ἀποδημεῖ, πα-
5 [ραχρῆμα ἐκεῖνος τῆ]ς τε ἀρχῆς [ἀποπαυέσ]θω καὶ ἔστω ἄτιμος καὶ [α]-
[ὐτὸς καὶ γένος ὡς ὁ] τὸν δῆμον καταλύ[ω]ν, καὶ ἐάν τις τήνδε τὴν πο[λ]-
[ιτείην ἐπιχειρεῖ καταλύειν τὴν νῦν οὔρην ἢ λέγων ἢ ἐπιψηφίζ[ω]-
[ν, ἄν τε ἄρχων ἄν τε] ἰδιώτης, ἄτιμος ἔστω καὶ τὰ χρήματα αὐτοῦ δ[ημ]-
[όσια ἔστω καὶ τῆς] Ἀρτέμιδος τῆς Ἀμαρυρίης ἱερὸν τὸ ἐπιδέκατ[ο]-
10 [ν καὶ ταφῆναι μὴ ἐ]ξέστω ἐν τεῖ γεῖ τεῖ Ἐρετριάδι καὶ ἄν τις [αὐτὸ]-
[ν ἢ τινα αὐτοῦ ἀπο]κτείνει,[18] καθαρὸς ἔστω χεῖρας καὶ αἱ δωρειαὶ [ἔ]-
[στων κατὰ ταὐτὰ κ]αθάπερ γέγραπται ἐν τεῖ στήλει ἐάν τις τὸν [τύ]-
[ραννον ἀποκτείν]ει. τοῖ δὲ λέγοντι παρὰ τοῦτα ἢ πρήττο[ν]τι κατ[α]-

---

17 For a description of the new fragment and its lettering, see Knoepfler (2001b: 214).
18 Dössel (2007: 115–16) restores the clause differently: καὶ ἄν τις [τὸν ἐ]πιχειροῦντα ἀπο]-
κτείνει, κτλ.

[ρᾶσθαι ἱερέας κα]ὶ ἱερίδας Διονυρίοις τε καὶ Ἀρτεμιρίοις μή[τ]-
15 [ε παῖδας ἐξ αὐτῶν] γυναῖκας τίκτειν κατὰ νόμον, μήτε πρόβατα μ[ή]-
[τε γῆν εὐθηνεῖσ]θαι· εἰ δὲ καὶ γίνοιντο, μὴ γίνεσθαι αὐτῶν [γ]υηρ[ί]-
[ους παῖδας, ἀλλὰ] τούσδε πανοικίει πάντας ἀπολέσθαι.[19] ἐάν τις ἐ[πι]-
[ψηφίζει ἢ γράφει] ἢ φέρει, ἄν τε ἄρχων ἄν τε ἰδιώτης, ὡς δεῖ ἄλλην τι-
[νὰ καθιστάναι πο]λιτείαν Ἐρετριᾶς ἀλλ᾽ ἢ βουλὴν καὶ πρυτανείη-
20 [ν ἐκ πάντων Ἐρετρ]ιῶν κληρωτὴν καθάπερ γέγραπται· ἂν δέ τις κ[αθ]-
[ιστεῖ ἢ τυραννίδα] ἢ ὀλιγαρχίην καὶ ἐγβιάρηται, παραχρῆμα βοη-
[θεῖν πολίτας ἄπαντ]ας τοῖ δήμοι[20] καὶ μάχην ἅπτειν τοῖς διακωλύ-
[ρουρι τὴν ἐκκληρίη]ν καὶ πρυτανείην, ἕκαστον ἡγείμενον αὐτὸν
[ἱκανὸν μάχεσθαι ἄνε]υ [π]αραγγέλματος. ἂν δέ τι συμβαίνει ἀδυνα-
25 [τέον κατασχεῖν τὸ Ἀγ]οραῖον παραχρῆμα ὥστ᾽ ἐ[ξ]ε[ῖν]αι τεῖ βουλεῖ
[καθῖσαι κατὰ νόμον ἢ ἂν] ἀποκλεισθεῖ ὁ δῆμος τῶν τειχέων, καταλ-
[αμβάνειν χωρίον τι τῆ]ς Ἐρετριάδος ὅ τι ἂν δοκεῖ σύνφορον εἶνα-
[ι πρὸς τὸ ἐκεῖ συνελθεῖ]ν τοὺς β[οη]θέοντας πάντας· καταλαβόντα-
[ς δὲ ὑποδέχεσθαι τὸν ἐλθ]όντα καὶ βολόμενον τῶν Ἑλλήνων βοηθε-
30 [ῖν τοῖ δήμοι τοῖ Ἐρετριῶν.] ἂν δέ τις Ἐρετριῶν μὴ βοηθήρει τοῖ δή-
[μοι, εἰσαγγέλλειν τεῖ πρυ]τανείει καθάπερ γέγραπται καὶ μάχη-
[ν συνάπτειν αὐτοῖ· ὁπόροι] δ᾽ ἂν Ἐρετριῶν καταλαβόντες τι τῆς χώ-
[ρης τ᾽ αὐτόνομον καὶ ἐλεύθ]ερον ποιήρωρι τὸν δῆμον τὸν Ἐρετριῶ-
[ν, τούτοις μέρος τι διαδιδ]όσθω τῆς γῆς καὶ τῆς οὐσίης τῶν ὑπομε-
35 [ινάντων ἄρχεσθαι τεῖ τυρα]ννίδι ἢ ἄλλει τινὶ πολιτείει ἀλλ᾽ ἢ β-
[ουλεῖ ἐκ πάντων κληρωτεῖ.] *vacat*

(Old Fragment)

Gods.

The *probouloi* and the *strategoi* proposed: for the good fortune of the *dēmos*
of Eretria: in order that concord and friendship with one another may be
established in the city, resolved by the council and the *dēmos*. The tyrant,
his offspring, and whoever makes an attempt at tyranny shall be without
rights. And whoever kills a member of the tyrant's faction or the tyrant, if
he is a citizen, . . . shall be given to him . . . and stand near the altar his . . .
bronze statue. And he shall have a front seat at the festivals that the polis
sponsors and public maintenance in the town hall as long as he lives. And
if the killer of the tyrant or the leader of an oligarchy dies, to his children,
should they be male, to each shall be given the written reward whenever
they reach the legal age. And should they be daughters, each shall receive
one thousand drachmas as a dowry whenever they turn fourteen.

19 Parker (2005: 154), following a suggestion of Peter Thonemann, tentatively suggests μὴ
γίνεσθαι αὐτῶν [ὅ]γηρι|[ν μηδὲ τέρψιν, αὐ]τοὺς δέ πανοικίει κτλ.
20 Gauthier (2004: 251) suggests a different restoration: βοη||[θεῖν πάντας Ἐρετρι]ᾶς τοῖ
δήμοι κτλ.

(New Fragment)

> Otherwise, whoever wishes . . . to the council or to the holy places in . . . or
> a councilor or magistrate, although the council forbids him, travels abroad,
> he shall be deprived of office immediately and be without rights, both he and
> his offspring, because he is dissolving the *dēmos*. And if someone attempts
> to dissolve this regime—the one now in existence—by making a proposal or
> putting a measure to vote, should he be a magistrate or a private citizen, he
> shall be without rights and his property shall be confiscated with one tenth
> consecrated to Artemis Amarynthos, and he shall not be buried in the land
> of Eretria. And if someone kills him or his family member, his hands shall be
> pure and he shall receive the rewards for these things just as is written in the
> stele if someone kills the tyrant. And against one speaking or acting contrary
> to these [measures] the priests and priestesses shall pronounce a curse at the
> Dionysia and Artemisia that [their] wives do not bear their sons as is cus-
> tomary (κατὰ νόμον) nor [their] flock nor land flourish; and if [sons] are
> born, that they are not their legitimate sons, but that all of them, together
> with their house, be utterly ruined.[21] If someone, either magistrate or private
> citizen, puts it to a vote, writes up a draft, or votes that the Eretrians must
> establish some regime other than a council and *prytaneia* appointed by lot
> from all Eretrians just as is written; and if someone establishes either a tyr-
> anny or an oligarchy and uses force, all citizens must assist the *dēmos* im-
> mediately and join in battle against those who will prevent [a meeting of]
> the assembly and *prytaneia*, each considering himself competent to fight
> without an order. But, if it is impossible to secure the Agoraion immediately
> in order for the council to convene according to the law, or if the *dēmos* is
> shut out of the walls, secure some Eretrian stronghold, whatever seems ad-
> vantageous for all helpers to arrive at; after securing [the stronghold], re-
> ceive any Greek who arrives and wishes to help the *dēmos* of Eretria. And if
> an Eretrian does not help the *dēmos*, impeach him before the *prytaneia* just
> as is written and join in battle against him. To the Eretrians who secure some
> territory and make the *dēmos* of Eretria autonomous and free shall be dis-
> tributed a part of the land and property of those who remained behind to be
> ruled by a tyranny or some regime other than a council appointed by lot
> from all.

---

21 It is tempting—and perhaps correct—to conclude that the expression κατὰ νόμον refers to
legitimacy, as opposed to bastardy, in this context. But that interpretation would seem to be incon-
gruent with the following clause that refers to the possibility that wives of men under the curse
might, despite the curse, give birth to boys. In that case, the curse declares, in Knoepfler's restoration, that such boys would be μὴ γνηρίους (i.e., illegitimate: not the biological son of the woman's
husband). Thus the Eretrian law appears to use the noun νόμος in its old sense as "custom." On the
meaning of γνήσιος (in the Eretrian dialect = γνήριος) as both legitimate and blood related, see
Ogden (1996: 17–18).

Eretrian pro-democrats clearly promulgated their tyrant-killing law in order to defend their democracy against attacks launched by anti-democrats (variously referred to in the law as tyrants, partisans of tyrants, and, obliquely, as oligarchs). It is also clear that the threat posed by those anti-democrats was very serious: one need note only that the law envisions as a distinct possibility the anti-democrats shutting "the *dēmos*" out of the city walls. One might thus wonder whether or not the promulgation of this tyrant-killing law actually helped the Eretrian democrats maintain control of their polis. The primary objective of this chapter is to answer that simple question. Doing so, however, will require a thorough analysis of the law's provisions and its historical and sociopolitical context.

This chapter defends the following thesis: the promulgation of the Eretrian tyrant-killing law played an important role in defending Eretria's newly reinstated democratic regime against internal subversion during the years immediately following the Athenian led liberation of 341. The arguments in support of that thesis are presented in three sections. In the first section, I argue that the Eretrian pro-democrats quite likely would have lost control of their polis shortly after the Athenian-led liberation, if no serious attempt were made to facilitate their efforts to mobilize in defense of their regime (i.e., to solve a revolutionary coordination problem). I next argue that, by promulgating their tyrant-killing law, the Eretrian democrats greatly increased the likelihood that they would successfully mobilize in defense of their regime (i.e., overcome a potential revolutionary coordination problem) and thus likely would have deterred anti-democrats from attempting a coup. And in the final section, I argue that the Eretrian democrats maintained secure control of their polis, under very difficult circumstances, for several years after they promulgated their tyrant-killing law.

Threats to Stability

The comments presented in this section demonstrate that the Eretrian pro-democrats quite likely would have lost control of their polis shortly after the Athenian-led liberation of 341, if no serious attempt were made to facilitate their efforts to mobilize in defense of their regime. Counterfactuals are problematic, of course: it is impossible to say for certain what would have happened if something else did not happen. It is important to note, however, that it is, in fact, necessary to answer a counterfactual in order to determine whether or not any attempt to solve a particular problem actually "worked." For example, in order to determine whether or not the United States' massive bank bailout of 2008 stabilized that country's financial system, one must first determine what would have happened to their financial system if no action had been taken. Only after it was demonstrated that the banking system would have failed if nothing had been done could someone determine persuasively whether or not, and to what extent, the bailout helped prevent that failure. The same logic applies to the study of the Eretrian tyrant-killing law.[22]

This section's argument rests on two complementary points. The first point is that, during the generation prior to the Athenian-led liberation of 341, Eretrian democrats had been consistently unable to maintain control of their polis, instead regularly being subdued by strongmen. The historical record is clear on that point. The Eretrians joined the Second Athenian League in 377 as a democratically governed polis.[23] But quite likely in 370, and certainly by 366, they lost control of the polis to a strongman named Themison.[24] The date of Themison's fall from power is not known. It is almost certain, however, that Eretrian democrats again controlled the polis in 357/6, after the Athenians invaded Euboia in either 358/7 or 357/6 (Knoepfler [1995: 334n100]) and drove out the Thebans.[25] But their regime was not long lasting: by 352, Menestratos, another autocrat—whom Demosthenes (23.124) politely referred to as a *dynastēs*—dominated Eretrian politics.[26] He fell quickly too; and by 349, another strongman, not the *dēmos*, named Ploutarchos controlled the polis. When Ploutarchos fell from power (perhaps in 344/3), the Eretrian democrats governed their polis yet again.[27] But, true to form, they retained control for only a matter of months: in 343 (perhaps in the summer), a faction led by Kleitarchos and two other men seized control of the polis.[28] Thus during the generation prior to the Athenian led liberation, the Eretrians had three different (all failed) democratic regimes covering (collectively) about twelve years (377–370, 357–353, 344–343) and four

22   For an informative discussion on the role of counterfactuals in historical inquiry, see Morris (2005).

23   Eretria in the Second Athenian League: *RO* 22 (line 81). Knoepfler (1995: 321–22nn45–46) presents some evidence and reasoning to suggest that the Athenians liberated Euboian cities from Spartan dominance in the spring of 377. There is very little evidence for internal Eretrian politics during the second third of the fourth century. However, Knoepfler (2001a: 84–88) suggests that the proxeny decree *IG* XII, 9, 187B, a decree of the *boulē* and *dēmos*, should be dated to around 370. In his discussion of that decree, Knoepfler considers a possible anti-tyranny context.

24   Themison took Oropos from the Athenians in 366: Diod. Sic. 15.76.1; Xen. *Hell.* 7.4.1; Dem. 18.99; Aischin. 2.164; 3.85. As noted by Knoepfler (2004: 405–6), Themison was the leader of a pro-Theban faction. He likely came to power soon after the battle of Leuktra (371), when the Eretrians left—at least de facto—the Second Athenian League, allied with Thebes and, "with all the cities of Euboia" (Xen. *Hell.* 6.5.23), invaded Sparta.

25   Diodoros (16.7.2) wrote that all of Euboia was in stasis in 358/7, torn apart by pro-Thebans and pro-Athenians. The Athenians, led by Timotheos, invaded the island and expelled the Boiotians (Dem. 8.74–75; 21.174 [cf. 22.14]; Aischin. 3.85). The Athenians made treaties with the four major cities of Euboia (*RO* 48). On the inscription recording that treaty, see Knoepfler (1995: 335–37). On Thebes's treaty of surrender to the Athenians: Aischin. 3.85; Dem. 21.174; 22.14.

26   As Knoepfler (2002: 197n262) notes, Xen. *Vect.* 3.11 might refer to Menestratos.

27   On this nontraditional dating of the fall of Ploutarchos's regime, see Picard (1979: 240–45). The traditional date of his fall is 348. For a clear presentation of the traditional view, see Parke (1929).

28   Dem. 9.57–58. See Ellis (1976: 164 and 282–83nn22–23) for the date of this coup.

different "strongman" regimes covering about eighteen years (370–357, 353–349, 349–344, 343–341).

The second complementary point is that, after the Athenian-led liberation of 341, would-be Eretrian strongmen, enjoying Philip's support and encouragement, almost certainly would have attempted to overthrow the recently reinstated Eretrian democracy. In defense of that point, one might note, first, that Philip had a motive to assist a would-be Eretrian strongman's efforts to overthrow the Eretrian democracy. The fact that he sent mercenary forces to Eretria on three different occasions within one year clearly demonstrates that Philip thought that the control of that city was in his strategic interest. And it is also possible that Philip believed that his credibility was at stake: Macedonian sympathizers in other poleis might no longer trust him if he did not follow through with his commitment to the strongmen in Eretria. In addition to motive, Philip would have had ample opportunity to assist would-be Eretrian strongmen in overthrowing the Eretrian democracy. As the previous paragraph suggests, there seems to have been no shortage of Eretrians who wanted to dominate their polis. And even an apparently pro-democratic leader could be "flipped" and support a narrow oligarchy; such was quite likely the case, for example, with the "tyrant" Kleitarchos.[29] And finally, the chances were quite good that a would-be Eretrian strongman would succeed in taking control of the city: the Eretrians clearly had a bad track record of defending their democracy; and the fact that they recently lost control of the polis once again might very well have lowered their moral even further.[30] It would thus be worth the risk to stage a Macedonian-backed coup.

Thus Eretrian democrats repeatedly failed to maintain control of their polis during the years preceding the Athenian-led liberation of 341, and there is very good reason to believe that, in the postliberation period, their ability to maintain control would be severely tested. On might reasonably conclude, therefore, that Eretrian democrats quite likely would have lost control of their polis shortly after the Athenian-led liberation, if no serious attempt were made to facilitate their efforts to mobilize in defense of their regime.

---

29 This is suggested by the fact that Kleitarchos led a popular revolution against the tyrant Ploutarchos. The evidence: Schol. Dem. 5.5 ("Ploutarchos was tyrant of Eretria. Kleitarchos rose up in rebellion against him and then the citizens joined in with him."). Kleitarchos almost certainly posed as a democratic champion. It is also likely that he posed as a tyrant killer—he struck the first blow, and then the citizens (earlier afraid of Ploutarchos and his mercenaries) joined him.

30 There is no reason to conclude that Eretrian strongmen enjoyed widespread support. First, there were rebellions against their rule (e.g., against Ploutarchos [scholion to Dem. 5.5] and Kleitarchos [Dem. 9.57–58]). Second, the strongmen relied on mercenaries (e.g., Ploutarchos [Dem. 9.57]). Third, they relied on outside support (Themison relied on Thebes; Ploutarchos relied on Athens; Kleitarchos relied on Macedon).

The remaining comments in this section describe (what would appear to be) a typical, Macedonian-supported coup—including the coup at Eretria—during the years immediately preceding the Athenian-led liberation of 341. Such a description, at the very least, will provide both important historical context and insight into the mechanisms of Philip's imperial success, at least as with regard to Greek cities. There is, however, a potential payoff for this section's argument. I demonstrate that Philip, in order to gain control of a Greek polis, induced and then exploited a revolutionary coordination problem among its citizens. It might not be unreasonable to suspect, then, that were Philip and his supporters to stage a coup in Eretria—which, per the reasoning presented above, they would likely attempt—they would in some way follow the pattern that Philip had previously followed with success on other occasions, including, again, in Eretria.

It must be noted that the evidence used in the following description is found almost entirely in Demosthenes's *Third Philippic*. The reason: that speech is the only source that describes in any detail the manner by which Philip installed puppet regimes in a Greek polis. This is, no doubt, an unfortunate situation. Beyond the fact that much of what he wrote cannot be independently corroborated, Demosthenes is a potentially tainted source. He had, first of all, a strongly held worldview: namely, no democracy would choose to side with Philip and against Athens; if it did, it was corrupted. And he had a political agenda: namely, to persuade the Athenian *dēmos* to see things his way and thus adopt his policies.[31] Those two points notwithstanding, the speech is of considerable evidentiary value since it was written by an astute observer of democratic politics virtually contemporaneously to the events described.[32] And it is also worth pointing out that this chapter's larger argument supports Demosthenes's analysis.

There appear to have been three stages in a typical pro-Macedonian coup. The aim of the first stage was to deceive the masses about Philip's actual intentions. In order to achieve that objective, Philip, for his part, would profess his goodwill to the citizens of the poleis that he intended to subject. He claimed, for example, to be an ally to the citizens of Eretria, and to the people of Phokis, and Thessaly; he sent messages of friendship to the Oreitai and of reassurance to the Olynthians.[33] Meanwhile, the pro-Macedonian conspira-

---

31 Aischines referred (2.14) to Demosthenes as a "Philip hater" (*misophilippos*) and sarcastically declared (2.8) that everybody but Demosthenes is a traitor. The same orator asserted at length (3.82–83) that Demosthenes intentionally interpreted any of Philip's actions in a negative light.

32 Demosthenes delivered his *Third Philipic* in the spring of 341. The anti-democratic coups at Oreos and Eretria likely took place in the summer of 343: see note 28 of this chapter. Philip began the mercenary invasions of Euboia in the summer of 342: see note 1 of this chapter.

33 See Dem. 9.10–14: Demosthenes wrote that Philip "deceived" (ἐξαπατᾶν) the Olynthians (sending ambassadors to assure them of his good intentions), the Phokians (pretending to be their ally), the Thessalians (pretending to be a friend and ally), and the people of Oreos (sending words

tors in the target cities would "speak on Philip's behalf."[34] Demosthenes does not provide specifics. But it is quite likely that such individuals would repeatedly remind their fellow citizens of Philip's apparent intention and argue that friendship with Macedon would be advantageous for the polis.[35]

In the second stage of a typical pro-Macedonian coup, the conspirators intimidated the population. The conspirators began this stage simply by slandering anybody who opposed pro-Macedonian policies. Such men, they would assert, are warmongers, intent on dividing the population and, ultimately, on destroying the polis. And since it appeared to many citizens that Philip was a friendly ally, only a particularly brave individual would risk becoming unpopular by advocating a hard-line anti-Macedonian policy.[36] If an individual insisted on advocating such policies, the conspirators would ratchet up their intimidation and propose that he be expelled from the city or silenced in some other way. And the populace, convinced that Philip is a friend, would ratify the proposal: again, they believed that they were preserving the city by eliminating rabble-rousers. This apparently happened in several cities: Olynthos (Dem. 9.56) (where the *dēmos* was persuaded to expel Apollonides), Oreos (Dem. 9.59–60) (where the *dēmos* was delighted to see Euphraios imprisoned), Eretria (Dem. 9.57) (where advocates of an anti-Macedonian policy were expelled).[37]

After successfully implementing the first two stages of the coup, the conspirators could have been reasonably sure that their fellow citizens would be unable to respond effectively to a coup due to a coordination problem. As a result of the deception campaign, individuals would think that the vast majority support explicitly pro-Macedonian policies. As a result of the intimidation campaign, individuals would be deterred from publically stating or otherwise demonstrating what they actually think. As a result, individuals who suspected that some of their fellow citizens were orchestrating a coup would both falsify their preferences and raise their revolutionary thresholds. Demosthenes describes that dynamic well with respect to the coup at Oreos (Dem.

---

of goodwill). For his deception in Eretria: Dem. 9.58 (where it is reasonably clear that Philip claimed to be an ally [*symmachos*] to the Eretrians). Also note: Philip's deception—as a means to take a city—was the theme of Demosthenes's speech to the Messenians in 344 (6.20–25). Philip's deception is also emphasized in Dem. 2.6–7.

34　See Dem. 9.63; cf. 9.53 (with reference to Athens in particular); cf. 9.57 (where the Eretrian prodemocrats are referred to as "those speaking on behalf of themselves [i.e., in the best interests of the Eretrians]").

35　Demosthenes often asserted that Philip's agents intentionally deceive their fellow citizens about Philip's actual intentions: Dem. 19.259–62 (it is described as the spread of an epidemic [*nosēma*]); 19.68, 300; 18.47–49, 247, 294–96; 8.52–53.

36　With respect to Athens, Demosthenes wrote (9.7), "there is grave danger that anyone who proposes and urges that we shall defend ourselves may incur the charge of having provoked the war."

37　For intimidation of anti-Macedonian speakers, see Dem. 3.32; 6.3; 8.68–69; 10.17.

9.61): "Then having all the liberty of action they [i.e., the conspirators] desired, they intrigued for the capture of the city and prepared to carry out their plot, while any of common folk who saw what they were at were terrorized into silence (ἐσίγα καί κατεπέπληκτο), having the fate of Euphraios before their eyes."

In the final stage of a coup, Philip sent a small force to help the conspirators seize control of the polis. This was the most risky stage, of course. But, as just noted, the populace likely would not be able to mobilize en masse in defense of their democracy due to a revolutionary coordination problem. Speaking generally about the third stage of a coup, Demosthenes wrote (9.50), "When, relying on this [small, light] force, he attacks some people that is at variance with itself, and when through distrust (δι᾽ ἀπιστίαν) no one goes forth to fight for his country, then he brings up his artillery and lays siege." With respect to the coup at Oreos, Demosthenes wrote (9.61), "so abject was their condition that, with this danger looming ahead, no one dared to breathe a syllable until the enemy, having completed their preparations, were approaching the gates; and then some were for defense, the others for surrender." And it is to be noted that Philip sent only 1,000 mercenary forces to support the "tyrants" in Eretria (Dem. 9.58). At that time, Eretria likely could mobilize between 4,200 and 5,000 hoplites.[38] It would thus appear that Philip correctly expected that the Eretrians would not be able to mobilize effectively in defense of their democracy.

Pro-Macedonian coups no doubt exhibited a considerable amount of variety. Each city had its own internal dynamic. And Philip likely had to alter his approach due to changing circumstances and his immediate needs. To the extent that Demosthenes can be believed, however, the different coups followed a general pattern: a campaign of deception and intimidation encouraged individuals to falsify their preferences and raise their revolutionary thresholds; a light military campaign capitalized on the resulting coordination problem.

Response to Threats: The Tyrant-Killing Law

The comments presented in this section demonstrate that, by promulgating their tyrant-killing law, the Eretrian democrats greatly increased the likelihood that they would be able to mobilize in defense of their regime and thus likely would have deterred anti-democrats from attempting a coup. The validity of that thesis depends, of course, on the extent to which the law facilitated coordinated mass action: the more thoroughly it did so, the more likely

---

38 Reber, Hansen, and Ducrey (2004: 652). Note, too, that there was a procession in Eretria's Artemesia of 3,000 hoplites, 600 cavalry, and 60 chariots: Strabo 10.1.10, C448; Knoepfler (2002: 176n148). See, too, Hansen (2006b).

anti-democrats would have been deterred from staging a coup. The operative question, then, is, how thoroughly did the Eretrian tyrant-killing law facilitate the democrats' efforts to coordinate in defense of their regime?

As will be demonstrated, the promulgation of the tyrant-killing law established four separate "layers of defense" for the newly reinstated Eretrian democracy. Three of those layers are "particular," in that they facilitate coordinated mass action at specific moments in a coup. The aim of the first particular layer was to prevent conspirators from successfully overthrowing the democracy. If anti-democratic conspirators somehow breached that layer, the second particular layer became operational: its objective was to prevent the participants of the successful coup from consolidating their control of the polis. The third particular layer became operational if the participants in the coup breached the second layer of defense and consolidated their control of the city: its objective was to overthrow the consolidated regime. The remaining layer, which is discussed first, is "general." It facilitated pro-democracy mobilization at any time in a coup, from its beginnings as a conspiracy to the period after the coup members have consolidated their control of the city.

GENERAL LAYER OF DEFENSE

Old Fragment and Lines 13–17 in New Fragment

The promulgation of the Eretrian tyrant-killing law provided a general layer of defense for the Eretrian democracy by increasing the likelihood that, should members of an anti-democratic faction either attempt to stage a coup or succeed in such an attempt, some individual (or individuals) would subsequently commit a conspicuous and violent act of defiance—"kill a tyrant"— and thereby spark a pro-democracy revolutionary bandwagon. The Athenians promulgated the decree of Demophantos in order to accomplish that same objective, of course. It is thus not at all surprising to discover that the Eretrians followed the same two-step process as that used by the Athenians: (1) lower the revolutionary thresholds of moderately risk-averse individuals by generating common knowledge of widespread credible commitment to defend the democracy; (2) incentivize particularly brave individuals to lower their revolutionary thresholds to zero. The Eretrian democrats, however, went to greater lengths than did the Athenians to achieve those ends. The following comments validate that assertion by comparing the "tyrant killing" (or "spark and bandwagon") provisions in the Eretrian tyrant-killing law to those found in the Athenian decree of Demophantos.

One clear and significant difference between the Eretrian tyrant-killing law and the Athenian decree of Demophantos is the fact that the Eretrian law explicitly incentivized noncitizens to "kill a tyrant." Evidence for that assertion is found in lines 6–7 of the old fragment, where the law, listing the rewards that will be given to a tyrant killer, states, "if he is a citizen." The use of that conditional indicates—virtually without any doubt—that the law also appealed to noncitizens. The question is thus: what group or groups of noncitizens were incentivized?

It is reasonable to conclude that the Eretrian law incentivized both free foreigners (*xenoi*) and slaves (*douloi*) to become tyrant killers. The case for free foreigners is simplest. To begin with, if the law incentivized only one noncitizen group, it would be free foreigners since they were only one level of status below citizens. And additional support is found in the fact that the Ilian tyrant-killing law (chapter 6) explicitly incentivized *xenoi* to kill tyrants (lines 28–29). The case for inclusion of slaves is only slightly less solid: they, too, were incentivized in the law from Ilion (lines 31–32); two well-known laws from late-fifth-century Thasos incentivized slaves to act in defense of the ruling regime (*ML* 83, lines 2 and 10); there are examples in the literary record of slaves having been rewarded—or promised rewards—for fighting in defense of a city's democracy.[39]

The generosity (or size) of what might be called the "tyrannicide incentive package" constitutes another important difference between the Eretrian tyrant-killing law and the decree of Demophantos. The decree of Demophantos simply states that the tyrannicide, if he lives, will receive the cash value of one-half of the "tyrant's" property; but if he dies, he and his descendants will be treated like Harmodios and Aristogeiton and their descendants. Unfortunately, there are only three rewards in the Eretrian law that are known for certain—i.e., not restored in Knoepfler's text: (1) public maintenance (*sitēsis*: line 9); (2) something concerning children (line 11); (3) something concerning daughters (line 13) and likely connected to the word "drachmas" in line 14. It is thus reasonably clear that the tyrant killer, should he survive, would receive (at least) public maintenance (*sitēsis*), while, if he died, his children would be taken care of. It is important to note here, however, that Knoepfler has persuasively argued (2001b: 210) that lines 5 to the end of the old fragment record only the rewards that would be given to a citizen tyrannicide—the rewards for noncitizen tyrant killers having been recorded in the lost lines of the law that followed the old fragment and preceded the new fragment (about four or five lines).[40] That strongly suggests that the law recorded additional rewards for the citizen tyrant killer: there is too much space within which to record only the three aforementioned rewards. And citing compelling epigraphic and literary parallels, Knoepfler has (with reason: 2001b:

---

39 According to the *Ath. Pol.* (40.2) Thrasyboulos proposed, unsuccessfully, a measure to give citizenship to all individuals who "joined in the return from the Piraeus." Importantly, [Aristotle] notes that many "clearly were slaves" (cf. Aischin. 3.195). In Rhodes (Diod. Sic. 20.100) the democrats gave citizenship to slaves who helped the city resist Demetrios's famous siege. (Note, however, that, in both cases, these honors were apparently announced after the slaves had already participated.)

40 Knoepfler (2001b: 213).

211–13) restored two rewards: (1) a statue in the tyrannicide's likeness would be erected somewhere in the city;[41] (2) the tyrannicide would receive a front-row seat at festivals (i.e., *proedria*). It is also reasonably suggested that the citizen tyrannicide would receive a cash payment.[42]

It is impossible to know for certain what rewards the Eretrians were prepared to give to a noncitizen tyrant killer. But, again, a comparison with the law from Ilion might be helpful. That law states (lines 28–31) that a free foreigner (*xenos*) would receive the same rewards as a citizen tyrannicide *and* could become a citizen. A slave, on the other hand, would receive his freedom and half the cash payment that would be given to a citizen or free foreigner tyrannicide (lines 31–36). It is by no means certain that the Eretrians did the same. But it is not unreasonable to suspect that they did something similar.

Before discussing the final difference between the Eretrian tyrant-killing law and the Athenian decree of Demophantos (again, just concerning the tyrant-killing "spark" and "bandwagon" dynamic), it is important to determine which individuals were legitimate targets of assassination. The old fragment clearly (i.e., not restored) marks as legitimate targets "the tyrant" (line 6) and anyone who "makes an attempt at tyranny" (line 5). Two points suggest, however, that the law authorized the assassination of any (prominent) member of a nondemocratic regime. First, Knoepfler has restored (line 6) "whoever kills a member of the tyrant's faction (τυραννίζοντα) or the tyrant" and, in lines 10–11, "if the killer of a tyrant or the leader of an oligarchy dies." Those are reasonable restorations: (1) the participle τυραννίζοντες is found in a nearly contemporaneous speech written for an Athenian audience ([Dem]. 17.7), and its meaning ("member of the tyrant's faction") is virtually identical to that of "whosoever shall help to install a tyrant," which is found in the decree of Demophantos; (2) "leader of an oligarchy" is found in the Ilion tyrant-killing law (lines 19–20). Second, by the 340s, to many Greeks—not just Athenians—the concept of "the tyrant" was broad and could include the members of any nondemocratic regime. For example, the leader of the democratic revolution in Rhodes in 395 (*Hell. Oxy.* 10, 2 = column xi, 12–28) encouraged his fellow citizens "to attack the tyrants as quickly as possible."[43]

41 Statues were a well-established reward for tyrannicides: Harmodios and Aristogeiton in Athens; Metapontion (Berve 1967: 159); Xen. *Hier.* 4.5; Ilion (chap. 6); Erythrai (chap. 5), Konon in Athens (Dem. 20.70). And it is worth pointing out that there is evidence for the Eretrians erecting statues of individuals—but not tyrannicides—just a few years after the promulgation of their anti-tyranny law (*IG* XII, 9, 196 and 198).

42 A cash payment as a reward for tyrant killing or acting in defense of the ruling regime was standard: Ilion (chap. 6); both laws from Thasos (*ML* 83); a decree from mid-fifth-century Miletos (*ML* 43); Demophantos (chap. 1). It should also be noted that the Eretrian law likely also deemed the tyrant slayer to be "pure," although that is not restored in Knoepfler's text.

43 It is to be noted that this is the only direct quote in the extant remains of the Oxyrhynchos

And after the famous assault on Thebes in 379 (Xen. *Hell.* 5.4.9), the revolutionaries encouraged their fellow citizens to rally to their side because "the tyrants are dead."

The means by which the Eretrians generated common knowledge of credible commitment to defend the democracy constitutes the final significant difference between their tyrant-killing law and the decree of Demophantos. The decree of Demophantos, of course, required all citizens to swear a one-time oath by tribes and demes.[44] The Eretrian law did not require the citizens to swear an oath. Instead, it mandated that Eretria's priests and priestesses utter a curse calling for the total destruction of all individuals "speaking or acting" contrary to the law's provisions. Two points are important.

The first point is that the priests and priestesses pronounced the curse at both the Dionysia and the Artimisia. The Dionysia was held in the city of Eretria on 12 Lenaion; the Artimisia was held in Eretria's countryside about two months later (end of Anthesterion).[45] It is quite reasonable to suppose, therefore, that virtually every citizen, whether he lived in the *asty* or the *chora*, heard the curse. The performance context for the oath's pronouncement is unknown. But it is quite likely that the law was displayed, read, or—at the very least—repeatedly referred to.[46] And the "audience" likely made signs of commitment to enforce the law or to show their support of the curse's sentiment.

The second point is that the priests and priestess pronounced the curses annually. This is not stated explicitly, but it is certainly implied. Doing so provided an opportunity for each Eretrian both to reaffirm publically his commitment to uphold the tyrant-killing law and to observe his fellow citizens reaffirm publically their own commitment. Widespread support for the tyrant-killing law—that is, to defend the democracy—would thus be main-

---

Historian. Bruce (1967: 100) suggests that an eyewitness informant might have provided the quote of the short speech to the historian.

44   For a detailed discussion of the oath of Demophantos's ritual, see the section in chapter 1 titled "Reconstruction of the Oath Ritual."

45   On the dates for the Dionysia and the Artimisia: Knoepfler (2001b: 232). It is important to note that citizens from Chalkis and Karystos regularly attended Eretria's Artimisia. See Knoepfler (1972). The primary evidence is Livy 35.38 and Paus. 1.31.4–5.

46   Knoepfler (2001b: 199 with notes 23–24) suggests that the extant stele was placed in the temple of Artemis Amarynthos—halfway between Porthmos and Eretria. His evidence: (1) several stelai set up in that temple have been found in the vicinity of Aliveri (most notably the important *lex sacra* [*RO* 73]); (2) the tyrant-killing law mentions a 10 percent tax that would be given to Artemis and the curse was pronounced at the Artimisia. (Although he notes [2001b: 199n25] that the lengthy swamp clearing inscription [*IG* XII, 9, 191A] was placed in the sanctuary of Apollo despite the fact that it contains the "10 percent to Artemis" stipulation.) In the second part of his editio princeps (2002: 191–92) Knoepfler suggests that the Eretrians inscribed the law on two stelai (like the law of Eukrates: see chapter 3)—one placed in the temple of Artemis, the other in the temple of Dionysos.

tained as common knowledge. And that would be very important in a "young" democracy where credibility of commitment could be doubted.

It thus appears that the Eretrian democrats established a solid general layer of defense for their new democracy. On the one hand, they directly incentivized all male members of their larger society to kill any (prominent) member of a nondemocratic regime or participant in an anti-democracy coup. On the other hand, they ensured that widespread credible commitment to uphold the tyrant-killing law (i.e., to defend the democracy) remained common knowledge. Success could not be guaranteed, of course. But they did greatly increase the likelihood that, at anytime while the democracy is threatened or overthrown, someone would "kill a tyrant" and thus spark a revolutionary bandwagon that would overwhelm the anti-democrats.

FIRST PARTICULAR LAYER OF DEFENSE

Lines 3–13 in New Fragment

The promulgation of the Eretrian tyrant-killing law provided the first particular layer of defense by increasing the likelihood that a sufficient number of democrats would successfully respond to subversive activity *before* anti-democrats actually overthrew the democracy. It did so by explicitly criminalizing two subversive acts.

The first subversive action criminalized (lines 3–6) is unauthorized traveling abroad by a member of the council or (likely) a magistrate (*archōn*). There could be any number of reasons why the Eretrians criminalized such behavior. But perhaps the single most important objective was to prevent individuals with institutional authority from communicating with foreign agents or Eretrian exiles. A councilman or magistrate, for example, might formulate a plan with such individuals to overthrow the Eretrian democracy. And, upon returning to Eretria, he could use the power of his office to implement it. Thus the law equates such unauthorized travel with "dissolving the *dēmos*."[47]

The second subversive action criminalized in this section of the law (lines 6–13) is proposing (λέγων) or putting to vote (ἐπιψηφίζων) a bill that would dissolve the regime in control of Eretria. The objective here is to prevent a "legal" coup where—like what happened in Athens in 411—the assembly simply votes to change the regime. It thus should be noted that the law does not call Eretria's legitimate regime a democracy. Instead, it refers (lines 6–7) to "this regime—the one now in existence." And later in the law (lines 19–20), the legitimate regime is described as one with a "council and *prytaneia* ap-

---

47 Knoepfler (2001b: 218) also suggests that this provision was intended to prevent individuals from meeting with exiles. As an additional possibility, he suggests that it could have been intended to prevent individuals from fleeing the city in the event of a coup.

pointed by lot from all Eretrians."[48] The Eretrians did so in order to prevent anti-democrats from using the word "democracy" in order to mask a proposal that really established some sort of oligarchy. A great example of such a trick occurred, again, in Athens during the coup of the Four Hundred when Peisandros cynically suggested in the assembly that the Athenians adopt "another type of democracy" (Thuc. 8.53.1).[49]

The punishments for committing either subversive act correspond to how immediately the act threatened the Eretrian democracy. The first act—unauthorized travel abroad—did not constitute an immediate threat. Thus the punishment was comparably mild: a guilty man would be stripped of his office immediately, and both he and his family would be deprived of their political rights (i.e., be declared *atimoi*). The second act (active involvement in a proposal to dissolve the regime in control of Eretria), on the other hand, represented an immediate threat. Thus an individual guilty of that crime would be punished severely: he would lose his political rights, his property would be confiscated, he could not be buried in Eretrian soil, and—quite remarkably—he *and his family* may be killed, the killer being rewarded just like a tyrannicide.

As noted above, the criminalization of the two subversive acts increased the likelihood that a sufficient number of democrats would successfully respond to subversive activity *before* anti-democrats actually overthrew the democracy. It is reasonable to suppose that neither of the two aforementioned subversive acts was illegal before the law's promulgation: individuals had the freedom to propose (and the *dēmos* the freedom to ratify) any motion; magistrates had complete freedom of movement. If that were the case, it would have been very difficult for democrats to coordinate in response to such acts even if many suspected that the actors were working to subvert the democracy: there would be confusion about what others think is acceptable behavior. By criminalizing those two acts, however, the Eretrians knew that such behavior was, in fact, widely viewed as unacceptable. And they also knew what to do in response (and that that response enjoyed widespread support). Thus, if a councilman traveled abroad without permission, the as-

---

48   For comments on the Eretrian council and *prytaneia*, see Knoepfler (2002: 157–61). The council likely had either 240 or 300 members (i.e., either 40 or 50 from each of the six tribes). The *prytaneia* likely performed a function similar to the *prytaneis* in Athens (i.e., preside over the council).

49   Based on these provisions, one can reconstruct (speculatively) the steps of a coup feared by the Eretrian democrats. First, conspirators travel abroad to coordinate a plan (with Philip, his representatives, or exiles). Second, the conspirators return and use the power of their office to implement the plan. Third, in a meeting of the assembly they successfully move that the Eretrians change their regime. Fourth, they call in foreign troops (who are waiting) and use their own partisans to protect the new "legal" regime. Compare this speculation with the conspiracy headed by Perillos and Ptoiodoros in Megara (Dem. 19.295).

sembly would be much more likely to remove him from office and deprive him of his political rights. And if someone participated in a resolution to change the regime, a supporter of the democracy would be much more likely to assassinate him. In both scenarios, the conspirators would fail.

SECOND PARTICULAR LAYER OF DEFENSE

Lines 17–24 in New Fragment

The promulgation of the tyrant-killing law provided the second particular layer of defense by increasing the likelihood that supporters of the Eretrian democracy would respond *immediately* and in sufficient numbers to a successful coup and thereby prevent the coup members from consolidating their control of the city.[50]

The Eretrian lawmakers envisioned two scenarios in which anti-democrats might succeed in overthrowing the Eretrian democracy. First, the assembly might actually vote to dissolve the democracy. Specifically, the law envisions (lines 17–20) a scenario wherein someone puts to a vote (ἐπιψηφίζει), drafts (γράφει), or votes for (φέρει) a bill that would change the regime.[51] It might appear as though there is a redundancy here since, just a few lines earlier (in the provisions concerning the first particular layer of defense), the law addressed a scenario wherein someone makes a proposal or puts to the vote a bill that would dissolve the current regime. The difference is that the earlier provision focuses on attempts to stage a legal coup, while the later provision focuses on a successful attempt to stage a legal coup.

The second scenario envisioned by the democrats (lines 20–21) is the use of brute force. Specifically, the law addresses someone establishing either a tyranny or oligarchy and using force (ἐγβιάρηται: literally "to force out"). It is quite possible, of course, that, in drawing up this provision, the Eretrians imagined any scenario wherein anti-democrats used force in order to overthrow the democracy. Two points, however, might suggest that the Eretrians had something more specific in mind. First, the immediately preceding provision considered the possibility that anti-democrats might establish a nondemocratic regime by a vote in the assembly. Second, the provision that immediately follows refers to participants in either of the two scenarios covered in the "second layer of defense"—that is, the use of assembly procedure and the use of force—as those "who will prevent [a meeting of] the assembly and *prytaneia*." It is quite possible, then, that the Eretrians envisioned a scenario

---

50 It should be noted that line 17 contains the law's only extant asyndeton (ἐάν τις). Knoepfler (2001b: 214–15) argues that that asyndeton marks the beginning of the law's second part: the first part of the law focused on protection of the democratic regime; the second part focused on the means to reestablish a democratic regime after a coup.

51 For φέρειν to mean "vote," see Xen. *Hell.* 2.4.9 (φέρειν τὴν ψῆφον).

wherein anti-democrats used force in order to expel their opponents from the assembly before a vote on regime change.

The promulgation of the Eretrian tyrant-killing law increased the likelihood that Eretrians would respond adequately to a successful coup by explicitly ordering all citizens to mobilize quickly in defense of their democracy. The moments immediately following a coup are crucial in determining who will control the state. If democrats respond slowly—if they wait, looking around for others to act—the coup members will have time to intimidate, misinform, and ultimately atomize the population. They will have time, that is, to consolidate their control of the city. If the pro-democrats are able to mobilize quickly, however, they could overwhelm their (likely numerically inferior) opponents. But that is easier said than done: the mobilization must be large-scale; military leaders might be dead or unable to issue orders. The Eretrian democrats thus issued—in the law—the mobilization order in advance. Quite revealingly the law reads, "all citizens must assist the *dēmos* immediately and join in battle against those who will prevent [a meeting of] the assembly and *prytaneia*, each considering himself competent to fight without an order." The hope is that there would be a leaderless uprising, a riot, throughout Eretria.[52] And the coup members would be defeated before they were able to solidify their control of the city.

THIRD PARTICULAR LAYER OF DEFENSE

Line 24 to End of New Fragment

Promulgation of the tyrant-killing law provided the third particular layer of defense by increasing the likelihood that the pro-democrats would eventually be able to regain control of the polis in the event that anti-democrats successfully solidified their control of the polis.

The law articulates two scenarios—both of which indicate that the anti-democrats have consolidated their control of the city—wherein the third layer of defense would become operational. In the first scenario (lines 24–26), the anti-democrats prevent the members of the council from convening in the Agoraion. It is not entirely clear why the law focused on such a scenario. Perhaps the citizens normally looked to the council for guidance and

---

52 It is interesting to compare this provision with a mid-fifth-century law from Erythrai (*I. Erythrai* 2c). The law from Erythrai lists punishments for any individual who "does not come when the *prytaneis* issue a public order" (ὃς ἄμ μὴ ἔλθηι ἐπ[α]νγγελάντων τῶν πρυτάνεων) (lines 11–15). As the editors note (pp. 31–32), the law quite likely refers to situations where the polis is threatened. What happens, however, if the *prytaneis* are unable to issue an order? The provision in the Eretrian tyrant-killing law addresses that possibility: Eretrians are to fight even without having received orders from officials.

instructions. Thus, should the council be unable to perform that function, the democrats would be powerless. In the second scenario (line 26), the anti-democrats actually shut the *dēmos* out of the city walls. Knoepfler suggests that such a drastic development might take place during a large-scale civic festival.[53]

Promulgation of the tyrant-killing law increased the likelihood that the democrats would overthrow a consolidated nondemocratic regime by explicitly ordering all Eretrians to form a pro-democracy resistance movement. Specifically, the law requires (lines 26–30) every Eretrian to "secure some Eretrian stronghold, whatever seems advantageous for all helpers to arrive at; after securing [the stronghold], receive any Greek who arrives and wishes to help the *dēmos* of Eretria." The law does not state where the democrats should convene. But that is quite reasonable: if the law publicized the location beforehand, the anti-democrats almost certainly would secure it in the early moments of the coup. Operational flexibility was essential. (The location would spread by word of mouth in the event of a coup.)

It perhaps goes without saying that an individual Eretrian would have required a good reason to join a resistance movement. Participation would be dangerous, disruptive, and time-consuming. Thus one might be tempted to "free ride," that is, to not participate in the struggle but to benefit should it succeed. Why would an individual choose to participate? There are three complementary reasons.

The first and most fundamental reason that an individual would choose to participate is that the resistance movement would have a reasonably decent chance of success, should an adequate number of individuals join. To begin with, many—most likely most—Eretrians had already participated in resistance movements: such movements are known to have been conducted against Ploutarchos (348) and Kleitarchos (342–341).[54] Thus people knew the drill, as it were. In addition, the Eretrians had reason to expect support from the citizens of other poleis. The Athenians, it will be recalled, were treaty bound (*IG* II² 230) to assist the Eretrian *dēmos* in the event of a coup. And Chalkis (led by Kallias) almost certainly would provide assistance too. (Eretria was part of the Euboian League led by Chalkis [Aischin. 3.85–105]; see above in the introduction to this chapter.)

Financial considerations also would have motivated an individual to participate in the resistance movement. The law is very clear on this point (lines 32–36). If an individual joined the movement and the movement succeeded,

---

53 Knoepfler (2002: 176–77). He cites as precedent: Hdt. 1.150 (eighth-century Smyrna) and Aen. Tact. 17.1–4 (Argos in 417).

54 Resistance movement against Ploutarchos: Schol. Dem. 5.5. Resistance movement against Kleitarchos: Dem. 9.57–58.

he would receive a portion of the property and movable goods that belonged to those individuals who did not join. The flip side of that provision, of course, is that anybody who did not join in the movement would lose his property. Thus poor individuals had the opportunity for financial gain. Rich Eretrians would be motivated to keep what they had.

The final complementary reason why an individual would choose to join the movement is that all participants were legally obliged to attack anyone who did not participate. The law does not order participants to attack anyone actively defending a nondemocratic regime. Instead, it orders (lines 30–32) the participants to attack anybody who "does not help the *dēmos.*" Thus an individual could not hope to play it safe by neither joining the resistance movement nor defending the nondemocratic regime. Each individual would have to choose which side he would actively fight for.

After taking into consideration the three aforementioned factors, a typical, moderately risk-averse individual might reasonably conclude that a sufficient number of his fellow citizens will join the resistance movement and that, as a result, the movement would prevail. Thus, after he saw a few men "run to the hills," he would decide to do likewise, believing that others would follow him. And others would, in turn, follow him for the same reason. Thus the resistance movement would enjoy more and more support and quite possibly overwhelm Eretria's nondemocratic regime.

The analysis presented above demonstrates that the Eretrian pro-democrats, by promulgating their tyrant-killing law, utilized a strategy commonly referred to as "defense in depth." The law, that is, did not simply establish a single line of defense for their democracy. Instead, it established multiple lines of defense, each of which became operational at particular "progression points" in a coup: one line sought to disrupt a coup even before the democracy was overthrown; another line sought to prevent the members of a successful coup from consolidating their control of the polis; another line sought to dislodge a consolidated anti-democratic regime; and another, the "general layer of defense," sought to facilitate large-scale pro-democracy mobilization whenever anti-democrats threatened to overthrow, or succeeded in overthrowing the Eretrian democracy. The Eretrian tyrant-killing law is thus considerably more sophisticated than it might appear at first reading.

Considering how thoroughly the tyrant-killing law facilitated coordinated mass action in defense of the Eretrian democracy, one might reasonably suspect that anti-democrats would be deterred from staging a coup. One cannot know for certain, of course. But the pro-democrats greatly increased the probability that a coup would fail. And the degree to which they increased that probability is (roughly) the greater degree to which anti-democrats would begrudgingly choose to cooperate with the newly reinstated Eretrian democracy.

Stability

The comments presented in this short section demonstrate that the Eretrian democrats maintained secure control of their polis—in a very difficult environment—for several years after they promulgated their tyrant-killing law. The chronological terminus for the discussion is 323—i.e., the death of Alexander. Several points argue in favor of that terminus. First, it is reasonable to conclude that the law's impact decreased over time: it would thus become increasingly irrelevant to extend the period of time examined. In addition, the death of Alexander marks the beginning of a new era in Greek history—when Alexander's "successors" fought with and against each other for supremacy—wherein Eretria's internal dynamics might very well have been both qualitatively and quantitatively different than in the years prior. And finally, evidence that sheds light on the fortunes of Eretria's democracy in the years after Alexander's death is both sparse and ambiguous.

The first point in support of this section's argument is that Eretrian democrats were optimistic about the viability of their regime a couple of years *after* the Athenian-led liberation. Evidence in support of that point is found in an Eretrian decree (*RO* 73) promulgated in circa 338.[55] The decree, which establishes the basis for augmenting the city's festival for Artemis, reflects optimism and confidence. Effort is made, for example, to attract foreigners to compete in various musical competitions and participate in an elaborate procession and sacrifice. The final sentence of the decree (lines 41–45), however, is particularly telling: "write up the decree on a stone stele and stand it in the sanctuary of Artemis, in order that the sacrifice and the musical festival for Artemis shall happen in this way for all time, with the Eretrians being free, prospering and ruling themselves" (ἐλευθέρων ὄντων Ἐρετριέων καὶ εὖ πρηττόν|των καὶ αὐτοκρατόρων). Eretrian democrats almost certainly would not have articulated such a sentiment during the years preceding their liberation.[56]

---

55 This date is suggested by Knoepfler (2004: 409–11). In his editio princeps for the Eretrian tyrant-killing law (2001b: 207), however, Knoepfler suggests that *RO* 73 was promulgated up to six years after the anti-tyranny law. In *RO*, the inscription is dated circa 340.

56 It is also worth pointing out as potential evidence in support of this section's argument that the Eretrians likely fought against Macedon at Chaironeia. The only evidence for their possible participation is found in a passage in Demosthenes (18.237) wherein the orator boasts about the success he had in making alliances with many powers that fought at Chaironeia. Included among those powers are "the Euboians." Sealey (1993: 197–98) suggests that the Euboian contingent at Chaironeia might have been considerable because of the Athenian liberation of Eretria and Oreos and subsequent formation of the Euboian League. That is certainly plausible; but the size—or even existence—of the Eretrian contingent is unknowable. It is certainly reasonable to assume, however, that the Eretrians did fight against Philip at Chaironeia. Thus the situation was quite different than it was a couple of years earlier when Eretria was, according to Demosthenes (18.71), Philip's "base of operations from which to attack Attica."

It is important to emphasize the fact that the decree does not simply reflect postliberation euphoria. The Eretrians, again, likely promulgated the decree a couple of years after the fall of Kleitarchos. Thus enough time had elapsed for the Eretrians to assess the viability of the new, postliberation status quo. And they certainly appear to have been quite positive.

The second point in support of this section's argument is that Eretrian democrats maintained control of their polis after the battle of Chaironeia and throughout the reign of Alexander. That they had such control during the reign of Alexander is adequately attested epigraphically—there is no doubt.[57] It is true that the there is no evidence that surely sheds light on Eretrian politics immediately after Chaironeia. But there is no reason whatsoever to suppose that the Eretrian democracy was overthrown after Chaironeia and reestablished early in the reign of Alexander.[58]

It is quite remarkable that anti-democrats did not reclaim control of Eretria after the battle of Chaironeia. There can be little doubt that they would have liked to stage a coup d'état. And one would think that they had the opportunity to do so. To begin with, the Eretrian pro-democrats were, at least during the previous generation, unable to defend their regime against attacks launched by their domestic adversaries. In addition, Eretrian pro-democrats likely would not have received support from an outside power (e.g., Athens or Chalkis); they would have had to defend their regime by themselves. And finally, Philip quite likely made it known that he was not at all averse to pro-Macedonian, anti-democratic coups in the wake of his victory at Chaironeia. Demosthenes, for example, wrote (18.65) that, after his victory, Philip destroyed, wherever he could, "the prestige, the authority, the independence, and even the regime of every city alike." And there is reason to suspect that

57 There are perhaps four inscriptions that both date to the reign of Alexander and demonstrate that the *dēmos* controlled Eretria. The first inscription is Knoepfler's *Décrets érétriens* no. 1: a decree, dated circa 335, honoring a man [Krates?] from Sikyon. Although the enactment formula reads "it seems best to the *ekklesia*" and [Krates] is praised for being a good man to the polis (i.e., not the *dēmos*) of Eretria (lines 5–7), the decree was proposed by Exekestos the son of Diodoros, a prominent democrat (he proposed, for example, the aforementioned *lex sacra* [*RO* 73]). The second inscription is *IG* XII, 9, 197: a decree of the *dēmos*, dated circa 323, honoring two of Alexander's men, who might have assisted Eretria during the Lamian war (Eretria did not join the Athenians in that war). For that inscription, see Knoepfler (2001a: 170–74). The third inscription is *IG* XII, 9, 222: a decree of the *dēmos*, dated 335–330, honoring Philoxenos, a high-ranking official for Alexander. For that inscription, see Knoepfler (2001a: 97–104). And the fourth possible inscription is the *lex sacra* (*RO* 73) discussed above. It could date to as late as 334.

58 Such a scenario would entail four steps: (1) an anti-democratic coup after Chaironeia; (2) the sanctioning of the new non-democratic regime by Philip and the Korinthian League (see the introduction to chapter 3); (3) a successful counter-coup by pro-democrats almost immediately after the death of Philip; (4) Alexander sanctioning that new democratic regime. This is possible, but by no means probable: one might expect some indication in the sources of such events; one might suspect that Alexander would not sanction a regime on the Greek mainland whose members overthrew a regime recently sanctioned by his father.

many cities suffered pro-Macedonian, oligarchic coups in the wake of Philip's victory, likely with Philip's active support.[59] One might reasonably conclude, therefore, that, if Eretrian anti-democrats did not assume control of their polis, they either tried and failed or did not try because they thought they would fail. In either case, their failure (actual or expected) would have been due to the Eretrian pro-democrats.

The evidence presented above demonstrates that the Athenian-led liberation of 341 marked a turning point in the history of Eretria's fourth-century democracy.[60] As noted in the "Threats to Stability" section of this chapter, during the thirty years before 341, the Eretrians had three different democratic regimes covering (collectively) about twelve years (377–370, 357–353, 344–343) and four different "strongman" regimes covering about eighteen years (370–357, 353–349, 349–344, 343–341). The story after 341 is quite different: the democrats maintained control of the polis for eighteen years straight. And, at least during the first few of those years, one might reasonably conclude that the pro-democrats' ability to maintain that control was severely tested by their domestic opponents.

Conclusion

Philip II posed the most serious threat to democratic governance on the Greek mainland since—at least—Sparta's victory in the Peloponnesian War. On the one hand, he could threaten a democratically governed polis from the outside: he had accumulated sufficient military and economic resources to simply overpower a polis.[61] On the other hand, and perhaps most notewor-

---

59 Solid evidence exists for coups in Akarnania (Diod. Sic. 17.3; *RO* 77) and Troizen (Hyp. *Athenogenes* 29–36). The later coup is rather fascinating. Immediately after Chaironeia, the Athenians requested assistance from Troizen (Lykourg. *Leok.* 42). But Athenogenes, who had just fled Athens, and Mnesias of Argos staged an anti-democratic coup before the city could send aid. The exiled Troizenians fled to Athens and were granted citizenship. On Philip's postvictory arrangements, see Roebuck (1948). He suggests that pro-Macedonians also staged coups in Megara and the islands of Korkyra, Leukas, and Kephallenia. Philip directly intervened in Thebes: he established a garrison (Diod. Sic. 16.87.3) and formed a council of 300 from returned exiles (Justin 9.4.6–10). Philip also placed a garrison in Ambrakia (Diod. Sic. 17.3) and, perhaps, in Korinth.

60 Note that one cannot attribute Eretria's stability to the Athenian invasion alone: they invaded Eretria before (e.g., 357), and the democracy in that city subsequently failed. Something else was at work after the Athenian invasion of 341: the tyrant-killing law. Note, however, that Dössel (2007) has argued that the Eretrian tyrant-killing law is actually a composite text, containing three separate laws: the first (and oldest) is contained in the old fragment; the second (and second oldest) began sometime before the extant lines of the new fragment and concluded in line 17 of the new fragment, just after the curse; the third begins with the asyndeton in line 17 and continues to the end of the new fragment. Her arguments are cogent, and her conclusion should be taken seriously. But I still conclude that the stele recorded a single law, one that established a well-thought-out "defense in depth" (supra) strategy to defend the democracy.

61 Key to Philip's economic strength was control of the Krenidean mining communities (later

thy, he could threaten a democratically governed polis from the inside. He appears to have known that democracy's weak link was the difficulty its supporters had in mobilizing effectively in its defense. And he certainly knew that he could find reliable partners in the various cities to help him exploit that vulnerability. Indeed, such a partnership would be "win-win": Philip would acquire loyal puppet regimes on the cheap; anti-democrats would be able to dominate their domestic opponents. It thus was with reason that Demosthenes feared for the future of democracy.[62]

Eretrian pro-democrats, however, demonstrated that it was possible to counter Philip's attempts to overthrow a democratic regime from the inside. Their main weapon, of course, was a thoroughly crafted tyrant-killing law—a tool that facilitated coordinated mass action by the (majority) pro-democrats in response to a coup attempt by the (minority) anti-democrats. Philip, despite the promulgation of that law, likely still could overthrow the Eretrian democracy. But he would have to do so from the outside. And that would be much more costly.

It is tempting to connect the success of the Eretrian democrats to the subsequent popularity of tyrant-killing legislation. Arguments from silence are problematic, of course. But it is quite striking to note, first, that all extant (i.e., on stone) tyrant-killing enactments were promulgated during the late Classical and early Hellenistic periods—that is, during a period wherein the nature and extent of a king's influence in the domestic affairs of the various Greek poleis was being worked out for the first time. Second, the law from Eretria is the earliest such enactment. Perhaps the Eretrians (and, of course, the Athenians) taught the wider Greek world that tyrant-killing law could facilitate pro-democrats' efforts to maintain control of their city—and not just in Athens.

---

renamed Philippoi) in 356. See Ellis (1976: 68–70) and Worthington (2008: 45–47). The mines produced 1,000 talents per annum.

62 See [Dem.] 10.4 for a clear articulation of that fear: "Philip's faction, those who hanker after tyrannies and oligarchies have everywhere gained supremacy, and I doubt whether of all the states there is any stable democracy (πόλις δημοκρατουμένη βεβαίως) left except our own."

The Law of Eukrates

Introduction

In early August 338, Philip II defeated an Athenian-led coalition in the battle of Chaironeia. The Athenians and their allies—the most important of whom were the Thebans—could not have expected a better chance for victory. They had, first of all, a large number of infantry and cavalry: as many, if not more, than Philip's 30,000 infantry and 2,000 cavalry. Second, their position, a lone line stretching across the river plain, was strong, superior to Philip's: they could both prevent Philip's forces from marching southward down the valley and, since they held the important Kerata pass, conduct a safe retreat if needed. But they lost badly. Of the 6,000 Athenian participants, 1,000 died and 2,000 were taken prisoner. The allies fared no better. The Athenians and their allies were simply no match for the well-drilled, well-armed, and well-led Macedonian phalanx. And with there being no plausible hope of fighting Philip under more favorable circumstances, the significance of the battle was clear: Philip was indisputably the master of the Greek mainland.[1]

Philip was conspicuously lenient to the defeated Athenians. It is true that he forced them to join the Korinthian League—an institution by means of which he maintained his control of the conquered Greek poleis.[2] And it is

---

1 For modern discussions of the battle (and citations of the ancient evidence), see Ellis (1976: 197–98); Cawkwell (1978b: 144–49); Griffith (1979: 596–603); Hammond (1989:115–119); Sealey (1993: 196–98); Worthington (2008: 147–51).

2 Philip founded this league in the winter of 338/7 (Diod. Sic. 16.89). All member states sent representatives to a common council (*synedrion*) that was charged with (inter alia) maintaining a common peace, adjudicating disputes between members (see, for example, *RO* 82), and preserving the integrity of each member state's constitution (*politeia*). But Philip, as holder of the office of *hegemōn*, controlled the council: his approval was likely necessary for a bill (*dogma*) to be ratified, and he probably could propose bills too. In addition to the *synedrion* and the office of the *hegemōn*, there were officials called "those appointed for the common safety" ([Dem.] 17.15). Those men (Antipater might have served on this board) likely were charged with ensuring that the citizens of member states were abiding by the league's charter. For the oath-bound duties of member states, see *RO* 76 and [Dem.] 17. For a short description of the Korinthian League, see Cawkwell (1978b: 169–76) and Heisserer (1980: xxiii–xxvii). On the post-Chaironeia peace, see Ryder (1965). For Philip's settlements with various poleis after Chaironeia and before the foundation of the Korinthian League, see Roebuck (1948).

also true that he forced them to disband their (at that time anemic) naval confederacy. But, on the other hand, he returned the ashes of their dead soldiers with dignity (sending Alexander and Antipater as escorts); he returned their captured soldiers without ransom (indeed, he gave them new clothing); he allowed the Athenians to maintain control of the important islands of Lemnos, Imbros, Skyros, and Samos; and, most importantly, he did not make any overt move (or support any such move) to dissolve their democracy.[3]

Nevertheless, in the spring (or summer) of 336 an Athenian named Eukrates successfully proposed a law against tyranny and subversion of the Athenian democracy. A nearly perfectly preserved stone stele engraved with that law was found in Athens in May of 1952. Its vivid articulation (both pictorially and verbally) of Athenian democratic ideology has made it one of the most famous inscriptions from classical Athens.[4]

ΣΤΟΙΧ. 36

ἐπὶ Φρυνίχου ἄρχοντος· ἐπὶ τῆς Λεωντίδος ἐν-
άτης πρυτανείας· ἧι Χαιρέστρατος Ἀμεινίου
Ἀχαρνεὺς ἐγραμμάτευεν· τῶν προέδρων ἐπεψή-
φιζεν Μενέστρατος Αἰξωνεύς. Εὐκράτης Ἀρισ-
5 τοτίμου Πειραιεὺς εἶπεν· ἀγαθῆι τύχηι τοῦ δ-
ήμου τοῦ Ἀθηναίων, δεδόχθαι τοῖς νομοθέται-
ς· ἐάν τις ἐπαναστῆι τῶι δήμωι ἐπὶ τυραννίδι
ἢ τὴν τυραννίδα συγκαταστήσηι ἢ τὸν δῆμον τ-
ὸν Ἀθηναίων ἢ τὴν δημοκρατίαν τὴν Ἀθήνησιν
10 καταλύσηι, ὃς ἂν τὸν τούτων τι ποιήσαντα ἀπο-
κ⟨τ⟩είνηι ὅσιος ἔστω. μὴ ἐξεῖναι δὲ τῶν βουλευτῶν τῶν τῆς Βουλῆς τῆς ἐξ Ἀρείου Πάγου καταλ-
ελυμένου τοῦ δήμου ἢ τῆς δημοκρατίας τῆς Ἀθήνησιν ἀνιέναι εἰς Ἄρειον Πάγον μηδὲ συνκα-
15 θίζειν ἐν τῶι συνεδρίωι μηδὲ βουλεύειν μηδὲ περὶ ἑνός· ἐὰν δέ τις τοῦ δήμου ἢ τῆς δημοκρατίας καταλελυμένων τῶν Ἀθήνησιν ἀνίηι τῶ-
ν βουλευτῶν τῶν ἐξ Ἀρείου Πάγου εἰς Ἄρειον Π-
άγον ἢ συνκαθίζηι ἐν τῶι συνεδρίωι ἢ βολεύη-
20 ι περί τινος, ἄτιμος ἔστω καὶ αὐτὸς καὶ γένος
τὸ ἐξ ἐκείνου, καὶ ἡ οὐσία δημοσία ἔστω αὐτοῦ
καὶ τῆς θεοῦ τὸ ἐπιδέκατον. ἀναγράψαι δὲ τόν-

---

3 For Philip's settlement with Athens, see Ellis (1976: 199–200, 295–96nn80–87).

4 It is, for example, on the cover of several well-known books: Ober (1989); Murray and Price (1991); Ober and Hedrick (1996); Arnaoutoglou (1998); Bakewell and Sickinger (2002); Cataldi (2004); Gagarin and Cohen (2005). News of the inscription's discovery was published in the *New York Times* (May 26, 1952).

δε τὸν νόμον ἐν στήλαις λιθίναις δυοῖν τὸν γ-
ραμματέα τῆς βουλῆς καὶ στῆσαι τὴμ μὲν ἐπὶ τ-
25 ῆς εἰσόδου τῆς εἰς Ἄρειον Πάγον τῆς εἰς τὸ βο-
υλευτήριον εἰσιόντι, τὴν δὲ ἐν τῆι ἐκκλησία-
ι. εἰς δὲ τὴν ἀναγραφὴν τῶν στηλῶν τὸν ταμίαν
δοῦναι τοῦ δήμου : ΔΔ : δραχμὰς ἐκ τῶν κατὰ ψη-
φίσματα ἀναλισκομένων τῶι δήμωι. vacat

In the archonship of Phrynichos; in the ninth prytany of Leontis; to which
Chairestratos son of Ameinias of Acharnai was secretary; of the *proedroi*
Menestratos of Aixone was putting to the vote. Eukrates son of Aristotimos
of Piraeus proposed: For the good fortune of the *dēmos* of Athens, be it resolved by the *nomothetai*: If any one rises up against the *dēmos* for a tyranny
or joins in setting up the tyranny or overthrows the *dēmos* of Athens or the
democracy at Athens, whoever kills the man who has done any of these
things shall be undefiled. And it shall not be permitted to any of the councilors of the council of the Areopagos, if the *dēmos* or the democracy at
Athens is overthrown, to go up to the Areopagos or to sit together in the
meeting or to deliberate about anything at all; and if—when the *dēmos* or
the democracy at Athens has been overthrown—any of the councilors of
the Areopagos does go up to the Areopagos or sit together in the meeting
or deliberate about anything, he shall be without rights, both himself and
his descendants, and his property shall be made public and the tithe given
to the Goddess. This law shall be written up on two stone stelai by the secretary of the council, and placed one at the entrance to the Areopagos as
you enter the council-house and the other in the assembly; for the writing-
up of the stelai the treasurer of the *dēmos* shall give 20 drachmas from the
dēmos's fund for expenditure on decrees.[5]

Two peculiar aspects of Eukrates's law are noticeable more or less immediately. The first such aspect is the date of its promulgation: the ninth prytany
in the archonship of Phrynichos (spring/summer 336). It would make sense,
for example, if the Athenians promulgated a tyrant-killing law during the
run-up to the battle of Chaironeia: at that time, Philip was subverting democracies and installing "tyrants" in various poleis; and Demosthenes repeatedly warned his fellow citizens that some Athenians were Philip's agents
and actively working to overthrow their own democracy.[6] It also would be
understandable if the Athenians promulgated a tyrant-killing law immediately after the battle of Chaironeia. Those were chaotic and desperate times.

5 Text and translation: *RO* 79 (but changing *RO*'s "the people" to *dēmos*). Editio Princeps:
Meritt (1952). Other editions include: Pouilloux (1960: no. 32); Schwenk (1985: no. 6). English
translations (without Greek text): Harding (1985: no. 101); Arnaoutoglou (1998: no. 65).
6 See, for example: [Dem.] 7.17; Dem. 8.61; 9.53; 10.68; 19.225–27, 299.

And it would have been reasonable for Athenian democrats to fear that pro-Macedonians would take advantage of the uncertainty and, perhaps in coordination with outside forces, orchestrate a coup d'état.[7] Eukrates, however, did not propose his law in one of those two periods. Instead, he made his legislative proposal nearly two years (twenty-two months) after the battle of Chaironeia, by which time it must have been clear that Philip's celebrated postvictory leniency was genuine.[8]

The second peculiar aspect of Eukrates's tyrant-killing law is its focus on the council of the Areopagos.[9] If the Athenian democracy is overthrown, the Areopagites are forbidden from ascending the hill of Ares, sitting in session, and deliberating about anything whatsoever. And if an Areopagite did engage in such activities, both he and his offspring (*genos*) would be declared *atimos* (i.e., without political rights or privileges).[10] One should compare those provisions with the decree of Demophantos, the clear model for Eukrates's law.[11] The earlier decree does not focus on a particular political institution. Instead, it prohibits *all* magistrates from serving during a coup; and

7 For a presentation of the evidence for post-Chaironeia Athens, see Worthington (1992: 246–49). Among other measures, Demosthenes proposed the fortification of the city and Piraeus (Dem. 18.248), and Hypereides proposed to enfranchise *atimoi*, metics, and slaves (Hyp. F 18 [Loeb]).

8 It is certainly worth pointing out, however, that the Korinthian League authorized Philip's invasion of the Persian Empire in the Archonship of Phrynichos (Diod. Sic. 16.89). Perhaps Eukrates feared that Philip would seek to increase his control over Athens—the most powerful Greek city on the Aegean Peninsula—before marching too far eastward.

9 On the Areopagos, especially in the time of the promulgation of the law of Eukrates, see the section of this chapter titled "The Areopagos."

10 The meaning of *atimos* here is unclear. As is well known, originally an *atimos* was an outlaw and could thus be killed with impunity. Yet, later, an *atimos* was a man who had lost only certain rights. Demosthenes (9.44) noted this change in a way that suggests that people had forgotten that the word originally meant outlawry. Thus one might conclude that the word is used in its more lenient sense in Eukrates's law. However, use of the archaic sense of *atimia* seems more likely. First, since the law of Eukrates is traditional legislation (going back to the old legislation—called a *thesmos*—quoted in *Ath. Pol.* 16.10), the archaic flavor of *atimia* would be welcomed; see the section in chapter 1 titled "Solution to Coordination Problem." And, second, because Areopagites who convened after the democracy was overthrown would most likely be considered to be "joining in establishing a tyranny" (line 8 of Eukrates's law), they presumably could be killed with impunity, which, again, is the archaic sense of *atimia*. On *atimia*, see Hansen (1976).

11 For a comparison of the language of the decree of Demophantos and the law of Eukrates, see Table 1.1 in chapter 1. It should be noted that, subsequent to the promulgation of the decree of Demophantos, provisions concerning the overthrow of the democracy (*katalusis tou dēmou*) became part of the *nomos eisangeltikos* (part of which is quoted, apparently verbatim, in Hypereides's speech *In Defense of Euxenippos* [7–8]). The significance of that transfer concerns the punishment for the crime: pursuant to the decree of Demophantos, a guilty man may be assassinated, while the *nomos eisangeltikos* states that a suspect is to be denounced and subsequently tried in a *dikasterion*. Thus Eukrates's law restored the self-help provision for *katalusis tou dēmou* found in the decree of Demophantos. For the likely rationale behind that change, see the section in this chapter titled "The

should a magistrate act contrarily, he is declared a *polemios* (enemy), his assassination is encouraged, and his property is to be confiscated.

This chapter has two related objectives, each of which addresses (inter alia) one of the two aforementioned peculiar aspects of Eukrates's tyrant-killing law. The first objective is to identify the tyrannical threat that the Athenians faced in the spring of 336. As we will see, the nature of the threat largely accounts for the fact that Eukrates proposed his law later than one might have expected. This chapter's second objective is to explain how the promulgation of Eukrates's law would neutralize the tyrannical threat that confronted the Athenians. As would be expected, the law's sharp focus on the council of the Areopagos played an important role. But so too did the process by which Eukrates's law was ratified and the placement of the two stelai upon which it was inscribed.

The Tyrannical Threat

In order to identify the tyrannical threat facing the Athenians in 336, it is first necessary to appreciate this fundamental, strategic fact: in the years immediately following the battle of Chaironeia, Athenian security was, to a large extent, in Macedonian hands. It is true that Philip could not easily conquer the city of Athens: it was well fortified and the Athenians still had a large navy. But Philip had the most powerful army in the Greek world and was a master at siege warfare; and it is almost certain that other poleis would not have come to Athens's defense. In any event, Philip was in a position to cause the Athenians great harm. The Athenians were in no real position to cause Philip such harm.

Given their vulnerability, it is not at all surprising to discover that the Athenians went to great lengths to obtain and retain the goodwill of prominent Macedonians or friends of such Macedonians. The currency was public honor. As would be expected, the Athenians honored Philip lavishly. Among his many honors, the Athenians placed an equestrian statue in his likeness in the agora (Paus. 1.9.4).[12] But the Athenians' "flattering policy," as suggested, was much more broadly based. There exist, for example, two inscriptions honoring two different Macedonians that date to the archonship of Phrynichos: *Tod* 180 (for Alkimachos); *Tod* 181 (for a man in Philip's court whose name is lost). And it is quite possibly in that same year (337/6) that the Athenians notoriously honored a number of Macedonians en bloc (Hyp., *Ag.*

Tyrannical Threat." With respect to the date for the *nomos eisangeltikos*, Ostwald (1955: 115–19) suggests after the fall of the Thirty. Hansen (1999: 213) agrees with that date.

12 In addition: he was granted citizenship (Plut. *Dem.* 22.3); and, after granting him an honorific crown, the Athenians promised—a promise made at the wedding of Philip's daughter Kleopatra—to punish anyone who might plot against him (Diod. Sic. 16.92.1–2).

Philippides). More examples could be mentioned.[13] Now, the overwhelming majority of the Athenians hated the Macedonians, of course; indeed, they publically honored Philip's assassin (Aischin. 3.160; Plut. *Dem.* 22.2). The Athenians engaged in such activity simply because they thought that it would buy them security.[14]

The tyrannical threat confronting the Athenians in 336 was that individuals might take advantage of Athens's dependency on Macedonian goodwill in order to insinuate themselves into positions of extralegal authority. Again, a friendly relationship with the hegemonic power was an essential precondition for Athenian security. It is obvious, however, that hard-line anti-Macedonians—those prominent in the pre-Chaironeia period—could not secure such a relationship: they had led Athens to war against Philip, rejecting his repeated attempts to make peace. It was their political opponents, men accused by leading democrats in previous years of being traitors, who will have performed that function. Consequently, Athenian democrats were caught in a catch-22: the success of such (potentially subversive) men was necessary for the security of the democracy; yet, if those men were too successful in gaining Macedon's goodwill, they could undermine the democracy since democrats would be beholden to them. Such men could become de facto above the law; and in democratic Athens, a man above the law was considered a tyrant.[15]

Two speeches delivered after the battle of Chaironeia and (perhaps) more or less contemporarily with the promulgation of the law of Eukrates support the explanation of the tyrannical threat just stated. The first speech is [Demosthenes's] *On the Treaty with Alexander* (delivered in the assembly). The second speech is Hypereides's *Against Philippides* (delivered in a *dikasterion*).[16]

---

13 The Athenians honored, for example, the pro-Macedonian Euthykrates from Olynthos (Hyp. frag. B.19.1).

14 Arrian (*Anab.* 1.1.3) provides a particularly fine glimpse into the Athenians' use of honors to buy security. After the assassination of Philip, the Athenians planned to revolt from the Macedonians. But, after Alexander approached Athens with an army, the Athenians "conceded to him honors still greater than had been given to Philip."

15 Demades is a fine example. He captured the goodwill of prominent Macedonians and was thus quite powerful in Athens. For example, he convinced Alexander to drop his demand, after the sack of Thebes, that the Athenians hand over several prominent political figures. The Athenians rewarded him for that success with a statue and *sitēsis*. But he was also considered to be dangerous and to have successfully proposed decrees (several of which honored Macedonians and friends of Macedonians) that were seen as being against the interests of the *dēmos* (e.g., Din. 1.101; *Tod* 181 provides a list of decrees moved by Demades). See Worthington (1992: 271–72) for ancient sources and modern discussions. For the general dynamic, see Aischin. 3.250.

16 The date of both speeches is debatable. Hypereides's speech is likely exactly contemporary with the law of Eukrates (see the Loeb introduction to the speech for an explanation). [Demosthenes's] speech is notoriously difficult to date; scholars have dated it anywhere between 336/5 (before Alexander's destruction of Thebes) and 330. Cawkwell (1961) dates it to 331 BCE. Ostwald (1955: 124) dates it to the winter of 336/5.

In *On the Treaty with Alexander*, [Demosthenes] argued that the Athenians should declare war on Alexander (30). The justification for that conclusion was that Alexander had transgressed the formal terms (*synthēkai*) of the Korinthian League's charter: he intervened in the political affairs in Messene, Pellene, and Sikyon; he intercepted Athens's grain fleet in the Black Sea; he sailed a ship into the Piraeus. Much of the speech, however, focuses on the purportedly subversive, enabling activity conducted inside Athens by men who the speaker claims are Macedonian sympathizers. Significantly, the orator refers to such men as οἱ τυραννίζοντες (7)—"those in the tyrant's faction." (It will be recalled that Knoepfler restored that participle in the Eretrian tyrant-killing law [line 6, old fragment].) Also, the speaker claims that those men have "the armies of tyrants as their bodyguard" (25). The actions of those men constituted Athens's tyrannical threat.

According to [Demosthenes], the pro-Macedonians worked to *gradually* subvert the Athenian democracy—the operative concept thus being subversion by evolution rather than subversion by revolution. He notes two complementary methods of attack. The first method was to urge the Athenians to uphold their treaty obligations with Macedon (5, 12, 21) despite the fact that, as noted above, Alexander repeatedly transgressed its terms, often to the detriment of the Athenians. Such subversive individuals (cynically) made arguments grounded in concerns over justice: the Athenians, they asserted, would violate the terms of their sacred oath should they wage war against Macedon and thus would rightly be punished. [Demosthenes], however, believed that their objective was sinister: to normalize Athenian acquiescence such that, over time and gradually (κατὰ μικρόν: 27), they would become accustomed to such a state of affairs and totally subservient to Macedon.

Whereas the first method of attack focused on Athens's foreign policy, the second complementary method focused on her domestic matters, in particular the rule of law. Apparently, pro-Macedonians compelled the Athenians to rescind certain laws, to release men condemned in the courts, and to countenance other illegal acts (12). [Demosthenes] did not explain how they did that. But if the allegations were true, those actions represented a serious attack on the Athenian democracy: some people (both those who did the compelling and those subsequently freed) would be essentially above the law—thus the *dēmos* not fully in control of the polis's domestic affairs (i.e., not *kurios*).[17] It is important to realize, however, that the speaker is not only concerned that the rule of law (and thus the power of the *dēmos*) is being undermined. He is concerned that his fellow citizens do not realize that that is happening. They are, he asserts, too lazy to understand the cumulative effects. And that ill-informed quiescence, according to the speaker, is precisely

---

17   The orators often noted that law upholds the rule of the *dēmos*: Dem. 21.223; Aischin. 3.6, 233–35; Lykourg. *Leok.* 4.

what the Macedonian sympathizers hope to capitalize on. As he puts it, they hope that the democrats will not "be sensible of the change from democracy to tyranny or of the overthrow of a free constitution" (14).

Hypereides wrote his speech *Against Philippides* in response to the Athenians' grant of an honorary crown to an unknown number of prominent Macedonians. For reasons now unknown, the grant of those crowns was technically illegal (4–5).[18] Nevertheless, the *proedroi* put the motion to a vote in the *ekklesia*. Hypereides suggests that they did so out of a sense of compulsion (5). He does not elaborate on that suggestion, but it is almost certainly the case that the Athenians considered such gestures essential for maintaining good relations with Macedon. The most important point here, however, is that Philippides later proposed that the *dēmos* crown the *proedroi* for—of all things—"being just toward the *dēmos* of Athens and following the law" (6). In response to that subversive and insincere pretext, Hypereides accused Philippides of making an illegal motion and delivered his speech *Against Philippides* in order to persuade a jury to convict him.

Philippides's proposal to honor the *proedroi* clearly threatened to make a mockery of the rule of law. Why did he do it? Hypereides had an answer: "he has chosen to be the slave to tyrants and give orders to the *dēmos*" (10). That is, as author of the proposal, he could become more influential with prominent Macedonians and thus, because Athenian security depended on the goodwill of Philip, more powerful in Athens and potentially (per this chapter's hypothesis) above the law. This interpretation is strengthened by Hypereides's fear that the *dēmos* might let Philippides get away with it and thus mock the rule of the law because he is "useful" (χρήσιμος: 10); that is, he could (likely continue to) secure Macedonian goodwill. One might suppose, then, that Philippides was testing the extent to which the *dēmos* would bend the rule of law. If he got away with it once, the reasoning goes, he could do so again. Soon such *paranomia* (illegality) would become acceptable to his and his associates' benefit; they could become tyrants.[19]

Based upon the evidence presented above, the tyrannical threat of 337/6 is fairly intelligible: individuals might take advantage of Athens's dependency on Macedonian goodwill in order to insinuate themselves into positions of

---

18 One of course thinks of the indictment lodged by Aischines against Ktesiphon for proposing that Demosthenes be crowned in the Dionysia for his work—after the battle of Chaironeia—as Commissioner for the Repair of Walls (Aischin. 3). There the alleged illegality was threefold: (1) Demosthenes had not yet undergone his financial audit (*euthynai*) for his time in office; (2) the crown was to be awarded during the Great Dionysia and thus in the theater of Dionysos (instead of in the Pnyx, as required by law); (3) Demosthenes did not deserve such an honor.

19 One thinks here of Aristotle's advice (*Pol.* 1307b31–37) that small breaches of the law must be vigorously addressed—"for transgression of the law creeps in unnoticed, just as a small expenditure occurring often ruins men's estates . . . for the mind is led astray by the repeated small outlays."

extralegal authority.[20] It was a subtle threat and moved gradually. It would have, however, a profound cumulative effect: people might be afraid or otherwise reluctant to lodge an *eisangelia* or a *graphē paranomōn* against a man with close ties to prominent Macedonians, for example; and if someone did lodge an *eisangelia* or a *graphē paranomōn*, people might be unwilling to convict. Over time, the notion of the rule of law would be eroded; there would be a handful of people above the law. Athens would still look like a democratically governed polis. But it would really be an oligarchic Macedonian client state.[21]

Eukrates's Solution

The comments presented in this section explain how the promulgation of the law of Eukrates addressed the tyrannical threat identified in the previous section. Generally speaking—and as one might reasonably expect after reading the analysis of the decree of Demophantos and the Eretrian tyrant-killing law—the law deterred anti-democrats from defecting from the democratic status quo by facilitating mass action in support of the democracy. It is the particular means by which Eukrates's law achieved that general end that must be elucidated.

NOMOTHESIA: GENERATION OF COMMON KNOWLEDGE

Since the end of the fifth century, the Athenians distinguished sharply between a decree (*psēphisma*) and a law (*nomos*). Decrees were promulgated by a simple majority in the assembly and addressed particular, nonrecurring matters. It was pursuant to a decree, for example, that the Athenians honored an individual or mobilized for battle. Laws, on the other hand, articulated general norms to which all Athenians were beholden. Thus murder or theft (inter alia) were prohibited by law, not by decree. And unlike decrees, laws were not promulgated by the assembly. They were promulgated by the *nomothetai* in a rather lengthy and very public procedure called *nomothesia*.[22]

There were three primary stages in the *nomothesia* procedure that ended with the ratification of Eukrates's law.[23] In the first stage, Eukrates wrote his

---

20 For statements in the oratorical corpus that support this conclusion (apathy, subversion by evolution), see: Aischin. 3.250–51; Dem. 18.45–46, 149; 19.224–28.

21 One should note that—per this chapter's hypothesis—it is unnecessary to posit a large "pro-Macedonian" faction to suppose that Macedonian interests were vigorously advanced in Athens.

22 It is to be noted that, before the end of the fifth century, the Athenians did not distinguish between a decree and a law. Thus the decree of Demophantos was a law, not a decree, in the fourth-century sense: it articulated general norms to which all Athenians were beholden.

23 Eukrates apparently availed himself of the so-called repeal law in order to propose his legislation: (1) the law does not date to the first prytany, so the law is not a result of the "review law";

proposed legislation on white boards that were then placed in front of the statues of the Eponymous Heroes (in the southwest corner of the agora). As noted by Demosthenes (24.36; cf. 20.94) the purpose of that practice was to inform the citizens of the possible legislation before the matter was discussed in a more formal setting. Subsequent, informal, conversations would allow individuals to consider both the spirit and letter of Eukrates's law: to discuss the tyrannical threat and how the law might counter it. The Athenians thus formulated and sharpened the arguments that would be employed in the subsequent stages.

In the second stage, Eukrates's proposal to change existing law on *katalusis tou dēmou* (overthrow of the *dēmos*) was discussed in the assembly on at least two different occasions. The first discussion considered the question of whether or not to proceed with the *nomothesia* process (Dem. 3.10–13; Dem. 20.94). Since Eukrates's law was eventually ratified, the *dēmos* obviously considered his proposal worthy of further discussion.[24] At the second meeting of the assembly, the *dēmos* determined the number of *nomothetai* (law commissioners: those who ultimately ratified Eukrates's legislative proposal), their pay, and, likely, when they would meet.[25]

In the third stage, Eukrates prosecuted and five men defended the current law (again, on *katalusis tou dēmou*) before the panel of *nomothetai*. It is not known how many *nomothetai* sat in judgment, but, given the importance of Eukrates's law, it was likely over one thousand. After hearing the arguments on both sides, a majority of *nomothetai* voted by a show of hands in favor of Eukrates's proposal and it became law on the spot (Dem. 24.33).

It is thus clear that, as a result of the *nomothesia* process, discussion of both the letter and the spirit of Eukrates's law would have permeated Athenian political discourse.[26] It is not a stretch to assume, then, that much of the important content of that discourse was common knowledge. The exact content of that discourse is obviously unknown. It is reasonable to suppose, how-

---

(2) there is no reason to think that the *thesmothetai* initiated the procedure as a result of using the "inspection law." On *nomothesia* in the fourth century, see, above all, Hansen (1999: 161–77). See also MacDowell (1975); Hansen (1985); Rhodes (1985b).

24 The *dēmos* likely also chose five advocates to defend the old law—in this case, provisions concerning *katalusis tou demou* contained in the *nomos eisangeltikos*—at this assembly (Dem. 24.36).

25 The evidence for this step must be inferred from Dem. 24.21 (describing the step in the so-called review law). All potential *nomothetai* had already sworn the heliastic oath for that year (and were thus also eligible to be jurors in the *dikasteria*). The *nomothetai* for a particular case (e.g., deciding on Eukrates's legislative proposal) were selected by lot from those eligible men who presented themselves for service on that particular day.

26 The *boulē* was also involved in the *nomothesia* process: not only did it establish the agenda for the *ekklesia*, it also had a legislative secretary (*Ath. Pol.* 54.4; Hansen [1999: 256–57]). Therefore the *ekklesia*, the *boulē*, *ho boulomenos* (the interested citizen), and *nomothetai* were formally involved in the discussion. And that is in addition to informal discussion that would have begun after Eukrates placed his proposal on the white boards.

ever, that two major issues—corresponding to the two basic sections of the law—dominated: (1) tyrant killing (lines 7–11), in particular the relationship between the law of Eukrates and the decree of Demophantos; and (2) the activities of the Areopagos (lines 11–22). Thus the following comments offer informed speculation on what the Athenians might have said about those two issues during the lengthy *nomothesia* procedure.

TYRANT KILLING

Since the law of Eukrates explicitly echoes language found in the oath of Demophantos, we can assume that there was a considerable amount of public discussion about that oath (and decree) during the *nomothesia* procedure that ultimately ratified Eukrates's law. What did the Athenians talk about? Fortunately, two fourth-century speeches contain some analysis of that decree and oath: Lykourgos's *Against Leokrates*, 124–27 (330 BCE) and Demosthenes's *Against Leptines*, 159–62 (355 BCE).

Lykourgos delivered his speech *Against Leokrates* in order to persuade an Athenian jury to convict a certain Leokrates for treason (*prodosia*). The alleged treasonous act was leaving Athens immediately after the Athenian defeat at the battle at Chaironeia. Leokrates first sailed to Rhodes. Two years later, he moved to Megara, where he lived for six years working as a grain merchant. Then, finally, after eight years abroad, he returned to Athens. Lykourgos subsequently indicted him.

Lykourgos faced a significant obstacle in his effort to gain a conviction: Leokrates likely did not break a law that existed at the time that he left Athens.[27] Lykourgos countered this difficulty by suggesting to the jurors that no applicable law existed at that time because previous lawmakers could not even have imagined that an Athenian would commit such a crime. If they had experienced such traitorous activity—the logic goes—they certainly would have criminalized it. Thus Lykourgos had to argue that the jurists should condemn Leokrates based upon what their ancestors would have done—that there was an implied precedent. Consequently, much of the speech attempts to demonstrate the existence of that precedent.

Lykourgos read five inscriptions to the jury, each of which recorded a death sentence against a traitor, in an attempt to demonstrate that the jurors' ancestors would have executed Leokrates. The first inscription recorded the Athenians' action taken against Phrynichos, a prominent figure of the Four Hundred (411).[28] After his burial, the Athenians dug up his

---

27   This conclusion is based on the facts that (1) Leokrates was spared conviction by one vote (Aischin. 3.252) and (2) Autolykos, an Areopagite, was condemned for removing his wife and children from Athens after Chaironeia (Lykourg. *Leok.* 53, frag. 9). Thus it would appear that the law was passed after Leokrates left Athens and before Autolykos sent away his wife and children.

28   On Phrynichos during the coup of the Four Hundred, see the section in chapter 1 titled "Mobilization."

body, convicted him of treason, and removed his bones from Attic soil; they even executed and denied burial to the two men who defended him in his posthumous trial (112–14). The second inscription authorized the Athenians to melt down a statue of Hipparchos, the first Athenian ostracized (487 BCE), and to turn it into a pillar on which to inscribe the names of traitors (117). The third inscription recorded a decree of the *dēmos* that condemned to death any Athenian who moved to then (i.e., post-413) Spartan-occupied Dekeleia (an Attic deme) during the Peloponnesian War (121). The fourth inscription recorded the fact that, before the battle of Salamis (480), the *bouleutai* killed with their bare hands an Athenian who merely attempted to speak treasonously (122). And the last inscription Lykourgos read recorded the decree of Demophantos.

Lykourgos explained to the jurors that, after the coup of the Four Hundred, their ancestors sufficiently understood the method utilized by defectors and thus crafted an adequate solution to it (124–25).[29] First, they established by decree and oath that anyone who kills a man who aims at tyranny or *katalusis tou dēmou* shall be *hosios* (blameless). The orator explained that their ancestors wanted all citizens to live in such a way as to avoid any suspicion of subversive activity. To put it another way, they realized that, if widespread commitment to killing defectors were common knowledge, men would be deterred from even appearing to act undemocratically. Second, after swearing the oath, they inscribed its text on a stele and placed it in the Bouleuterion to be a reminder of what one's attitude toward traitors should be. Lykourgos concludes his discussion of the decree of Demophantos with the following exhortation.

> You have memorials (*hypomnēmata*), you have examples (*paradeigmata*) of the punishments they meted out, embodied in the decrees concerning criminals. You have sworn in the decree of Demophantos to kill the man who betrays his country, whether by word or deed, hand or vote. I say "you"; for you must not think that, as heirs to the riches bequeathed by your ancestors, you can yet renounce your share in their oaths or in the pledge your fathers gave as a security to the gods, thereby enjoying the prosperity of their city. (127)

Josiah Ober's essay "Historical Legacies: Moral Authority and the Useable Past" presents some useful concepts with which one might more fully appreciate the persuasive force of Lykourgos's exhortation.[30] As implied by the title, the essay examines how one might borrow positive moral authority (of the

---

29 It should be noted that Lykourgos mistakenly wrote (124) that the decree of Demophantos was promulgated after the fall of the Thirty. That is certainly a peculiar error. Perhaps he attempted to link the famous decree with that famous "tyranny."

30 Ober (2005b: 43–68).

past) in order to persuade an individual or individuals to perform a particular act. Ober focuses on three types of appeals to past action. He calls the first use "record of past judgments." This is basically an appeal to someone's reputation: if some individual is known to have been correct and fair many times and on many issues in the past, one might cite his or her assessment on the given topic (i.e., borrow his or her authority) in order to bolster one's own argument. For example, one might cite former chairman of the Federal Reserve Paul Volcker's assessment of America's struggling economy in order to convince another person of the validity of one's own assessment on the subject ("my opinion is similar to Paul Volcker's").[31] He calls the second use "precedent." This is an appeal to a past action or decision and its consequences in order to bolster one's own argument about something else that, although perhaps somewhat different, is analogous in some important way. For example, the supporters of the modern gay rights movement might co-opt the powerful logic behind the civil rights movement of decades ago. But it is the third use, called "action as exemplum and legacy gift," that is directly relevant here.

The effectiveness of a citation of a past "action as an exemplum and legacy gift" results from the belief that certain actions committed by members of a previous generation have given the present generation something of considerable value. The present generation thus possesses that valuable possession as a legacy gift. Consequently, out of respect, the members of the present generation feel compelled to act in a certain way (to imitate) in response: to deem the past action as an exemplum and to commit to pass on the legacy (i.e., the valuable possession) to future generations. One who wishes to persuade members of the present generation to act in a certain way thus might appeal to the moral authority of those past actions to bolster his or her argument.

It is clear that, in his efforts to persuade the jurors to convict Leokrates of treason, Lykourgos sought to borrow the moral authority of the "Demophantos moment." Their forefathers' oath was an "action as exemplum"—Lykourgos called it a *paradeigma*. The resulting freedom and prosperity of 330 BCE (i.e., the "riches") was the legacy gift. Thus Lykourgos encouraged

---

31   It should be noted that Ober presents the scenario differently. In the dynamic presented above, individual A appeals to the moral authority of individual B in order to persuade individual C. In Ober's dynamic, individual B accepts a decision made by individual A because of individual A's moral authority. The variation on Ober's presentation is made because it brings this type of use of moral authority (i.e., "record of past judgment") in line with the following two types mentioned below in the text. The fundamental dynamic is not changed. Indeed, the altered presentation is in line with Ober's general configuration on the borrowing of moral authority: "So the social fact of moral authority emerges from a three-way relationship: an external source, an individual or institutional borrower, and the public that determines whether or not the loan is valid" (Ober [2005b: 51]).

the jurors to live up to that ideal and to pass on the legacy gift to future generations by killing Leokrates. And Lykourgos made the whole concept very concrete by telling the jurist "you took the oath." Now it is almost certain that none of the jurists swore Demophantos's oath: most, if not all, were not even born yet. His point, again, was that, since the jurists were heirs to riches (i.e., the legacy) secured by the oath to kill defectors, they too must kill defectors (i.e., act like their ancestors did or swore to do) to secure the legacy for future generations.

The second more-or-less contemporary reference to the decree of Demophantos is found in Demosthenes's speech *Against Leptines* (159–62). Demosthenes delivered that speech in order to persuade a panel of jurists to repeal a law earlier proposed by Leptines that revoked all earlier grants of *ateleia* (exemption from public burdens)—except for descendants of Harmodios and Aristogeiton—and forbade such grants from being made in the future. Demosthenes objected to the law on the grounds that honoring important benefactors with *ateleia* contributed to state security; should that practice be taken away or somehow diminished, all Athenians would suffer.

Demosthenes referred to the decree of Demophantos in order to bolster his argument that the prerogative to grant future grants of *ateleia* should not be abrogated. He notes that, according to the decree of Demophantos, future tyrant killers are to be treated like the descendants of Harmodios and Aristogeiton and thus receive a grant of *ateleia*. Thus, should Leptines's law stand, the Athenians could not observe their oaths: a future tyrant killer would not be treated "like the descendants of Harmodios and Aristogeiton" (as stated in the decree of Demophantos). He then raises the possibility that some people might not be troubled with the de facto annulment of the decree of Demophantos since, in their opinion, the need for tyrant killers has long passed. Demosthenes rejects that view on the general grounds that one cannot predict the future and thus must be prepared for all possibilities. He cites the history of Syracuse as an example: although that city was once powerful and democratically governed, its citizens nevertheless fell to a tyrant (Dionysos I). Thus Demosthenes asserts that the Athenians must keep the decree of Demophantos fully valid in order to prevent such an event from happening in Athens.

The persuasive force of Demosthenes's reference to the decree of Demophantos—and the necessity to keep it valid—hinged on what Ober (2005b) calls the prudential force of historical citation. The reasoning is quite simple: if something worked in the past, all things being equal, it likely will work in the present. Demosthenes assumed, that is, that the relevant sociopolitical conditions inside the Athens of 355 had not changed from the time of the promulgation of the decree of Demophantos (410). Thus the Athenians of 355 must both assume that someone might attempt to become tyrant of Athens and retain the decree of Demophantos so that such threats may be adequately dealt with.

One might reasonably suppose that public discussion about the decree of Demophantos that took place pursuant to the proposal of Eukrates's tyrant-killing law echoed the themes articulated by Lykourgos and Demosthenes in their respective speeches. That is, in the *ekklesia*, in the agora, during the trial in front of the *nomothetai*, and elsewhere the Athenians repeatedly heard it professed (inter alia) that (1) they owe it to their ancestors to stay true to Demophantos's oath; (2) since tyrant killing (as codified in Demophantos's decree) worked in the past, it will work in the present too. Consequently, one might conclude that the commitments to killing tyrants—defending the democracy—were widespread and credible and that such commitment was common knowledge. And that commitment would have been particularly emphatic since it was codified in law.

The generation of common knowledge of widespread credible commitments to killing tyrants (i.e., enforcing the law of Eukrates) greatly increased the likelihood that the Athenians would be able to mobilize in defense of their democracy: should the democracy be overthrown, an individual might rationally choose to "go first" and thereby set in motion a revolutionary bandwagon. Yet, as discussed in the previous section, the tyrannical threat confronting the Athenians in 337/6 was subtle and slow moving; the democracy might not be overthrown in a single, spectacular event (like the assembly at Kolonos in 411, for example). The concern, again, was subversion by evolution rather than subversion by revolution. There had to be, then, a way for the people to know that the democracy was, in fact, overthrown. Thus the second provision of Eukrates's law.

THE AREOPAGOS

The council of the Areopagos was composed entirely of ex-archons. At the end of their year in office, each of the nine archons underwent his *euthynai* wherein both his financial accounts and (potentially) his behavior in office were publically examined. If an archon successfully passed that examination, he was subjected to another scrutiny conducted by the current members of the Areopagos. If the archon passed that second examination, he was admitted to the council of the Areopagos, where he served for the rest of his life. Thus the number of Areopagites serving at any given time varied. But it likely averaged 150 members.

For over a century prior to the promulgation of the law of Eukrates, the Areopagos's powers were quite limited. The epochal year was 462/1. Before that year (at least from 594), the council wielded considerable powers in its somewhat nebulous role as the "guardian of the regime (*politeia*)" (*Ath. Pol.* 25.2). The details are not certain, but the council likely could overturn decisions made by both magistrates and the citizen assembly. After 462/1, as a result of the reforms of Ephialtes, the council was stripped of such broad authority. It became, primarily, a court for premeditated homicide trials.[32]

Within the years immediately preceding the promulgation of the law of Eukrates, the Areopagos's powers were greatly augmented. Perhaps most significantly, the Areopagos was authorized to participate in the new procedure of *apophasis*, a procedure that adjudicated crimes against the state. An *apophasis* could originate by a decree of the *dēmos* or—quite importantly—on the initiative of the Areopagos itself. Either way, the Areopagos would conduct a preliminary inquiry into the alleged crime and then report both its findings and its recommendation to the assembly. If the Areopagos recommended acquittal, no further action was taken. If the Areopagos recommended a guilty verdict, however, the assembly subsequently decided whether or not to refer the matter to the courts. If the matter was referred to the courts, the court pronounced the final verdict.[33]

Demosthenes's account (18.132–133) of the Areopagites' involvement in the case against Antiphon nicely demonstrates the use of the *apophasis* procedure within the larger context of the Macedonian threat. Antiphon, an Athenian recently deprived of his citizenship, allegedly promised Philip that he would burn down Athens's dockyards. Before he could do so, however, Demosthenes found him hiding in the Piraeus and brought him before the *ekklesia* for a trial. The *dēmos* (i.e., the *ekklesia*) acquitted him. But the council of the Areopagos, "having become aware of the matter and seeing your [i.e., the *dēmos*'s] inopportune ignorance," arrested him and brought him into court for another trial. This time he was convicted and executed.[34]

Although the matter has been debated, there is reason to believe that a decree authored by Demosthenes after the battle of Chaironeia gave the Areopagos even more power (i.e., in addition to their role in *apophasis*). In a speech titled "Against Demosthenes," Deinarchos wrote (62), "And yet in the past, Demosthenes, you proposed that the council of the Areopagos should be given absolute authority to punish (κυρίαν εἶναι κολάσαι) anyone who offended against the laws, in accordance with the ancestral laws." That is, no doubt, a vague assertion. But it is quite possible that, per Demosthenes's decree, the council was given the power to adjudicate criminal cases without appeal. As suggested by Mogens Hansen, henceforth a prosecutor

---

32   For the Areopagos council, see Wallace (1989). The stripping of the Areopagos's power was part of the full democratization of Athens: henceforth, there would be no check on the assembly.

33   On the *apophasis*, see Wallace (1989: 113–15); Worthington (1992: 357–62); Hansen (1999: 292–94).

34   Wallace (1989: 113–15) sought to reconcile Demosthenes's account of the Antiphon affair with Plutarch (*Dem.* 14.4). Thus he concludes that Demosthenes brought Antiphon before the Areopagos; the Areopagos, that is, did not initiate the matter. That is debatable since, according to the known rules, either the assembly or the Areopagos initiated an *apophasis* procedure.

could choose to try his case in front of the Areopagos instead of the other *dikasteria*.[35]

Given the increase in its powers, it is not at all surprising to discover that the Areopagos played a rather large and proactive role in Athenian politics during the years immediately preceding the promulgation of the law of Eukrates. Their action against Antiphon has already been mentioned. In addition, they vetoed Aischines's appointment as Athens's advocate (*syndikos*) to the Amphictyonic Council and secured, instead, the appointment of the obviously more pro-democratic Hypereides (Dem. 18.134); they imprisoned the general Proxenos, likely for military procrastination in 346; they had Charinos expelled for treasonous activity that benefited Macedon; after Chaironeia they relieved Charidemos of his position as general in charge of defense of the city and gave it to Phokion (Plut. *Phok.* 16.1–3). And most notoriously, they ordered the execution of those who attempted to leave the city after the battle of Chaironeia (Lykourg. *Leok.* 52, 53; Aischin. 3.252).

One should interpret the singling out of the Areopagos in Eukrates's law in light of that council's increased powers and proactive presence in Athenian politics. As noted at the beginning of this chapter, the second provision of Eukrates's law focused on the Areopagites' actions "while the *dēmos* or the democracy at Athens has been overthrown." Specifically, each councilor is prohibited from climbing up the hill of Ares, joining others in a meeting of the council, and deliberating about anything whatsoever. If an Areopagite committed any of those acts, both he and his *genos* would be *atimos*. This provision is, again, in peculiar contrast to the decree of Demophantos, the model for Eukrates's legislation: it generically forbade all magistrates (thus including the Areopagites) from executing any of their duties during a coup. Why did Eukrates single out the council of the Areopagos is his tyrant-killing law?

Robert Wallace (1989: 180–83) has nicely summarized and critiqued three answers to that important question. According to the first answer, the intention behind the provision was to prevent the Areopagites from willingly cooperating in a pro-Macedonian coup. The reasoning in support of that conclusion consists of three steps: first, Philip sponsored oligarchic, or "tyrannical," coups elsewhere (e.g., in Euboia, see chapter 2); second, some Athenians might have suspected that the Areopagites were Macedonian sympathizers since, as noted above, the council, after the battle of Chaironeia, overrode the appointment of the overtly anti-Macedonian Charidemos to

---

35 See Hansen (1999: 291–92). Wallace (1989: 115–19) presents the possibility that Demosthenes's decree was the decree that instituted *apophasis*—that is, the powers of the Areopagos council were augmented once, not twice, during the period of Athenian resistance to Macedonian imperialism. But Wallace himself acknowledges the difficulties posed by that conclusion (especially Deinarchos's claim that, pursuant to Demosthenes's decree, the Areopagos had "absolute authority to punish"). Hansen's conclusion should be accepted.

the generalship and chose Phokion—a man willing to work with the Macedonians both before and after Chaironeia—in his place; third, Eukrates was apparently ardently anti-Macedonian: according to Lucian (*Dem. Enc.* 31), the only evidence on Eukrates other than his law, he (along with other prominent anti-Macedonians) was executed on Antipater's orders after Athens lost the Lamian War (322).

The weakness of the first answer is that the totality of the evidence clearly indicates that the Areopagites were anti-Macedonian and thus would have had no desire to participate in a pro-Macedonian coup. Indeed, the only possible indication of any pro-Macedonian tendencies would be their aforementioned effort to appoint Phokion as general. But Wallace has demonstrated that Phokion was a pragmatic democratic patriot, not a Macedonian sympathizer: a man clearly more suited to deal with Philip than the fiery and overtly anti-Macedonian Charidemos. And, as Wallace points out, the *dēmos* itself elected Phokion as general in 338, before the battle of Chaironeia. The Areopagites' post-Chaironeia support of Phokion was thus grounded in prudence, not ideology.

According to the second answer, the Athenians promulgated the law of Eukrates in response to the stipulation that, upon joining the Korinthian League, a polis's regime (*politeia*) must not be changed ([Dem.]. 17.10). The apparent intention behind the law was thus to prevent the Areopagos council from participating in a coup that altered the regime in place in Athens at the time that the Athenians swore the oath for the Korinthian League. Like the crowning of prominent Macedonians, the law was part of the "politics of loyalty to Philip."[36]

The weakness of the second answer is that it suggests the possibility of Areopagite participation (or acquiescence) in a coup that was both anti-democratic and anti-Macedonian. It is hard to envision a faction to whose members such a coup would appeal. Indeed, the available evidence suggests that Athenian anti-democrats in this period were (to various degrees) "pro-Macedonian." And even if there were an anti-democratic faction that was not initially pro-Macedonian, its members almost certainly would have to become pro-Macedonian after a coup: the survival of their new regime would almost certainly require outside support—support only Philip could reliably give. In short, overthrowing the Athenian democracy implied support for Macedon.

The third answer does not necessarily situate the law within a specifically Macedonian context. Instead, the promulgation of Eukrates's law, according this interpretation, represents an attack on Demosthenes by his political enemies, men who were concerned with the aforementioned decree he authored that gave the Areopagos the authority to adjudicate cases.[37] The cri-

---

36   Mossé (1970: 75–76).
37   Sealey (1958) and *RO* (79) advance this view.

tique of this position is rather straightforward: a much better response would be to repeal Demosthenes's decree since doing so would both limit the power of the Areopagos and hurt Demosthenes politically.

After rejecting each of the three aforementioned positions, Wallace presented his own explanation for the singling out of the Areopagos council in Eukrates's law. He suggests that Eukrates was motivated by a general concern over the council's recent activities. One possible concern—one for which he admits there is no evidence—could have been the council's conspicuous support for the creation of the new and very powerful office called the Controller of the Finances. The *dēmos*, he suggests, might have been afraid lest the council collaborate with the holder of that office and thus wield extraordinary executive authority. Wallace also suggests that the people might have concluded that the council's order to execute the citizens who fled after the battle of Chaironeia, although apparently legal (Lykourg. *Leok.* 52), was undemocratic. Wallace thus concludes rather generally, "Eukrates' measure may be regarded as a restatement of Athens's commitment to its democratic government, and a warning to the Areopagos insofar as any future actions by it might threaten that government."

The basic weakness in Wallace's position is that there is no real reason to suppose that the Areopagos council threatened the Athenian democracy. The previous comments have already both noted that the council was staunchly anti-Macedonian and suggested that, were the Athenian democracy overthrown, the new regime would almost certainly be required to be pro-Macedonian. And there is an abundance of evidence demonstrating that the Athenians held the council in high regard.[38] Within that general understanding, both of Wallace's points may be countered. First, there is no evidence for collusion between the council of the Areopagos and the new office of the Controller of the Finances. There is no evidence that there was *not* such a fear, of course. But surely one is not required to prove a negative in order to refute speculation. Second, although some democrats—indeed, maybe a majority—might have thought that the Areopagites went overboard in ordering the execution of those who fled Athens after Chaironeia, that council was nonetheless punishing individuals for not protecting the democracy.

Cynthia Schwenk (following Homer Thompson) advanced an explanation of the Areopagos provision not discussed by Wallace.[39] Noting the greater prestige enjoyed by the council at the time, she suggests that the law was promulgated in order to prevent the council from unwillingly granting legitimacy to a nondemocratic regime. This is certainly a reasonable interpreta-

---

38   For example, Aischin. 3.20, 1.92; Dem. 23.65; Lykourg, *Leok.* 12; Din. 1.9.

39   Schwenk (1985: 33–41). It should be noted that Wallace (1989: 267n13) refers to Schwenk's conclusion. He states that she accepted answer number one (i.e., that advanced by Meritt and Ostwald).

tion. And one may strengthen it by noting that, since the Areopagites served for life, the council could not be stacked (e.g., by Philip) with new members in a superficially democratic manner.[40] Consequently, the convening of that council demonstrated political continuity—and thus political legitimacy—in a way that no other organ of government could.

This chapter advocates a new interpretation of the Areopagos provision, one that complements Schwenk and Thompson's. The interpretation is based on this simple observation: the Athenians would have interpreted the Areopagites' failure to convene as a sign that—at least according to the Areopagites—the democracy had been overthrown or was severely threatened. The democrats, already committed to "killing tyrants," would then mobilize to defend their regime. Is it reasonable to conclude that that was (one of) Eukrates's intention?

Two complementary points suggest that the law of Eukrates established the Areopagos council as a "signaling institution." To begin with, doing so would be consistent with Athenian understanding of the Areopagos's primary function. It will be recalled, for example, that the Athenians in Eukrates's day believed that the Areopagos council originally was established to serve as "the guardian of the *politeia*" (e.g., *Ath. Pol.* 25.2; cf. 8.4). Also relevant is the fact that, shortly before the promulgation of Eukrates's law, the *dēmos* gave the Areopagos the authority to be on the lookout for crimes against the state (*apophasis*). And finally, the council of the Areopagos was already empowered by the decree of Teisamenos (Andok. *Myst.* 83–84) to ensure that the magistrates enforced Athens's laws; and it will be recalled that one aspect of the 337/6 tyrannical threat was the gradual erosion of the rule of law.[41]

The second complementary point is that the Areopagos council would be an effective "signaling institution." As we have seen, the case against Antiphon demonstrated the council's willingness to be on the lookout against pro-Macedonian activity. (And note, again, what Demosthenes wrote about the council: "having become aware of the matter and seeing your inopportune ignorance.") In addition, meetings of the council were conspicuous, in full view of everybody in the agora, the busiest place in Athens; thus news of the failure of the council to meet would disseminate rapidly.[42] Also significant is the fact that the council could not quickly be stacked and then con-

---

40   Noted by Knoepfler (2001b: 215n94).

41   One might also note that, around the middle of the fourth century, the Athenians started to rely on expert management of important governmental affairs (e.g., the Controller of the Finances and the Board for the Theoric Fund). Appointing the Areopagos to watch for subversive activity would be in line with that trend.

42   The council met on the terrace just north of the summit of the "hill of Ares": Wallace (1989: 215–18). Also important is the fact that the Areopagites were very prominent individuals—all were ex-archons—and many would have served in the council for years. Consequently, individuals who did not go to the agora would also quickly notice or learn of the councilors' refusal to

trolled: as mentioned above, all of its members were ex-archons. And finally, only one member's refusal to attend a meeting of the council might convince other members that they, too, should refuse to attend, lest they be charged with breaking Eukrates's law. The operative dynamic, that is, would be like the revolutionary bandwagon discussed by Timur Kuran. Unlike rebellion against a regime, however, one would not require a particularly low revolutionary threshold to "go first" (here, not attend a meeting of the council) since there likely was no punishment for incorrectly concluding that the democracy had been overthrown.[43]

PLACEMENT OF STELAI: *HYPOMNĒMATA* AND *PARADEIGMATA*

By the time Eukrates proposed his tyrant-killing law, the Athenians had a long tradition of commemorating or authorizing the punishment of traitors by erecting stelai in prominent public places. Lykourgos, it will be recalled, mentioned five such stelai during his prosecution of Leokrates, one of which carried the decree of Demophantos. And there were many more, the "Attic Stelai," which recorded the sale of the property of the Thirty Tyrants, being perhaps the most well known.[44] Such monuments were thus established fixtures of Athenian public space; almost every citizen would have seen them many times and knew that others saw them many times too. Consequently, they collectively performed the very important political function of generating and maintaining as common knowledge the fact that the *dēmos* punishes defectors and that such punishment is necessary in order to maintain the democratic regime. Indeed, the presence of the older stelai, some being over one hundred years old when Eukrates proposed his law, concretely symbolized political continuity and the necessity of sanctioning defectors to achieve that end.

The Athenians drew upon that epigraphic tradition when they chose to place two stelai carrying Eukrates's law in two different, strategically important locations. As will be demonstrated below, the public presence of those two stone stelai facilitated coordinated action and was thus an important part

---

convene. One might also note, of course, that individual Areopagites could publically announce why they had chosen not to "climb the hill of Ares."

43 One should note, however, that if the democracy were clearly overthrown by intimidation and force, it would take an individual with a low threshold to "go first" and not climb the hill of Ares; it would be tantamount to rebelling against a regime.

44 Attic Stelai: *ML* 79. Other well-known, similar monuments include the "stele commemorating the wrong-doing of the tyrants [i.e., the Peisistratidai] that was set up on the acropolis of Athens" (Thuc. 6.55.1); a stele recording the banishment of the followers of Isagoras due to their attempt at tyranny (Schol. Aristoph. *Lys.* 273); decrees concerning Phrynichos and other prominent members of the Four Hundred ([Plut.], *X orat.* 834b). And although not concerning an Athenian, the *dēmos*'s decree against Arthmios of Zeleia was quite popular (Dem. 9.41–45; 19.271–72; Aischin. 3.258; Din. 2.24). For the decree against Arthmios of Zeleia, see Worthington (1992: 309–10).

of how the law of Eukrates "worked." Before engaging in that discussion, however, an analysis of the famous sculptured relief is in order.

The sculptured relief adorning the stele engraved with Eukrates's law depicts two figures, a male and a female (see Figure 3.1).[45] The male is almost certainly personified Dēmos. He is middle aged and bearded but, as his exposed chest reveals, of considerable physique. He sits upright on a throne with his feet on a footrest and he holds—or was to have held—a scepter in his left hand. He looks like Zeus. The younger woman is most likely personified Dēmokratia. She has long coifed hair and wears a highly girted chiton. She stands immediately to Dēmos's left and holds a crown over his head. The overall mood is dignified and serene.

One might interpret the sculptured relief as a visual articulation of three political themes, each of which likely was repeatedly stressed during the lengthy *nomothesia* procedure that promulgated Eukrates's law. The first theme is that the *dēmos*—not some outside force (i.e., Philip)—is the sovereign authority in Athens. The key iconographic move here is the apparent identification of Dēmos with a scepter-bearing king. In the Greek's historical tradition, the scepter was the symbol of a king's authority over the laws (*themistes*) of his community. To draw on speech act theory, the scepter rendered the king's speech felicitous: as he held it, he would pronounce what is lawful (*themis*) and, subsequently, people would act accordingly.[46] The sculptured relief depicts the *dēmos* as having that authority in Athens: what it says is law. And that is certainly a fitting message to accompany a law against tyranny—a law that addresses the fundamental question of who rules Athens.

External evidence supports this interpretation. First, there was a long tradition of conceiving of the *dēmos* as an autocrat. In Aristophanes's *Knights*, for example, the *dēmos* is referred to as a tyrant (1114), a monarch (1330), and a king (1333). Both Isokrates (7.26) and Aristotle (*Pol.* 1274a7) refer to the *dēmos* as being "like a tyrant." Demosthenes called the *dēmos* a despot (3.30; 23.209). And Aischines (3.233) referred to each Athenian as a king because of his authority to enforce law. Second, orators often stressed the fact that that the *dēmos* controls their polis through making and enforcing law.[47]

---

45 On the sculptured relief, see Lawton (1995: 99–100n38, with plate 20); Blanshard (2004); Ober (2005c: 222–24).

46 In Homer's *Iliad*, Odysseus articulates the ideology of kingship particularly well (2.204–6): "No good thing is a multitude of leaders; let there be one leader, one king, to whom the son of crooked-counseling Kronos has given the scepter and *themistai* so that he may take counsel for his people." It is interesting to note that, according to Theophrastos (*Char.* 26.2) the only Homeric line known by the "oligarchic man" is the line just quoted. Perhaps the sculptured relief adorning Eukrates's law is to be interpreted as the *dēmos* (the collective) agreeing with that basic sentiment but for democratic ends: *dēmos* is the one, unitary ruler in Athens. On the power of kings' speech in Archaic Greece, see Detienne (1996).

47 See Ober (1989: 145–46) on the conflation of *dēmos* and *dikastai*.

Figure 3.1. Law of Eukrates, 337/6. Photo by permission of the American School of Classical Studies: Agora Excavations.

Demosthenes's *Against Meidias* (223–24) is a good example. He asks, "Why are you jurists powerful and authoritative (*kurioi*) in all state-affairs?" The answer, he says, is "the strength of the laws," by which he means enforcing law.[48] It is thus not too surprising that a sculptor would depict the *dēmos* as a scepter-bearing king in order to represent the *dēmos* as sovereign. And a typical Athenian would have understood the message.

The decision to depict the *dēmos* as a king should be interpreted in light of Philip's success. Since the later decades of the fifth century, the theoretical advantages of kingship (or one man rule) over democracy were known to the Athenians: the king ruled efficiently, the *dēmos*—as a collection of individuals—ruled inefficiently.[49] But for generations, the superiority of kingship could be disputed, since the Athenians, the most powerful democracy, defeated the Persians, the most powerful monarchy, not to mention the fact that several kings (Macedonian, Thracian) were pushed around by Athens from time to time. But Philip was different. As Demosthenes noted (18.235; 1.4), he was exceptionally able to capitalize on the advantages of kingship. And of course he defeated democratic Athens. Thus, in the early 330s, the figure of the king would have represented power and success.[50] So it is not altogether surprising that the Athenians, in a bit of wishful thinking, depicted the sovereign *dēmos* as a powerful king.

The second theme articulated by the sculptured relief is that all of Athens's political conduct should bring honor to the (sovereign) Athenian *dēmos*. Thus Dēmokratia (an active political regime) crowns a sitting Dēmos. That message would have been particularly poignant considering how controversial the politics of crowing were at the time. As noted earlier in the chapter, the Athenians honored many prominent Macedonians and friends of Macedonians after the battle of Chaironeia. And many Athenians resented that. Thus they made sure, for example, to honor the arch anti-Macedonian Demosthenes. And Hypereides, another prominent anti-Macedonian, sharply criticized (Frag. 19) the motives behind the honoring of certain Macedonians and their friends. The sculptured relief reflects that push back: all grants of honor, it suggests, are to advance the interests of—indeed, bring honor to—the *dēmos*.[51]

48 Laws preserve democracy: Aischin. 3.6; Dem. 21.188, 24.206. Note that Aristotle (*Pol.* 1285b30) describes an absolute monarch as πάντων κύριος. That is how Demosthenes (21.223) described the jurors. And note, too, that Demosthenes (18.201) describes Philip as κύριος ἁπάντων.

49 Hdt. 3.82 is the classic, early formulation, admittedly articulated by a non-Athenian. An early Athenian discussion is Eur. *Supp.* 411–25.

50 Kingship seen as the optimal regime in the mid-fourth century: Plato, *Resp.* 473B–D; Isok. 3.16–26. Also note that Isokrates (5.14–16) called on Philip to unite the Greeks because he, as king, was powerful enough to do so.

51 Note Demosthenes's (18.120) observation that the *dēmos* publically proclaims the granting of crowns in order to encourage other individuals to serve the polis.

The third theme articulated by the sculptured relief is that the *dēmos* and thus its democracy cannot be overthrown permanently. Thus both the Dēmos and Dēmokratia are depicted as immortal gods. Such a depiction in not entirely unexpected, since it is well known that a cult of Dēmokratia flourished in the 330s.[52] Hypereides, in his speech *Against Philippides* (8), however, explains *why* the Athenians might have concluded that the *dēmos* was immortal.

> You have concluded that one person will be immortal, yet you sentenced to death a city as old as ours, never realizing the simple fact that no tyrant has yet risen from the dead while many cities, though utterly destroyed, have come again to power. You and your party took no account of the history of the Thirty or of the city's triumph over her assailants from without and those within her walls who joined in the attack upon her.

Hypereides cites the successful mobilization against the Thirty as evidence that Athens, as a democratic city, is immortal: even if overthrown, the democrats can still defend their regime. As demonstrated in chapter 1, the success of the mobilization against the Thirty was due, in part, to the decree and oath of Demophantos. Now, the law of Eukrates explicitly echoes that decree and oath. Eukrates's law thus reminded everybody of that earlier decree's success, thereby increasing the likelihood that the Athenians could "do it again." The sculptured relief symbolized that capability.

The three themes articulated by the sculptured relief are historically important, since they reveal the mentality of the times. Issues of sovereignty, political practice, and regime persistence were important. But it is also important to remember that the two stelai were reminders (*hypomnēmata*) that the Athenian citizens are committed tyrant killers and that the members of the Areopagos must not convene if the democracy is overthrown. The following comments explain how seeing the inscribed stelai would actually help defend the Athenian democracy.

The *nomothetai* ordered that two stelai carrying Eukrates's law be placed in two separate locations. One stele was to be placed "at the entrance to the Areopagos as you enter the council-house." That was, so far as can be determined, the first time the Athenians ordered an inscribed stele to be placed at that location. The stele thus would have been startlingly conspicuous; each Areopagite was essentially "forced" to look at it—and thus to consider its significance—each time he entered the chamber. Another stele carrying Eukrates's law was to be placed "in the *ekklesia*." This too was a highly unusual, if not unique, placement order. Unlike the placement order for the Areopagos copy, however, there is no indication of where "in the *ekklesia*" the stele was to be

---

52 In 333/2, the *boulē* erected a statue of Dēmokratia; the *strategoi* are known to have sacrificed to Dēmokratia in 332/1 and 331/0. See Raubitschek (1962: 238–43).

placed. But it is reasonable to conclude that it was placed near the speaker's bema, facing the audience: (1) if it were to be placed at the entrance to the Pnyx, the placement order would have said so, like the placement order for the Areopagos;[53] (2) there is evidence that stelai stood near the bema in the Pnyx.[54]

The Athenians likely placed a stele at the entrance of the Areopagos in order to provoke two reactions. First, an Areopagite who suspected that the democracy had been overthrown, but was not confident enough to stay home, might, after seeing the sculptured relief, turn away at the last minute and not enter the council chamber. If he did so, he would have committed a highly dramatic, highly visible public act.[55] Consequently, another councilor, after observing his colleague's reaction, might not enter the council-house either, lest he be punished for breaking Eukrates's law. A miniature revolutionary bandwagon of Areopagites thus might ensue. Second, an Areopagite who was concerned for the democracy, but was not fully convinced that it was overthrown, might be emboldened enough to suggest to his colleagues that they conduct a formal investigation—i.e., an *apophasis*—into the cause of his concern.

The stele placed in the *ekklesia* would have controlled the dynamic of debate in the Pnyx in favor of the pro-democrats. It would have been common knowledge that every individual saw the stele and thus that everybody was, to some degree, thinking about its significance. Each audience member, therefore, would be more emboldened to shout down speakers who proposed or supported potentially subversive motions. Were one to do so (perhaps referring to the law and stele in the process), others, who were thinking the same thing, might vocally support him; soon the whole *ekklesia* could erupt. Consequently, pro-Macedonian orators—men who certainly understood the operative dynamics—would be much less likely to advocate positions that could spark such outrage. And thus the democracy would be more difficult to subvert from the speaker's bema.

Conclusion

This chapter sought to explain how the promulgation of the law of Eukrates facilitated the Athenians' efforts to defend their democracy against the then current tyrannical threat. As one would expect, it did so, in part, by convincing individuals to lower their revolutionary thresholds in the hope that, should there be a coup, an individual who had lowered his threshold to zero

---

53　It should also be noted that, if Pnyx III had not yet been completed by 337/6—a reasonable possibility—there would have been two entrances to the Pnyx (i.e., to Pnyx II). See Hansen (1999: 353–54).

54　Kourouniotes and Thompson (1932: 162).

55　Ober (2005a: 21–22) makes this important point.

would "kill a tyrant" and spark a revolutionary bandwagon. As noted, however, the tyrannical threat of 337/6 was subtle and slow moving—the operative concept being subversion by evolution not by revolution. Thus democrats might not realize that their regime is essentially overthrown. In order to counter that serious problem, Eukrates's law charged the Areopagites with being on the lookout: they were to notify the broader population if, in their opinion, the conspirators' straw broke, or severely threatened to break, the democracy's back. And finally, the Athenians placed a stone stele inscribed with Eukrates's law in two strategic locations to serve as a clear reminder of the democrats' credible commitment to defend their regime.

In conclusion, it is worth asking whether or not the promulgation of the law of Eukrates assisted the Athenians' efforts to defend their democracy. Their democracy was overthrown in 322, of course. But that *katalusis tou dēmou* ("overthrow of the *dēmos*") was not the result of internal subversion: the regime change was forced on the Athenians by an outside power (Macedon) and maintained by foreign troops stationed in the Piraeus.[56] Thus, the relevant time within which to evaluate the law's effectiveness is the fourteen years between its promulgation (336) and Athens's surrender to Antipater (322). One need not doubt that, during those years, anti-democrats wanted to defect and dominate the polis with Macedon's at least tacit support: anti-democrats in several other poleis did so; and Athenian democrats, obviously, were very concerned with the possibility of a coup.[57] But Athenian anti-democrats did not make such a move. Why not? The simplest answer is that they concluded that their attempt would fail—that the democrats would successfully mobilize against them. And it was to force that calculation, of course, that the democrats promulgated the law of Eukrates.

In this light one should note a significant difference between the law of Eukrates and both the decree of Demophantos and the Eretrian tyrant-killing law. Those two promulgations promised great honors to the tyrant killer. According to the decree of Demophantos, the tyrant killer would receive the monetary value of half the "tyrant's" property, and, should he be killed, he would be treated like Harmodios and Aristogeiton and his descendants treated like their descendants. And the honors prescribed by the Eretrian law were no less grand. If Knoepfler's restorations are correct, the tyrant

---

56   For the overthrow of the Athenian democracy in 322, see Diod. Sic. 18.18.4–5; Plut. *Phok.* 27–28.

57   For pro-Macedonian, anti-democratic coups after the battle of Chaironeia, see the section of chapter 2 titled "Stability." One should note here that Demosthenes, likely shortly before his trial concerning the Harpalos affair (spring of 323), impeached Kallimedon for consorting with Athenian exiles in Megara with the intention of overthrowing the democracy. He also alleged that there was a conspiracy threatening the dockyards (Din. 1.94–95). See Worthington (1992: 264–66). Other evidence alleging the existence of pro-Macedonians after the battle of Chaironeia: Hyp. *Euxen.* 22; Hyp. *Phil.* 8–9; Dem. 18.52, 297, 323.

killer would receive *proedria*, *sitēsis*, a cash payment, and a statue in his likeness would be erected in a conspicuous location; and should he die while killing the tyrant, the state would provide for his children. The law of Eukrates, on the other hand, prescribes no such positive, selective incentives for the tyrannicide, only the assurance that he would not be prosecuted. Why would that be the case?

One part of the answer might be that, in the Athens of 337/6, tyrannicide was not considered to be an especially daring act. The driving logic behind that conclusion is quite simple: incentives are offered in order to encourage people to do something that they might not otherwise do. The question thus becomes, why would an individual democrat need an incentive to kill a tyrant? One reason—likely the most significant reason, it seems—would be to counter the weight of his concern that, should he commit that act, an insufficient number of people would follow him. The greater his uncertainty, the greater the incentive required to make tyrant killing potentially worth the risk. It thus stands to reason that the absence of incentives in Eukrates's law reflects the widespread belief that the democrats—a majority of the population—will fight to defend their regime. This does not mean that any democrat would be as likely as any other democrat to kill a tyrant. It means that would-be tyrannicides would come from the (relatively large) pool of proactive democrats, not the (very small) pool of extraordinarily brave, proactive democrats. That is, Athenian democrats became increasingly more confident, more aware of their collective strength, between the promulgation of the decree of Demophantos and the law of Eukrates.

Tyrant-Killing Legislation in the Early Hellenistic Period

4

The Anti-Tyranny Dossier from Eresos

Introduction

The earliest extant inscriptions from Eresos record punitive actions taken by the Eresian *dēmos* against tyrants and their descendants. There are, in all, six texts—five of which are fragmentary—written on two nearly identically sized stones.[1] The first two texts concern a trial, ordered by Alexander the Great, of Agonippos and Eurysilaos, two men who ruled Eresos as "tyrants" in 333. The third, fourth, and fifth texts record the official responses to the requests of certain descendants of tyrants—the two aforementioned tyrants and others who ruled as tyrants before Agonippos and Eurysilaos—to return to Eresos: text 3 (circa 324) establishes a public trial on the matter pursuant to an order of Alexander the Great; text 4 (circa 317) is a royal transcript from King Philip Arrhidaios forbidding the return of the exiles; text 5 (circa 305) is a fragment of a letter from King Antigonos to the people of Eresos wherein he apparently supports the Eresians' decision to refuse the exiles' return. The sixth text, dated circa 300, is a decree of the *dēmos* validating all the actions taken by the Eresians against the tyrants and their descendants during the previous three decades.

This dossier is arguably more challenging to interpret than the texts examined in the previous three chapters. The decree of Demophantos, the Eretrian tyrant-killing law, and the law of Eukrates are single enactments, promulgated in a single moment in time. Their interpretation, therefore, required a rather straightforward negotiation of one text and its particular historical

---

1   For generations, scholars have worked under the impression that the two extant stones were originally part of a single, large stele (see Heisserer [1980: 28] for an Illustration). But Heisserer (1980: 27–32) has demonstrated that the two extant stones did not originally form a single stele. (See now, however, Ellis-Evans [2012].) Heisserer refers to the two stones as beta and gamma. He posits a lost stone (which he refers to as alpha) that recorded both an anti-tyranny law and an agreement to join Eresos in the Korinthian League. Stone beta has legible writing only on its right lateral (text 1 below). Stone gamma has legible writing on its obverse (text 2 and much of text 3), right lateral (end of text 3, text 4, and most of text 5), and reverse (end of 5 and all of 6). Note that earlier editors (e.g., *OGIS* 8 and *Tod* 191) concluded that the dossier contained seven—not six—texts: they concluded that the opening lines of gamma's right lateral was not a continuation of the text that begins near the end of gamma's obverse; that is, they concluded that what this chapter (following Heisserer) calls text 3 was really two different texts.

context. The dossier from Eresos, however, contains several different types of texts (decrees of the *dēmos*, a royal letter, a royal transcript) inscribed over a thirty-year period characterized by extraordinary change: 332, the likely date of the first text, was a quite different world than 300, the rough date of the last text. Yet the events documented in the dossier are clearly related, part of a single story or experience: a point emphasized by the fact that the Eresians had the texts inscribed on the same stones. The challenge, then, is to create a single, unified interpretation of the dossier that accounts both for the whole and its particular parts.

I argue below that the "anti-tyranny dossier" documents Eresos's transition from an unstable, nondemocratically governed polis to a stable polis governed by an authoritative *dēmos*. The argument is presented in three parts. The first and longest part interprets the actions recorded in the first two texts of the dossier. Therein I argue that Alexander ordered the Eresians to try the two tyrants in order to establish the pro-democrats' threat credibility and thus stabilize the new democratic regime. The second part interprets the actions recorded in the third, fourth, and fifth texts. The argument in that section is that the exiles' attempts to return to Eresos were potentially destabilizing because they suggested that exogenous factors (i.e., events outside of Eresos's new unilateral deterrence game set up by the trial) might undermine the *dēmos*'s threat credibility. The third part interprets the action documented in the sixth text. I argue that the pro-democrats, now confident that the kings would not intervene on behalf of tyrants, proactively ended their potentially destabilizing struggle with tyrants by definitively proclaiming the permanent credibility of their threat.

Establishment of a New Game

This section interprets the actions recorded in the earliest two texts of the dossier. Here are the texts and translations of Rhodes and Osborne (*RO* 83).

TEXT 1

ΣΤΟΙΧ. 17

[παρ]ήλετο τὰ ὅπλ[α καὶ|ἐξ]εκλάισε ἐκ τᾶς [πό|λι]ος πανδάμι,
5 ταὶ[ς|δὲ] γύναικας καὶ τ[αὶς‖θ]υγάτερας συλλάβ[ων|ἦ]ρξε εἰς
τὰν ἀκρόπ[ο|λ]ιν· καὶ εἰσέπραξε|δισχιλίοις καὶ τρι[α]|κοσίοις
10 στάτηρα⟨ς⟩· τὰ[ν]‖δὲ πόλιν καὶ τὰ ἶρα [δι|α]ρπάξαις μετὰ τῶν|
[λ]αίσταν ἐνέπρησ[ε|κ]αὶ συγκατέκαυσε|σώματα τῶν πολί[ταν.‖
15 κ]ρίνναι μὲν αὖτον|[κ]ρύπται ψάφιγγι [κα|τ]ὰ τὰν διαγράφαν τ[ῶ|
20 β]ασιλέως Ἀλεξάνδ[ρω|κ]αὶ τοῖς νόμοις· [αἰ δέ‖κ]ε
καταψαφίσθηι [κα|τ'] αὖτω θάνατος, ἀ[ντι|τι]μασαμένω

25 Εὐρυ[σι|λ]άῳ τὰν δευτέραν [κρί|σ]ιν πο
ήσασθαι διὰ || [χ]ειροτονίας,
τίνα|[τ]ρόπον δεύει αὖτον [ἀ|π]οθάνην. λάβεσθαι δ[ὲ|κ]αὶ

30 συναγόροις τὰ[ν]|πόλιν δέκα, οἴτινε[ς||ὀ]μόσαντες Ἀπόλ[λω|ν]α
Λύκειον ὄ[μ]α σ[υνα|γ]ορήσοισι [τᾶ πόλι ὄπ|πω]ς κε δύνα[νται ---]||

—he seized their arms and shut them all out of the city, and he arrested their
women and their daughters and confined them in the acropolis; and exacted
two thousand three hundred staters; and he looted the city and the sanctuaries with the pirates and set fire to them and burned the bodies of the citizens.
Try him by a secret ballot according to the transcript (*diagraphē*) of king
Alexander and the laws; and, if he is condemned to death, when Eurysilaos
has made his counter-assessment a second trial shall be held by show of
hands, on the manner by which he is to be put to death. The city shall take
ten advocates (*synagoroi*), who shall swear by Apollo Lykeios that they will
perform their advocacy for the city as best they can ---

TEXT 2

ΣΤΟΙΧ. 36

[---------- 17---------- τοὶς πολ]ιορκήθε[ντας]
[εἰς τὰν] ἀ[κρ]όπολιν [ἀ]νοιϙο[μ]ό[λη]σε·² καὶ τοὶ[ς πο]-
[λίτα]ις δισμυρίοις στάτηρας εἰσέπραξε· [καὶ]
[τοὶ]ς Ἕλλανας ἐλαίζετ[ο]· καὶ τοὶς βώμοις ἀ[νέ]-

5 [σ]καψε τῶ Δίος τῶ [Φ]ιλιππί[ω]· καὶ πόλεμον ἐξε[νι]-
[κ]άμενος πρὸς Ἀλέξανδρον καὶ τοὶς Ἕλλανας
τοὶς μὲν πολίταις παρελόμενος τὰ ὄπλα ἐξε-
κλάισε ἐκ τᾶς πόλιος [πα]νδάμι, ταὶς δὲ γύνα[ι]-
κας καὶ ταὶς θυγάτερας συλλάβων καὶ ἔρξα[ις]

10 ἐν τᾶ ἀκρόπολι τρισχιλίοις καὶ διακοσίο[ις]
στάτηρας εἰσέπραξε· τὰν δὲ πόλιν καὶ τὰ ῐρ[α]
διαπράξαις μετὰ τῶν [λα]ίσταν ἐνέπρησε κα[ὶ]
σ[υ]γκατέκαυσε σώματα [τῶν] πολίταν· καὶ τὸ τ[ε]-
λεύταιον ἀφικόμενος πρὸς Ἀλέξανδρον κατ[ε]-

15 ψεύδετο καὶ διέβαλλε τοὶς πολίταις. κρῖνα[ι]
[μ]ὲν αὖτον κρύπται ψάφιγγι ὀμόσαντας περ[ὶ]
[θ]ανάτω· αἰ δέ κε καταψαφίσθη θάνατος, ἀντιτ[ι]-
μασαμ[έ]νω Ἀγωνίππω τὰν δευτέραν διαφόραν
ποήσασθαι, τίνα τρό[π]ον δεύει αὖτον ἀποθα-

20 νην. αἰ δέ κε καλλάφθε[ν]τος Ἀγωνίππω τᾶ δίκα
κατάγη τίς τινα τῶν Ἀγωνίππω ἢ εἴπη ἢ πρόθη

2 Dittenberger (*OGIS* 8) restored this line differently: [τάν τε ἀ[κ]ρ]όπολιν [ἀ]νοικο[δ]όμ[η]-
σε κτλ. *IG* XII, 2 526 prints: [ὶς τὰν ἀ]κ[ρ]όπολιν [ἀ]νοικο[δ]όμ[η]σε κτλ.

περὶ καθόδω ἢ τῶν κτημάτων ἀποδόσιος, κατά-
ρατον ἔμμεναι καὶ αὖτον καὶ γένος τὸ κήνω
[κ]αὶ τἆλλα ἔ[ν]οχος ἔστω τῶ νόμω [τῶ] ⟨ἐπὶ τῶ⟩ τὰν στάλλαν
25 ἀνέλοντι τὰν περὶ τῶν τυράννων καὶ τῶν ἐκγ[ό]-
[ν]ων. ποήσασθαι δὲ καὶ ἐπάραν ἐν τᾶ ἐκλησία α[ὔ]-
[τικ]ᾳ τῶ μὲν δικάζοντι καὶ βαθόεντι τᾶ πόλε[ι]
ϙαὶ τᾶ δικαία εὖ ἔμμεναι, τοῖς δὲ παρὰ τὸ δίκα[ι]-
[ο]ν τὰν ψᾶφον φερόντεσσι τὰ ἐνάντια τούτων.
30 ἐδικάσθη. ὀκτωκόσιοι ὀγδοήκοντα τρεῖς· ἀπ[ὸ]
ϙαύταν ἀπέλυσαν ἔπτα, αἱ δὲ ἄλλαι κατεδίκασ-
ϙαν.   *vacat*

—he—those who had been besieged in the acropolis; and he exacted twenty thousand staters from the citizens; and he committed piracy against the Greeks; and he dug up the altars of Zeus Philippios; and he made war on Alexander and the Greeks, and from the citizens he seized their arms and shut them all out of the city, and he arrested their women and daughters and confined them in the acropolis; and he exacted three thousand two hundred staters; and he looted the city and the sanctuaries with the pirates and set fire to them and burned the bodies of the citizens; and finally he arrived before Alexander and told lies against and slandered the citizens. Men on oath shall try him on a secret ballot for death; and, if he is condemned to death, when Agonippos has made his counter-assessment the second disputation shall be held, on the manner by which he is to be put to death. If, when Agonippos has been convicted in the trial, any one restores any of Agonippos' family or speaks or makes a proposal concerning return or the restoration of possessions, he shall be accursed, both himself and his descendants, and in other respects he shall be liable to the law against one who destroys the stele about the tyrants and their descendants. A solemn prayer shall be made in the assembly immediately, that it may be well with one who judges and supports the city with a just vote, but with those who cast their vote contrary to justice the opposite of these things. It was judged: eight hundred and eighty-three [voters]; of these seven [votes] acquitted, the others condemned.

These two texts concern a trial, ordered by Alexander the Great, of Agonippos and Eurysilaos, two men who ruled Eresos as "tyrants" in 333. There are several significant aspects of this trial. And we will have the opportunity to discuss many of them later in this chapter. But two preliminary points are particularly important for present purposes.

First, it is quite likely that all or at least most of the citizens of Eresos served as jurors in these trials. In defense of that assertion, note, first, that 883 people cast a vote (text 2, line 30). The exact population of Eresos is unknown, of course. But it was a small polis. And 883 is a relatively large number—too big to have represented a real subset of the citizen population.[3] One should also note that, according to the indictment, the two men looted "the city" (text 1, lines 9–12; text 2, lines 11–12), seized weapons from "the citizens" (text 1, line 1 [implied]; text 2, line 7), exacted ransom money from "the citizens" (text 1, lines 7–9 [implied]; text 2, lines 2–3), burned the bodies of "citizens" (text 1, lines 13–14; text 2, line 13), and—at least with respect to Agonippos—slandered "the citizens" before Alexander (text 2, lines 13–15). Since all of the citizens were victims either directly or indirectly of the alleged crimes, it is reasonable to suppose that virtually all of them wanted to sit in judgment of the accused.[4]

Second, Agonippos and Eurysilaos were likely accused (inter alia) of breaking a law against tyranny. Again, this is not explicitly stated in the dossier. However, as text 6 makes clear, the Eresians conceived of the trials against Agonippos and Eurysilaos as trials against tyrants: the two are explicitly called tyrants (lines 6–7, 29–30) and reference is made about the "votes against the tyrants" (line 35). In addition, the Eresians clearly had a "law against tyrants"—it is mentioned in the dossier three times.[5] And finally, text 6 states that the law against tyrants played a role in the trial of Agonippos and Euysilaos: it states (lines 15–17) that "their descendants should be liable to the law on the stele" (i.e., the law against tyrants). One thus might conclude that the Eresians recorded Agonippos's and Eurysilaos's crimes in texts 1 and 2 in order to support the charge that those two men actually did rule as tyrants and thus violated the anti-tyranny law.

Very little is known for certain about Eresos's law against tyranny. Since it is mentioned in the indictment of Agonippos (text 2, lines 24–25), it must have been promulgated sometime before his trial (i.e., before 332).[6] A rea-

---

3 Hansen, Spencer, and Williams (2004: 1024) suggest that Eresos had at least one thousand adult citizens and a total population of about four thousand citizens, plus foreigners and slaves.

4 Note that, according to the stipulation articulated in text 2 (lines 26–29), a prayer was to be made "in the assembly" concerning the conduct of the trial of the two tyrants. Note, too, that, with respect to the later trial of the descendants of "the former tyrants," those descendants told Alexander that they were willing to stand trial in Eresos "before the *damos*" (ἐν τῶ δά[μω]: text 3, line 40); the judges in that trial are referred to as "the citizens who are judging" (text 3, lines 10–11); text 6 (lines 21–22) states that "the *damos*" should decide whether or not they would be allowed to return. All of this suggests that the trials referred to in this dossier took place in the assembly convened as a law court. And it is reasonable to suppose the space where the assembly met was large enough to hold all, or at least most, of the roughly one thousand citizens.

5 Text 2 (lines 24–5); text 6 (lines 26–27, 31–32). The law is alluded to in text 6 (lines 16–17), where mention is made of a "law in the stele." In text 6 (lines 31–32) the law against tyranny is referred to as "the law against the tyrants that is written on the old stele." Thus the law referred to in text 6 (lines 16–17) is almost certainly the anti-tyranny law.

6 Actually, text 2 (24–25) refers to "one who destroys the stele about the tyrants and their descendants." That clearly is the law: as mentioned in the previous note, in text 6, the law against tyrants is said to be "on the old stele." Note the destruction of stelai by pro-Persian oligarchs in 333 in Tenedos (Arr. *Anab.* 2.2.2) and Mytilene (Arr. *Anab.* 2.1.4).

sonable guess would be 336, just after Eresos joined the Korinthian League:
(1) cities that joined the league were obliged to maintain the regime that was
in power when they joined ([Dem]. 17.10); (2) anti-tyranny legislation was
promulgated in order to preserve (democratic) regimes; (3) anti-tyranny legislation appears to have been somewhat popular on the Greek mainland at
that time.[7] With respect to the law's content, all that can be said definitively is
that it mandated both that the descendants of tyrants be exiled and that the
property belonging to the tyrants and to the descendants of tyrants be confiscated (text 6, lines 14–18, 23–28; text 2, lines 20–26).[8]

One might speculate about the content of the Eresians' anti-tyranny law.
First, the law likely was against tyranny in general and not only against particular individuals who ruled Eresos as "tyrants" before the law was promulgated. It is true that the law is referred to in the dossier as the law against
"the" tyrants (τόν τε νόμον τὸμ περὶ [τ]ῶν τυράννων: text 6, line 31; τόν τε
ν[ό]μο]ν τὸν κατὰ τῶν τυράννων: text 6, lines 26–27). One might be tempted
to conclude, therefore, that the law from Eresos was roughly similar to the
well-known mid-fifth-century decree from Miletos (*ML* 43). That decree
outlawed at least three named men—almost certainly for political crimes—
and offered a reward to anybody who might kill them. But several points
argue against comparing too closely the law from Eresos and the decree
from Miletos. To begin with, there is no reason to suppose that the law from
Eresos contained the names of particular men: it is always referred to simply
as the law against the tyrants. Second, all known laws against tyranny—that
is, laws that explicitly use the word tyranny or tyrant—are against tyranny
in general. Third, the decree recorded as text 6 of the dossier—a text that
dates to circa 300—states (lines 29–32) that the law against the tyrants shall
remain *kurios* (permanently valid): that certainly could suggest that the law
was of a general nature, not just aimed at men who perhaps were dead in
300. And finally, the *Ath. Pol.* refers (16.10) to Athens's earliest anti-tyranny
laws as (literally) "the laws concerning the tyrants" (οἱ περὶ τῶν τυράννων

---

7 Heisserer (1980: 67n32) doubts that the Eresians promulgated their anti-tyranny law in 336
because it is referred to in circa 300 (text 6, line 32) as being inscribed on an "old stele." He thus
suggests that it might have been promulgated when Eresos joined the Second Athenian Confederacy (an unknown date, but post-377: *RO* 22 line 117) or at the end of the Social War (355). Knoepfler (2001b: 206n47) is of a similar mind: he prefers the restoration [λιθίν]α ("stone") instead of
[παλαί]α ("old") since, in his opinion, it is strange to qualify a law still on the books as "old." It
should be noted, however, that the Eresians of circa 300 referred to the Eresians of 332 as their
"ancestors" (*progonoi*) (text 6, lines 34–35). Bosworth (1980: 179) suggests, without argument, that
the Eresians promulgated their anti-tyranny law in 332, after the fall of Agonippos and Eurysilaos.

8 It is true that the Eresians conducted a trial. But the trial was ordered by Alexander (text 6,
lines 9–12) and conducted according to the laws (plural) (text 1, line 19; text 3, lines 7, 14–15; text
6, line 14). One need not conclude, therefore, that the anti-tyranny law mandated a trial. Do note,
however, that text 6 states (lines 24–25) that the Eresians held the trial concerning the descendants
of the former tyrants according to "the law" (singular) and Alexander's order.

νόμοι); and it certainly appears that those laws addressed tyranny in general, not specific tyrants.[9]

It is also likely that the law from Eresos sanctioned the assassination of a tyrant or anybody who makes an attempt to become a tyrant. In support of that assertion, one might simply note that all known laws against "tyranny" sanction such an assassination. And the aforementioned decree from Miletos also sanctioned assassination. In fact, it appears that sanctioning the assassination of men who committed crimes against the state was commonplace in Greek poleis.[10]

Alexander's rationale for ordering (all of) the Eresians to try the two tyrants is not self-evident and thus needs to be explained. As is noted below, the king had physical control of both Agonippos and Eurysilaos while he was in Egypt. The easiest and most efficient means to eliminate them, therefore, would have been to kill them right there.[11] Alexander also could have ordered the two men to stand trial before the *synedrion* of the Korinthian League. Eresos, after all, was a member state of that league before Agonippos and Eurysilaos staged their coup. And the league's charter specifically forbade regime change among its member states ([Dem.] 17.10). Thus Agonippos and Eurysilaos had broken the law, as it were: a transgression that the *synedrion* would adjudicate. And it is quite important to note that Alexander likely did use the *synedrion* to adjudicate such crimes: that body might have determined the fate of Thebes in 335 (Diod. Sic. 17.14.1);[12] and—perhaps in 334 (or in 332)—Alexander ordered the *synedrion* to try the participants of a coup in Chios (*RO* 84 lines 14–15).[13] Nevertheless, Alexander chose neither

---

9   Note the decree of nearby Nasos (*OGIS* 4). It dates to 319–317 and refers (lines 106–10) to their "law concerning *katalusis tou damou*" (τῶ νόμ|[ω π]ερὶ τῶ καλλ|[ύο]ντος τὸν δᾶ||[μον]). Thus the neighbors of Eresos had a "general" law against subversion of the democracy: so too, quite likely, the Eresians—their anti-tyranny law.

10   See, for example, the mid-fourth-century decree from Amphipolis (*RO* 49). Like the aforementioned mid-fifth-century decree from Miletos, it orders the permanent exile of two men and authorizes their assassination "wherever they are found" (lines 7–9).

11   Note, in this regard, that Alexander sent Apollonides and his captured Chian associates to Elephantine Island (Arr. *Anab.* 3.2.7). While this is not an execution, it is an example of Alexander delivering justice personally at the same time that he ordered Agonippos and Eurysilaos to stand trial in Eresos.

12   This is questioned by Bosworth (1980: 89–90). Drawing attention to Arr. *Anab.* 1.9.9 (wherein "the allies" [τοῖς ξυμμάχοις] are said to have decided Thebes's fate) and Diodoros's abuse of the word *synedrion*, he suggests that an ad hoc assortment of league members rendered the famous verdict.

13   Matters surrounding the handling of the captured pro-Persian Chians are disputed. The dispute arises because (1) in Alexander's "First Letter to the Chians" (*RO* 84, lines 13–15), the king ordered those men to be tried by "the *synedrion* of the Greeks" (i.e., the *synedrion* of the League of Korinth); (2) Arrian (*Anab.* 3.2.7) notes that Alexander—in 332—sent captured Chians (among whom was included Apollonides) to the city of Elephantine in Egypt. Resolving the matter depends on the date of Alexander's letter to the Chians. Heisserer (1980: 83–95) dates it to 334. Thus, in

course of action. Instead, he decided to send Agonippos and Eurysilaos to Eresos to stand trial before (all of) its citizens for (inter alia) breaking an antityranny law. Why did he do that? What was his objective, and how would the trial obtain it?

It is argued below that Alexander ordered the Eresians to try the two tyrants in order to establish the pro-democrats' threat credibility and thus stabilize the new democratic regime. The first part of the argument briefly presents the historical context within which Alexander issued the order and demonstrates that that one might reasonably suspect—even before explicitly considering the trial's sociopolitical effect—that Alexander's goal in ordering the trial was to stabilize the polis: to prevent, that is, attempts at regime change. The argument's second part explains how the trial could help achieve that end.

HISTORICAL CONTEXT

The Macedonian conquest of western Asia Minor provides the historical context within which the "tyranny trials" in Eresos must be interpreted.[14] Philip II began the invasion in the spring of 336 with great fanfare: it was authorized by the *synedrion* of the Korinthian League and advertised as a campaign both to punish the Persians for their ancient crimes (Diod. Sic. 16.89) and to liberate the Greek cities of Asia Minor (Diod. Sic. 16.91.2; cf. Isok. 5.123). But the king was assassinated only a couple of months later (around July 336) leaving the campaign's future—indeed the future of the Macedonian state—in doubt. But Alexander, Philip's son, quickly demonstrated, to both his domestic and foreign enemies alike, that he firmly controlled Macedon.[15] Thus the aforementioned *synedrion* dutifully gave him permission to continue the invasion of Persia (Diod. Sic. 17.4.9; Arr. *Anab.* 1.1.2).[16] And he, of course, brought it to a successful conclusion.

It is helpful to conceptualize the war in western Asia Minor as consisting of simultaneously played and interrelated "games." One game was "exterior."

Heisserer's view, there were two sets of captured pro-Persian Chians: the first (captured in 334) were, indeed, tried by the *synedrion*; the second (captured in 332) were sent by Alexander to Egypt. Bosworth (1980: 268) accepts the more traditional (i.e., pre-Heisserer) date of 332 for Alexander's first letter to the Chians. He thus suggests the possibility that the *synedrion*—per Alexander's order as contained in his letter to the Chians—deliberated on the matter but was unable to come to a conclusion. Thus they sent the men to Alexander, who, in turn, sent them to Elephantine Island. Bosworth compares that possibility with the actual dealings with the Spartans in 330: Antipater submitted the matter to the *synedrion* and the *synedrion* subsequently referred the matter to Alexander (Diod. Sic. 17.73.5–6; Curt. 6.1.19–20; Aischin. 3.133).

14   For Alexander's conquest of Asia Minor, see Badian (1966).

15   For the difficulties facing Alexander after the assassination of Philip, see Diod. Sic. 17.2–4. Arrian (*Anab.* 1.1.1–3) largely ignores the matter.

16   Like his father, Alexander announced that his intention was to liberate the Greek cities of Asia: Diod. Sic. 17.24.1

It was played by Persia and Macedon on the big board of western Asia Minor and the eastern Aegean. The goal of that game was to dominate an entire region. The other games were "interior." They were played inside the various Greek poleis located on the aforementioned big board. Those games also had two players: an anti-democrat faction and a pro-democratic faction. The goal of both of those collective players was to dominate their polis. Very importantly, both Persia and Macedon actively supported opposing players of the various interior games: Persia supported the anti-democrats; Macedon supported the pro-democratic faction.

Generally speaking, developments in the exterior game affected developments in the various interior games. They did so by affecting the threat credibility of the interior games' two factions. For example, if the Persians had the upper hand in the exterior game, they would be better able to support militarily a polis's anti-democratic faction. That faction would thus have increased threat credibility (and capability). That is, they likely could more effectively respond to a coup. The pro-democratic faction, consequently, would "cooperate" with the oligarchic regime: defecting would be too risky. If the Macedonians subsequently gained the upper had in the exterior game, however, the anti-democratic faction's threat credibility would be greatly diminished because the Persians would be less likely to support them militarily. The pro-democrats' threat credibility, on the other hand, would be greatly augmented, since their benefactor, the Macedonians, would be better able to support them militarily. The pro-democratic faction would thus calculate that it is worth the risk to defect from oligarchic status quo. And a new democratic equilibrium would be established and maintained due to the pro-democrats' threat credibility: now it would be too risky for the anti-democrats to defect.

Table 4.1 demonstrates the relationship between the exterior game and Eresos's particular interior game. It should be noted at the outset, however, that the development of Eresos's internal events is not entirely clear and has been debated: the issue of contention being the number of different tyrannical regimes and when and how they were established. The following remarks conform to the traditional interpretation as modified by Heisserer and accepted by Rhodes and Osborne.[17]

---

17 There are three basic historical interpretations. The traditional interpretation (advanced by Pistorius and then modified by Heisserer) argues for three tyrannical periods, each of which is followed by a pro-Macedonian democracy: (1) before Eresos joined the Korinthian League; (2) in 335, after Memnon's gains in the Troad; (3) in 333, after Memnon's naval counter offensive. According to this interpretation, Philip established or at least strongly supported a democratic regime in Eresos when the city joined the Korinthian League and Memnon did, in fact, engage in naval operations in 335 (and took Eresos). Bosworth (1980: 179; 1988: 192–93) offered a second interpretation according to which two different tyrannical regimes dominated Eresos back to back: Hermon, Heraios, and Apollodoros ruled from some unknown time until circa 338; Agonippos and Eurysi-

Table 4.1. Persian and Macedonian Games

	Exterior	Interior
336	*Macedonian success* Parmenion and Attalos begin the invasion of Asia (Diod. Sic. 16.91.2) in spring/summer (maybe March) 336 with, according to Polyainos (v 44.4), 10,000 men. The campaign, although poorly documented in extant sources, is apparently quite extensive: activity is recorded in the Troad, the bay of Elaia (Diod. Sic. 17.7.8–10), as far south as Ephesos (Arr. *Anab.* 1.17.10–12), where a democracy was set up.[a]	*Democrats' success* The "former tyrants" (Apollodoros, Hermon, and Heraios) are deposed and democratic rule is established. In gratitude, the democrats erect altars to Zeus Philippios and enroll the city in the Korinthian League.
335	*Persian success* Philip II is assassinated (July 336) only months after Parmenion began his campaign (Diod. Sic. 16.93). Alexander is thus forced to secure his control of Europe. Memnon, Darius's admiral, taking advantage of the disorder, erases nearly all of Macedon's gains of the last year. Parmenion likely retained control only of the area around Abydos, an essential beachhead for the Macedonians on the east side of the Hellespont (Arr. *Anab.* 1.11.6).	*Anti-democrats' success* The recently established democratic regime is quite likely deposed and the aforementioned "former tyrants" reestablished as masters of Eresos.
334	*Macedonian success* This year's campaign—the first in which Alexander personally participated—starts out auspiciously with the Macedonian victory at the river Granikos (May/June 334) (Arr. *Anab.* 1.13–16).[b] Alexander then marches through the interior of Asia Minor and, after a brief stay at Sardeis, arrives in Ephesos.[c] After overseeing the reestablishment of a democracy there (Arr. *Anab.* 1.17.10), he sends Alkimachos with a force to the Aeolic and Ionian cities still subject to Persian rule. According to Arrian (*Anab.* 1.18.1–2), "He ordered oligarchies everywhere to be overthrown and democracies to be established. He restored the laws in each city and ended tribute." The mission is attested at Erythrai, Kolophon, Priene, and Pontos.[d] (Alexander then takes Miletos and engages in a costly and ultimately fruitless siege of Halikarnassos.)	*Democrats' success* The "former tyrants" are once again—that is the second time—deposed and the *dēmos* once again—also for the second time—put in control of Eresos. It is quite possible that the former tyrants are exiled on the order of Alexander; the situation thus parallels that in Chios (*RO* 84, lines 10–14).

Table 4.1. (*continued*)

	Exterior	Interior
333	*Persian success* In the spring of this year, Memnon, with 300 ships (Diod. Sic. 17.29.2), leads a very extensive naval counter offensive in the Aegean "to divert the war into Macedon and Greece" (Arr. *Anab.* 2.1.1). The success is massive. All the cities in Lesbos are taken (Mytilene after a protracted siege during which Memnon dies of illness), Tenedos (Arr. *Anab.* 2.2.3) and Chios fall (Arr. *Anab.* 3.2.3), most of the Cyclades send envoys in submission (Diod. Sic. 17.29.2), and there are Persian gains as far south as Miletos (Curt. 4.1.37), Kos (Arr. *Anab.* 2.13.4), and Halikarnassos (implied in Arr. *Anab.* 2.13.6).[e] (Alexander was in Pamphylia, then Phrygia, then Cilicia.)	*Anti-democrats' success* Arrian simply writes (*Anab.* 2.1.1) that Memnon "won over" (*prosēgageto*) the cities of Lesbos with the exception of Mytilene. But, as texts 1 and 2 of the "anti-tyranny dossier" show, the Eresian *dēmos* was violently overthrown and Agonippos and Eurysilaos installed as heads of a new regime.[f]
332	*Macedonian success* Alexander's victory at Issos (circa November 333) marks the beginning of the end of the exterior game in the Aegean and coastal Asia Minor.[g] Around the time of the siege of Tyre (which began around July 332), he orders massive cleanup operations on land (e.g., Paphlagonia, Lykaonia) and sea (e.g., Tenedos, Chios, Mytilene, Kos, Lesbos) (Arr. *Anab.* 3.2.3–6; Curt. 4.5.13–18).	*Democrats' success* Fortunately, Arrian notes activity on Lesbos at this time. Hegelochos, he wrote, "won over the other cities by agreement (*homologia prosēgageto*: *Anab.* 3.2.6)." Like earlier (i.e., 333, interior game), this word almost certainly glosses over the harsh, violent reality; there likely was an internal struggle like that which occurred at that time, in similar circumstances, in Chios (Curt. 4.5.14–18). Regardless, Agonippos and Eurysilaos are ousted and the *dēmos* is—for the third time—put in control of the polis.

a. It is to be noted that, during this campaign, Parmenion "took by storm the (Greek) city of Gryneion and sold its inhabitants as slaves." And he also besieged Pitane (Diod. Sic. 17.7.9). There clearly were limits to Macedon's policy of "liberation."

b. Arrian (*Anab.* 1.11.3) wrote that Alexander marched to the Hellespont with "not much more than 30,000" infantry "and over 5,000 cavalry." For the size of Alexander's army, see pp. lxix–lxxxii in the first volume of Brunt's Loeb translation of Arrian's *Anabasis* and Bosworth (1980: 98–99).

c. At Sardeis, Alexander granted the Lydians their ancestral laws and declared them free. But there was still to be a satrap (Asander) and tribute. For this development, see Bosworth (1980: 128–29) and Badian (1966: 44–45).

d. For the evidence of Alkimachos's mission, see Bosworth (1980: 134–36). Badian (1966: 53) concluded that Alkimachos's order was to join the cities of Ionia and Aeolis to the Korinthian League. One should also interpret the decree of the *dēmos* of Zeleia (*Syll.*³ 279) in this context: Dittenberger suggests that its tyrant Nikagoras (Ath. 7 289c; Clem. Alex. *Protr.* 4 54) was overthrown after Granikos.

e. For this campaign, see appendix II (pp. 453–56) in vol. 1 of Brunt's Loeb edition of Arrian's *Anabasis*. Badian (1966: 48–49) argues that the Persians attacked Priene and might even have taken Naulochos: he interprets the Priene decree (*RO* 86)—a decree wherein Alexander hands over to the (Greek) citizens of Priene the harbor town Naulochos while laying personal claim to the countryside and the land of the (non-Greek) Myrseloi and Pedieis—as punishing Priene's non-Greek community for cooperating with Memnon.

f. The events recorded in texts 1 and 2 of the dossier are remarkably similar to contemporaneous events in Mytilene recorded by Arrian (*Anab.* 2.1.5), a nice check on Arrian.

g. Date of the battle of Issos: Bosworth (1980: 219).

At the conclusion of his naval campaign, Hegelochos brought the captured leaders of the pro-Persian regimes in his theater of operation to Alexander, who was then in Egypt. According to Arrian (*Anab.* 3.2.7), Alexander then made the following interesting and historically significant decision: "Alexander," he wrote, "sent the tyrants to the cities from which they came, to be treated as the citizens pleased." This is when and how the "tyrants" Agonippos and Eurysilaos ended up on trial in Eresos.

Thus, by 332, Alexander had essentially conquered the Aegean and western Asia Minor. Yet the recently conquered territory was volatile, littered with Greek poleis torn apart by years of stasis. Such a situation constituted a potential threat: the regimes in those cities could be overthrown and the cities subsequently ally with Persia and/or cities on the Aegean mainland. Supply routes from the west could be threatened. One would certainly expect, then, that Alexander sought to secure the dominance of his favored players (i.e., pro-democrats) in the various cities.[18]

There is a considerable amount of evidence that demonstrates Alexander's involvement in postconquest stabilization efforts (i.e., efforts to consolidate the pro-democrats' control of the Greek poleis in western Asia Minor). Cases are known, for example, in Priene, Mytilene, Ephesos, Chios, and (likely) Erythrai and Zeleia.[19] Alexander's well-known "First Letter to the Chians" (*RO* 84) is a particularly good example. Therein the king made it clear (line 17) that his desired end was reconciliation, apparently between two factions: the few, who were supported by Persia during the previous several years (many of whom had since been exiled), and the many who were supported by Macedon. However, Alexander insisted that the Chians have a democracy and that they elect law drafters who were to craft laws "so that nothing may be contrary to the democracy or to the return of the exiles" (lines 5–6). Inter-

---

laos succeeded them and ruled until they were expelled by Alexander's forces in 332. In this interpretation, Agonippos and Eursilaos were originally loyal to Philip but medized during Memnon's naval campaign in 333. Lott (1996) offered the third interpretation according to which there were two separate tyrannical periods: (1) Hermon, Heraios, and Apollodoros came to power circa 338 and ruled until they were expelled by Alexander's forces after the battle of Granikos in 334; (2) Agonippos and Eurysilaos seized power in 333 during Memnon's naval campaign, but were expelled by Alexander's forces in 332. In this interpretation, Philip supported a tyranny in 338 and Eresos did not fall to Memnon's forces in 335.

18　One must note the war of 331, led by Agis III of Sparta. For a discussion, see Cartledge and Spawforth (2002: 22–24). It was limited to Peloponnesian states, but the danger could have spread. Also note Diodoros's comments at 17.48.5–6. Many Persian military officers who escaped from the battle of Issos continued to fight against Alexander: "some got to important cities and held them for Darius, others raised tribes and furnishing themselves with troops from them performed appropriate duties in the time under review."

19　Priene (*RO* 86), Mytilene (*RO* 85), Ephesos (Arr. *Anab.* 1.17.10–12), Chios (*RO* 84), Erythrai (*I. Erythrai* 10), Zeleia (*Syll.*³ 279). Also note Alexander's action at Mallos (Arr. *Anab.* 2.5.9).

estingly—and a sign of Alexander's then micromanaging style—the new laws were to be brought to Alexander; presumably he intended to inspect them himself.

It is thus reasonable—in light of the known historical context and both literary and epigraphic sources—to suspect that Alexander ordered the Eresians to try their tyrants (332) in order to stabilize the polis under the newly established democratic regime. It was an attempt, that is, to make his "player" dominant in Eresos's particular interior game. The next question, then, is clear: how could the trials help achieve political stability?

ANALYSIS

In order for the tyranny trials to have any stabilizing impact, they ultimately had to convince individual democrats to lower their revolutionary thresholds. That assertion is based, first, on the simple fact that, in order to stabilize their regime, the pro-democrats required a credible threat: they needed to convince anti-democrats that any coup attempt would fail and its participants would be harshly punished. Anti-democrats thus would be deterred from attempting a coup. Second, to acquire such a credible threat, the pro-democrats had to ensure that they could quickly mobilize a sufficient number of men in response to an anti-democratic coup. They had to ensure, that is, that they would not be handicapped by a revolutionary coordination problem wherein each individual waits for a prohibitively large percentage of the population to act in defense of the democracy before he does.

The cumulative effect of three important phases of the tyranny trials would have convinced Eresian pro-democrats to lower their personal revolutionary thresholds and thus would have established a credible threat. The first phase was the presentation of the advocates' (συναγόροι: text 1, line 28) case. The presentation of that case should not be viewed as an attempt to "prove" to the citizens of Eresos that Agonippos and Eurysilaos committed the acts listed in texts 1 and 2 of the dossier: everybody knew that they did. Instead, the advocates' task was to explain *why* the citizens of Eresos should punish the two "tyrants."[20] There is no way to know how they made their case. But they likely stressed that the citizens, should they vote to condemn the two men, would send a message to everybody—pro-democrats and anti-democrats alike—that the citizens of Eresos will defend their democracy and enforce the anti-tyranny law. As a result of this phase of the trial, then, every Eresian would have known what message he would be sending with his vote; the final verdict would thus be clearly interpreted by all.

The second important phase of the trials was the announcement of the verdict. The vote was overwhelming, of course: 876 to 7. Equally important,

---

20   On the important role of punishment in a democratic polis, see Allen (2000).

however—perhaps more important—is the fact that the vote was taken by secret ballot (text 1, lines 15–16; text 2, lines 15–16). Thus there was no "voter intimidation." Each individual therefore understood that the verdict revealed the genuine private preferences of the citizens of Eresos. Consequently, the verdict generated common knowledge of widespread, genuine support for enforcing their anti-tyranny law and defending the democracy from its internal enemies. The Eresians thus sent the message identified in the preceding paragraph.

The third important phase of the trial is the application of the punishment. The texts do not indicate how the two men were executed; they just state that the citizens of Eresos were to vote to determine the manner of execution (text 1, lines 19–27; text 2, lines 17–20). It certainly would be helpful for this section's argument if the tyrants were executed publically in front of a large and cheering crowd. One might note, in this regard, Polybios's opinion about what *should* have happened to Aristomachos, the tyrant of Megalopolis: "He should have been led round the whole Peloponnesus and tortured as a deterrent spectacle" (2.60.7).[21] And it is certainly reasonable to suppose that the Eresians wanted everybody to see for himself the harsh fate that awaits tyrants. According to Plutarch (*Tim.* 34), for example, the people of Messana brought their children to the theater to witness the torture and execution of their former tyrant Hippo. Regardless of the manner of their execution, however, the execution, banishment of family, and confiscation of property would have demonstrated to all—and was thus made common knowledge—that the pro-democratic majority will back up the threats codified in their anti-tyranny law; they will defend their democracy.

After the trial was completed, the Eresians inscribed the indictments, a description of the trial's procedure, and the verdict on a stone stele that was almost certainly placed in a conspicuous location. That act of commemoration performed a very important service: it maintained as common knowledge the widespread commitment to defend the democracy and enforce the anti-tyranny law—the commitment that was made in the trial. If nothing were done to retain the memory of the trial, people might soon wonder whether or not the pro-democrats were still fully committed to defending their regime. Should there be such doubt, individuals would be less certain that, should they act in defense of the democracy, a sufficient number of individuals would follow them. They would thus raise their revolutionary thresholds, thereby undermining the pro-democrats' threat credibility. But the presence of the stone stele worked against such "memory decay." Just see-

---

21 The translation "tortured as a deterrent spectacle" (μετὰ τιμωρίας παραδειγματιζόμενον) is suggested by Walbank (1957: 266).

ing the stone maintained the common knowledge of the trial, of course. And citizens in various political settings could refer to the stone and what it represented. The message: "We all know that we are still committed." As a result, each individual would maintain his (post-trial) relatively low revolutionary threshold and the credibility of the pro-democrats' threat would thereby be upheld.

The tyranny trials were a major, complex political event in Eresos's history and thus might be viewed from a number of perspectives. From a symbolic perspective, the trials constituted a collective act of "tyrannicide" and thus placed the refoundation of their democracy within a well-established political narrative. In this light, it is interesting to compare the tyrannicide in Eresos with that of Harmodios and Aristogeiton (the tyrannicide model). Harmodios and Aristogeiton individually killed a tyrant and the Athenians subsequently erected statues of the two that proudly displayed how they killed the tyrants and thereby brought democracy to Athens. In the case of Eresos, the community of citizens killed the tyrants. Thus the Eresians erected a symbol of the democratic community: a stele. And it, too, indicated how the tyrants were killed: by a trial.

Viewed from another perspective, the tyranny trials laid the foundation for the rule of law in democratic Eresos. The Eresians were likely tempted to murder Agonippos and Eurysilaos right away, in which case they would have been, essentially, a lynch mob that got the right men.[22] The dossier, however, emphasizes the democratic principles of the rule of law and established procedure—that is, principles of governmental restraint. And the trial of Agonippos and Eurysilaos was a particularly good object lesson: (1) those two would have been considered the least deserving of a trial according to the laws; (2) the correct outcome was reached: a guilty verdict and subsequent execution. The trial thus built respect for law and the institution of the *dikasterion*. The system "worked."

The significance of such interpretations notwithstanding, the primary function of the tyranny trials was to establish the democrats' threat credibility and thus deter anti-democrats from staging a coup. We must remember that, at the time of the trials, the Eresian pro-democrats had only recently reestablished their regime. And it is reasonable to assume that there were individuals who wanted the democracy to fail. Thus the dominant question of the day must have been, are the pro-democrats sufficiently committed to defend their regime? The trials, like Athens's oath of Demophantos, were the mechanism whereby they generated and publicized that commitment. As a result, an individual could be reasonably sure that, if he acted to defend the new regime, others would follow him.

22 Compare what happened in nearby Methymna (Curt. 4.8.11).

Basis of the New Game Questioned

This section interprets the historical significance of the actions recorded in texts 3, 4, and 5 of the dossier. The texts and translations are of Rhodes and Osborne.[23]

TEXT 3

ΣΤΟΙΧ. 36

[ἔ]γνω δᾶμ[ο]ς. περὶ ὧν οἱ πρέσβεες ἀπαγγέλλοισ[ι]
[ο]ὶ πρὸς Ἀλέξανδρον ἀποστάλεντες καὶ Ἀλέ-
35   ξανδρος τὰν διαγράφαν ἀπέπεμψε· ἀφικομέ-
νων πρὸς αὗτον τῶν ⟨τῶν⟩ πρότερον τυράννων ἀπογ[ό]-
νων Ἡρωίδα τε τῶ Τερτικωνείω τῶ Ἡραείω κα[ὶ Ἀ]-
γησιμένεος τῶ Ἑρμησιδείω, καὶ ἐπαγγελλα[νέ]-
[ν]ων πρὸς Ἀλέξανδρον ὅτι ἕτοιμοί ἐστι δίκ[αν]
40   [ὑ]ποσκέθην περὶ τῶν ἐγκαλημένων ἐν τῶ δά[μω]·
[ἀγάθα τύχα δ]ἐ[δο]χθ[αι] τῶ δάμω· ἐπειδὴ ἁ[--6--]

TEXT 3, CONCLUDED

ΣΤΟΙΧ. 17

[-------- c. 14 -------- ποή|σασθαι δὲ καὶ ἐπάραν|ἐν τᾶ ἐκλησία αὔτι|κα
τῶ μὲν δικ]αίω [ὑπ|άρχο]ντι καὶ βαθόεν|[τι τᾶ] πόλει καὶ
5   τοῖς|[νόμο]ισι τᾶ δικαία εὖ||[ἔμμε]ναι καὶ αὔτοισι|[καὶ ἐκγόνοισι],
τῶ δὲ|[πα]ρὰ τοὶς νόμοις κα[ὶ]|τὰ δίκαια δικαζόν|τεσσι τὰ
10   ἐνάντια. ὄ||μνυν δὲ τοὶς πολίτ[αις]||τοὶς δικάζοντας·|[ν]αὶ
δικάσσω τὰν [δίκαν|ὄ]σσα μὲν ἐν τοῖς [νό|μ]οισι ἔνι κὰτ τοὶ[ς
15   νό||μο]ις, τὰ δὲ ἄλλα ἐκ [φιλο|π]ονίας ὡς ἄριστα κ[αὶ|δ]ικαιό⟨τατα·
καὶ τιμά|[σ]ω, αἴ κε κατάγνω, ὄρθω[ς]||καὶ δι⟨καί⟩ως. οὔτω ποήσω||
20   ναὶ μὰ Δία καὶ Ἅλιον.

The *damos* decided. Concerning what is reported by the envoys sent to Alexander, and Alexander sent back his transcript; when there arrived before him the descendants of the former tyrants, Heroidas son of Tertikon son of

---

23   The first part of text 3 is inscribed on the last lines of the obverse of gamma, immediately after text 2; thus its first line is line 33. The second part of text 3 constitutes the earliest lines of the right lateral of gamma; thus it begins with line 1. Text 4 continues right after text 3 on the same right lateral of gamma: thus the line numbering. And the majority of text 5 completes the rest of the right lateral of gamma: thus the line numbering. The very last lines of text 5, however, constituted the earliest lines on gamma's reverse: thus the line numbering. Note that, in my translation, I print the Greek word *dēmos* (or the Aeolian *damos*) instead of *RO*'s translation "the people."

Heraios and Agesimenes son of Hermesidas, and they offered to Alexander that they were willing to submit to judgment before the *damos* concerning the charges: For good fortune be it resolved by the *damos*: Since . . . A solemn prayer shall be made in the assembly immediately, that with one who is just and supports the city and the laws with a just vote it may be well, both with him and with his descendants, but with one who judges contrary to the laws and justice the opposite. The citizens who are judging shall swear: "I shall judge the case, as far as it lies within the laws, according to the laws, and in other respects industriously, as well and as justly as possible; and if I condemn I shall assess rightly and justly. I shall do this, by Zeus and Sun."

TEXT 4

ΣΤΟΙΧ. 17

    vac. Φιλλίπω. *vac.*|αἱ μὲν κατὰ τῶν φυγά|δων κρίσεις αἱ κριθε[ί]|σαι
25 ὑπὸ Ἀλεξάνδρου‖κύριαι ἔστωσαν. καὶ|[ὣ]ν κατέγνω φυγὴν
    φε[υ|γ]έτωσαμ μέν, ἀγώγιμο[ι]|δὲ μὴ ἔστωσαν. *vac.*

Of Philip. The trials of the exiles tried by Alexander shall be valid; and those whom he condemned to death shall be exiled but shall not be liable to seizure.

TEXT 5

ΣΤΟΙΧ. 17

30 πρότανις Μελίδωρος.‖βασιλεὺς Ἀντίγονος|Ἐρεσίων τῆι βουλῆι|
35 καὶ τῶι δήμωι χαίρειν.|παρεγένοντο πρὸς ἡ|μᾶς οἱ παρ᾽ ὑμῶν πρέ[σ]‖βεις
    καὶ διελέγοντ[ο],|φάμενοι τὸν δῆμον|κομισάμενον τὴν παρ᾽ [ἡ]|μῶν
40 ἐπιστολὴν ἣν ἐγρ[ά|ψ]αμεν ὑπὲρ τῶν Ἀγωνίπ‖[π]ου υἱῶν ψήφισμά
    τε π[οι|ήσ]ασθαι, ὃ ἀνέγνωσα[ν|ἡμῖ]ν, καὶ αὐτοὺς ἀπε|[σταλκέναι] . .
    λσ[-- c.5 --]|------------

TEXT 5, CONCLUDED

ΣΤΟΙΧ. 36

1 [. . . . δη]μο . ηκ[-----------15-----------ἐ]πὶ τῆ[ι . . . .]
    [-----------------23------------------]ν Ἀλεξάν[δρωι ἐν]-
    τυγ[χ]άν[ετε-----------16----------] ἔρρωσ[θε]. *vac.*

Prytanis Melidoros. King Antigonos to the council and *dēmos* of Eresos, greetings. The envoys from you came before us and made speeches, saying that the *dēmos* had received from us the letter which we wrote about the sons of Agonippos and had passed a decree, which they read to us, and had sent them . . . *dēmos* . . . you encounter Alexander (?) . . . Farewell.

These texts document three failed attempts by descendants of tyrants to return to Eresos in the years after the trial of Agonippos and Eurysilaos. The first attempt (recorded in text 3) likely came in the wake of Alexander's famous "exile decree" of 324 (Diod. Sic. 18.8.2–5). Upon hearing of the decree, descendants—grandsons—of the "former tyrants" apparently traveled to meet with the king in order to ascertain whether or not they could end their period of exile. The Eresian *dēmos*, in response, sent envoys to Alexander to explain why the descendants should not be allowed to return. Presumably to counter the Eresians' response, the exiles expressed their willingness to stand trial in order to determine whether or not they would be allowed return home.[24] Alexander thus sent a transcript ordering the Eresians to conduct a trial on the matter. The exiles, as revealed in text 6 of the dossier, lost their case.

The second failed attempt (recorded in text 4) likely came in the wake of King Philip Arrhidaios's exile proclamation of 319 (Diod. Sic. 18.56.1–8). Announced in the tough, chaotic times of the early period of Alexander's successors (the *diadochoi*), this text too ordered exiles—except those exiled for blood guilt or impiety, and certain named individuals—to return to their native poleis. Apparently, although not explicitly stated in the dossier, the same descendants who tried and failed to return to Eresos five years earlier requested permission from Philip to return.[25] In response, the Eresians most likely sent envoys once again to officially contest the exiles' request. And Philip acquiesced to the *dēmos*, issuing a transcript that slightly altered Alexander's decision of 324: the descendants of the former tyrants were to remain in exile, but they would no longer be susceptible to arrest.

The particular context for the third attempt (recorded in text 5) is not known. The letter, however, must have been written between 306 (when Antigonos assumed the title of king) and 301 (when Antigonos died). Antigonos is not known to have issued an exile decree, but it is certainly possible that he did so. It is also possible that the descendants of Agonippos thought that the new king might acquiesce to an individual request not pursuant to a royal proclamation. In any case, it appears that King Antigonos wrote a letter to the Eresians in their support.[26] In response, the *dēmos* of Eresos passed a decree that their ambassadors read to the king. The content of that decree is

24 Perhaps these exiles were driven out of Eresos before the Eresians passed their "law against the tyrants" (336?). Thus they might have argued that they should be affected neither by that law nor by the trial of 332.

25 This is argued by Heisserer (1980: 62–67).

26 This conclusion is based in large part on the possible meaning of ὑπέρ ("on behalf of") (line 39). But note that the same preposition is used in text 6 (lines 18–19) referring to Alexander's letter to the Eresians concerning the trial of the descendants of the "former tyrants." It is, perhaps, doubtful that Alexander wrote a letter of support for those men in 324. Both Welles (1974: 14) and Magie (1950: 874n60) conclude that Antigonos initially supported the descendants of Agonippos.

not known, but it almost certainly both praised the king and requested that the descendants of Agonippos not be allowed to return to Eresos. King Antigonos granted their request.

THE PROBLEM

It is quite clear that the Eresians were concerned with the prospect of the exiles' return home. The basis of that concern, however, is not clear. What were the Eresian democrats so worried about?

To understand the basis of their concern, it first is important to realize that pro-democrats likely would interpret the exiles' return as an indication that the exiles had strong political support from the king. The key point here, of course, is that the king would have personally granted the permission—the exiles went directly to him. Pro-democrats thus would naturally have wondered why the king overruled their earlier decisions. And it would have been reasonable to conclude, even if incorrectly, that the exiles and the king cut some sort of deal whereby Eresos would be governed by a "pro-monarch," nondemocratic regime—a regime in which the exiles would play an important role. First, why would the king grant the exiles' (descendants of tyrants, it must be remembered) request in the first place? Second, some kings (e.g., Lysimachos) were known to support oligarchy.[27] And finally, the exiles likely had supporters in the city: they likely would not have wanted to return if they had no supporters; seven people had the courage to vote for the acquittal of Agonippos and Eurysilaos (that might suggest deeper support for a nondemocratic regime); in text 2 (lines 20–22), concern is expressed that someone might propose the recall of the tyrants' descendants; in text 6 (lines 35–39), concern is expressed that the descendants of former tyrants might somehow return to Eresos.

If there was even the perception that the king supported the exiles, the democrats' threat credibility would have been diminished and the recently established democratic equilibrium potentially jeopardized. The democrats' threat required individuals to believe that, should they risk their lives to defend the democracy, a sufficient number of additional individuals would follow them. If the exiles returned, however, people would reasonably conclude that others would not follow them, should they defend the democracy in response to a coup attempt: it would be foolish to (potentially) confront the king. And it is important to note that, even if it an individual doubted that the king actually would support an anti-democratic coup, he might think that other Eresians believed that he would. Thus individual pro-democrats would raise their personal revolutionary thresholds; a greater number people would now have to defend the democracy before they do. And if that dynamic were perceived, the democrats' threat would not be deemed credible and the anti-

27 On Lysimachos, see Lund (1992).

democrats would be more likely to defect and reestablish a nondemocratic regime.

THE SOLUTION

The democrats had to respond to these challenges vigorously. They had to ensure the exiles' attempt to return would not result in individual democrats raising their revolutionary thresholds and thus diminishing the credibility of their collective threat.

In each of the instances, the democrats' response consisted of two complementary parts. First, they generated common knowledge of continued widespread credible commitment to defend the democracy (i.e., to enforce their anti-tyranny law). They achieved that end by means of both a thorough discussion of the matter in the citizen assembly—gathered as a law court in the first instance—and a concluding vote. Like in the original trial of Agonippos and Eurysilaos, the pre-vote discussion ensured that every citizen was fully aware of what was happening and understood its significance for the survival of the democracy. Thus each meeting was, essentially, a referendum on whether or not the Eresians wanted to keep (and were thus willing to defend) the democracy—to uphold their anti-tyranny law. And each time, of course, the answer was "yes."

Second, the Eresians made common knowledge the fact that the particular king in question (first Alexander, then Philip, then Antigonos) decided *not* to support the exiles' request. The Eresians accomplished that objective by engraving each king's decision on a stele; and they no doubt announced that decision in a meeting of the assembly. All citizens thus could read what the king decided. But inscribing the king's decision performed another important function: it increased the likelihood that the king would not renege on his promise; were he to contemplate a change in policy, the Eresians could show him his earlier decision. It was literally written in stone.[28]

In hindsight, the exiles' repeated attempts to return likely strengthened the Eresian democracy. Simply put, those attempts provided opportunities for each citizen to publically reaffirm his commitment to defend the democracy and to learn of his fellow citizens' continued commitment. Individuals would thus be more likely to trust that their fellow citizens would, in fact, follow them should they defend their democracy against a coup d'état. Indi-

---

28 A great example of this use of publicly placed writing is found in lines 13–18 of *I. Ilion* 33. Meleagros, the Seleukid governor of the Hellespont satrapy, wrote to the *dēmos* of Ilion that Aristodikides of Assos (a "friend" of the king) had chosen to attach his newly received land to the territory of Ilion. At the end of the letter, Meleagros wrote, "You, however, would do well to vote all the usual privileges to him and to make a copy of the terms of his grant and inscribe it on a stele and place it in the sanctuary in order that you may retain securely for all time what has been granted" (trans. Burstein). For a detailed examination of the use of inscribed documents in the mediation between Hellenistic poleis and the superpower kings, see Ma (2000).

viduals, that is, lowered their personal revolutionary thresholds even lower than they were immediately after the initial tyranny trials. As a consequence, the pro-democrats' threat was that much more credible and anti-tyranny ideology sunk that much deeper into the Eresians' collective consciousness.

The New Game's Basis Definitively Secured

This section interprets the action recorded in the sixth text of the dossier. The text and translation are those of Rhodes and Osborne.[29]

TEXT 6

ΣΤΟΙΧ. 36

[ἔ]γν[ω δᾶμος. περὶ ὦν ἀ βό]λ[λα] προεβόλλε[υσε ἢ ἔδο]-
5 [ξ]ε ἢ [μ]ετέδ[οξε τᾶ βόλλα, καὶ οἰ] ἄνδ[ρ]ες οἰ χ[ειροτο]-
[ν]ή[θεν]τε[ς πάν]τα [τὰ γράφεντα] κατὰ τῶν τυρ[άν]-
γων [κα]ὶ τ[ῶν ἐ]μ πό[λει οἰκη]θέντων καὶ τῶν ἐκγ[ό]-
[νω]ν [τῶν τούτων παρέχ]ονται καὶ ταῖς γράφαι[ς]
[ε]ἰσ[κομίζοισ]ι εἰς τὰν ἐκλησίαν· ἐπειδὴ καὶ π[ρό]-
10 [τε]ρον ὀ βασίλευς Ἀλέξανδρος διαγράφαν ἀποσ-
[τέ]λλαις π[ροσέτ]αξε Ἐρ[εσίοις κρῖναι ὐπέρ τ[ε]
[Ἀγ]ωνίππω καὶ Εὐ[ρυσ]ιλ[ά]ω, τί δεῖ πά[θ]ην αὔτοις· [ὀ]
[δὲ δᾶμος ἀκο]υ[σ]αις τὰ[ν] διαγράφαν δικαστήριο[ν]
[καθί]⟨σ⟩σα[ι]ς κ[ατὰ] τοὶς νόμοις ὀ ἔκριν[ν]ε Ἀγώνι[π]-
15 [π]ομ μὲν καὶ Εὐρυσιλ[αο]ν τε[θ]νάκην, τοῖς δὲ ἀπο[γό]-
[νοις] αὔτων ἐνόχοις [ἔμμε]ναι τῶ νόμω τῶ ἐν τᾶ
[στ]άλλα, τὰ [δ]ὲ ὐπάρχον[τα π]έπρασθαι αὔτων κατὰ
[τ]ὸν νόμον· ἐπιστέλλ[αντος] δὲ Ἀλεξάνδρω καὶ ὐ-
πὲρ τῶν Ἀπολλ[οδ]ωρε[ίων] ⟨κ⟩αὶ τῶν κασιγνήτων [αὔ]-
20 [τ]ω Ἔρμωνος καὶ Ἡραίω τῶν πρότερον τυραννη-
σάντων τᾶς πόλιος καὶ τῶν ἀπογόνων αὔτων, γ[νω]-
ναι τὸν δᾶμον πότερο[ν δόκ]ει καταπορεύεσθ[αι]
αὔτοις ἢ μή· [ὀ] δὲ δᾶμος ἀκούσαις τᾶς διαγράφα[ς]
δικαστήριόν τε αὔτοισι συνάγαγε κατὰ τὸν [νό]-
25 [μο]ν καὶ τὰν διαγράφαν τῶ βασιλέως Ἀλεξάνδρ[ω],
[ὂ ἔ]γνω λό[γ]ων ῥηθέντων παρ᾽ ἀμφοτέρων τόν τε ν[ό]-
[μο]ν τὸν κατὰ τῶν τυράννων κύριον ἔμμεναι κα[ὶ]
[φ]εύγην αὔτοις κὰτ [τὰ]μ π[όλιν]. δέδοχθαι τῶ δάμ[ω]·
[κ]ύριομ μὲν ἔμμεναι κατὰ [τῶν] τυράννων καὶ τῶ[ν]

---

29 This text, recorded on the reverse of gamma, immediately follows text 5. Thus it begins with line 4. Note that I have maintained the Greek word *damos* instead of *RO*'s "the people."

30 [ἐ]μ πόλι οἰκηθέντων καὶ τῶν ἀπογόνων τῶν το[ύ]-
   [τ]ων τόν τε νόμον τὸμ περὶ [τ]ῶν τυράννων γεγρά[μ]-
   [μ]ενον ἐν τᾶ στάλλα τᾶ [παλαί]α καὶ ταὶς διαγρά-
   [φ]αις τῶν βασιλέων ταὶς κατὰ τούτων καὶ τὰ ψα-
   [φ]ίσματα τὰ πρότερον γράφεντα ὑπὸ τῶν προγό-
35 [ν]ων καὶ ταὶς ψαφοφο[ρ]ίαις ταὶς κατὰ τῶν τυράννων. [αἰ]
   [δ]έ κέ τις παρὰ ταῦτα ἀλίσκηται τῶν τυράννω[ν ἦ]
   τῶν ἐμ πόλι οἰκηθέντων ἦ τῶν ἀπογόνων τῶν [τού]-
   των τις ἐπιβαίνων ἐπὶ τὰν γᾶν τὰν Ἐρεσίων [. . .]
   [.]ω τὸν δᾶμον βουλεύσασθαι καὶ πρ[------ c.9------]
40 [. .]αλλ[--- 5---]τα[--------------c. 24--------------]

The *damos* decided. Concerning the matters about which the council made
a preliminary consultation [*probouleuma*], or the council made a resolution
or a revised resolution, and the men who have been elected produce all that
has been written against the tyrants, both those who lived in the city and
their descendants, and convey the documents to the assembly: Since previously also King Alexander sent back a transcript and ordered the Eresians to
hold a trial concerning Agonippos and Eurysilaos, as to what should be
done to them; and the *damos* heard to transcript and set up a law-court in
accordance with the laws, which sentenced Agonippos and Eurysilaos to
death, and that their descendants should be liable to the law on the stele, and
their belongings should be sold in accordance with the law; And when Alexander sent a letter also about the family of Apollodoros and his brothers
Hermon and Heraios, who were previously tyrants over the city, and their
descendants, that the *damos* should decide whether it resolved that they
should journey back or not; and the *damos* heard the transcript and convened a law-court for them in accordance with the law and the transcript of
Alexander, which decided after speeches had been made on both sides that
the law against the tyrants should be valid and that they should be exiled
from the city; Be it resolved by the *damos*: That there shall be valid against
the tyrants, both those who lived in the city and their descendants, the law
against the tyrants that is written on the old stele and the transcripts of the
kings against them and the decrees previously written by our ancestors and
the votes against the tyrants. If contrary to this any of the tyrants, either
those who lived in the city or their descendants, is caught setting foot on the
land of Eresos --- the *damos* shall deliberate and ---

Text 6 records a decree of the Eresian *dēmos* validating "all that has been written against the tyrants, both those who lived in the city and their descendants." Four documents are mentioned. The first document is "the law against
the tyrants that is written on the old stele." As noted at the beginning of this
chapter, we do not know for certain the date of that law's promulgation; and
we know very little about its provisions. The second group of documents

listed in the decree is "the transcripts (*diagraphai*) of the kings" against the tyrants. The only explicitly mentioned transcripts in the dossier are from Alexander: one ordering the Eresians to try Agonippos and Eurysilaos (texts 1 and 2), the other ordering the Eresians to try the descendants of the "former tyrants" in order to determine whether or not they will be allowed return to Eresos (text 3). But Philip Arrhidaios's judgment (text 4) is almost certainly a transcript, and Antigonos's letter (text 5) might have contained one too. The third group of writings mentioned consists of previous decrees promulgated against the tyrants. Texts 3 and 6 are clearly decrees: they contain the generic motion formula "the *dēmos* decided." And texts 1 and 2 are likely parts of decrees too: they publicly declared how the *dēmos* will try the two tyrants. And there were likely additional decrees that are no longer extant: formal decrees of banishment and property confiscation, for example.[30] The fourth group of documents listed in text 6 consists of "the votes against the tyrants." That obviously refers to the jury votes in the trial against Agonippos and Eurysilaos (texts 1 and 2) and the trial of the descendants of the "former tyrants" (text 3).

The most salient context for this decree (text 6) is the widespread conclusion that, in the future, kings would not interfere in Eresos's interior game. The fact that three different kings in one generation decided not to interfere supports that conclusion, of course. But the Eresians had more to rely on than simply the particular decisions of individual kings: the logic of the modern legal concept of *stare decisis* seems to have taken root. The only *legitimate* action for a king vis-à-vis involvement in Eresos's interior game concerning tyrants and their descendants, that is, was to follow Alexander's precedent—namely, to let the Eresians decide the matter for themselves. In support of that conclusion, one might note, first, that both Philip's transcript (text 4) and Antigonos's letter (text 5) refer to Alexander. The exact context of the Antigonos's reference is unknown. But he quite likely was explaining the rationale of his own decision: he will follow the precedent established by Alexander.[31] Second, the decree recorded in text 6 cites Alexander's rulings as the source

---

30   Such texts were likely inscribed on the parts of the two stones that are no longer legible. Heisserer (1980: 64) also suggests that Alexander's order (in 334) that the tyrants be exiled and rendered subject to arrest (*agogimoi*) was inscribed on stone beta.

31   Note that the verb ἐντυγχάνω (found in the present tense in Antigonos's letter, lines 2–3) can mean, in addition to "encounter" (as found in *RO*'s translation), "appeal to" (+ dative), as found in *RC* 2. Importantly, Alexander's name is in the dative case: Ἀλεξάν[δρωι] (line 2). Thus the sense could be "appeal to Alexander." Also, there appears to be general agreement that the subject of εν]|τυγ[χ]αν[is the Eresians: Paton, in *IG* XII, 2, 526 (followed by Heisserer and *RO*) restored the second person plural finite verb: ἐν]|τυγ[χ]άν[ετε; *Tod* 191 and *OGIS* 8 restored the plural participle in the nominative case: ἐν]|τυγ[χ]άν[οντες; Welles (*RC* 2) restores a participle but is noncommittal on its case and number: ἐν]|τυγ[χ]αν[οντ–16–. It is thus possible that the general sense is "your appeal to Alexander's precedent is persuasive." For a brief discussion of the first three lines of the reverse of stone gamma, see Heisserer (1980: 55–56).

of authority of both the Eresians' decisions and the decisions of the subsequent two kings:

> Since previously also King Alexander sent back a transcript and ordered the Eresians to hold a trial concerning Agonippos and Eurysilaos, as to what should be done to them. . . . And when [or since] Alexander sent a letter also about the family of Apollodoros and his brothers Hermon and Heraios. . . . Be it resolved by the *damos*: That there shall be valid against the tyrants . . . the law against the tyrants . . . and the transcripts of the kings.

The pro-democrats' realization that the Hellenistic kings would not interfere in their internal actions against tyrants and the descendants of tyrants had very significant consequences. Simply put, the pro-democrats acquired a much firmer control of their polis. There no doubt would be future exogenous events that threatened to undermine the democratic equilibrium. But perhaps the single most significant exogenous threat had been royal intervention on behalf of the anti-democrats. And now it was reasonably certain that the kings' policies in that regard would be predictably benign; they had been "endogenized" (i.e., made part of the known variables of the interior game). It thus follows that, if the democrats had a clearly credible and capable threat, it would be quite unlikely that anti-democrats would defect: to do so would be irrational.

This decree (text 6) thus records the *dēmos*'s attempt to demonstrate—one last time—the credibility of their threat against tyrants, thereby securing as permanent the basis of the "new game" established by Alexander a generation earlier. The means toward that end, predictably, was the generation of common knowledge of credible commitment via discussion and subsequent vote in an assembly of citizens. The same dynamic as described in the first and second sections of this chapter was in play; thus there is no need to articulate its generic characteristics again. But it is important to appreciate how impressive that assembly meeting must have been. Each text was (most likely) brought before the audience, read out loud, discussed, and then deemed by majority vote to be *kurios*. The meeting was an opportunity, then, for the Eresians to affirm the past thirty years of democratic rule and thus the *dēmos*'s control of the polis. Nobody would doubt the anti-tyranny stance of the Eresian *dēmos*.

Soon after the assembly adjourned, the Eresians had their decree inscribed on the same stones that recorded the original trial against the tyrants and each of the subsequent "anti-tyranny episodes" that transpired during the subsequent thirty years. But this would be the final installment, the last action against tyrants. The *dēmos*'s threat was clearly credible, and thus defection was clearly irrational. After one generation, the new game was secure.[32]

---

32 Unfortunately, there are very few extant inscriptions from Eresos, and the few that do exist are not precisely (or even roughly) dated. However, the inscriptions do suggest that the *dēmos* was

Conclusion

The events analyzed in this chapter underscore the importance for pro-democrats to maintain their threat credibility. A dramatic, foundational "moment"—such as a public trial or oath against tyrants—certainly was essential: it established the initial credible commitment. But, due to the passage of time and changing circumstances, individuals may begin to doubt whether or not their fellow citizens remain committed. As a consequence, individual pro-democrats might lack the confidence to potentially risk their life in the defense of their democracy; thus they raise their revolutionary threshold. If anti-democrats detected that dynamic, they would conclude that the pro-democrats could not respond adequately to a coup. That is, they would conclude that the pro-democrats' threat was not credible. Those anti-democrats would thus defect and try to establish a nondemocratic regime. To fight against that, pro-democrats had to continually generate common knowledge of widespread credible commitment to defend their democracy.

The need to maintain threat credibility would be particularly important for new democracies. The citizens of older, more established democracies benefit from the accumulated effect of past commitment demonstrations—by word or, most effectively, by deed. That is not to say that established democracies did not have to ensure that their threat remained credible. It is just that the regime likely would receive the benefit of the doubt: individuals, pro-democrats and anti-democrats alike, would more likely assume that the citizen population is defined by a "pro-mobilization" threshold sequence. Defending the democracy would thus be rational; staging a coup would be irrational. The citizens of new democracies, however, would not have such a reservoir of trust. They thus would readily doubt that their fellow citizens have maintained their commitment to defend the regime. In such an epistemic environment, it would be foolish for an individual to keep a low revolutionary threshold: he could not really be sure that, if he acted in defense of the democracy, a sufficient number of his fellow citizens would follow him. One would thus expect the citizens of new democracies to expend a considerable amount of energy to maintain common knowledge of widespread credible commitment to defend the democracy.

It is thus quite interesting to note that Alexander promoted anti-tyranny ideology during his conquest of—and attempt to democratize—the cities of western Asia Minor. This chapter analyzed one particular example, of course: it was Alexander himself who sent "the tyrants to the cities from which they came, to be treated as the citizens pleased" (Arr. *Anab.* 3.2.7). Those men al-

---

in control of the polis after 300. The following texts likely date to the Hellenistic period and give an indication that the *dēmos* controlled Eresos: *IG* XII, 2: 527, 528, 529, 530; Supplement to *IG* XII: 120 (before 190 BCE), 121 (3rd/2nd c. BCE), 122 (209–204 BCE). No extant text from this period indicates that the *dēmos* was not in control of the polis.

most certainly were sent back to their home poleis with some sort of written document that authorized and justified their execution specifically *because* they were "tyrants." Alexander was thus sending a very clear message that "tyrants" are bad for the community and thus must be killed. And by brutally punishing them, the citizens of the various poleis would have internalized and normalized that anti-tyranny ideology.

Alexander also promoted anti-tyranny ideology in a proclamation he made after his victory in the battle of Gaugamela (331). According to Plutarch (*Alex.* 34), Alexander sought to increase his prestige among the Greeks. He thus "wrote to the states saying that all tyrannies are now abolished and that henceforth they might live under their own laws" (ἔγραψε τὰς τυραννίδας πάσας καταλυθῆναι καὶ πολιτεύειν αὐτονόμους). This proclamation certainly was read aloud in the assemblies of the newly democratic poleis. And it is quite reasonable to suppose that the pro-democrats in those cities inscribed the proclamation—or, perhaps more likely, a decree or law pursuant to the proclamation—on a prominently placed stone stele: thus the anti-tyranny proclamation would have become a concrete, permanent fixture of the newly democratic public space. A possible analogy here would be Philip Arrhidaios's exile decree (Diod. Sic. 18.56.1–8): it specifically ordered the citizens of the various poleis to pass a decree not to engage in war with each other and not to act in opposition to the king's rule.

A final (potential) example of Alexander's promotion of Athenian-style anti-tyranny ideology concerns the returning to Athens of the original statues of Harmodios and Aristogeiton. The matter is confused. Arrian wrote that Alexander returned the statues to the Athenians but gave two different dates: 331, during Alexander's first stay in Babylon (*Anab.* 3.16.7–8), and 325/4, during his second stay at Babylon (*Anab.* 7.19.2). Pausanias, however, wrote (1.8.5) that Antiochos I returned the statues. And Valerius Maximus (ii 10, *ext.* 1) attributed the deed to Seleukos. In an attempt to reconcile the conflicting accounts, Bosworth (following the original suggestion of C. Seltman) concluded that the statues were returned to Athens during the joint reign of Seleukos and Antiochos I (292–281) and that Alexander "merely promised" to do so.[33] That is certainly a reasonable position. But it should be noted that Pliny (*NH* 34.70) agrees with Arrian in attributing the deed to Alexander. In any case, if Alexander did not do it, he certainly was thought to have done it and thus (most likely) publicized widely his "promise" throughout the Greek world. (And it would be fine propaganda for Alexander to make his promise widely known: he is the ultimate tyrant killer.)

It is reasonable to conclude that Alexander heavily promoted anti-tyranny ideology to facilitate his efforts to democratize the cities of western Asia Mi-

---

33 Bosworth's comments (1980: 317). It might be relevant to note that Seleukos I and Antiochos I returned a statue of Apollo to Miletos that was taken by Darius I (Paus. 1.16.3, 8.46.3).

nor.[34] He utilized it, that is, to support his favorite faction—pro-democrats—in the various internal games. First of all, the democracies in those cities would certainly be new: Persia controlled the western coast of Asia Minor since (at least) the King's Peace of 387/6. The pro-democrats in the various cities would thus likely have required assistance in establishing a collective credible threat to deter supporters of the "old guard" from reestablishing a nondemocratic regime.[35] Second, as demonstrated in this chapter, Alexander himself ordered the citizens of Eresos to try their "tyrants" in order to establish a credible threat for the supporters of Eresos's new democracy. And finally, Alexander almost certainly knew that the Athenians and the Eretrians had recently demonstrated that tyrant-killing law could facilitate the pro-democrats' efforts to maintain control of their polis.[36] It thus simply makes sense that he would use it to advance his interests in Asia Minor.

If Alexander heavily promoted anti-tyranny ideology, one would expect to find multiple examples of its use by supporters of the newly constituted democracies of Asia Minor to defend their democratic regime. The next two chapters analyze two significant instances: in Erythrai and in Ilion. Both of those instances should—and will—be interpreted within the general historical and theoretical framework articulated in this chapter. And we will return, at the conclusion of chapter 6, to assess the role of tyrant-killing law in the democratization of Hellenistic western Asia Minor.

---

34   It must be stressed that the Alexander was not doctrinaire in his liberation/democratization policy. Parmenion, for example, enslaved the small Aeolic town of Gryneion (Diod. Sic. 17.7.9). But that occurred before Alexander commanded the forces in Asia Minor (see Badian [1966: 39–40]). And Thebes was a democracy when Alexander had it destroyed. But it, of course, was on the Greek mainland. Note, too, Alexander's maltreatment of Soli (in Kilikia) during the run-up to the battle of Issos (Arr. *Anab.* 2.5.5–8): he put a garrison in the city and fined the citizens 200 talents (because they favored Persia) and then "granted them democracy." As Bosworth notes (1980: ad loc.), this notorious incident demonstrates that a grant of democracy was not necessarily a grant of freedom. Arrian appears to contrast Alexander's treatment of Soli with his subsequent treatment of Mallos (Arr. *Anab.* 2.5.9).

35   There surely was internal competition for control of the various poleis. The epigraphic record in several cities makes this clear. For example, Mytilene (*RO* 85), Erythrai (*I. Erythrai* 10), Chios (*RO* 84). Alexander's democratization policy was unwelcomed by anti-democrats.

36   For an analysis of the laws from Eretria and Athens, see, respectively, chapters 2 and 3. Note, too, that Phanias of Eresos (a student of Aristotle, who was Alexander's tutor) wrote a book titled τυράννων ἀναίρεσις ἐκ τιμωρίας ("the slaying of tyrants out of vengeance") (Athen. 3.90e; 8.33a, 10.438c). Alexander clearly understood the potential power of anti-tyranny ideology.

The Philites Stele from Erythrai

Introduction

Alexander's conquest of western Asia Minor marked a dramatic turning point in Erythraian politics. For the previous fifty-four consecutive years (386–332) and for seventy-two of the previous eighty years (412–394 and 386–332), oligarchs controlled that polis.[1] By the end of the 330s, however, the democrats were in control. What many Erythraians likely considered to be the natural and immutable political order had been completely upended.

This chapter analyzes the Erythraian democrats' efforts to maintain control of their polis in the face of efforts by their anti-democratic opponents to reinstate the pre-Alexander status quo. The following inscription (*I. Erythrai* 503), henceforth referred to as the "Philites stele," is the starting point for the inquiry.[2]

---

1 That oligarchs controlled Erythrai from 412 to 394 must be inferred from several sources: (1) Thuc. 8.5.4–8.6; 8.14.2 (the Erythraians revolted from Athens in 412); (2) Xen. *Hell.* 3.4.2 (after the Peloponnesian war [404], the Spartan Lysander established decarchies in the Greek cities of Asia Minor); (3) *RO* 8 (the *dēmos* of Erythrai honors Konon in 394 after he defeated the Spartans in a naval battle near Knidos—the *dēmos*, no doubt, subsequently assumed control of the polis); (4) Diod. Sic. 14.84.2–3 (the Erythraians, after the battle of Knidos, expelled their Spartan-supported garrison—cf. Xen. *Hell.* 4.8.1–2).

That oligarchs controlled Erythrai from 386 to circa 334–332 also must be inferred from several sources: (1) *RO* 17 (a decree of the Athenian *dēmos*, dated to circa 386, wherein it is made clear [lines 11–14] that the *dēmos* of Erythrai does not want to be "handed over to the barbarians"—i.e., handed to the Persians pursuant to the King's Peace); (2) Xen. *Hell.* 5.1.31 (according to the terms of the King's Peace, the "poleis in Asia" belonged to the king of Persia); (3) *RO* 56 (an honorary decree dated to the mid-350s promulgated by the Erythraian *boulē*—*not* the *dēmos*—for Maussollos of Karia for being [lines 3–4] "a good man regarding the *polis*" [i.e., not the *dēmos*]); (4) HD 28 B (an honorary decree, dated 365–355, promulgated by the Erythraian *boulē*—again, *not* the *dēmos*—for Maussollos's brother Idrieos for being [lines 5–6] "a good man regarding the polis"); (5) *RO* 68 (an alliance, dated circa 350–342, with Hermias of Atarneus, perhaps in preparation for war against the Persians; the customary oath was to be "taken care of" [lines 18–19] by the generals of Erythrai—perhaps a sign of oligarchy). Alexander subsequently (334–332) established democratic rule, as is noted generally by Arrian (*Anab.* 1.18.1–2) and is borne out in Erythrai's epigraphic record: *I. Erythrai* 21. Note that the context of *I. Erythrai* 7, an Athenian decree concerning Erythrai dated 366/5, is unknown: it need not suggest that Erythrai was governed by a democracy.

2 Text and translation: Heisserer (1979: 282–83). Note, however, that I have retained the Greek word *dēmos* in the translation; Heisserer translated *dēmos* as "the people." Editio princeps:

Non-ΣΤΟΙΧ.

Ἔδοξεν τῆι βουλῆι καὶ τῶι δήμωι· Ζωίλος Χιάδου εἶπεν· ἐπειδὴ οἱ ἐν τῆι ὀλιγαρχίαι τῆς εἰκόνος τῆς Φιλίτου τοῦ ἀποκτείναντος
τὸν τύραννον τοῦ ἀνδριάντος ἐξεῖλον
5 τὸ ξίφος, νομίζοντες καθόλου τὴν στάσιν
καθ᾽ αὑτῶν εἶναι· ὅπως ἂν ὁ δῆμος φαίνηται
πολλὴν ἐπιμέλειαν ποιούμενος καὶ μνημο-
νεύων ἀεὶ τῶν εὐεργετῶν καὶ ζώντων
καὶ τετελευτηκότων, ἀγαθῆι τύχηι δεδόχθαι
10 τῆι βουλῆι καὶ τῶι δήμωι· τοὺς ἐξεταστὰς το[ὺ]-
ς ἐνεστηκότ[α]ς ἐγδοῦναι τὸ ἔργον διαστολὴν
ποιησαμένους μετὰ τοῦ ἀρχιτέκτονος, καθότι
συντελεσθήσεται ὡς πρότερον εἶχεν· ὑπηρετε[ῖ]
ν δὲ αὐτοῖς τὸγ κατὰ μῆνα ταμίαν. ὅπως δὲ καθαρὸς
15 ἰοῦ ἔσται ὁ ἀνδριὰς καὶ στεφανωθήσεται ἀεὶ ταῖς
νουμηνίας καὶ ταῖς ἄλλαις ἑορταῖς, ἐπιμελεῖσθαι
τοὺς ἀγορανόμους.
Ἔδοξεν τῆι βουλῆ καὶ τῶι δήμωι· Ζωίλος Χιάδου
εἶπεν· ἐπειδὴ ἐν τῶι πρότερον ψηφίσματι προσε-
20 τάχθη τῶι ἀγορανόμωι ἐπιμελεῖσθαι τῆς εἰκόνος
τοῦ ἀνδριάντος τοῦ Φιλίτου, ὅπως στεφανω-
θήσεταί τε καὶ λαμπρὸς ἔσται, ὁ δὲ ἀγορανόμος
φησὶν εἰς ταῦτα πόρου δεῖσθαι, ἀγαθῆι τύχηι
δεδόχθαι τῆι βουλῆι καὶ τῶι δήμωι· τὸ μὲν καθ᾽ ἔ-
25 τος εἰς ταῦτα διδόναι τὸ ἀνάλωμα τοὺς
[κα]τὰ μῆνα ταμίας, ἐπιμελεῖσθαι δὲ τὸν
[ἀγορα]νόμον, εἰς δὲ τὸν λοιπὸγ χρόνον οἱ ἀ[γ]-
[ορανόμο]ι πωλοῦντες τὰς ὠνὰς προστι[θέ]-
[τωσαν τὴν πο]ίη[σιν] τῶν στεφά[νων -----]
30 [-----------]τε[---------]

It was resolved by the council and the *dēmos*. Zoilos the son of Chiades proposed: since the members of the oligarchy took away the sword from the
statue, which was a portrait of Philites the tyrannicide, thinking that the
erection of the statue was a protest against themselves, and in order that it be

Kirchhoff (1863: 265–68). The provenance of this inscription has been debated, because its chain of
custody is not known for certain: see Heisserer (1979: 289). Some of the earliest editors (e.g., Kirchhoff [1863] and Michel [1900–27: no. 364]) suggested that the decree was promulgated in Chios.
Engelmann and Merkelbach, in their edition of the text (*I. Erythrai* 503), follow Wilhelm (1915)
and suggest that the Philites stele was promulgated in Klazomenai. But Heisserer (1979) has given
cogent arguments for Erythraian origin.

apparent that the *dēmos* takes great care and remembers forever its benefactors, both living and dead, with good fortune it was resolved by the council and the *dēmos*: the current *exetastai* are to invite bids for the work, having made specification with the municipal architect whereby it shall be completed as it was previously; and the monthly treasurer is to assist these official. The clerks of the market are to take care that the statue will be free of verdigris and will be crowned always at the festivals of the first of the month and at the other festivals.

It was resolved by the council and the *dēmos*. Zoilos the son of Chiades proposed: since in the previous decree it was assigned to the clerk of the market to take care of the portrait, namely the statue of Philites, so that it will be crowned and will be shining, but the clerk of the market reports that funds are needed for this, with good fortune it was resolved by the council and the *dēmos*: for this year the monthly treasurers are to provide the expenses for this project, and the clerk of the market is to take care of it, but in the future the clerks of the market selling the contracts (are to add the making) of the crowns. . . .

The earliest historical event alluded to in this inscription is a successful democratic coup d'état. The previous, nondemocratic regime was, apparently, some sort of "tyranny." At any rate, after securing control of the polis, the victorious democrats erected a statue in the image of an otherwise unknown man named Philites "the tyrant killer."[3] That statue, unfortunately, has not been found. Yet several important points may be inferred about it from information provided in the decree.

First, the statue of Philites was quite likely an explicit imitation of the Athenians' statue of Harmodios sculptured by Kritios and Nesiotes. In defense of that assertion, one should note that Philites is explicitly called a "tyrant killer" (Φιλίτου τοῦ ἀποκτείναντος τὸν τύραννον, lines 3–4). And Harmodios, of course, was known as a tyrant killer.[4] Much more suggestive is the fact that the sword (ξίφος) was a very important feature of the statue of Philites—so much so that the oligarchs removed it. Now, the most recognizable feature of Kritios and Nesiotes's statue of Harmodios was the raised right arm bearing a sword (ξίφος). In Aristophanes's comedy *Lysistrata* (lines 630–35), for example, the male chorus leader, after announcing that he will carry his sword (ξίφος), humorously poses just like the statue of Harmodios to signal his readiness to combat tyranny. And, importantly, a (likely) mid-fifth-century electrum stater from Kyzikos depicts Harmodios with a sword in his

3 Gauthier (1982: 216) notes that an ἀνδριάς (lines 4, 15, 21 in the Philites stele) is a statue in the form of a man, while an εἰκών (lines 2–3 and 20 in the Philites stele) is a statue in the form of a particular man, a portrait.
4 Most notably in the so-called tyrannicide *skolia* (Ath. 15.695a).

raised right hand.[5] Philites was thus almost certainly depicted as delivering what B. B. Shefton (1960) has called "the Harmodios blow."[6]

Second, the statue of Philites was made out of bronze. It is true that the Philites stele does not state that explicitly. And it is also true that, when referring to statues, Erythraian decrees often state the material that they are made of.[7] But the Philites stele does state that the statue has ἰός (14–15) that must be removed in order to make it "shiny" (λαμπρός, line 22). That almost certainly indicates that the statue was made of bronze: one would be less inclined to refer to a marble statue as "shiny"; it is difficult to imagine what the ἰός, a word that can also mean "poison," would be on a marble statue. And one should also note that the Kritios and Nesiotes statues of Harmodios were made of bronze.[8]

Finally, the Erythraians almost certainly placed the statue of Philites in the agora. The best evidence in support of that assertion is that the *agoranomoi*— officials formally in charge of transactions that take place in the agora—were chiefly responsible for "taking care" (ἐπιμελεῖσθαι) of the portrait-statue.[9] Also suggestive is the fact that there are extant decrees of the Erythraian *dēmos* (e.g., *RO* 56 lines 11–13; *I. Erythrai* 28 lines 51–53; *IEryth*McCabe 19 lines 11–12) that order a statue (εἰκών) of an honored man placed in the agora. And finally, the Athenians placed the Kritios and Nesiotes statue of Harmodios in their own agora.[10]

Sometime after the democrats erected the statue of Philites, oligarchs staged their own coup d'état and took control of Erythrai. Presumably shortly

---

5 For the coin from Kyzikos, see Brunnsåker: (1971: 99–100 with plate 23). For evidence of the popularity of the Athenian tyrannicides outside Athens in the post-Classical period, see the texts discussed in Trypanis (1960) and Lebedev (1996). And recall, from the conclusion to chapter 4, that Alexander heavily promoted anti-tyranny ideology during his conquest of western Asia Minor.

6 Many scholars have suggested that the statue of Philites echoed the Athenian model: Dittenberger (*Syll.*[3] 284); Engelmann and Merkelbach (*I. Erythrai* 503); Ober (2005c: 229).

7 A great example is *RO* 56. In that inscription (lines 11–14) it states that a statue of Maussollos will be made out of bronze, while a statue of his wife Artemesia will be made out of stone. The Philites stele likely does not refer to the material of the statue because it orders not the creation of a statue but the repairing of an already-existing statue.

8 See Brunnsåker (1971: 143–64). It is to be noted that the Roman copies of the Kritias and Nesiotes statue group of Harmodios and Aristogeiton, because they are made out of heavier stone, might not replicate exactly the bronze originals.

9 See, for example, *I. Erythrai* 15, which records a law on the sale of wool. It clearly demonstrates that the *agoramomoi* were in charge of transactions in the agora. Also, *I. Erythrai* 104 records the dedication by an *agoranomos* of his scales to Dēmos.

10 For the evidence of the placement of the Kritios and Nesiotes statue of Harmodios and Aristogeiton, see Brunnsåker (1971: 33–41). It is interesting to note here that Xenophon, *Hier.* 4.5, wrote that citizens of various poleis placed statues of tyrant killers in holy places. He gives no examples. And no examples are known.

after their victory, the members of the new regime "took out" (ἐξεῖλον, line 4) the sword from the statue of Philites. One might wonder whether or not they simply removed the sword. Perhaps they broke it off or did some sort of damage in the process of removal: that would explain the apparent difficulty the democrats later expected to encounter in repairing the statue. The most important point, however, is that the oligarchs did not destroy the statue of Philites. Thus, during the rule of an oligarchic regime, there stood, in the agora, a statue of Philites the tyrant slayer delivering the famous "Harmodios blow"—without a sword.[11]

At some point after the oligarchs "took out" the sword from the statue of Philites, the democrats staged yet another coup and reestablished their democratic *politeia*. Soon thereafter, members of that regime—assuming that the order contained in the decree was carried out—restored the sword to the statue of Philites, cleaned the statue of verdigris, and arranged for it to be crowned at the beginning of every month and at all religious festivals. It is interesting to note here that several extant Athenian vases depict the Athenian statues of Harmodios and Aristogeiton wearing wreaths. And Brunnsåker has suggested that the Athenians might have crowned both statues during the Panathenaic festival—the festival at which Harmodios and Aristogeiton assassinated Hipparchos (514). It thus certainly appears that the Erythraian democrats were, once again, following the Athenian tyrannicide model.[12]

Based on an analysis of the events referred to in the Philites stele and their likely historical contexts, this chapter argues that the creation and subsequent manipulation of the statue of Philites played an important role in the foundation, contestation, and ultimate securement of the democracy that was established in Erythrai in the wake of Alexander's conquest of western Asia Minor. The defense of that thesis is rather straightforward. I first argue

---

11   Compare Lykourgos's account (*Leok.* 117) of how the Athenian *dēmos* treated the statue of Hipparchos: they melted it down and turned it into a stele upon which they inscribed the names of traitors. Wilhelm (1915: 33) notes an interesting law from Rhodes, apparently quoted by Dio Chrysostom (31.82), against violating a statue—including the taking of a spear out of the statue's hand. Even today, tearing down a statue is an important postrevolution event: consider the Americans (and Iraqis) tearing down the statue of Saddam Hussein after the fall of Bagdad in April 2003.

12   Brunnsåker (1971: 150, 102–6). The earliest, a black-figure *lekythos*, dates to 470–460 and possibly depicts the Antenor statue group: Österreichisches Museum, Vienna, Inv. 5247 = Brunnsåker (1971: 102, plate 23 no. 5). The others all date to around 400: Pelizäus-Museum, Hildesheim, Inv. 1253 and 1254 = Brunnsåker (1971: 104–5, plate 23 nos. 6a and 6b); Museum of Fine Arts, Boston, Inv. 98.936 = Brunnsåker (1971: 105–6, plate 24 no. 7). One might also note that according to the *Ath. Pol.* (58.1) the Athenian *polemarchos* made offerings to Harmodios and Aristogeiton. There is no telling if the people of Erythrai had a similar practice, but it is not unlikely: (1) they seem to have treated Philites as quasi-divine figure; (2) there is evidence that the Erythraians worshiped Dēmos starting (most likely) post-280; see below in this chapter's section titled "Repairing the Statue circa 281."

that both anti-democrats and pro-democrats manipulated the statue of Philites in order to affect the ability of the pro-democrats to mobilize in defense of the democracy. The important implication of that argument is that both sides considered the manipulation of the statue of Philites—that is, control of its message—to play an important role in determining whether or not there would be democracy in Erythrai. I then argue that the statue of Philites was erected and subsequently manipulated during a fifty-year period that immediately followed the establishment of democracy in Erythrai in the wake of Alexander's conquest of western Asia Minor. The manipulation of the statue, that is, was part of a domestic struggle to determine whether or not the post-Alexander status quo would hold. And in the chapter's final section, I argue that, after the pro-democrats repaired and provided for the repeated crowing of the statue of Philites, democracy remained the "normal" regime type in Erythrai.

Manipulation of the Statue: Why?

The comments presented in this section explain why the oligarchs and, subsequently, the democrats manipulated the statue of Philites in the wake of their respective coups. Previous interpretations have focused on the oligarchs' manipulation.[13] It will be clear, however, that the actions of both the democrats and the oligarchs must be considered in order to assess fully the statue's significance in Erythraian politics.

THREE PREVIOUSLY PUBLISHED INTERPRETATIONS FOR THE OLIGARCHS' MANIPULATION

Engelmann and Merkelbach offered an interpretation of the oligarchs' treatment of the statue that is based on their translation of the phrase (lines 5–6) "νομίζοντες καθόλου τὴν στάσιν|καθ᾽ αὐτῶν εἶναι." They translate that phrase as follows: "weil sie meinten, der Zwist sei jedenfalls zu ihrem Vorteil." Engelmann and Merkelbach thus supposed that the oligarchs removed the sword in order to provoke conflict (stasis) between their domestic opponents. Democrats, that is, would attack supporters of tyranny in the belief that they had vandalized the statue of the democratic hero. And members of the tyrannical faction would retaliate. Members of the oligarchic faction might then take advantage of the chaos and seize control of the polis. Thus the conflict (stasis) would be to their benefit (καθ᾽ αὐτῶν).

---

13   Berve (1967), Heisserer (1979), and Wilhelm (1915) do not offer an explanation for the manipulation of the statue. However, in defense of the latter two scholars, their works focused on the fundamental questions of the inscription's date and provenance. Friedel (1937: 81–82), noting the oligarchs' (supposed) solidarity with tyranny, simply asserts that the oligarchs mutilated a symbol of a powerful *dēmos*.

Engelmann and Merkelbach's explanation for the oligarch's treatment of the statue is not persuasive. To begin with, the preposition κατά (καθ' in the inscription) plus a noun in the genitive case (here, the αὐτῶν) almost always means "against"—not "for the benefit of."[14] Second, the noun stasis (which they translate as "Zwist"), when used in reference to a statue, almost certainly means placement, erection, or stance; and one should note in this regard that the verb ἵστημι (from which the noun stasis is derived) was regularly used—including in Erythrai—in the phrase "to set up a statue."[15] Thus the phrase νομίζοντες καθόλου τὴν στάσιν καθ' αὐτῶν εἶναι should be translated "thinking that the placement [of the statue] is entirely against them." Engelmann and Merkelbach's theory thus collapses.

Josiah Ober's interpretation of the oligarchs' manipulation of the statue is predicated on the fact that democrats tended to consider any nondemocratic regime to be a "tyranny."[16] Thus Ober suggests that the Erythraian oligarchs removed the sword but allowed the statue to stand as part of a well-intended attempt to challenge that overly simplified and potentially dangerous bipolar political taxonomy. On the one hand, oligarchs, according to this explanation, agreed with the democrats that tyranny is harmful to the polis: thus they allowed the statue of the tyrant killer to stand. Yet, on the other hand, they asserted that (moderate) oligarchy is not tyranny and is, in fact, beneficial for the polis: thus they took out Philites's sword aimed entirely "against them" (i.e., against oligarchs and thus oligarchy). The oligarchs' treatment of the statue would thus be an appeal to the political center in order to end conflict by marginalizing, and thus rendering impotent, all extremists, tyrannical and democratic.

Ober's explanation is quite interesting but not entirely convincing. The first weakness is that it is not in sympathy with the basic dynamic of a standard stasis situation in a Greek polis. Generally speaking, one would expect to find the two opposing sides locked in a zero-sum game for control of the polis: thus the losers are killed or exiled by the victor. Such behavior in a stasis situation was on display in chapters 1 (Athens), 2 (Eretria), and 4 (Eresos); and—importantly—the citizens of Erythrai certainly had experience of such behavior.[17] It is perhaps best to assume, then, without evidence

14 Smyth ([1920] 1956: §1690).

15 The first definition for στάσις in LSJ is "placing, setting; erection of a statue." For epigraphic examples of the use of στάσις in this sense, see Gauthier (1982: 218n15). Examples of Erythraian decrees containing the phrase εἰκόνα στῆσαι: RO 8 (lines 14–15), RO 56 (lines 11–12), I. Erythrai 28 (lines 52–53); also, the phrase τὸν δεῖνα ὁ δῆμος ἔστησεν occurs on the inscription for two statue bases: I. Erythrai 25 and 26.

16 Ober (2005c: 228–30). The widespread equation between oligarchy and tyranny by non-Athenians is clear. See, for example, Rhodes in 395 (Hell. Oxy. 10, 2 = column xi, 12–28), Eretria in 341 (their tyrant-killing law, lines 20–21), Ilion circa 280 (their tyrant-killing law, lines 53–54).

17 See RO 17 for a clear depiction of a zero-sum-game stasis situation in Erythrai (387/6 BCE). On stasis, see Gehrke (1985) and Hansen and Nielsen (2004: 124–29).

to the contrary, that significant political actions in a stasis situation are motivated by a desire to dominate, not a desire to reconcile or compromise.[18] The second weakness in Ober's interpretation is that it is too complicated. The simplest—and one would think most probable—interpretation is that the oligarchs were straightforwardly insulting Philites and, by extension, the democrats. That interpretation would avoid the rather sophisticated interpretive move whereby the sword's symbolic significance is separated from the symbolic significance of the rest of the statue. And one might also note that if the manipulation of the statue were not meant to insult moderate democrats, the oligarchs presumably would not have neglected the statue and allowed it to gather verdigris.

Philippe Gauthier has offered an interpretation of the oligarchs' manipulation that is based, in large part, on information provided in the Ilian tyrant-killing law and Lykourgos's speech *Against Leokrates*.[19] The Ilion law explicitly encourages individuals to kill tyrants or leaders of an oligarchy (19–24); oligarchs and tyrants, that is, were conceptually equivalent. In Lykourgos's speech, the orator claims (51) that, whereas the Athenians erect statues of tyrant killers and victorious generals in the agora, the citizens of other states erect statues of athletes. Based on those two texts, Gauthier suggests that, upon taking control of the polis, the oligarchs were concerned about the fact that a statue glorifying and encouraging the assassination of nondemocratic leaders stood prominently in the agora. They would have liked to destroy the statue, but concluded that doing so would provoke a democratic uprising. Thus they formulated a subtler, long-term plan. In the dead of night, they took out the sword, thereby transforming the portrait (εἰκών) of Philites the tyrannicide into a generic statue (ἀνδριάς) of an athlete.[20] Over time, the oligarchs hoped, the people of Erythrai would forget about the political significance of the statue and thereby evacuate the statue of its "power."

Gauthier's interpretation is, in its details, not entirely convincing. Perhaps the biggest weakness is that it simply would be too difficult to "reinvent" the statue. The statue of Philites, like the statues Harmodios and Aristogeiton in Athens, was clearly very well known to all democrats. Thus they would quickly notice such a large-scale alteration and respond accordingly. Another weakness in Gauthier's interpretation is that the oligarchs were almost certainly neglecting the statue conspicuously: the oligarchs, presumably, would not let the statue of a heroic athlete gather verdigris. In short, the oligarchs were insulting the statue and, by extension, the democrats.

---

18   The Erythraians did make an attempt at reconciliation and amnesty in circa 330 (*I. Erythrai* 10), but, per the historical argument offered below, that amnesty was over thirty years before the oligarchs manipulated the statue of Philites.

19   Gauthier (1982: 219–21).

20   Inscribed statue bases for athletes in Erythrai: *I. Erythrai* 87 (3rd or 2nd BCE), 88 (190/180). *I. Erythrai* 89 (early imperial) records an honorary decree for an athlete.

The details of his interpretation notwithstanding, Gauthier quite likely identified the oligarchs' actual intention behind the manipulation of the statue: to change the message that it sent to the people of Erythrai in order to prevent individual democrats from becoming tyrant killers and rising up against the regime. The following comments expand upon that important insight.

THIS CHAPTER'S INTERPRETATION

I argue below that both oligarchs and democrats manipulated the statue of Philites in order to affect the ability of the democrats to mobilize in defense of their democracy. The oligarchs did so in order to negatively affect the democrats' ability; the democrats did so in order to positively affect it. To substantiate that assertion, the following comments examine the oligarchs' actions first, the democrats' reaction second.

MANIPULATION BY THE OLIGARCHS

By removing the sword from the statue of Philites while allowing the statue itself to stand, the oligarchs widely publicized to all the inhabitants of Erythrai two complementary, negative messages about tyrannicide.[21] First, they advertised that tyrannicide, qua rebellion that ushers in democracy, will fail. The symbolism is clear and straightforward: without a sword, Philites (i.e., rebellion) looked impotent, unable to harm anyone, much less overthrow a nondemocratic regime. And it is quite important to note that history "backed up" the statue's new symbolic significance: the democracy ushered in by Philites did, in fact, fail.

Second, by removing the sword from the statue, the oligarchs advertised that tyrannicide, qua "going first," is very costly. The would-be tyrannicide would die, of course: Philites did (presumably). But the oligarchs' alteration of the statue showed that the would-be tyrant killer would pay an even higher price than death. Indeed, contemplating the image of Philites with a missing sword and gathering verdigris (a sign of neglect) would force an individual to conclude that, should he "go first," he will die *and* be remembered forever as a failure, a source of shame to both his ancestors and descendants.

---

21 The population of Erythrai almost certainly fluctuated and can be only crudely estimated. But, in the late fourth century, Erythrai's city walls enclosed 135 hectares (see note 37 on the walls). Also, Rubinstein (2004: 1073) designates Erythrai as size "5" (= 500 km² or greater). With that information, one might apply Hansen's "shotgun method" (2006a) to determine the approximate population of Erythrai in the later fourth century. Doing so produces a total population—in the late fourth century—of 30,375 persons: (1) 67.5 hectares of inhabited intramural space [i.e., one-half of the 135 total hectares enclosed by the city walls]; (2) 150 people lived in each hectare of inhabited intramural space; (3) two-thirds of the total population of size "5" poleis lived outside the city walls. Thus 67.5 × 150 × 3 = 30,375. This very well might be underestimating the population: the territory of Erythrai contained five dependent poleis (Rubinstein [2003: 1074]).

The manipulation of the statue of Philites thus appears to have been the propaganda component of the oligarchs' "regime maintenance" strategy. That manipulation generated and maintained common knowledge that "democracy failed and thus resistance is futile." If people believed that, or even if they thought that others did, they would be less likely to join a pro-democracy rebellion in its early moments: they would doubt that a sufficient number of people would follow them. And particularly bold individuals would be much less inclined to commit the initial, quite daring act of tyrannicide. Instead, a dynamic like that in Athens during the coup of the Four Hundred would take root: (1) individuals falsify their preference and raise their revolutionary thresholds; (2) an ignorance cascade sweeps through the population; (3) pro-democrats are paralyzed by pluralistic ignorance. And, as chapter 1's discussion about threshold sequences demonstrated, even slight increases in individuals' revolutionary thresholds can be devastating: they could transform a pro-mobilization threshold sequence into an anti-mobilization threshold.

It must be admitted that, for their propaganda campaign to be effective, the oligarchs also must have implemented some sort of intimidation campaign. There is no direct evidence for such a campaign in Erythrai. But one might reasonably infer its presence. To begin with, regimes with only minority support, generally speaking, must both misinform and intimidate the population in order to retain control of the state: (1) if they only punished individuals for publicly defying the regime, those individuals could still discover that they are part of a majority that is ready and willing to rebel; (2) if they relied solely on misinformation—i.e., publicly asserting that the regime enjoys overwhelming popular support—individuals would take the risk to dissent publicly and thus discover whether or not their fellow citizens actually support the regime. In addition, one might suspect that the democrats did not fix the statue earlier because they were afraid to do so. And finally, the oligarchs likely would not insult the democrats so directly unless they had an adequate backup force.[22]

MANIPULATION BY THE DEMOCRATS

By repairing the statue and crowning it at the beginning of every month and at all festivals, the democrats accomplished two complementary, instrumen-

---

22   It would help my argument if Welles's suggestion (*RC* p. 83) that Lysimachos had a garrison in the city were true. (It will be argued below that the oligarchs removed the sword from the statue of Philites after the battle of Ipsos.) Welles based his conclusion on Meyer's assertion (1925: 35–36) that Lysimachos had a royal mint in Erythrai. But more recent works on Lysimachos's mints (Thompson [1968]; Mørkholm [1991]) do not include Erythrai as a location for a royal mint. Erythrai did issue coins after the battle of Ipsos: Mørkholm (1991: 92). But they were not royal coins. It might be worth noting, however, that Lysimachos did have royal mints at Teos (40 miles from Erythrai by land) and Smyrna (60 miles away, but easily accessible by sea). If those cities were garrisoned, soldiers stationed there easily could have provided backup for the Erythraian oligarchs.

tal ends. First, they countered head-on both aspects of the oligarchs' "anti-tyrannicide" propaganda. On the one hand, by restoring the sword, they proclaimed that tyrannicide, qua rebellion that ushers in democracy, does, in fact, "work": Philites (i.e., rebellion) is shown as powerful, determined. And, just as when the oligarchs manipulated the statue, recent history corroborated that assertion: not only did the democrats' most recent rebellion succeed, but, by glorifying Philites after retaking control of the polis, the democrats appear to suggest that the democracy now in power originated in the Philites-led revolution; oligarchy, that is, was merely an unfortunate interlude. On the other hand, by crowning the statue so frequently, the democrats ensured that everybody knew that an act of tyrannicide, qua "going first" and initiating a pro-democracy mobilization, would be greatly rewarded. There is no telling what specific rewards a tyrannicide would receive (other than, presumably, a statue), but they clearly would have been spectacular: Philites was treated as quasi-divine.

Second, Erythraian pro-democrats generated common knowledge of widespread commitment to support the democracy. The ritual conditions under which the democrats crowned Philites are not known and likely varied according to the particular occasion. However, the democrats of Erythrai almost certainly ceremoniously crowned the statue in front of a large crowd of spectators after announcing why they did so: "We crown Philites because he gave us democracy." Applause or some sort of sign of mass approval likely followed. Thus everybody in attendance would know the political commitments of his fellow citizens and perhaps those of the larger Erythraian society.[23] And it is important to note that such "tyrannicide ceremonies" were repeated presumably well over twelve times a year, thereby ensuring that that sentiment was preserved as common knowledge. As noted at the end of chapter 4, maintenance of such common knowledge would be particularly important for "new" democracies. (One wonders if the oligarchs previously sought to atomize the population by having few festivals—fewer opportunities for democrats to congregate and discover the preferences of their fellow citizens.)

It is thus reasonably clear that pro-democrats manipulated the statue of Philites in order to increase the likelihood that they would be able to mobilize en masse in response to a coup d'état. The repeated commitment rituals would convince individuals to lower their revolutionary thresholds and participate in a pro-democracy rebellion earlier than they otherwise would have (because they believe that others will follow). And the glorification of Philites would convince particularly brave individuals that it would be worth the risk to strike the first blow and "kill a tyrant." In short, Erythraian pro-democrats

---

23   Recall Plato's observation (*Leges* 738 D–E) noted in chapter 1, note 63: polis-sponsored festivals are an excellent occasion for people to get to know each other.

sought to induce a "pro-mobilization" threshold sequence. Challenging their regime would thus be a very risky proposition.

The previous discussion demonstrated that both the oligarchs and the democrats manipulated the statue of Philites in order to affect the democrats' ability to mobilize in defense of their democracy. The statue was not simply a static, bronze object. It was a tool—a medium—for generating and maintaining common knowledge about Erythraian (revolutionary) politics.[24] The oligarchs used it to send the message that "resistance is futile." If that were widely believed, resistance would be unlikely. The democrats used it to send the message "resistance will succeed." If that were believed, large-scale resistance would be more likely. Indeed, to the extent that the ability of the majority to mobilize determined whether or not a polis would be governed democratically, one might make the following conclusion: both oligarchs and democrats considered the manipulation of the statue of Philites—that is, control of its message—to play an important role in determining whether or not there would be democracy in Erythrai.

Creation and Subsequent Manipulation of the Statue: When?

Scholars generally agree that the events referred to in the Philites stele occurred in the aftermath of important moments in the early Hellenistic period.[25] But they do not agree on which moments. Dittenberger concluded (*Syll.*[3] 284) that the events followed Alexander's conquest of western Asia Minor (i.e., circa 334–332): they would thus follow the implementation of Alexander's democratization policy discussed in chapter 4.[26] Heisserer disagreed with Dittenberger primarily on the grounds that the Philites stele does not mention the name Alexander (as is the case, for example, in Alexander's "letter to the Chians" [*RO* 84] and the "anti-tyranny dossier" from Eresos [*RO* 83]). Heisserer (1979: 291–93), instead, dates the events referred to in the stele to the confusing aftermath of the battle of Ipsos (i.e., post-301), when, as happened in Priene, a tyrant might very well have capitalized on the disorder before Lysimachos solidified his control of the region.[27] En-

24 According to Plutarch (*Arat.* 45.3), statues of tyrants and their opponents played an important role in the politics of late-third-century Argos. Statues of its former tyrants had been cast down and statues of the anti-tyranny liberators of the Akrokorinth subsequently (i.e., post-243) erected. But later, Antigonos Doson re-erected the statues of Argos's former tyrants and cast down the statues (except that of Aratos) of the liberators of the Akrokorinth.

25 Gauthier (1982: 215n4), however, suggests that all attempts to date the events (beyond placing them in the third century) are futile.

26 This position is followed by (inter alios) Badian (1966: 62–63n19) and Ellis (1976: 222).

27 Lund (1992: 127) agrees with this general context. For the tyrant (named Hiero) at Priene from 300 to 297, see *I. Priene* 37, lines 66ff., 109ff.; Paus. 7.2.10; *Syll.*[3] 363; *I. Priene* 11 and 12 (this last inscription records honors for a certain Evander of Larissa and is almost certainly associated with Hiero's fall).

gelmann and Merkelbach (*I. Erythrai* 503), however, suggest —based on the Philites stele's letterforms—that the relevant events occurred circa 280, just after the battle of Kouroupedion, when Erythrai became part of the Seleukid empire.[28]

Dating the relevant events is potentially complicated by Heisserer's conclusion that the Philites stele is a commemorative text. It might not have been inscribed, that is, immediately following the *dēmos*'s initial order to repair and clean the statue. Heisserer bases his conclusion on two points. First, the stele's two decrees have an abbreviated enactment formula. The full formula for Erythrai's democratically promulgated decrees is "resolved by the council and the *dēmos*, a motion of the generals, prytanies, and exetastai" (ἔδοξεν τῆι βουλῆι καὶ τῶι δήμωι· στρατηγῶν, πρυτάνεως, ἐξεταστῶν γνώμη). The enactment formula for both decrees in the Philites stele, however, is "resolved by the council and the *dēmos*" (ἔδοξεν τῆι βουλῆι καὶ τῶι δήμωι). Second, the Philites stele does not record historical information: one might expect that the decree would make some mention of important historical circumstances such as the fall of the tyrant or the fall of the oligarchy, for example. Heisserer's conclusion will be disputed below. But it does open up the (small) possibility that the events referred to in the Philites stele occurred well before the stele itself was inscribed, for which the latest plausible date is the third quarter of the third century.

The following comments argue for the following, lengthy historical sequence. First, the Erythraian democrats erected the statue of Philites following Alexander's conquest of western Asia Minor (i.e., circa 332). Second, the oligarchs removed the sword from the statue in the aftermath of the battle of Ipsos (i.e., post-301). Third, the democrats repaired the statue after the battle of Kouroupedion (i.e., post-281). That is Dittenberger, Engelmann and Merkelbach, and Heisserer were all partially correct—but incorrect in placing all of the events into a short period of time. However, on the (quite slim) chance that Heisserer's commemorative text theory is correct, I assess briefly two possible pre-Alexander dates for the events referred to in the Philites stele. If nothing else, the discussion will provide an opportunity to explore additional periods of stasis in Erythrai's history.

PRE-ALEXANDER POSSIBILITIES

The combination of three pieces of evidence might suggest that the events referred to in the Philites stele occurred in the mid-fifth century, while Erythrai was part of the Athenian Empire. The first piece of evidence is the famous Erythrai Decree (*ML* 40), traditionally dated between the 460s and

---

28   Engelmann and Merkelbach thus accepted Wilhelm's dating (1915: 32) of the first decades of the third century.

450s.[29] That decree indicates that the Athenians intervened in Erythraian affairs, almost certainly after an oligarchic coup, and (re)established a democratic regime. Significantly, the decree refers to the domestic opponents of the democracy established by the Athenians as "tyrants" (το[ῖ]ς τυράννοις: line 33). Second, two fragmentary inscriptions (both a part of *IG* I³ 15) suggest that, shortly after the promulgation of the aforementioned Erythrai Decree, the Athenians intervened in Erythraian political affairs once again to support the democracy there: the Erythraian pro-democrats, that is, lost control of their polis once again.[30] And the third piece of evidence is the early- to mid-fifth-century Electrum stater from Kyzikos that is stamped with an image of Harmodios and Aristogeiton.[31] That coin is important because it suggests that the Erythraians could have known about the Athenian statue of Harmodios in the mid-fifth century, when the events referred to in the aforementioned Erythrai Decree occurred.

The evidence just presented supports a simple scenario. After the Athenians intervened in Erythrai and established democratic rule, the Erythraians erected the statue of Philites; he will have played a leading role in the struggle against the "tyrants." In the wake of the subsequent counter coup, the oligarchs removed the sword from the statue of Philites but allowed the statue itself to stand. And, finally, after the Athenians intervened once again and reinstalled the democratic regime, the democrats repaired the statue and arranged for its regular crowning.

Far from referring to mid-fifth-century events, several points might suggest that the events referred to in the Philites stele occurred after Konon's victory over the Spartans in the famous naval battle near Knidos (394). To begin with, both the Athenians and the people of Erythrai honored Konon by erecting a statue in his likeness.[32] The Athenians placed their statue in their

---

29 Virtually every aspect of this important decree is problematic due, in large part, to the fact that the stone is lost and scholars are completely beholden to Boeckh's publication (*CIG* 73b [p. 891]) that presented a copy of a drawing of the stone's text made by Fauvel (which is also lost). For a detailed study of the decree and its historical context, see Highby (1936). Rhodes (2008: 501)—who now rejects the old three-barred sigma orthodoxy—dates the Erythrai Decree to the late 450s. Lewis, in *IG* I³ 14, dates it to circa 453–452. Mattingly (1996: 367n23) also dates it to circa 453–452.

30 This is the conclusion of *ML* 40. It is followed by *IG* I³ (15 a, d), Mattingly (1996: 397), Rhodes (2008: 501). It is tempting to connect the promulgation of *I. Erythrai* 1 and 2 to these mid-fifth-century difficulties. The former sets strict term limits for secretaries. The latter outlaws certain (political, presumably) acts committed by magistrates (it appears), establishes procedures for trying transgressors, and articulates penalties for individuals who do not appear when summoned by the *prytaneis*.

31 For the electrum stater, see the introduction to this chapter with note 5.

32 The statue in Erythrai: *RO* 8. The Athenians eventually erected statues of both Konon and his son Timotheos in both the agora and the acropolis. See *Tod* 128 for a short discussion and presentation of the evidence (Paus. 1.3.1; Isok. 9.57; Aischin 3.243; Dem. 20.70; Nep. *Timoth.* 2.3).

agora—the first statue of an individual placed there since those of Harmodios and Aristogeiton. According to Demosthenes (Dem. 20.68–70), the Athenians did so because they "felt that he too, in breaking up the empire of the Lakedaimonians, had ended no insignificant tyranny." Second, it is highly likely that Erythraian pro-democrats referred to those who ruled the polis before the battle of Knidos as "tyrants": the people of Rhodes—liberated with Konon's help shortly before the battle of Knidos—certainly did (*Hell. Oxy.* 10, 2 = column xi, 12–28). And finally, there is evidence for stasis in Erythrai a few years after the battle of Knidos (*RO* 17).

Based on the evidence just presented, one might construct the following scenario. Before the battle of Knidos, oligarchs—called "tyrants" by the pro-democrats—controlled Erythrai. After Konon's naval victory, the emboldened pro-democrats staged a successful coup and overthrew the nondemocratic regime. Philites "the tyrant killer" struck the all-important first blow of that coup. In order to demonstrate their gratitude, the Erythraians erected, in their agora, statues of both "tyrannicides," Konon and Philites; Konon "killed" the regional tyrant (i.e., Sparta); Philites killed the local, Erythraian tyrant.[33] The subsequent regime changes and consequent manipulations of the statue of Philites occurred in the troubled run-up to the King's Peace.

Both pre-Alexander dates for the events referred to in the Philites stele should be rejected. The interpretations, first of all, are somewhat forced. There is no mention of tyrannicide in the fifth-century evidence, just of tyrants. And in any case it must be remembered that the Athenians, not the Erythraians, promulgated the Erythrai Decree: maybe the democrats of Erythrai did not commonly refer to their domestic enemies at that time as tyrants. And with respect to the early-fourth-century scenario, there is no *direct* evidence for tyranny—much less tyrannicide—in Erythrai whatsoever. In addition, Heisserer's commemorative text theory, the validity of which potentially justifies a pre-Alexander context, is likely false. It will be recalled that Heisserer based that theory on two points: (1) the decrees recorded in the Philites stele have an abbreviated enactment formula; (2) the decrees do not contain historical detail. One might counter both points. First, several public, democratically promulgated decrees from Erythrai contain only the abbreviated enactment formula (e.g., *RO* 8, *I. Erythrai* 24, 27). Second, it is just as reasonable to conclude that a commemorative text would *include*— not exclude—historical detail concerning the tyranny and the oligarchy.

---

33   In this interpretation, the erection of the statue of Philites would be more or less contemporary to the building of the temple of Aphrodite Pandemos. The inscription (*IEryth*McCabe 32.5) referring to the building of the temple is dated V/IVb. A reasonable and compelling context would be shortly after the battle of Knidos: the temple would commemorate the re-foundation of Erythrai's democracy. Note that the construction of that temple was for "the protection of the *dēmos*": lines 4–5.

Moreover, if the text were abbreviated and commemorative one might wonder why the Erythraians chose to retain, and thus commemorate, all of the procedural matters recorded in the second decree.[34]

As indicated above, the following comments argue that the events referred to in the Philites stele occurred in the wake of watershed moments of the early Hellenistic period. The argument is, admittedly, circumstantial. It has to be: the only (possible) hard fact is that the stele likely was inscribed in the third century. But circumstantial cases can be compelling. And there is enough evidence, when it is viewed it its entirety, to make such a case.

ERECTION OF THE STATUE IN WAKE OF ALEXANDER'S CONQUEST

The cumulative weight of three points suggests that the Erythraians erected the statue of Philites in the wake of Alexander's conquest of Asia Minor. First, in the wake of Alexander's conquest there was a (presumably violent) democratic revolution in Erythrai.[35] A decree of the *dēmos* (*I. Erythrai* 21)—dated to circa 334–332—honors a certain Phanes because he "contributed money at no interest for both the expulsion (*ekpempsis*) of the soldiers and the destruction of the acropolis" (lines 7–10). That is, he provided money both to bribe occupying forces to leave the city and to destroy the fortifications on the acropolis so that such forces could not occupy the city in the future. And another inscription (*I. Erythrai* 10), almost certainly contemporary with *I. Erythrai* 21, carries a decree calling for the return of exiles and an amnesty. It thus appears that the people of Erythrai experienced what the citizens of other cities of Asia Minor experienced at that time: a democratic revolution followed by attempts to stabilize the new political order.[36]

The second point is that the Erythraians embarked upon a large-scale building project in the wake of Alexander's conquest. Most substantially, they built both a city wall and a theater,[37] almost certainly a theater of Dionysos.[38]

34   Heisserer's theory is apparently accepted by Rhodes and Lewis (1997: 368). Neither Gauthier (1982: 215n4) nor Lund (1992: 127, 239n73) accepts it.

35   In spring 332 Chios fell (Arr. *Anab.* 3.2.3)—see Bosworth (1980: ad loc.); it is quite likely, as suggested in the commentary on *I. Erythrai* 21, that Erythrai fell shortly before that.

36   For examples of this dynamic, see the section titled "Historical Context" in chapter 4. It would be nice if *I. Erythrai* 51 dated to this time: it contains fragments of a loyalty oath.

37   Epigraphic evidence for wall building: *I. Erythrai* 22, 23. The walls were in place by 315 when Seleukos failed to take the city (Diod. Sic. 19.60.4). Prepelaos—Lysimachos's general—also failed to take the city in 302 (Diod. Sic. 20.107.5). The walls were nearly three miles long (Magie [1950: 79])—protecting the city on the landward side—and enclosed 135 hectares (Rubinstein [2004: 1075]). It is quite possible that the building of this wall followed immediately the destruction of the fortification on the acropolis referred to in *I. Erythrai* 21.

38   The construction of a theater in the later years of the fourth century (C4l) is noted by Rubinstein (2004: 1075), citing (the not terribly helpful) *TGR* iii. 451. Ömer Özyiğit (2003: 118) notes that the theater in Phokaia (discovered in 1991) is the oldest theater in Anatolia—built 340–330. He notes that that theater is very much like the theater in Erythrai, which he dates to the last quarter of

It is also likely that they conducted a review of their roads and (it appears) other infrastructure at this time.[39] It is thus not too much to say that, for the Erythraians, the years after Alexander's conquest constituted an era of re-foundation, both for the city and for the democracy.

The third point is that Alexander heavily promoted anti-tyranny ideology both during and in the wake of his conquest of western Asia Minor. The evidence was presented in the conclusion to chapter 4. I recite the basics here as a simple reminder: (1) the post-Gaugamela "tyranny proclamation" (Plut. *Alex.* 34); (2) his (no doubt very publically announced) intention to return to Athens the original statues of Harmodios and Aristogeiton (Arr. *Anab.* 3.16.7–8; 7.19.2); (3) Alexander's decision, made in Egypt, to send "the tyrants to the cities from which they came, to be treated as the citizens pleased" (Arr. *Anab.* 3.2.7).

Based on the previous three points, one might construct the following scenario. For decades before Alexander's conquest, democracy supporters in Erythrai were out of power; the oligarchs, although the minority, were firmly in control, likely cowing the majority into submission. Alexander's arrival in the region fundamentally changed that dynamic. Now the masses were confident enough to rise up against the oligarchs and perhaps did so in a sudden burst of collective action.[40] Philites will have played a key role in that uprising; he might very well have been the man who "went first" by striking down a prominent oligarchic leader. The democratic revolution succeeded, but Philites died. And the *dēmos*, inspired by the anti-tyranny ideology promoted by Alexander and struck by its congruity to their present situation, considered Philites to be their own "Harmodios." Thus they erected a bronze statue of him in the agora as an important part of their postliberation/refoundation democratic building project.

---

the fourth century. The earliest epigraphic reference to Erythrai's theater is *I. Erythrai* 24, line 32 (277/5). It might be worth pointing out that the Erythraians appear to have begun announcing honors "in the Dionysia" in the later fourth century: *I. Erythrai* 21, lines 13–14 (334–332); *I. Erythrai* 13, line 5 (fourth/third century); restored in *I. Erythrai* 24, line 31 (277/275); *I. Erythrai* 27, lines 21–22 (ca. 274) orders "the [presidents of the Dionys]ia" to make sure honors are announced; *I. Erythrai* 35, line 13 (mid-third century) has "announce the crown in the Dionysia and Seleukeia." In contrast, the earliest honorary decrees from Erythrai do not mention the festival of Dionysos: *RO* 8 (394); *RO* 56 (mid-350s, if not before the Social War); *HD* 28 B (mid-350s, if not before the Social War). It is thus quite likely that, in the wake of Alexander's conquest, the Erythraians built a theater of Dionysos.

39 *I. Erythrai* 151 is a list of public roads. It likely should be dated post-340 since it uses εἰς, not ἐς. It easily could be post–Alexander's conquest. Line 1 might refer to water reservoirs, as suggested by Rubinstein (2004: 1075).

40 The dynamic here presented purposely echoes Arrian's account (*Anab.* 1.17.11) of Alexander's arrival near Ephesos in 334: "The Ephesian *dēmos*, relieved from fear of the oligarchs (*oligoi*), rushed to kill those who had been for calling in Memnon, those who had plundered the temple of Artemis, and those who threw down the statue of Philip in the temple and dug up the tomb of Heropythes, the liberator of the city, in the marketplace."

THE OLIGARCHS' MANIPULATION, POST-301

The combination of two points strongly suggests that the oligarchs "took out" the sword from the statue of Philites sometime in the wake of Lysimachos's victory at the battle Ipsos (i.e., post-301).[41] The first point is that a nondemocratic regime governed Erythrai after that battle. The existence of that regime, unfortunately, must be inferred. But the cumulative weight of the evidence makes a very strong case.

Erythrai's epigraphic record strongly suggests that anti-democrats controlled the city soon after the battle of Ipsos. There are several extant public inscriptions that date to the latter third of the fourth century when Erythrai was clearly governed democratically.[42] Likewise, there are several extant public inscriptions that date to the 270s and 260s that indicate that the *dēmos* controlled the city.[43] There are, however, no extant public inscriptions that are securely dated to the first two decades of the third century.[44] Since de-

---

41 See Magie (1950: 90–93, 917–24nn4–18) for the complexity in Ionia after the battle of Ipsos.

42 *IEryth*McCabe numbers are not in brackets, while *I. Erythrai* numbers are in brackets: 35 [10], 17 [21], 39/40 [22], 42 [23], 264 [151]; these perhaps should be included too: 59 [206], 24 [13], 22 [34], 27 [11].

43 *IEryth*McCabe numbers are not in brackets, while *I. Erythrai* numbers are in brackets: 11 [30], 12 [27], 18 [28], 19 [not in *I. Erythrai*], 21 [24], 23 [29], 37 [31], 114 [25], [119] (not in *IEryth*McCabe). And, according to my arguments articulated below, 34 [503 = the Philites stele] should be dated to the period too.

44 There are thirty-five inscriptions dated (or potentially so) to the third century in *IEryth*McCabe and *I. Erythrai*; the numbers in brackets refer to the inscription's number in *I. Erythrai*: 11 [30], 12 [27], 13 [114], 18 [28], 19 [not in *I. Erythrai*], 21 [24], 22 [34], 23 [29], 24 [13], 34 [503], 37 [31], 50 [160], 60 [201], 67 [215], 73 [33], 77 [32], 83 [212], 95 [26], 114 [25], 117 [87], 119 [53], 134 [234], 124 [54], 143 [210a], 154 [302], 172 [353], 175 [355], 187 [365], 260 [55], 268 [192], 270 [191]; four inscriptions contained in *I. Erythrai* are not found in *IEryth*McCabe: [35], [36], [119], [431] (this last might not be Erythraian). None of them is securely dated to the years 301–281. Eleven of those thirty-five inscriptions do *not* record public documents: 134 [234], 124 [54], 143 [210a], 154 [302], 172 [353], 175 [355], 187 [365], 260 [55], 270 [191], 83 [212], 67 [215]. That leaves twenty-four (out of the original thirty-five) inscriptions that are potentially dispositive. Sixteen of those twenty-four inscriptions are dated post-281: 11 [30], 12 [27], 13 [114], 18 [28], 19 [not in *I. Erythrai*], 21 [24], 23 [29], 34 [503], 37 [31], 50 [160], 114 [25], 117 [87], [35], [36], [431], [119]. That leaves eight public inscriptions that *possibly* date to the first two decades of the third century: 22 [34], 24 [13], 60 [201], 73 [33], 77 [32], 95 [26], 119 [53], 268 [192]. Three of those inscriptions might actually date to the fourth century: 22 [34] = IVe/IIIb; 24 [13] = IV/III; 268 [192] =IV/III. Three of the remaining five are simply dated to the third century generally, with there being no reason to date them to the first two decades of that century: 73 [33], 95 [26], 119 [53]. One of the remaining two, 77 [32], is dated IIIb (*IEryth*McCabe) or similarly "erstes Drittel des 3. Jahrh. v. Chr." (*I. Erythrai*). It almost certainly is to be dated to the 270s: it records a dedication of the city's generals to Dēmos, and there are two extant decrees of the *dēmos*, dated to the 270s, that honor the city's generals for their work defending the city against the Celts—see the section titled "Repairing the Statue circa 281." That leaves one inscription: 60 [201], a list of priesthoods sold. But it is dated 300–260.

mocracies tended to inscribe more than did nondemocratic regimes (Aischin. 3.103–5), it is reasonable to suppose that this epigraphic drought corresponds to a change to a nondemocratic regime in the years following the battle of Ipsos.[45]

Another indication of a post-Ipsos oligarchy is the fact that the democrats of Erythrai did not enjoy Lysimachos's rule. (Lysimachos took control of much of Asia Minor in the years after Ipsos.) A brief extract from a letter from King Antiochos (I or II, thus dating between 280 and 246) to the *dēmos* of Erythrai (*I. Erythrai* 31) is particularly telling. The passage reads (lines 21–23), "And since Tharsynon and Pythes and Bottas [i.e., Erythrai's ambassadors to the king] declared that both in the time of Alexander and of Antigonos your city was autonomous and exempt from tribute...." The contrast between the praise of Alexander and Antigonos, two autocrats known for their support of democracy, and the conspicuous omission of Lysimachos is strong inferential evidence that Lysimachos did not support the Erythraian *dēmos*.[46]

A final indication of a post-Ipsos oligarchy is that one might reasonably conclude that Lysimmachos *would* support a nondemocratic regime in Erythrai. To begin with, Lysimachos did tolerate or even support nondemocratic regimes in Ionia: the case of Hiero, the tyrant of Priene (circa 300–297), is a good example.[47] In addition, we know that Lysimachos had a man from Miletos placed as "general in charge of the cities of Ionia" (στρατηγὸς ἐπὶ τῶν πόλεων τῶν Ἰώνων: *Syll.*[3] 368, line 3). That might suggest that the Ionian cities suffered some restriction of their freedom. And, finally, the Erythraians successfully prevented Prepelaos, Lysimachos's general, from taking their city in 302 (Diod. Sic. 20.107.5). Lysimachos thus had reason to be angry with (and thus punish) democratic Erythrai after the battle of Ipsos.[48]

---

45   On democratic Athens and epigraphic production, see Hedrick (1999). The late fourth century is particularly striking. Habicht (1997: 71) notes that there is only one significant extant inscribed assembly decree dating to the period of Demetrios of Phaleron's rule (317–307), while there are over one hundred extant inscribed assembly decrees that date to the period 307–301, when Athens was democratic and protected by Demetrios Poliorketes.

46   Magie (1950: 924n18) asserts that the failure of the ambassadors to mention Lysimachos's name does not support the conclusion that the Erythraians did not enjoy Lysimachos's rule. Magie suggests that the Erythraians did not mention Lysimachos because he was an enemy of Seleukos, Antiochos I's father: mentioning Lysimachos's good deeds might thus offend Antiochos. This need not stand; one might conclude that—if Lysimachos had supported democracy at Erythrai—the Erythraians would be inclined to tell that to Antiochos ("even Lysimachos did").

47   See Lund (1992: 122–23) for the arguments for and against. On Hiero, see note 27. Heisserer (1979: 293) notes that Douris likely established his tyranny in Samos in the early years of the third century and that there might have been tyrants in both Chios and Teos at that time.

48   It is also possible that the Erythraians supported Demetrios during his 287/86 campaign in Asia Minor. If they did, Lysimachos likely would have punished them like he punished the people of Miletos (the only city securely known to have supported Demetrios—but we know that other Ionian cities did too: Plut. *Demetr.* 46. 2–5). See Magie (1950: 92, 922–23nn14–15).

The second point in support of the thesis that the oligarchs "took out" the sword from the statue of Philites sometime after the battle Ipsos is simple but very important: there is no evidence that the democratic regime established in Erythrai in the late 330s was overthrown before the battle of Ipsos. All of the evidence, if fact, suggests that the post-Alexander status quo held until Lysimachos's famous victory. Thus, if, as seems most likely, the pro-democrats erected the statue of Philites in the late 330s, the members of a nondemocratic regime would not have had an opportunity to desecrate it until circa 300. The statue stood safely in the agora for more than one generation.

Based on the known facts and the interpretation thereof, one might construct the following scenario. The oligarchs were very upset with the democratic revolution of circa 332 and wanted to restore the pre-Alexander status quo. They took advantage of the chance afforded by Lysimachos's victory at Ipsos. There was now (post-301) a big difference, however. Earlier, the oligarchs likely faced a depoliticized, disorganized, and intimidated *dēmos*; thus they (i.e., the oligarchs) could relatively easily manipulate them. After the battle of Ipsos, they faced a politicized *dēmos* "armed" with a revolutionary ideology that facilitated mobilization. And the oligarchs surely knew that, should the pro-democrats mobilize, the polis likely would be governed democratically. Thus in a shrewd move, the oligarchs attacked head-on the tyrannicide ideology, publicizing its ineffectiveness and thus undermining its "power" as a pro-coordination tool.

REPAIRING THE STATUE CIRCA 281

The cumulative weight of several points suggests that the democrats repaired and arranged for the regular crowning of the statue of Philites after Seleukos's victory at the battle of Kouroupedion (281). To begin with, the *dēmos* clearly was in control of the polis after that battle.[49] As noted above (note 43), there are several extant public inscriptions dated between the 270s and 260s that indicate that the *dēmos* was in control of the city. Indeed, one of those inscriptions, *I. Erythrai* 29 (line 12), refers to the city's *dēmokratia*. There clearly was a regime change: "those in the oligarchy," to use the phrase found in the Philites stele, were overthrown and the democrats reestablished their control. Thus, in circa 280 a regime came to power whose members almost certainly would have repaired the statue of Philites if it was broken.[50]

---

49   For information on post-Kouroupedion Asia Minor, see Magie (1950: 93–94, 924–26 nn19–20).

50   The Erythraians appear to have celebrated the new political order with the inauguration of the Seleukeia. The editors for *I. Erythrai* 35 assert that Erythrai's first such festival began after Kouroupedion and before Seleukos's death. Note, too, that the people of Erythrai added a stanza to a hymn to Asklepios: Seleukos is hailed as the son of Apollo. See Magie (1950: 924n19) for the evidence.

It is important to note—and this is the second point—that there is no evidence to suggest that the oligarchy established after the battle of Ipsos fell before circa 280. As already noted, an oligarchic regime appears to have been firmly in control during those years. Thus, if the statue of Philites was desecrated sometime after 300 (as argued in the previous section), the earliest opportunity pro-democrats had to repair it was circa 280.

The third (admittedly indirect) point is that, after circa 280, the democrats of Erythrai apparently started to worship Dēmos. There are eight inscriptions that document this practice: each records that someone or some group of people made a dedication "to Dēmos."[51] Although none of the inscriptions are definitively dated, several points suggest, as noted, that the practice began shortly after the battle of Kouroupedion. First, the earliest extant inscription that refers to the practice (I. Erythrai 32) is roughly dated to the early third century (I. Erythrai = "Erstes Drittel des 3. Jahrh. v. Chr."; IErythMc-Cabe = "IIIb"). Second, there is no reason to believe that the practice began before circa 280—as noted above, oligarchs controlled the polis during the first two decades of the third century. Third, as was also demonstrated above, democracy was refounded in Erythrai in circa 280: that gives a possible motive for beginning the practice (see below). Fourth, 280 is within the "Erstes Drittel des 3. Jahrh. v. Chr." and "IIIb." Fifth, there are two extant decrees of the *dēmos* praising their generals that date to the early 270s or 260s (I. Erythrai 24, 29), and the Erythraian generals are the first individuals known to have made offerings to Dēmos (I. Erythrai 32).

But how does the apparent fact that the people of Erythrai started worshiping Dēmos circa 280 suggest (indirectly) a circa 280 date for the restoration of the statue of Philites? The answer is simple: a date of circa 280 for both events would suggest that the people of Erythrai began to use religious ritual to honor both Dēmos and the democracy after the battle of Kouroupedion. We do not know for certain why they began such a practice. But one should note that the Erythraian *dēmos* was severely threatened in the years immediately following 280: their democracy was just recently reinstated—certainly to the displeasure of the anti-democrats—and the Celts were attacking Erythraian lands with great success. One inscription indicates (I. Erythrai 24 lines 13–15), for example, that the Erythraians were forced to pay tribute to the Celts. Another (I. Erythrai 28 lines 14–18) refers to both Erythraian hostages given to the Celts and Erythraian captives taken by the Celts. And yet another (I. Erythrai 29 lines 7–8) refers to "war surrounding the polis." Given such a situation, it makes sense that the Erythraians would start worshiping Dēmos in order to somehow protect their polis and new

51   *I. Erythrai* numbers are in brackets, *IEryth*McCabe numbers are not: 77 [32] (IIIb), 73 [33] (III), 82 [102] (II/I), 75 [217] (ca. I), 76 [103] (I), 74 [104] (late Hellenistic), 76.5 [not in *I. Erythrai*] (Hellenistic), 68.5 [not in *I. Erythrai*] (no date).

regime.[52] If that were the initial rationale for worshiping Dēmos, it would also make sense to start "worshiping" (the statue of) Philites at that time too: he was instrumental for the foundation of democracy and embodied the ideology necessary to defend the refounded democracy. His statue might have served as a sacred object in a new cult of democracy.

A fourth point is that 281 is an acceptable "inscribing date" for the Philites stele. Wilhelm, as noted above, concluded that the letterforms date to the first decades of the third century. Heisserer concluded (perhaps led by a conviction that the Philites stele is a commemorative text) that the letterforms could be dated between circa 275 and 200. And Lund noted that both the letterforms and the pronounced apices find parallels in early-third-century texts; she sees no reason to date it to the later third century.[53] There is nothing that would exclude an early-third-century date.[54]

Based on the information just provided, one might construct the following scenario. The democrats were very upset by the fact that they had been overthrown after the battle of Ipsos and desired to secure the post-Alexander (democratic) status quo.[55] They got their chance and succeeded after the battle of Kouroupedion. But they knew that, because they were out of power for so long, a lack of confidence would hinder their capability to defend their regime: they likely were effectively atomized (or estranged) as a result

52 One should note here that, in worshiping Dēmos, the Erythraians were following, to some extent, Athenian practice. For the Athenian practice, see Raubitschek (1962: 240–41). A few inscriptions are worth noting here. First, *IG* II² 1496 lines 131–32, 140–41 records that the Athenian generals sacrificed to *dēmokratia* in 332/1 and 331/0. As noted above, it was generals who made the first known dedication to Dēmos in Erythrai. Second, both *IG* II² 4676 and *IG* II² 5029a refer to a priest of Dēmos in Athens. Both of those inscriptions date to the third century. The Erythraians could have been inspired by contemporary Athenian practice.

53 Lund (1992: 239n73). Lund cites *RC* (pp. li–liii) and Sherwin-White (1985: 73). Note, too, Heisserer's comments (1979: 291n32) about the decree's linguistic characteristics: the consonant assimilations before palatal mutes (lines 11, 14, 27) suggest an inscribing date before Koine became too influential; the *spiritus asper* in an uncompounded form (lines 24–25) suggests early influence of Koine. Thus the linguistic characteristics are consistent with an early Hellenistic date.

54 An additional, and admittedly very suppositious, point in support of a 280 date involves the statue's verdigris (i.e., its ἰός). If the statue was shiny (λαμπρός) when the democrats lost control of the polis after the battle of Ipsos, and if the verdigris was not in its very earliest stage of development when the Philites stele was promulgated, and if the Philites stele was promulgated shortly after the democrats regained control of the city, all previous attempts at dating are undermined: they suggest that the oligarchs were in power for too short of a period (i.e., not long enough for verdigris to develop). We would thus be compelled to devise a different chronology, one fundamentally different from those offered heretofore.

55 It is likely that the democracy established in circa 280 was configured as a return to the democracy established in the wake of Alexander's conquest of western Asia Minor. Philites is the founder of the Erythraian democracy: he committed the foundational act of tyrannicide. One might thus note that the *dēmos* decreed (*I. Erythrai* 30 lines 22–23) that they would announce honors for king Antiochos (I or II) in the festival of Alexander; the early-third-century democracy was a return to the post-Alexander, fourth-century democracy.

of roughly twenty years of the oligarchs' intimidation and disinformation policies.[56] Thus the democrats went to considerable lengths to ensure that they would generate and maintain common knowledge of widespread credible commitment to defend the democracy: they had the statue of their tyrant-killing hero repaired and crowned at the beginning of every month and at all festivals.

The comments presented above argued that the creation and subsequent manipulation of the statue of Philites took place during a fifty-year period following Alexander's conquest of western Asia Minor. And it will be recalled that this chapter's first section demonstrated that both oligarchs and democrats considered the successful manipulation of the statue of Philites—that is, control of its message—to play an important role in determining whether or not there would be democracy in Erythrai. Thus one might conclude that both oligarchs and democrats believed that the successful manipulation of the statue of Philites played an important role in determining whether or not the democracy originally established in the wake of Alexander's conquest would control the polis. It is thus now important to determine whether or not the democracy reestablished in circa 280 persisted for a significant period of time.

The Postmanipulation Political Status Quo

Given the current state of the evidence, it is not possible to determine conclusively how long the democracy reestablished in Erythrai in circa 280 remained in power. The literary sources refer to Erythrai infrequently and, when they do, do not mention internal matters. And Erythrai's epigraphic record is not as informative as one might like. Nevertheless, the following comments defend this thesis: after the democrats repaired and provided for the regular crowning of the statue of Philites, democracy remained Erythrai's "normal" regime type for several generations. I substantiate that thesis by dividing the available evidence into three separate chronological periods: 280–246, 246–201, early second century.

280–246

Two complementary points strongly suggest that Erythrai was a democracy from 280 until 246 (i.e., during the reigns of Antiochos I and Antiochos II). First, the public inscriptions that date to this period strongly suggest that the *dēmos* controlled the polis. There are several such inscriptions dated to the

---

56 This is the obvious goal of all minority regimes, tyrannical or oligarchic. Note, in this regard, [Aristotle's] assertion (*Ath. Pol.* 16.3) that Peisistratos explicitly pursued policies that encouraged farmers to refrain from engaging in public affairs; cf. also Aristotle's remarks at *Pol.* 1311a13–15.

reign of Antiochos I: *I. Erythrai* 24,[57] 25, 27, 28, 29 (perhaps—see note 59), 30 (quite likely: 270–260), 31,[58] 32, and 503 (the Philites stele), *IEryth*Mc-Cabe 19. And there are a couple such inscriptions that might date to the reign of Antiochos II: *I. Erythrai* 30 (possible: 270–260), 29,[59] 31 (possible, see note 58).

The second point is that it was (at least early) Seleukid policy to support democracies in Ionian cities.[60] Several inscriptions support this point. The first is *OGIS* 222, a decree (dated 268–262) of the Ionian League informing Antiochos I that the league has instituted a Birthday Festival in his honor. In lines 16–17, the decree orders the ambassadors to urge the king to maintain the Ionian cities as "free and democratic"; by doing so, it says, he will be following the policy of his ancestors (this could include Antigonos and maybe even Alexander, who is, in fact, mentioned in the decree). The second inscription is *OGIS* 226, a list of priestesses of Apollo Didymeios. In lines 5–6 it refers to Antiochos II's role (through the agent of Hippomachos, the son of Athenaios) in restoring (*katagein*) "freedom and democracy" to Miletos in 259/8; and that is after he drove out the tyrant Timarchos, a deed for which he was called "God" even in this inscription.[61] A third inscription is *OGIS* 229. It contains three decrees relating to a reconciliation (dated to 242) between Magnesia-by-Sipylos and Smyrna. (They had fought each other while Seleukos II—during the Third Syrian War—was in an area

---

57   Note that Dittenberger (*Syll.*[3] 410) restores, in line 17, τοῖς Πτολε]μαικοῖς and thus supposes that Ptolemy II took Erythrai in the First Syrian War. This restoration is accepted by neither Magie (1950: 928n23) nor Englemann and Merkelbach (*I. Erythrai* 24). One need not conclude that Ptolemy II controlled Erythrai during the First Syrian War.

58   This letter is dated by many (e.g., *OGIS* 223) to Antiochos I. Welles (*RC* 15) argues for Antiochos II. Magie (1950: 928n23) offers a sound rebuttal to Welles.

59   Dittenburger (*Syll.*[3] 442) dates this inscription to 261–248. This is accepted by Magie (1950: 928n23). That would give a context of the Second Syrian War. Englemann and Merkelbach (*I. Erythrai* 29), however, date the decree circa 270–260.

60   Ptolemy II's control of western Asia Minor was, in general, limited to Samos and south of Samos (i.e., Egyptian power did not then extend into the Erythraian peninsula). Samos and Miletos held by Ptolemy II: Magie (1950: 95, 926n21). It is possible that Ptolemy II held the Ionian city of Lebedos; it depends on whether or not the image on a coin is Ptolemy II or Ptolemy III: Magie (1950: 930n25). And for a brief time around the death of Antiochos I, Ptolemy II's son Ptolemy Epigonos rebelled from his father and held Ephesos (until the fall of Timarchos in Miletos). But by the peace of circa 253 (ending the Second Syrian War), all of Ionia was lost to Egypt: in *OGIS* 54, lines 5–8, Ptolemy III asserts that he inherited from his father (Ptolemy II) the kingdom of Egypt, Libya, Syria, Phoenicia, Cyprus, Lycia, Karia, and the Cyclades—i.e., not Ionia. On the gains of Antiochos II in the Second Syrian War, see McShane (1964: 45). McShane (1964: 33–35) states that Antiochos I allowed local autonomy in western coastal Asia Minor under his nominal control because he was busy elsewhere and he wanted to prevent Ptolemy II from making inroads in the region.

61   See too: App. *Syr.* 65. Grainger (2010: 121) suggests that this liberation started the Second Syrian War.

known as Seleukis.) Lines 10–11 of the first decree state that Seleukos II "confirmed" (*ebebaiōsen*) Smyrna's "autonomy and democracy."[62]

246–CIRCA 200

The second half of the third century, which saw the collapse of Seleukid control in western Asia Minor, is a very complicated period. And the political history of Erythrai during this period is virtually unknown. The following list provides the names, presented chronologically, of the powers that might have laid claim to the Erythraian peninsula during the half century following the death of Antiochos II.

Seleukos II (from 246 until setbacks in the Third Syrian War)

- Seleukos II tried to secure the allegiance of Ionian cities before he marched against Ptolemy II in Syria (summer of 246), after having lost Ephesos and parts of Thrace. (He left his fourteen-year-old brother Antiochos Heirax in charge of Asia Minor.) We see evidence of this attempt, first, in his relation with Miletos: *RC* 22 records the king's proposal to augment the city's privileges, the substance of which is unfortunately lost. And we see it, too, in his relationship with Smyrna: (1) *OGIS* 228, a decree from Delphi, grants Seleukos II's request that Smyrna and her temple to Aphrodite Stratonike should be "holy and inviolable" (ἱερὰ καὶ ἄσυλος) and notes (line 7) that the king decreed that Smyrna should be "free and pay no tribute"; (2) *OGIS* 229, a decree from Smyrna, both notes that Seleukos II confirmed that Smyrna shall have autonomy and democracy and even requests "the kings, dynasts, cities, and *ethnē*" to recognize the inviolability of the temple and the city (lines 10–12).[63]

Ptolemy III (after Seleukid setbacks in the Third Syrian War [246–242])

- In *OGIS* 54 (line 14), Ptolemy III boasts of taking Ionia. Polybios (5.34.7) suggests that Ptolmaic control extended up the costal islands up to the Hellespont. Cities near Erythrai known to have been taken by Ptolemy III: Miletos, Ephesos, Samos, Magnesia on Maeander, Priene, Kolophon, Lebedos (renamed Ptolemais), and maybe Teos.[64] Magie (1950: 99), however, notes that there is no solid evidence for Ptolemaic control on the mainland north of Lebedos. (Erythrai is north of Lebedos.)

---

62 Note that in the oath taken by the Magnesian soldiers, they swear (line 65—second text in the dossier) to join in guarding (*sundiatērein*) Smyrna's "autonomy and democracy."

63 See Magie (1950: 736n22, 934n29). Ma (2000: 44) also notes that Seleukos II sought the goodwill of Mylasa (a city south of Ionia).

64 For the evidence of Asia Minor cities taken by Ptolemy III, see Ma (2000: 44–45n65) and Magie (1950: 99, 936–37n31). Ma (2000: 45 with n. 66) also notes the possibility that Ptolemy III held Priapos, a town in the Troad.

Antiochos Heirax, the younger brother of Seleukos II (from the march of Seleukos II eastward in the Third Syrian War [246] until being driven out of Asia Minor by Attalos I circa 228)

- Heirax held the Troad, where he minted coins in several cities (Magie [1950: 937n32]). And his coinage is found at Sardeis (Ma [2000: 45n67]). He appears to have held the territory north of Lebedos.[65]

Attalos I. (after defeating Heirax circa 228 and until 222)[66]

- Polybios notes (5.77–8) that Attalos I, in his later campaign against Achaios in 218, acquired several cities: Kyme, Myrina (Smyrna in the manuscripts), Phokaia, Aigai, Temnos, Teos, Kolophon, Smyrna, Lampsakos, Alexandria Troas, and Ilion. With respect to Teos and Kolophon (both Ionian cities), Polybios wrote (5.77.6) that he secured their adherence "on the same terms as before" (ἐπὶ ταῖς συνθήκαις αἷς καὶ τὸ πρότερον). With respect to Smyrna (an Ionian city), Lampsakos, Alexandria Troas, and Ilion, the historian wrote (5.78.6) that those cities "preserved their loyalty to him" (διὰ τὸ τετηρηκέναι τούτους τὴν πρὸς αὐτὸν πίστιν). Thus Teos, Kolophon, Smyrna, Lampsakos, Alexandria Troas, and Ilion had already adhered to Attalos before 218, likely beginning circa 228. And it is possible that Kyme, Mryina, Phokaia (an Ionian city), Aigai, and Temnos did too.[67]

Achaios, likely the cousin of Antiochos III (from 223/2 to 218)

- He was appointed governor of cis-Tauric Asia Minor by Antiochos III. According to Polybios (4.48.10) he "recovered the whole of the country this side of the Taurus." Based on the passage from Polybios mentioned above (5.77–8) it is clear that Kyme, Myrina (Smyrna in the manuscripts), Phokaia, Aigai, and Temnos, Teos, and Kolophon adhered to Achaios. He minted coins in Sardeis.[68] A usurper from 220, he drove Attalos I back into Pergamum while still loyal to Antiochos III (Polyb. 4.48.2, 4.48.11). He was eventually besieged in Sardeis for two years by forces from both Attalos I and Antiochos III and executed (Polyb. 7.15–18; 8.15–21).

---

65 Heirax was likely co-ruler of Asia Minor. He subsequently fought a war against his brother, Seleukos II—the so-called Brothers' War. In that war, Hierax defeated Seleukos in a battle near Ankyra. As a result of that battle, Hierax ruled as an independent king in Asia Minor. The dates for the Brothers' War are contested. See Ma (2000: 46 with n. 68) and Magie (1950: 736–37n23).

66 For the inscriptions on Atallos's victories, see *OGIS* 273–79. See Magie (1950: 737–39n24).

67 See Ma (2000: 46n70) and Magie (1950: 939n36). Magie (1950: 739n26) notes that the cities of southern Ionia and Karia were controlled by Egypt at this time.

68 Ma (2000: 55) citing Mørkholm (1969: 15).

Attalos I (from 218—the date of his successful campaign against Achaios)

- Cities known—again from Polybios (5.77–78)—to have adhered to Attalos include Kyme, Phokaia, Aigai, Temnos, Teos, Kolophon, Smyrna, Lampsakos, Alexandreia Troas, Ilion. And we know that Erythrai was allied with Attalos I in 201, at the battle of Chios (Polyb. 16.6.5). It is thus likely that Erythrai became part of the symmachia formed by Attalos I in 218.[69]

There are several reasons to suspect that the *dēmos* controlled Erythrai at least most of the time during the chaotic years 246–200. The first reason is that the Attalids, who perhaps were the dominant power in the Erythraian peninsula for eighteen of those years, were friendly to Ionian states. We have, for example, a letter from Eumenes II to the Ionian League dated to the winter of 167/6 (*RC* 52) wherein he states (line 16) that he maintains his father's (Attalos I) policy in showing favor to the league. In addition, Polybios wrote a eulogy for Attalos I in which he stresses (18.41.9) that the king died fighting for the "freedom of the Greeks." And finally, modern scholars have argued that Attalos I upheld the freedom of the Greeks in his alliance. Magie wrote (1950: 102), "There is every reason to suppose that Attalos' allies maintained their position as free and independent states. McShane (1964: 67) wrote, "[T]he only consistent defender of the Greek cities from northern Ionia to Byzantium was the Attalid dynasty." And the same scholar wrote (1964: 86) that there likely were no garrisons in the Greek coastal cities in the Attalid alliance.[70]

A second reason is that the citizens of Ionian poleis could capitalize on the volatility of the times in order to maintain or obtain their freedom and thus govern themselves democratically. The aforementioned inscription from Smyrna (*OGIS* 229) provides a very interesting example of that dynamic. The

---

69   On the Attalid symmachy, see McShane (1964: 65–91). Egypt still controlled Samos, Ephesos, and the cities on the coast of Karia: Magie (1950: 102). Magie (1950: 11) concluded that Attalos "gained the support of the cities of the coast of Aeolis and northern Ionia as far south as Ephesus, which was probably held by a force of Egyptians." Note that a decree from Teos concerning Antiochos III (*Austin* 151) possibly dates to circa 203. Thus Antiochos III would have been in Ionia before his campaigns of 197 and 196. See Ma (2000: 260–65) for the arguments concerning the date of the Teian decree. Ma also suggests (2000: 72) that Antiochos III also took Kolophon and Lebedos (both Ionian cities). And it might be important to note the success of Philip V. He took Samos, Miletos, Magnesia on Maeander (Ionian cities). He besieged Chios (an Ionian city), but was defeated. And Philip made substantial gains in southwest Asia Minor. He does not appear to have taken Ionian territory north of Magnesia in these campaigns. For Philip's campaigns in 201–200: Magie (1950: 103–4, 747–50nn39–44), Ma (2000: 76–77).

70   McShane (1964: 70–72) argues that Attalos I had "treaties" (*synthēkai*) with the cities listed in Polyb. 5.77–78. The important cities around Pergamum were independent allies (*symmachiai*) of Attalos. The small cities (Elaia, Temnos, Atarneos, and Pitane—all close to Pergamum) paid taxes.

citizens remained loyal to Seleukos II during the Third Syrian War.[71] Thus the king strongly supported their democratic regime. The decree of Smyrna— quite interesting—states (line 7) that Seleukos II "knows how to return grati- tude to his benefactors" (ἐπιστάμενος χάριτας ἀποδιδόναι τοῖς ἑαυτὸν εὐεργετοῦσιν). This is a reversal of what one might expect to find, given the apparent discrepancy in power between a king and a city. The king, that is, should be the benefactor. Note, for example, the aforementioned letter from Eumenes II to the Ionian league (*RC* 52). In lines 23–24 of that letter the king writes, "in order that you might show that you always return fitting thanks to your benefactors" (ὅπως ἀεὶ φαίνησθε τὰς καταξίας τιμὰς τοῖς εὐεργέταις ἀπονέμοντες).[72]

The third and final reason to suspect that the *dēmos* controlled Erythrai is based on the city's (unfortunately meager) epigraphic record. There are pos- sibly nine third-century public inscriptions that do not definitively date to the reign of Antiochos I or earlier.[73] One (*IEryth*McCabe 268 = *I. Erythrai* 192) is exceptionally fragmentary and, in any event, is dated roughly to either the fourth or third century; thus it quite possibly dates to the period before the reign of Antiochos II. The eight remaining inscriptions indicate that the *dēmos* controlled the polis. Three are datable only to the third century.[74] Two are dated to the mid-third century.[75] One (if Erythraian) is dated to the late third century: *I. Erythrai* 431—not in *IEryth*McCabe. One (*IEryth*McCabe 117 = *I. Erythrai* 87) is very roughly dated to the third or second century. And the date of the final inscription (*IEryth*McCabe 13 = *I. Erythrai* 114) is disputed: *IEryth*McCabe dates it to the second century; *I. Erythrai* dates it to the third century. There is no epigraphic evidence for oligarchy in Erythrai in the years circa 246–200.

EARLY SECOND CENTURY

Several points suggest that Erythrai was a democracy during the first couple decades of the second century. Erythrai's epigraphic record is particularly suggestive. There are no extant inscriptions that suggest that Erythrai was not a democracy in those years. But there are at least five (and maybe seven) ex-

71   Rebuilt Smyrna was a member of the Ionian koinon in 289/8; there were thus thirteen members. On the Ionian league, see Magie (1950: 65–66, 868n50). Smyrna was destroyed in the Archaic period by the Lydians and turned into a few villages. It became a city and Ionian likely under Antigonos.

72   Ma (2000: 44 with n. 61) cites *OGIS* 229 (Smyrna) and *RC* 22 (Miletos) in order to demon- strate the power of cities at this time.

73   *IEryth*McCabe numbers are not in brackets, *I. Erythrai* numbers are in brackets: 73 [33], 95 [26], 117 [87], 119 [53], 13 [114], 268 [192], [35], [36], [431] (the last three are not included in *IEryth*McCabe.

74   *IEryth*McCabe numbers are not in brackets, *I. Erythrai* numbers are in brackets: 73 [33], 95 [26], 119 [53].

75   *I. Erythrai* 35 and 36 (neither is in *IEryth*McCabe).

tant inscriptions that suggest that the *dēmos* controlled Erythrai during those years.[76]

Second, Erythrai possibly did not fall to Antiochos III (at least not for any significant period of time); thus the king might not have had the opportunity to meddle in Erythraian domestic affairs. There is no direct evidence that the king took Erythrai during his campaigns of 197–196, although he did make significant gains in Ionia at that time.[77] (Indeed, it was the result of that campaign that Antiochos took most of cis-Tauric Asia Minor.) It is possible that Antiochos III held Erythrai during (part of) the Roman-Syrian War (192–188): in 191, his fleet sailed into Kissos, a port of Erythrai (Livy 36.43.10). But Erythrai had at least three ports (Kissos, Korykos [Livy 36.43.13], and Phoinikos [Livy 36.45.7]). And even if Kissos was right next to the *asty* of Erythrai, one need not conclude that Antiochos controlled the city: his fleet soon left and the Romans subsequently came "into the city" (Livy 36.45.7); and Livy—importantly—did not write that the Romans liberated Erythrai.[78] Also, Livy clearly indicates that Erythrai subsequently fought with the Romans in the naval action of 190.[79]

Finally, Erythrai was deemed a "free city" by the Romans after the peace of Apameia (188).[80] The Romans treated it very well, even signaling it out, for its

76   *IEryth*McCabe numbers are not in brackets, *I. Erythrai* numbers are in brackets: 5 [117], 10 [120], 9 [121], 8 [122], [88]. The latter is not in *IEryth*McCabe. An inscription that suggests the *dēmos* controlled Erythrai, 117 [87], might also date to the early years of the second century: it is dated III/II. And *I. Erythrai* 112 (not in *IEryth*McCabe) should be mentioned too: it dates to the first half of the second century and was clearly promulgated when the *dēmos* was in control of the city (line 18).

77   Ma (2000: 89) wrote, "Miletos (perhaps), Priene, Ephesos, and most or all of the coast up to the Erythrai peninsula." See also Magie (1950: 17–20, 755–64nn50–56; 105–7, 946–48 nn49–55).

78   One might draw a parallel with Athens: for fifty-eight years after the revolt of 287, the Athenians controlled the *asty*, but the Macedonians controlled the Piraeus. See Habicht (1997: 124). For the Athenian revolt, see Shear (1978).

79   Livy 37.8.5 (Roman forces at Erythrai trying to encourage other cities to join them); Livy 37.11.14 (Erythraian ships set sail to assist the Rhodian fleet—but it had been badly defeated); Livy 37.12.10 (after the Rhodian disaster, the Romans and Eumenes first sailed to Erythrai and then took the promontory of Korykos).

80   The terms of the peace of Apameia are not easy to determine precisely due to Polybios's imprecise account (21.45). Livy (38.39.7–17) essentially copies Polybios but does add one important phrase (38.39.10) about settlements granted by Rome to Ilion. And Livy also includes (37.56.2) a provision whereby Eumenes was to receive "the Milyae, and Lydia, and Ionia with the exception of those cities which had been free on the day when the battle [i.e., Magnesia] with King Antiochos had been fought." For this peace, see Magie (1950: 108–9, 950–51n60), Walbank (1979: 164–75), McShane (1964: 149–52). Note that Polybios also records (21.24.6–9 [= Livy 37.55.4–7]) the general instructions given by the Roman senate to the commissioners before the meeting at Apameia.

loyalty during the war with Antiochos III (Polyb. 21.45.6).[81] It subsequently would be left alone (for the time being) to prosper and conduct its own affairs as an official "friend" of Rome.[82]

The evidence presented above indicates that two moments were particularly important in the history of Erythrai's early Hellenistic democracy. The first moment was the foundation of democracy in circa 332. The importance there centers on origins: the long-ruling oligarchy was overthrown and the *dēmos* assumed power. The second important moment was the refoundation of the democracy in circa 280. The importance there is that the democracy "stuck," persisting into the Roman period. Democracy, that is, became the normal regime type for Erythrai after the Erythaians repaired their statue of Philites the tyrant killer.

Conclusion

Although focusing on events in a single Ionian city, this chapter highlights a fundamental dynamic involved in regime preservation for Greek poleis in general: affecting the revolutionary thresholds of the majority of the citizens. For a regime with only minority support to survive, the majority of the population must have relatively high revolutionary thresholds; more specifically, the population must be defined by an "anti-mobilization" threshold sequence. If they were, they would be unable to mobilize against the ruling regime. For a regime with majority support to survive, however, the majority of the population must have relatively low revolutionary thresholds; they must be defined by a "pro-mobilization" threshold sequence. If they were, they would be able to take advantage of their numerical superiority and mobilize in support of their regime. In short, control of a polis came down to affecting thresholds of the majority of the population—a struggle over the population's revolutionary threshold sequence.

That basic insight potentially accounts for many of the different institutions and practices, particularly those involved with managing publicly known information, of various regime types. As noted above, all regimes rely

---

81 Walbank (1979: 167) concluded that Erythrai fell into the category of "autonomous, but paid tribute to Antiochos, but helped Rome." The apparent basis of that conclusion, found on page 106, is Livy 36.43.10 (that Antiochos's fleet sailed to Kissos, a harbor of Erythrai). But, as suggested above in the text, that passage does not necessarily demonstrate that Antiochos controlled the *asty*.

82 For the beneficial situation of Rome's "friends" in Asia Minor during the half century following the peace of Apameia, see Magie (1950: 112–16). Note *Syll.*³ 591 (lines 33–35): Flamininus apparently made it known to the people of Lampsakos (196–195) that, "should he conclude friendship or alliance with anyone . . . he would protect the democracy, autonomy, and peace [of that city]." Lampsakos, like Smyrna in Ionia, played an important role in resisting Antiochos III in 196. See Livy 33.38.3.

on the generation of common knowledge to survive. Their survival, that is, depends on what people think others think. The question concerns the content of that common knowledge, and how it is generated and maintained. Nondemocratic regimes will have political institutions and practices that control common knowledge so that people raise their revolutionary thresholds and thus become atomized. Democratic regimes are the opposite.

6

The Ilian Tyrant-Killing Law

Introduction

Ilion, the site of legendary Troy, was in a fairly wretched condition by the end of the Classical period. To begin with, it was small and poor. Lykourgos (*Leok.* 62), for example, called Ilion "uninhabited" (*aoikētos*). And Strabo (13.1.26), referring to the Ilion of Lykourgos's day, called it a "village" (*kōmē*), and noted that its temple of Athena was "small and cheap" (*mikron kai euteles*).[1] In addition, by the last third of the fourth century, the Ilians had suffered through decades of extreme regional turbulence during which they were controlled by a series of foreign tyrants and other powers. Many of the specifics are unknown. But from the latter part of the fifth century until 399, Dardanian tyrants (Zenis, Mania, Meidias) dominated Ilion with Persian acquiescence (Xen. *Hell.* 3.1.10–16). From 399 to 387, it was garrisoned and under Spartan control (Xen. *Hell.* 3.1.16–19). The twenty-seven years that followed the King's Peace (i.e., 387–360) are particularly confusing; but, generally speaking, Ilion was once again controlled by Persian satraps or their agents, be they loyal to or in revolt from the Persian king.[2] And finally, from 360 to 334, Ilion was primarily in the hands of foreign mercenary generals.[3]

---

1 There are some signs, however, that Ilion's economic condition improved slightly starting around the middle of the fourth century. See Berlin (2002) and Lawall (2002).

2 Ilion, since it is was a polis on the mainland of Asia Minor, became part of the Persian Empire pursuant to the terms of the King's Peace (Xen. *Hell.* 5.1.31). The internal history of Ilion with respect to events in the Troad during this period is not well known. Ariobarzanes was the first satrap of Hellespontine Phrygia after the King's Peace, and thus the regional overlord of Ilion (Xen. *Hell.* 5.1.28). By 366 he was in rebellion against Artaxerxes II, as a leading figure in the so-called Great Satraps' Revolt (Diod. Sic. 15.90.3—falsely compressing events into the single year 362/1). Ariobarzanes was subsequently betrayed by his son Mithridates and executed in circa 361 (Xen. *Cyr.* 8.8.4; Arist. *Pol.* 1312a16). According to Diodoros (17.17.6), there was an overthrown statue of him by the temple of Athena at Ilion when Alexander arrived. After the capture of Ariobarzanes, Artabazos was appointed the lawful satrap of Hellespontine Phrygia and he appears to have held Ilion for a time (perhaps with his brothers-in-law, Mentor and Memnon): Dem. 23.154–58. He revolted (in 356) soon after Artaxerxes III assumed the throne in 359/8 (Diod. Sic. 16.22.1); in 352, he fled to Macedon, but was later pardoned by Artazerxes III (Diod. Sic. 16.52.3).

3 In 360, Charidemos of Oreos controlled Ilion (Dem. 23.154–58, Aen. Tact. 24.4–14, Polyaenus 3.14, Plut., *Sert.* 1.6, [Arist.] Oec. 2.30). (He had initially sided with Artabazos's brothers-in-law

In the closing decades of the fourth century, the people of Ilion had reason to conclude that both their political and material conditions would improve. Alexander's celebrated arrival into the city (334) marked the turning point: he sacrificed at the temple of Athena and declared the city free and without tribute and that it was to be governed democratically. He also apparently promised in 323, as part of his "last plans," to make the temple of Athena the largest temple in any Greek city.[4] Ilion also benefited while Antigonos ("the one-eyed") held much of Asia Minor: he likely founded the religious koinon of Athena Ilias that Ilion headed; a Panathenaic festival was inaugurated; and the people of Ilion built a theater, a new terrace wall, and (what might have been) a prytaneion. Ilion was becoming a real polis.[5]

Two generations after Alexander's conquest of western Asia Minor, the Ilians promulgated a tyrant-killing law. It is, chronologically, the latest known such law. And it is by far the most complex. Here is its text and an original translation—the bold numbers in parentheses mark the beginning of a new provision.[6]

---

against the Persian king during the former's period of revolt, but betrayed that alliance to gain control of Skepsis, Kebren, and Ilion.) Charidemos ruled Ilion for only one year. (*I. Ilion* 23 likely records the Ilians' gratitude to Menelaos the son of Arrabaios for his role in liberating the city from Charidemos in 359.) It then appears that Artabazos's brothers-in-law, likely with Artabazos himself, controlled Ilion for a couple of years (Dem. 23.157–58). And finally, from 355–334, the Athenian mercenary general Chares probably controlled Ilion along with Sigeion: many coins minted in Sigeion while Chares controlled it have been found in Ilion; when Alexander arrived at Ilion (334), Chares traveled from Sigeion to greet him (Arr. *Anab.* 1.12.1; Cook [1973: 180]; Berlin [2002]).

4   Alexander sacrificing at Ilion: Plut. *Alex.* 15; Diod. Sic. 17.17.6–18.1; Arr. *Anab.* 1.11.7–1.12.1; Strabo 13.1.26 (alone in placing the sacrifice after the battle of Granikos). The temple to Athena in Ilion as part of Alexander's "last plans": Diod. Sic. 18.4.5; cf. Strabo 13.1.26. Since Ilion was an Aeolic polis, it would have been democratically governed per Alexander's order (334) to Alkimachos: Arr. *Anab.* 1.18.1–2. Strabo wrote (13.1.26) that Alexander elevated Ilion to the status of polis. But Xenophon (*Hell.* 3.1.16) already referred to it as a polis.

5   The earliest evidence for the koinon at Ilion is *I. Ilion* 1, an inscription that includes five decrees of the koinon (each text begins with γνώμη τῶν συνέδρων) praising Malousios of Gargara. The decrees praise Malousios for (inter alia) providing funds to (1) send embassies to Antigonos (lines 8–9, 23–26 [where he is referred to as "king"]); (2) build a theater (lines 10, 28, 39). On the koinon at Ilion, see the comments in Billows (1990: 218–20) and Magie (1950: 869–71n53). There is no evidence linking Alexander and the koinon at Ilion, although it is reasonable, considering how interested he was with Ilion's temple of Athena, to suspect that he was somehow involved. For the terrace wall and "prytaneion," see Rose (1999: 46). On the improved fortunes of cities in the Troad under Antigonos, see McShane (1964: 24–25).

6   Text: Peter Frisch, *Die Inschriften von Ilion*, no. 25 with some changes (indicated in the notes). Frisch also provides a commentary and German translation. There are two other standard commentaries: (1) *IJG* (II: 22–57) (text, French translation, and a discussion that includes an investigation of some Athenian material); (2) *OGIS* 218 (text with Latin commentary). There are, in addition, several other important works on this law. Friedel (1937: 82–97) provides a (not reliable) Greek text for lines 19–106, 116–30, a German translation of much of the law (not, bizarrely, of lines 106–16), and comments. Berve (1967: 419–22) provides a quite brief overview of the law's provisions and short comment. Funck (1994) presents the law's possible historical and political

Non-ΣΤΟΙΧ.

Side I

[Lines 1–8 are lost]

 εντ[---]
10 .αστου[---]
.οι .οχοσ.υσα[---]
μα.γα . . . .σεαπ[--]
[---]
.π.λυσι[---]
15 .μ. κ̣α̣ὶ ἀρχ[---]
καὶ ἐν δημοκρατίαι .δυ[----------------------------]
νιολι..ρ[---------]ον[---]η[----------------------------]
τε α[ὐ]τὸν [---]νι[---- -]τωι [----]λ [-----]ο[--------]
(1) [ὃς δ᾽] ἂν ἀπ[οκτ]είνηι τ[ὸν τ]ύραννο[ν ἢ τὸν ἡ]-
20 γεμόνα τῆ[ς] ὀλιγαρ[χ]ίας ἢ τὸν τὴν δ[ημοκρα]-
τίαγ καταλύον[τ]α, ἐὰμ μὲν ἔναρχο[ς, τά]-
λαντον ἀργυρ[ί]ου λ[αμβάνειν παρὰ τῆς πό]-
λεως αὐθημερὸν ἢ τῆι δευτέραι, [κ]αὶ εἰκό[να]
χαλκῆν αὐτο[ῦ στ]ῆ[σ]α[ι τ]ὸ[ν δῆ]μον· εἶναι δὲ
25 αὐτῶι καὶ σίτη[σ]ιν [ἐ]μ πρυ[τα]νείωι, [ἕ]ως [ἂν] ζῆ[ι],
καὶ ἐν τοῖς ἀγῶ[σι] εἰς π[ρο]εδρίαν [κηρύ]σσεσ-
θαι ὀνομαστεὶ καὶ δύο δ[ρ]αχμὰς δίδοσθαι
αὐτῶι ἑκάστης ἡμέρας μέχρι ἂν ζῆι· ἐὰν δὲ
ξένος ἦι ὁ ἀποκτ[εί]νας, ταὐτὰ δίδοσθαι αὐτῶ[ι]
30 καὶ πολίτης ἔστω [κα]ὶ εἰς [φυλ]ὴν ἐξέστω αὐ[τ]ῶ[ι]
εἰσελθεῖν ἣν ἂν βούληται· ἐὰν δὲ δοῦλος ἦ[ι]
[ὁ ἀ]ποκτε[ί]νας, ἐπί]τιμος [ἔ]στω καὶ πολιτεί-
[ας μ]ε[τεχέτω κατὰ τὸν ν]όμογ καὶ τριάκοντα μ-
[νᾶς λαμβανέτω παρὰ τῆς πόλεως] αὐθημερὸν ἢ [τῆι]
35 [δευτέραι, καὶ μέχρι ἂν ζῆι ἑκάσ]της ἡμέρας λαμβά-
(2) [νέτω δραχμὴν------------------] τῆς ἀρχῆς οἱ με[..]
[--------------------------- τάλαντον ἀργ]υρίου λαμβανέ[τω]-
[σαν--------------------------------------] τριάκοντα μνᾶ[ς]
[---ἔσ]τω πολίτη[ς]

context. Koch (1996) provides an analysis of several of the law's provisions and situates the law in the general history of regime-preservation legislation. Dössel (2003) provides a text, German translation, and comments on several of the law's provisions. Maffi (2005) provides a through examination of several of the law's provisions and a French translation of some of the law's most controversial provisions. The editio princeps: Brueckner (1894). Somewhat surprisingly, this law is not included in any of the standard "sources in translation" books that cover the Hellenistic period (i.e., Austin [1981], Burstein [1985], Bagnall and Derow [2004]).

Side II

(3)   [---------------------τὰ δὲ]
40   [ἄ]λλα τῆς πόλεως εἶναι.
        [κα]ὶ εἴ τίς τι ἠδικήθη ὑπ᾽ αὐ-
        [τῶν], ἀπολαμβάνειν ἐντεῦ-
(4)   [θεν· ἐ]ὰν δέ τις τὸν τῦραν-
        [νον ἢ τ]ὸν ἡγεμόνα τῆς ὀλι-
45   [γαρ]χίας ἢ τὸν ⟨τὴν⟩ δημοκρατί-
        αγ καταλύσαντα τῶν συσ-
        στρατιωτῶν τις ἀποκτεί-
        νας εἰς δημοκρατίαγ κατα-
        στήσηι τὴμ πόλιν, ἀζήμιόν
50   τε αὐτὸν εἶναι ὧν ἔπραξεν
        μετ᾽ αὐτῶγ καὶ τάλαντον ἀρ-
        γυρίου λαμβάνειμ παρὰ τοῦ
(5)   δήμου. ὃς ἂν ἐπὶ τυράννο⟨υ⟩ ἢ
        ὀλιγαρχία⟨ς⟩[7] στρατηγήσηι
55   ἢ ἄλλην τινὰ ἀρχὴν ἄρξηι
        [ἥν]τιναοῦν, δι᾽ ἧς εἰς ἀργυ[ρί]-
        [ου λ]όγον ἔρχεται, ἢ ἐπιγρ[α]-
        [φὴν ἐ]πιγράψηι Ἰλιέων [τ]ινὶ ἢ
        [τῶν με]τοίκων, π[αρ]ὰ μηδε-
60   [νὸς τούτων ὠν]εῖσθαι μηδὲ
        [παρατίθεσθαι μ]ήτε γῆν μή-
        [τε οἰκί]α[μ μήτ]ε κτήνη μήτε
        [ἀνδ]ράποδα [μή]τε ἄλλο μη-
        [δ]ὲν μηδὲ φ[ερν]ὴν δέχεσθαι·
65   ὃς δ᾽ ἂν παρὰ [τού]των τινὸς πρί-
        ηταί τι ἢ παρ[αθ]ῆται ἢ φερ[ν]ὴν
        λάβηι ἢ ἄλλ[ως] πως κτήσηται,
        ται, ἄκυρον ε[ἶνα]ι τὴγ κτῆσιν
        καὶ τὸν ἀδικ[ηθέ]ντα ἰέναι εἰς
70   τὰ τοῦ ἀδικήσ[αν]τος ἀτιμη-
(6)   τεί, ὁπόταν θ[έλ]ηι. ἐὰν δέ τις
        τὸ δεύτερον [σ]τρατηγήσηι
        ἢ ἄλλην ἀρ[χὴν] ἄρξηι, ὅσ᾽ ἂν
        διαχειρίσηι χ[ρή]ματα, πάντα
75   ὀφείλειν ὡς δ[η]μόσια ὄντα·
        [ἐξ]εῖναι δὲ δι[κάσ]ασθαι τῶι
        [βουλο]μένωι ὡ[ς] περὶ δημοσί-

---

7 The stone reads τύραννον ἢ ὀλιγαρχίαν.

80

(7)

85

[ων ἐν τ]ῶι δικα[σ]τηρίωι, ὅταν
[βούλητ]αι, μέχ[ρι] τέλος δί-
[κης γέν]ηται [δη]μοκρατου-
[μένων Ἰλ]ιέων. [ὃς] δ᾽ ἂν ἐπὶ τυ-
[ράννου] ἢ ὀλιγα[ρ]χίας ἐκ τού-
[των χρήμα]τα δη[μό]σια δῶι ἢ λά-
[βηι, ἐξεῖν]αι δικ[άσ]ασθαι ὡς
[περὶ δημοσίων] χρημάτων, ὑπόδι-
[κος δὲ ἔστω----------------------]

Side III

(8)

90

95

(9)

100

105

(10)

ἐγ μιαροῦ γένωνται· καὶ τὰ ὄντα αὐτῶν
τὰ μὲν ἡμίση τῆς πόλεως ε[ἶ]ναι, τὰ δ᾽ ἡμίση τῶν παίδων τοῦ ἀποθανόντος, ἐὰν δὲ παῖ-
δες μὴ ὦσιν, εἰς οὓς ἂν τὰ χρήματα ἱκνῆται·
δίκην δὲ εἶναι περὶ τούτω[ν] ἀεί, μέχρι τέλος
δίκης γένηται δημοκρατουμένων Ἰλιέων·
ἐὰν δὲ δεθῆι ἢ ἐρχθῆι [ἢ] φεύγηι δεσμῶν,[8] τιμὰς
διπλασίας ὀφείλει[ν κ]αὶ ὅτι ἂν βλαβῆι διπλάσιον·
ἐὰν δὲ χρήματα ἐ[κ]τείσηι, διπλάσια ἀποτινέ-
[τ]ω ὁ κατηγορήσ[ας]· δίκην δὲ εἶναι περὶ τούτων
[ἀ]εί, μέχρι τέλ[ος] δίκης γένηται δημοκρατου-
[μ]ένων Ἰλιέω[ν. ἐ]άν τις ἐπὶ τυράννου ἢ ὀλιγαρχίας ἀποκτ[είνηι] τινὰ ἐν ἀρχῆι ὤν, πάντας τοὺς
τὴμ ψῆφ[ον προσθεμ]ένους ἀνδροφόνους εἶναι, κα[ὶ]
[ἐ]ξεῖ[ναι ἐπεξελθ]εῖν ἀεί, μέχρι τέλος δίκης
[γένηται δημοκρατουμέ]νων Ἰλιέων· καὶ ἐὰν τὴν
δίκ[ην ἀποφεύγηι τις, ψῆφον πρ]οσθέμενος[9] ὥστε ἀ-
ποκτεῖναι, ἄτ[ιμον εἶ]ναι καὶ φεύγειν αὐτὸγ
καὶ ἐκγόνους οἳ ἂν [ἐξ αὐτοῦ γ]ένωνται· φόνον
δὲ ἐπιγαμία(ι)ς[10] μὴ καταλλάσ[σεσ]θαι μηδὲ χρή-
μασιν· εἰ δὲ μή, ἔνοχον εἶναι τῆι α[ὐτ]ῆι ζημίαι. ἐ-
ὰν δέ τις τύραννος ἢ ἡγεμὼν ὀλιγαρχίας ἢ ὅσ-
τις Ἰλιέων ἀρχὰς συ[ν]αποδεικνύηι μετὰ τού[των]

---

8   Frish (followed by Dössel) punctuates this differently: [ἢ] φεύγηι, δεσμῶν τιμάς κτλ. See below, in the discussion of provision 8, for the significance of that alternative punctuation. The punctuation accepted here is standard (i.e., in Dittenberger).

9   Frish (followed by Dössel) restores this differently: ἐὰν τὴν | δίκ[ην μὴ νικήσηι, ψῆφον πρ]οσθέμενος κτλ. For a discussion of Frisch's restoration and the standard (in Dittenberger) restoration accepted here, see the discussion of provision 9 below.

10   Frish does not accept this standard (in Dittenberger) emendation. Instead he keeps the stone's ἐπιγαμίας. For a discussion of this emendation, see the discussion of provision 9 below.

ἢ ἄλλος πρὸ τούτων πρίηται γῆν ἢ οἰκίαν ἢ κτήν[η]
110   ἢ ἀνδράποδα ἢ ἄλλο ὁτιοῦν, ἀκύρως ἐωνήσθω κα[ὶ]
    (11) ἐπανίτω εἰς τοὺς ἀποδομένους. ἐάν τις ἐν ὀλι-
γαρχίαι κακοτεχνῶν περὶ τοὺς νόμους *vacat*
vacat βουλὴν αἱρῆται ἢ τὰς ἄλλας ἀρχάς,
ὡς ἐν δημοκρατίαι θέλων διαπράσσεσθαι τ[ε]-
115   χνάζων, ἄκυρα εἶναι καὶ τὸν τεχνάζοντα πάσ-
    (12) χειν ὡς ἡγεμόνα ὀλιγαρχίας. ὃς ἂν τύρανν[ος]
ἢ ἡγεμὼν γένηται ὀλιγαρχίας, ἢ τύραννον στ[ή]-
σηι ἢ συνεπαναστῆι ἢ δημοκρατίαγ καταλύσηι, ὅπου[11] ἄν τι ὄνομα ἦι τούτων, ἐάν τε ἐν τοῖς
120   ἱερ(ητ)εύσασιν ἐάν τε ἐν ἀναθήματι ἐάν τ᾽ ἐπὶ τάφο[υ],
ἐκκόπτειν παντόθεγ, καὶ ἐγ μὲν τῶν ἱερητευ-
κότων ἐκκόψαντας πωλεῖγ, καὶ τὸμ πριάμενον
ὄνομα ἐπιγράψασθαι ὅτι ἂν θέληι οἷς μέτεστι·
τὰ δὲ ἀναθήματα ὅσα μὲν ἂν ἰδίαι ἀνατεθῆι, ἐξα-
125   λείψαντας τοῦ ἀναθέντος τὰ ἐπιγράμματα βο[υ]-
λεύειν περὶ τοῦ ἀναθήματος τὸν δῆμον, ὅπως μ[ή]-
τε ἐκείνων ἐστήξει μηδὲ μνημεῖον μηθὲν ἔσ-
ται· ὅπου δὲ κοινὸν ἀνάθημα καὶ ἑτέρων ἐπι-
γέγραπται, ἄδηλον ποιεῖν ἐξαλείψαντας τ[ὸ]
130   **(13)** [ὄνομ]α τὸ ἐκείνου. ἐάν τις ἐπὶ τυράννου ἢ ὀλ[ι]-
[γαρχίας---------------------------------------]

Side IV

    (14) [----]ι [----]ηδιμ[----ἐὰν δὲ]
οἱ ἄρχοντες μ[ὴ κηρύξωσι τὸν]
στέφανον ἐν τοῖς [μεγάλοις Διο]-
νυσίοις ἢ μὴ συντελέ[σωσιν],
135   ὅπως ἀναγραφῶσιν κατὰ [τὸν νό]-
μον, ὀφειλέτω τῶμ μὲν ἀρχόν-
των ἕκαστος τριάκοντα στα-
[τ]ῆρας, βο[υλῆς δ᾽] ἕκαστος δέ-
[κα] στατῆρας, ὁ δὲ ταμίας στα-
140   [τ]ῆρας ἑκατόν· καὶ ἄτιμοι ἔστω-
[σαν] καθ᾽ οὓς ἂν τῶν γεγραμ-
[μέ]νων τιμῆς ἐ[πικ]αλῆται, ἕ[ως ἂν]
[κο]μίσω[ν]ται τὰ χρήματα οἱ ἐπι-
καλοῦντες· εἶν[αι δὲ] τὴν ἐφο-

---

11   This is the standard (in Dittenberger) emendation of the stone's οτου.

145 δον ἀεὶ ἐπὶ τοὺς ἄρχοντας καὶ
τὴμ βουλὴν τὴν ἐνεστῶσαν,
καὶ ἔστω τοῦτο πρῶτον ἔτος
καὶ τὰ ἐπίτιμα ταὐτὰ εἶναι
τοῖς ἐνεστῶσιν ἀρχείοις, ἕ-
150 ως ἂγ [κ]ομίσωνται τὰ χρήματ[α]
[κα]ὶ τὸν στέφανον οἱ ἐπικαλοῦν-
τες καὶ ἡ ἀναγραφὴ γένηται.

(15) ἐὰν δέ τις κομίζηται μὴ τὴν
δημοκρατίαγ κατασκευάζων
155 εἰσενέγκας ἢ ἀναλώσας ἢ μὴ
ὀφειλόμενα ἢ πλείω ἀπολάβηι,
ἀποτινέτω διπλάσια, ἐὰν δίκηι

(16) [ν]ικᾶται. καὶ ὃς ἂμ παρὰ τούτων
[λ]αβὼν ⟨μὴ⟩ ἀναλώσηι ὥστε ἡ δημο-
160 κρατία κατασταθῆι ἢ ὃς ἂμ [πα]-
ρὰ τούτω[ν] ἔχων μὴ ἀποδε[ίξηι]
[ἀ]ναλωμένα εἰς ταῦτα, διπλ[άσια]
ἀποτεισάτω ἅπερ ἂν λάβη[ι, ἐ]-

(17) ἂν δίκηι νικᾶται. ὧι δ᾽ ἂν ἐπικ[α]-
165 λῆται καὶ γραφῆι δίκη μὴ εἰσ[ε]-
νέγκαι ἢ μὴ ε[ἰσ]αναλῶσαι [κα]-
τὰ τὸν νόμον ἢ μὴ ὀφειλόμ[ενα]
ἢ πλείω ἀπολαβεῖν, μὴ στ[εφα]-
νούσθω μηδὲ ἀναγραφ[έσθω]
170 εἰς στήλην [----------------]γέ
νηται κα[ὶ------]π[----] τα[---]
[---------]σι[-------------]χρήματα

Side I

(1) Whoever kills a tyrant, a leader of an oligarchy, or someone overthrowing the democracy, if he is a citizen (*enarchos*), he shall receive a talent of silver from the polis on that day or the next, and the *dēmos* shall erect a bronze statue in his likeness. And he shall have free meals (*sitēsis*) in the prytaneion as long as he lives, and will be called by name to the front seat (*eis proedrian*) in the competitions, and two drachmas shall be given to him every day for as long as he lives. If the killer is a free foreigner (*xenos*), the same things shall be given to him, and let him be a citizen, and he shall be allowed to enroll in whatever tribe he wants. If the killer is a slave (*doulos*), let him be in possession of his rights (*epitimos*) and let him participate in the regime (*politeia*) according to the law, and let him receive thirty minae from the polis on that day or the next, and for as long as he lives let him receive a drachma each day . . . [12]

(2) . . . of office . . . they shall receive a talent of silver . . . thirty minae . . . let him be a citizen.

Side II

(3) . . . and the rest belongs to the polis. And if someone was somehow injured by them, he shall receive [compensation] from there.

(4) And if one of the fellow soldiers kills a tyrant, a leader of an oligarchy, or someone overthrowing the democracy and [subsequently] establishes democracy in the city, he shall not be punished for what he did with them, and he shall receive a talent of silver from the *dēmos*.

(5) Whoever—during a tyranny or oligarchy—holds the office of *strategos* or holds any office whatsoever which must provide an account of its finances, or registers the property of an Ilian or a metic for a tax, [it is forbidden] to buy from any of them or be entrusted with land, a house, flocks, slaves, or anything else and [it is forbidden] to accept a dowry [from them]. Whoever buys something from one of them, or in entrusted with [it], or accepts a dowry, or somehow else acquires [something], the acquisition is invalid and the victim shall take compensation from the offender's possessions without an appraisal, whenever he wants.

(6) If someone holds the office of *strategos* a second time or holds another office [sc., for a second time], he owes all the money he managed, since it belongs to the *dēmos*. And anyone who wishes—since the matter concerns the *dēmos*'s property—may plead the case in the law court whenever he wants until a trial concludes while the Ilians are governed democratically.

(7) Whoever—during a tyranny or oligarchy—gives or receives the *dēmos*'s money [acquired] from those [individuals], he may be judged [sc., in a law court],[13] and let him be liable to be tried. . . .

Side III

(8) . . . they are born from a defiled man. And half of their property shall belong to the polis and half to the children of the deceased; if there are no children, the money shall be given to his rightful heir. There may be a trial concerning

---

12   This translation starts with line 19: no sense can be made of the previous lines.

13   There is a minor problem here. In lines 76–78 the law reads, [ἐξ]εῖναι δὲ δι[κάσ]ασθαι τῶι| [βουλο]μένωι ὡ[ς] περὶ δημοσί|[ων ἐν τ]ῶι δικα[σ]τηρίωι. In lines 84–85 the law reads, ἐξεῖν]αι δικ[άσ]ασθαι ὡς|[περὶ δημοσίων] χρημάτων. It is thus tempting to read lines 84–85 as an abbreviation of lines 76–78—that is to assume an implied τῶι βουλομένωι in provision 7. I have chosen, however, not to translate lines 84–85 based on that assumption. This results in regarding the infinitive δικάσασθαι as in the middle voice in line 76 ("to plead one's case") and in a passive sense in line 84 ("to be judged"). But even if lines 84–85 abbreviate lines 76–78 (i.e., there is an implied τῶι βουλομένωι), there is virtually no difference in meaning.

those matters at anytime, until a trial concludes while the Ilians are governed democratically. And if someone is bound, or confined, or is a defendant facing imprisonment, [the accuser] owes twice the penalties and twice as much as the damage he caused. If he [i.e., the victim] paid money, the accuser must pay back double. And there shall be a trial concerning those matters at any time until a trial concludes while the Ilians are governed democratically.

(9) If—during a tyranny or oligarchy—someone, while serving as an office holder, kills someone, all of those who voted [sc., for the execution] are murderers, and one may prosecute [them] at anytime, until a trial concludes while the Ilians are governed democratically. And if someone goes into exile to escape a trial, since he voted to kill, he and his children shall be without rights and shall go into exile. And the murder shall not be atoned for either by intermarriage or money. If it is, he shall be beholden to the same penalty.

(10) If some tyrant or leader of an oligarchy, or whoever appoints the Ilians' magistrates with them, or someone else on their behalf buys land, or a house, or flocks, or slaves, or anything else whatsoever, the purchase is invalid and [the purchased items] shall be returned to the sellers.

(11) If, during an oligarchy, someone is selected to the *boulē* or the other magistracies by misusing the laws, desiring—by his contrivance—to accomplish it as though [he were selected] in a democracy, [the selection] is invalid and the contriver shall suffer as though he were a leader of an oligarchy.

(12) Whoever becomes tyrant or leader of an oligarchy, or sets up a tyrant, or joins in a revolt, or overthrows the democracy, wherever their names are [engraved]—if it is in the list of the priests, if it is on a votive offering, if it is on a tombstone—chisel them out from everywhere. After they have chiseled out [the names] from the priests lists, sell [sc., the space]. And the buyer shall engrave whatever name he wishes from those who are eligible. And with respect to the votive offerings dedicated privately, after they have struck out the dedicator's inscription, the *dēmos* shall deliberate about the votive offering so that it shall not stand as their [offering] and there will be no record. And wherever there is a public votive offering also inscribed [with the names] of others, make that individual's name invisible, after they have struck it out.

(13) If someone—during a tyranny or oligarchy— . . .

Side IV

(14) And if the archons do not announce the crown in the Great Dionysia, or do not provide funds to engrave a public record according to the law, each of the archons shall owe thirty staters, each member of the *boulē* ten staters, and the treasurer one hundred staters. And if an accusation concerning compensation is brought against any of those [magistrates] just mentioned,

they shall be without rights until those making the accusation receive the money in full. And there shall be access always to the magistrates and the standing *boulē*—and this shall be [permissible] during the present year—and the penalty shall be the same for the members of the standing special boards (*archeioi*) until those making the accusation receive the money in full and the crown, and a public record is made.

(15) If someone receives compensation although he did not contribute or spend money to establish the democracy, or recovered what was not owed or more [sc., that what was owed], he must pay back double if he is convicted in court.

(16) And whoever receives [sc., money] from them and does not spend it so that democracy is established, or whoever holding [money acquired] from them does not reveal the expenditures for those matters, he shall pay back double of what he received if convicted in court.

(17) Against whomever an accusation and indictment is made that he did not contribute or spend money according to the law, or recovered what was not owed or more [sc., than what was owed], he shall neither be crowned nor shall [his deeds] be recorded on a stele. . . .

The Ilian tyrant-killing law is long and complex, its extant portions alone containing roughly twice the number of words as the Eretrian tyrant-killing law and four and one-half times as many words as the law of Eukrates (Ilion: 1,078; Eretria: 534; Eukrates: 227). This chapter's first section thus focuses solely on the law's provisions in order to ensure that we know what the Ilian pro-democrats actually promulgated. The second section of this chapter then presents the law's likely historical context. Therein we will consider both the circumstances within which the law was promulgated and the nature of tyrannical threat that confronted the Ilians at that time. And the chapter's third and final section will determine whether or not the law was effective.

Analysis of the Law's Provisions

This section has two complementary objectives. The first objective is simply to ensure that we understand what each provision of the Ilian tyrant-killing law actually says. For a few of the provisions that is not too much of a problem. But in several places the law's language is vague and thus quite confusing. The second objective is to determine the rationale behind each provision—that is, to explain what the Ilians hoped to accomplish by including it in their law.

To assist in this analysis, I have divided the law's extant provisions into three large sections. It is perhaps unlikely that the Ilians thought of the law in such a way. Indeed, in my scheme, provision 11 is interpreted in conjunction with provisions 5–7 and provision 4 is tied to provision 1.[14] And one must not forget that no sense can be made of the law's first nineteen lines, roughly 15 percent of the original Greek text.[15] Nevertheless, the extant provisions seem to fall roughly into three sections, and imposing some sort of macro structure will help one acquire a synoptic view of a rather long and initially quite baffling law.

FIRST SECTION

The first extant section of the Ilian anti-tyranny law (provisions 1–4) specifically addresses "tyrant killing." The section has three parts.

The first part (provisions 1 and 4) of this section lists the rewards that will be given to an individual who kills a tyrant, a leader of an oligarchy, or someone overthrowing the democracy. The nature of the reward depends on the assassin's status.

- Citizen (*enarchos*):[16] he will receive a talent of silver, free meals in the prytaneion for life, heralding to a front-row seat in civic competitions, and a daily stipend of two drachmas, and a statue in his likeness will be erected.

---

14 The authors of *IJG* (II: 37) conclude that the law's language is clumsy and impure—a quality that makes the text rather confusing. They further conclude that the provisions are inserted without order.

15 One can only speculate about the content of these first lines. Friedel (1937: 84–85) suggests that, after some sort of prescript, the law articulated the legal position of a tyrant or oligarchic leader (e.g., he is *atimos* or *polemios*). Berve (1967: 422) suggests that the law stated that the tyrant can be killed; the tyrant's relatives are banned forever (if not killed); the tyrant's property and that of his family is confiscated; the Ilians must utter a curse on the tyrant and his family; the tyrant cannot be buried in Ilian soil. Koch (1996: 46n40) suggests that the first lines of the law would have contained a reference to the ruling king (which, according to Koch, was Seleukos I) or some explanation for why the Ilians promulgated such a law. Koch also suggests (1996: 47) that, in the lost opening section, there was an order to kill anti-democratic revolutionaries and an assurance of immunity for the assassin. Dössel (2003: 208) suggests that the opening lines ordered the confiscation of the anti-democratic leader's property, provided guidelines on what must be done with the property, and deemed such a leader to be an outlaw.

16 The meaning of *enarchos* is not immediately self-evident. *IJG* (II: 39) suggests that *enarchos* refers to a subject of Ilion's empire (*archē*). Dittenberger (*OGIS* 218) argued that, in this law, *enarchos* simply means "citizen" since it is most logical to divide a Greek polis's society into citizens, foreigners, and slaves. Dittenberger did suggest, however, that the use of the word *enarchos* to mean citizen indicates that, at some previous time, the Ilians had two citizenship statuses: high-level citizens (who were entitled to serve as magistrates) and low-level citizens (who were not so entitled). He cites the meaning of *entimos* as a potential parallel: it can mean "honored" or "in office" as well as (likely a later evolution) "eligible for honors or office." Friedel (1937: 83–84), Frisch (1975: ad loc.), Berve (1967: 420), Koch (1996: 46), and Dössel (2003: 202) all agree that an *enarchos* is a full citizen (*Vollbürger*). Funck (1994: 321–22) understands the word *enarchos* as maintaining, in addition to its larger sense of citizen, the more limited sense of "in office."

- Free foreigner (*xenos*): he will receive the same rewards as a citizen tyrannicide and will be made a citizen, enrolled in whatever tribe he chooses.[17]
- Slave (*doulos*): he will be freed, be allowed to participate in the regime (*politeia*), receive thirty *minai*, and (as reasonably restored) receive a daily stipend of one drachma. It is unlikely that he received full citizenship rights.[18]
- Fellow soldier of the tyrant (*sustratiōtēs*): he will be pardoned for the acts he did with the tyrant and will receive a talent of silver provided that he establishes democratic rule in the polis after killing the tyrant.[19]

There is precedent for several of the elements contained in the Ilians' "tyrannicide incentive package." Grants of the *megalai timai* (statue, *sitēsis*, *proedria*), for example, were a well-established reward for tyrant killing: the Athenians erected a statue of Harmodios and Aristogeiton and granted both *sitēsis* and *proedria* to their descendants (and recall that the oath of Demophantos mandates that, should someone die as a result of having killed a ty-

---

17   Friedel (1937: 86) suggests that the grant of citizenship is made explicit because of problems that might arise; he notes the situation in Athens after the fall of the Thirty. For a brief discussion of the rewards given after the fall of the Thirty, see *RO* 4 and the accompanying commentary.

18   Dittenberger (ad loc.), Frisch (ad loc.), and *IJG* (II: 40) concluded that the slave tyrannicide is given full citizenship rights. This is an understandable position: ἐπί]τιμος [ἔ]στω καὶ πολιτεί|[ας μ]ε[τεχέτω seems to suggest that. But several points argue against that conclusion. First, one might conclude that, just as a *xenos* tyrannicide is elevated one status level to become a *politēs*, a *doulos* tyrannicide is elevated one status level to become (in some sense) a *xenos*. (And note that Hansen [1998: 104] demonstrated that, in Athens, manumitted slaves became registered as metics—i.e., not as citizens—with their former master as *prostatēs*.) Second, since the slave tyrannicide receives a smaller cash payment than a free foreigner does, one might also conclude that his other rewards were smaller; also, note that the slave receives neither *sitēsis* nor *proedria*, although both the citizen and free foreigner do. Third, the law does not explicitly state that a *doulos* would become a *politēs*, but it does say so with respect to the *xenos* tyrannicide (line 30). Fourth, the law does not simply say "participate in the regime" but "participate in the regime according to the law" (πολιτεί|[ας μ]ε[τεχέτω κατὰ τὸν ν]όμογ). Perhaps the Ilians had a law on the rights of freed slaves vis-à-vis their ability to participate in the regime. Both Friedel (1937: 87) and Berve (1967: 420) suggest that the slave tyrannicide was elevated to the status of a metic. Koch (1996: 48) suggests that the slave tyrannicide was given some sort of limited citizenship ("die vorgesehene Hereinnahme von Fremden und—wenn auch eingeschränkt—von Slaven in die Bürgerschaft"). And this appears to be the position of Funck (1994: 321). Dössel (2003: 202) does not comment, but translates ἐπί] τιμος [ἔ]στω καὶ πολιτεί|[ας μ]ε[τεχέτω κατὰ τὸν ν]όμογ as "so soll er die Ehrenrechte erhalten und das Bürgerrecht gemäss dem Gesetz."

19   Koch (1996: 51) asserts that the pardon covers only actions committed in common with other anti-democrats, not any private crime he may have committed. That is a reasonable position: the law does state (lines 49–51), "he shall not be punished for what he did with them." But Koch's interpretation might be overly subtle: the distinction might be difficult to make. On a different note, Maffi (2005: 142–43) raises the interesting question of how a tyrant-killing mercenary soldier might subsequently help "establish democracy." He suggests that he would join exiled democrats in their fight to reclaim their polis.

rant, he will be treated like Harmodios and Aristogeiton and his descendants treated like the descendants of the two tyrannicides);[20] such incentives are restored by Knoepfler in the Eretrian tyrant-killing law (lines 8–15, old fragment). There also is precedent for a grant of a lump sum payment: the Athenians, it will be recalled (chap. 1, n. 54), began their festival of Dionysos by announcing that anybody who kills a tyrant will receive a talent (Ar. *Av.* 1072–75); in the mid-fifth century, the Milesians decreed (*ML* 43) that the assassin of certain named individuals will receive 100 staters; the Thasians included (late fifth century) a lump sum payment in their laws regarding informants (*ML* 83). And a third standard element is explicitly incentivizing noncitizens or even a member of the coup to defend the regime that was previously in power. As shown in chapter 2 (in the "General Layer of Defense" section), the Eretrian tyrant-killing law incentivized noncitizens to kill a tyrant; and the aforementioned law from Thasos also incentivized both slaves and the participants in a conspiracy (except the originator) to alert the authorities.[21]

In addition to those standard elements, the Ilion's incentive package contains a couple of unprecedented features. The first such feature is the grant of a daily stipend to a tyrannicide.[22] The Ilion tyrant-killing law is also unique in directly incentivizing the tyrant's soldiers to commit an act of tyrannicide.[23] But the late-fifth-century law from Thasos (*ML* 83) comes close: as noted above, it incentivized members of a conspiracy to inform the authorities about their plans.[24]

20 See the section in chapter 1 titled "The Oath of Demophantos" for the evidence. Friedel (1937: 85) asserts that the provisions of the decree of Demophantos do not allow for the erection of a statue of the tyrant killer. This is incorrect. The Athenians erected statues of Harmodios and Aristogeiton. And, according to the oath of Demophantos, the Athenians will treat a fallen tyrannicide "just like" Harmodios and Aristogeiton.

21 Note that Aeneas Tacticus (10.16–17) recommends that it be publicly announced that, should one of the associates (*sunontes*) kill "the exile, the monarch, or the general," he will be rewarded and guaranteed safe return to him home. As noted in the introduction to this book, Aeneas Tacticus is essentially recommending the promulgation of a tyrant-killing law. Note too that *I. Erythrai* 2 B (lines 14–end) perhaps provides incentives (or simply the authority) for individuals to inform magistrates about anti-regime behavior.

22 Berve (1967: 420) asserts without explanation that the daily stipend corresponds with the spirit of the Hellenistic period.

23 On mercenary soldiers killing a tyrant (their paymaster), note Xen. *Hier.* 6.11.

24 Note, too, the passage in Aeneas Tacticus noted above in note 21. A couple of possible striking omissions in the Ilion law's incentive package should be noted. First, there is no indication that the state will provide for a tyrannicide's children, should he die as a result of his deed. Second, there is no statement that a tyrannicide would be deemed "pure." This latter point is minor and certainly implied. And both features might very well have been included in a lost part of the law. On a different note, Frisch (1975: 74) concluded that the rewards are moderate when compared to those given by the Athenians to Harmodios and Aristogeiton: there is no prohibition in the Ilian

The Ilians clearly included provisions 1 and 4 in their law in order to increase the likelihood that, should anti-democrats overthrow or attempt to overthrow the democracy, someone would kill one of the coup's prominent members. That likelihood was increased, of course, by the fact that every male person in Ilion was explicitly incentivized to become a tyrannicide. Thus, wherever in the city a prominent member of a nondemocratic regime might go, there would be someone there who would be greatly rewarded for killing him. The "tyrant" would not be safe even around his own men. And the greater the number of opportunities for an assassination, the greater the likelihood that an assassination would occur.

There is an interesting potential consequence to provision 4 that should be noted. Since mercenary soldiers would receive a talent of silver for killing a prominent member of an anti-democratic regime, the regime might be forced to pay a higher price for mercenaries than it otherwise would. That does not automatically follow, of course. But, if we make the crucial assumptions that the mercenary soldier survives and that the assassination quickly leads to the establishment of a democracy, it likely would be more profitable for a mercenary soldier to kill the tyrant than to protect him (cf. Xen. *Hier.* 6.11). Knowing that, the tyrant might pay his mercenaries more money in order to alter their risk-reward calculus: the risk is still great, the reward less so.

All that can be said about provision 2, the second part of the law's first section, is that it records a monetary reward and, apparently, a grant of citizenship.[25] It should be noted, however, that the rewards listed in this provision are also included in provision 1: a talent (as restored) of silver, thirty minas, a citizenship grant. It thus appears that, like in provision 1, an individual's reward is based on his status. But for what is he to be rewarded? Frisch (1975: 73–74) suggests that the provision might have incentivized individuals to tell the authorities of a plot against the democracy. (And he suggests that the grant of citizenship might have been directed toward the metic population.) It is also possible that the provision stated the reward that the polis would give to the children of an individual who died as a result of killing, or trying to kill, a tyrant.

The fragmentary provision 3 allows for the confiscation of property, no doubt originally owned by a prominent member or members of a nondemo-

---

law against placing another statue by their statue, as there was in Athens (*Syll.*³ 320 lines 30–33); there is no grant of *sitēsis* for a tyrannicide's descendants, as there was in Athens (*IG* I³ 131).

25 Frisch restores—and I have accepted—ἔσ]τω πολίτης ("let him be a citizen") in line 39. Dittenberger leaves his text blank after μνᾶ[ς] and before [τὰ δὲ ἄ]λλα; *IJG* prints . . . τω πολίτη[ς. Frisch's restoration seems reasonable. But note that, in line 30, the Greek for "let him be a citizen" is πολίτης ἔστω, while, in 39, Frisch's restoration reverses the two words.

cratic regime.[26] All that can be said for certain is that the polis will take part of the property and use it to compensate victims for what they suffered during the tyranny. It is quite possible that the other part of the confiscated property, likely one-half of the original total, would be given to the tyrannicide (or maybe his children, if he died): perhaps the cash payments promised in provisions 1 and 4 would be taken from this money.[27]

SECOND SECTION

The second extant section of the law (provisions 5–13) prescribes punishments for certain actions committed while the Ilian democracy is overthrown. There are five parts to this complex and lengthy section.

ECONOMIC OR FINANCIAL MATTERS

Provision 5 is the first of four provisions (5, 6, 7, 10) that address economic or financial matters concerning which the anti-democratic regime is implicated. This particular provision forbids everybody from acquiring anything in any way from either magistrates who handle public money or individuals who levied a tax on citizens or metics. If someone does acquire something from such individuals, the law states that that acquisition shall be invalid and "the victim (τὸν ἀδικ[ηθέ]ντα) may take compensation from the property of the offender (τοῦ ἀδικήσ[αν]τος) without an appraisal" (i.e., without ensuring that the values are equal). This is not entirely clear. The "victim" is likely the person who originally owned a piece of property that was subsequently acquired by a financial magistrate or taxing official. The implication is that the property was acquired against the "victim's" will: it might have been confiscated, for example; or the victim might have been somehow forced to sell it at a low price. The identity of the "offender" is less apparent. But he likely is the person who unlawfully acquired items from the financial magistrate or taxing official. Thus the sequence of events envisioned in this provision seems to be this: (1) magistrate or taxing official acquired something from victim; (2) at a later date offender acquired that something from magistrate or taxing

---

26   Koch (1996: 50) rightly notes that this provision (i.e., about confiscated property) concerns the leaders of the anti-democrats, not those who held office while the democracy was overthrown or who—again, during a nondemocratic regime—voted to execute an individual. The law lists penalties for those individuals elsewhere (lines 54–86, 97–106). Frisch (1975: 74) suggests that, according to this provision, part of the tyrant's property would be given to the tyrannicide, part would be used to establish a fund for victims of the regime.

27   Thus Dittenberger (ad loc.) following *IJG*. It will be recalled that the decree of Demophantos also mandated that the slain tyrant's property be sold and that one-half of the money raised be given to the tyrant slayer. It is thus reasonable to conclude that the other half went to the polis of Athens. But the decree of Demophantos did not state what the Athenians should do with the money.

official; (3) the law thus states that victim might take compensation for his loss of that something from the property of offender.

The Ilian democrats likely crafted provision 5 in order to accomplish two related objectives. The first objective was to facilitate the "victim's" efforts to reclaim his property (apparently taken by the financial magistrate or taxing official). The logic is simple. Since it would be potentially quite costly for an individual (i.e., the offender) to somehow acquire property from the financial magistrate or taxing official, it is likely that, after the democracy is restored, the property would still be in the hands of those financial magistrates or taxing officials.[28] Thus the victim could easily reacquire his property. The second objective was to prevent the members of the regime from using the property that they acquired from any "victim" to buy political support. Potential supporters might not accept those items because, again, it would be too risky: they likely would lose something of greater value once the democracy is reinstated.

Provision 6 states that anybody who serves in any office twice must pay back all of the money he managed while in office.[29] Presumably the money referred to is the money that he spent during the illegal second term; although it is possible that the offender must pay back the money he spent during his first term too. The important point, however, is that the offending individual likely must pay back even the money that he spent on what otherwise would be considered justified expenditures.[30]

The Ilians crafted provision 6 in order to prevent the gradual overthrow of their democracy (i.e., *katalusis* by evolution, not by revolution). As Aristotle noted (*Pol.* 1308a19–24), repeated tenure in office was a well-known method for an individual to become tyrant. By adding this provision in the law, the Ilians, first, made it clear that repeated tenure is, in fact, illegal: it is quite possible that the Ilians did not previously have a law on that matter. Henceforth,

---

28   Dössel (2003: 211) helpfully draws attention to a passage in a speech by Aischines (3.21): in Athens, magistrates were not allowed to rid themselves of assets or lower their net worth until they had successfully completed their *euthynai*. The purpose was to ensure that the magistrate could pay any fines that may be levied against him. Maffi (2005: 145) also came to this conclusion, citing the passage in Aischines.

29   Maffi (2005: 147) argues that τὸ δεύτερον in the phrase ἐὰν δέ τις|τὸ δεύτερον [σ]τρατηγήσηι|ἢ ἄλλην ἀρ[χὴν] ἄρξηι (lines 71–73) should be translated "en deuxième lieu." That is, he does not believe that provision 6 focuses on magistrates who hold office a second time. Instead, he sees provision 6 as articulating the second part of a single provision that begins with (what I label) provision 5. The first part of that provision (= my provision 5) states that magistrates of a nondemocratic regime cannot rid themselves of any property; the second part (= my provision 6) states that, second (τὸ δεύτερον), those magistrates must pay back all the money they spent while in office. Maffi himself acknowledges (2005: 147) that this is a daring interpretation, without parallel. Indeed, the most natural reading of the Greek is "If someone holds the office of *strategos* a second time. . . ." Maffi's interpretation almost certainly should be rejected.

30   Thus Friedel (1937: 90).

there is a very clear "red line." Second, the Ilians ensured that holding office for over a year would be potentially quite costly: the offender would be forced to pay back twice the amount of money that he spent while in office.[31]

Provision 6 concludes with the stipulation that "anyone who wishes . . . may plead the case in the law court whenever he wants until the trial concludes while the Ilians are governed democratically." This stipulation, as noted by Dittenberger (ad loc.), had two significant consequences. First, it ensures that there would be no "statute of limitations" for the crime: anyone may initiate a trial at any time after the democracy has been restored. Second, it ensures that a defendant can be acquitted lawfully only under a democratic regime. Thus if there were a coup during the trial and the defendant was subsequently acquitted under the nondemocratic regime, he could be tried again when the democrats retake the polis.[32]

Provision 7 forbids individuals from giving or receiving of money ἐκ τού||[των. The meaning of ἐκ τούτων is not immediately clear: in lines 59–60, 65, 158, "from them," the translation offered for ἐκ τούτων, is παρὰ τούτων. Even Dittenberger chose not to offer an interpretation. But Friedel (1937: 90), Frisch (1975: ad loc.), Koch (1996: 57n73), and Dössel (2003: 203) are likely correct: ἐκ τούτων does mean "from them" and refers to the magistrates mentioned in provision 6 (i.e., those serving in a magistracy twice—although it might also refer to the individuals singled out in provision 5).

---

31   Koch (1996: 54–55) suggests that the Ilion law articulates a careful distinction with regard to the participation of magistrates in a nondemocratic regime. The first stage—when the revolution actually takes place—is addressed in provision 5. In that case, the office holder is not necessarily complicit in the revolution and is unsure of what he should do. He might stay in office even if he does not fully support the new regime. Thus the penalty would not harm a well-intended office holder (assuming, of course, that he did not acquire another individual's property). Provision 6 concerns the second stage, when it is clear that the democracy has been overthrown and that the office holder thus clearly *chose* to participate fully in the nondemocratic regime. In that case the "hurt" of the penalty is unavoidable: he must pay pack double the money that he managed because, by definition, he illegally appropriated the money. This is an interesting observation and is accepted, with some nuance, by Dössel (2003: 210 with n. 27). Maffi (2005: 146–47) rejects Koch's theory by noting that, if a democratically selected magistrate continued to hold his office after an anti-democratic coup, he would be deemed to have been complicit with the anti-democratic regime once the democrats regained control of the polis. Koch's theory probably should be rejected.

32   Dössel (2003: 211–12 with n. 30) suggests that the stipulation "while the Ilians are governed democratically" is included in order to prevent members of a successful anti-democratic coup from somehow using the provision against magistrates that had been selected during the previous democracy. Maffi (2005: 147–48), advances a very different interpretation of the phrase ὅταν||[βούλητ]αι, μέχ[ρι] τέλος δί[[κης γέν]ηται [δη]μοκρατου||[μένων Ἰλ]ιέων (lines 78–81). He does not believe that τέλος δί[[κης refers to a trial begun by the accusation of *ho boulomenos*. Instead he argues that it refers to the end of a period of time within which *ho boulomenos* can make his legal complaint to initiate a trial—what the Greeks called a *prothesmia*. Thus, in this interpretation, anybody can make an accusation against an official who worked in a non-democratic regime whenever he wants (ὅταν||[βούλητ]αι) from the time that the democracy is established until (μέχ[ρι]) an established closing date for such trials (i.e., τέλος δί[κης).

Should someone "give or receive" such money "from them," (1) he may be tried in a law court (the extant part of the law does not indicate the punishment); (2) he is also liable to something else (ὑπόδι|[κος δὲ ἔστω), the substance of which is lost.³³

The Ilians likely crafted provision 7 in order to accomplish two related objectives. The first objective is to prevent people from acting as a nondemocratic regime's "middlemen" (i.e., people who do things for the regime, in this case "give money" to other people). As a result of this provision, it might be too risky to perform such a service.³⁴ The second objective is to prevent people from doing business with the regime's middlemen: they would be "receiving" money from the middleman. They, too, might choose not to engage in such activity because of the risk involved (although, again, we do not know the penalty). Thus the intention behind this provision was to prevent regime members from both buying political support and benefiting economically from their unlawful position.³⁵

Provision 10 states that both high-level members of a nondemocratic regime (a "tyrant or leader of an oligarchy") and their agents (those who "appoint the Ilians' magistrates with them" and "those who act on their behalf") cannot buy anything.³⁶ If they do, the acquisition is invalid and the item must be returned to the seller.

33   Koch (1996: 57) believes that the subject of ὑπόδι|[κος δὲ ἔστω is the individual who made the accusation ("der Kläger") against someone for "giving or receiving money from them." His reasoning: ὑπόδικος δὲ ἔστω is not included in provision 6, where the accuser is explicitly referred to as *ho boulomenos* (a "volunteer" who takes initiative); thus provision 7 likely articulates some risk to the accuser. This is unlikely correct: (1) it is not necessary grammatically (the likely subject of ὑπόδικος is the same subject as that of the two finite verbs: δῶι and λάβηι ("gives" and "takes"); (2) one might seriously doubt that the law would specify any risk to a potential accuser: the whole law seems to be 100 percent with accusers and against the accused. Maffi (2005: 148–49) also rejects Koch's interpretation. Maffi then offers his own interpretation of lines 84–85. He does not think that ὑπόδι|[κος (which he suggests should be restored ὑπόδι|[κωι) begins a new clause but, instead, modifies the magistrate that may be tried in court. He translates, "Il sera loisible de l'appeler en justice comme s'il était responsable du vol de choses appartenant à l'Etate. . . ."

34   Frisch (1975: 76) suggests that the targets of this provision were the regime's "hangers-on" (Mitläufer).

35   Dössel (2003: 213) concludes that this provision was included in order to help ensure that property confiscated by a non-democratic regime would more likely be returned to its original owners after they returned from exile. She cites (2003: n. 33) an inscription from Mytilene (*RO* 85) as an example of the basic issue. One might also note Plut. *Arat.* 12–14 for a description of the dynamic in mid-third-century Sikyon. Dössel concludes that the guilty nondemocratic magistrates and those complicit with them would be responsible for reimbursing a third party that had lawfully purchased confiscated property.

36   Maffi (2005: 155–56) offers a very different interpretation of the clause ἐ|ὰν δέ τις τύραννος ἢ ἡγεμὼν ὀλιγαρχίας ἢ ὅσ|τις Ἰλιέων ἀρχὰς συ[ν]αποδεικνύηι μετὰ τού[των] (lines 106–8). He first notes that this provision (i.e., provision 10) is very similar to provision 5. Provision 5 seeks to prevent anybody from buying or in any way acquiring anything from anybody who, during a nondemocratic regime, served as any financial magistrate or taxed either an Ilian or a metic. Thus Maffi

The Ilians likely crafted provision 10 in order to accomplish, once again, two related objectives. The first objective was to ensure that an individual would not permanently lose something that he was forced to sell or something that was sold while he was in exile. (This "forcing" seems to be implied since the sold item would be returned to the seller; thus he appears to be considered a victim.) The second objective was to prevent anyone from permanently possessing that illegally purchased item. The targeted individuals here are neither the tyrant nor the oligarchic leaders: they would either be dead or living in exile once the democrats regained control of the polis. Instead, the likely targets were regime supporters and their families. The provision seeks to ensure that they would not continue to benefit financially from the tyranny after it has been overthrown.[37]

There is an interesting unanswered question here: would the original "seller," after he reacquires the item that he sold to the member of the nondemocratic regime, be required to return the money (to the polis?) that he made on the initial sale? One would think that he would have to do so. Otherwise, an individual could gain doubly (at the expense of the *dēmos*): he retains possession of both the item and the money—public money, likely—that the "tyrant" originally used to buy the item.

INDICTMENTS LODGED BY A LAY ACCUSER

Provision 8 articulates the punishments to be meted out against a lay accuser (ὁ κατηγορήσ[ας] [line 95]) who initiated legal action against another individual while the democracy is overthrown. Three scenarios are envisioned. In the first, the victim is executed after the trial.[38] The extant portions of the

believes that provision 10 should be interpreted as referring to all magistrates in a nondemocratic regime: they cannot buy anything; provision 5, that is, deals with illegal magistrates unloading property while provision 10 deals with illegal magistrates acquiring property. Evidence in support of his theory rests heavily on a very strained interpretation of ἢ ὅσ|τις Ἰλιέων ἀρχὰς συ[ν]-αποδεικνύηι μετὰ τού[των] (lines 107–8). He suggests it does not mean "or whoever appoints Ilion's magistrates with them"; instead it means "ou tout autre magistrat que quiconque des Iliens aura démontré avoir coopéré avec eux dans cette sorte d'opérations." This interpretation of the Greek is almost certainly incorrect.

37 Koch (1996: 50) wonders whether or not the person who bought something πρὸ τούτων (sc., the tyrant, leader of the oligarchy, or office-appointing official) would receive compensation once the democracy is reinstated—perhaps from the fund set up per provision 3. This is quite unlikely, since such an individual would have been complicit with the tyranny: he would have bought something "on behalf" of the regime leaders. Koch is led to this consideration, it appears, because he interprets, in note 55, πρὸ τούτων as meaning "in ihrem Auftrag."

38 Koch (1996: 60n80) does not believe that this provision concerns formal death-sentence trials. He suggests, instead, that the provision concerns anybody killed as a result of regime policy or practice during a nondemocratic regime. His reasoning is that provision 9 concerns executions subsequent to a trial. This is an understandable position. But provision 8 does appear to deal with court cases (thus the provision refers to ὁ κατηγορήσας and τιμαί) and provision 9 deals with executions specifically brought about by magistrates (and certainly appears to envision something

provision do not state the punishment that the lay accuser will suffer once the democrats regain control of this polis. But he almost certainly would be executed. The extant portions of the provision law do state, however that (1) the lay accuser's children are to be considered defiled (thus they are pariahs); (2) the victim's children (or his rightful heirs) shall receive one-half of the lay accuser's property, the other half given to the polis; (3) a trial on the matter my be convened at any time, the verdict of which must be rendered while Ilion is democratically governed.

It is difficult to determine the exact nature of the second scenario articulated in provision 8. There are actually two difficulties. The first concerns the nature of the punishment potentially inflicted on the defendant (i.e., the man unlawfully accused by ὁ κατηγορήσας). The meaning of ἐὰν δὲ δεθῆι ἢ ἐρχθῆι (line 92) seems clear: "if someone is bound or confined." The problem is the following verb: φεύγηι. Frisch translates it as "go into exile." He thus takes the following noun in the genitive case (δεσμῶν) to be dependent on τιμάς (see below).[39] I, however, translate φεύγηι as "to be a defendant [sc., in a trial]." And take the genitive δεσμῶν—"imprisonment"—to be the punishment that would be inflicted on the defendant should he be unlawfully convicted.[40] I prefer this interpretation because all three potential unlawful punishments listed in provision 8 would then explicitly concern some sort of confinement: binding, confining, being a defendant facing imprisonment. And, as is well known, the Greeks—or at least the Athenians—generally bound or kept people to prison only until they were executed or paid a fine.[41]

The second difficulty concerns the punishment that would be inflicted on the lay accuser once the democrats regain control of the polis. Here is the Greek (lines 92–93): τιμὰς | διπλασίας ὀφείλει[ν κ]αὶ ὅτι ἂν βλαβῆι διπλάσιον. Thus the lay accuser will owe twice the τιμαί and twice the βλάβη (literally, "twice the damage he caused"). What are the τιμαί? Perhaps the τιμαί refer to

---

different than a normal trial in the *dikasterion*; see below). Maffi (2005: 149–50 with n. 19) essentially agrees with Koch, although admitting that the provision might address executions pursuant to a trial.

39 *IJG* accepts the standard punctuation (which I too accept) whereby a comma is placed right after—not, as Frisch prefers, right before—δεσμῶν and translates (II: 31) "s'il a dû fuir pour échapper à la prison." This is possible. But one might expect the use of a preposition such as ἀπό: compare the restoration in line 102. Friedel (1937: 91) accepts the traditional punctuation yet translates it differently: "[Wenn aber ein Bürger . . .] zu einer Gefängnisstrafe verurteilt wurde." Berve (1967: 420) both appears to accept the traditional (i.e., not Frisch's) punctuation and interprets the language as Friedel did. Maffi (2005: 151) accepts the traditional punctuation and translates it as "[Si un homme . . .] s'est soustrait aux entraves." Koch (1996: 57) and Dössel (2003: 203), however, accept Frisch's translation.

40 For φεύγηι as "defendant" with the potential punishment in the genitive, see *LSJ* s.v. φεύγω IV. For the plural δεσμοί meaning "imprisonment", see Thuc. 7.82.2.

41 See *RO* 84B (lines 3–6) for an example—in Chios—of confining someone until he provided guarantors for assigned penalties.

the penalties that the victim suffered (or would have suffered) as a result of the unlawful trial's verdict. Frisch, as mentioned above, takes the δεσμῶν with τιμαί: thus "twice the penalties of imprisonment." That is a reasonable position, but it is, perhaps, too narrow: the penalties (τιμαί) likely included both the amount of time of confinement and any money that the victim might have paid to get out of prison or would have had to pay to get out of prison. What, then, does ὅτι ἄν βλαβῆι refer to? Maybe it refers to physical harm suffered by the victim. And it might also include any additional losses the victim incurred as a result of his imprisonment. In any case, the logic behind the punishment is "two eyes for an eye."[42]

In the third scenario covered in provision 8, the victim paid money (presumably) to the lay accuser. Should that happen, the lay accuser must pay twice the amount that the victim was forced to pay. The law seems to imply that the original victim would receive that money.[43]

The Ilian pro-democrats obviously crafted provision 8 in order to prevent individuals from using the courts while the democracy is overthrown. The provision does so, first, by making such action potentially quite costly: as noted above, the consequences will be twice as bad for the accuser as for his victim, if the democracy is reinstated. Second, by ensuring that there will not be a statute of limitations, it is more likely that the offender eventually will be punished for his actions. And finally, it appears—and this is significant—that the lay accuser will be punished even if his victim was actually guilty of the alleged crime.

CAPITAL "TRIAL" LODGED BY A MAGISTRATE (SPECIAL TRIBUNAL)

Provision 9 addresses a situation wherein a magistrate successfully convinces members of the regime to execute an individual. Should that occur, everybody who voted for the execution will be considered a murderer and may be tried in court once the democrats regain control of the polis. If a regime member who voted for the execution goes into exile to avoid the trial, he and his descendants will be deprived of their rights and must remain in exile.[44]

---

42 *IJG* translates (II: 31) "doubles amendes et doubles domages-intérêts." Friedel (1937: 91), Berve (1967: 420), and Koch (1996: 57) translate it similarly. Maffi (2005: 151) translates it like *IJG* yet he translates *timai* as "pénalité."

43 Koch (1996: 57–58) suggests that lines 94–95 (ἐὰν δὲ χρήματα ἐ[κ]τείσηι, διπλάσια ἀποτινέ|[τ]ω ὁ κατηγορήσ[ας]) seek to protect a former magistrate of an anti-democratic regime from having to pay his mandated penalty twice: the subject of ἐ[κ]τείσηι is thus the former magistrate of an anti-democratic regime. This interpretation likely should be rejected: as I noted above with reference to provision 7, the whole law seems to be 100 percent with accusers and against the accused.

44 Lines 102–3 are difficult. I have accepted the standard (Dittenberger) restoration: ἐὰν τὴν | δίκ[ην ἀποφεύγηι τις, ψῆφον πρ]οσθέμενος. In this case ἐὰν τὴν | δίκ[ην ἀποφεύγηι almost certainly means "if someone goes into exile to escape a trial" and the following participle, πρ]οσθέμενος, is causal: "since he voted." The law thus seeks to ensure that such an individual will still pay

And the relatives of the executed man are forbidden from accepting—from whom the law does not say—either money or offers of marriage to atone for the murder.[45] If a family member does accept money or a marriage agreement to atone for the execution, he himself, along with his descendants, must "pay the same penalty." That is not entirely clear, but it likely means that he and his children are to be exiled and deprived of their rights. It is possible, but perhaps unlikely, that they could also be tried as murderers, since that is the only other penalty articulated in this provision. But that penalty is articulated in the previous conditional sentence.

The apparent objective of provision 9 is to render special tribunals ineffective. It is necessary to realize that the votes referred to in this provision would have been conducted openly: if they were conducted by secret ballot, no one would know who voted for the execution and thus the provision would be impossible to enforce. In such a scenario, the votes of a few enthusiastic and influential radicals could put tremendous pressure on everybody else to vote for an execution: the less radical individuals think that others will also vote for the execution and thus do not want to be seen as dissenters. Thus the less radical individuals, too, would vote for the execution.[46] The harsh penalties

a very high price for his vote: the Ilians will punish his family. *IJG* (II: 31), Friedel (1937: 91), and Berve (1967: 420) interpret it similarly. If, however, τὴν|δίκ[ην ἀποφεύγηι means "be acquitted" or "escape conviction" (which is perfectly good Greek—cf. Ar. *Nub.* 167) the participle πρ]οσθέμενος must be concessive: "although having voted." But, in that case, the scenario is difficult to imagine: the law would seek to punish someone who, during a nondemocratic regime, (allegedly) voted for an individual's execution despite the fact that he (i.e., the person who voted for the execution) was subsequently acquitted in a trial held (almost certainly) under the reinstated democracy. Despite its difficulty, Maffi (2005: 154) suggests such an interpretation. Frisch restores the text differently: ἐὰν τὴν|δίκ[ην μὴ νικήσηι, ψῆφον πρ]οσθέμενος. In this case one might translate, "If he did not prevail at trial, although having voted to kill [the defendant]." This makes sense, especially when the following ὥστε ἀποκτεῖναι is recognized as a potential result clause, bordering on a purpose clause. Thus the law would seek to punish an individual—Frisch argues just the accuser (Ankläger)—who voted for an individual to be executed even if that individual was not actually executed. This interpretation (accepted by Koch [1996: 59–60] and Dössel [2003: 214]), however, likely should be rejected. First, later in the law (lines 157–58, 163–64) "to prevail in a trial" uses the dative, not the accusative: ἐὰν δίκηι νικᾶται. Second, the following stipulation that a "murder may not be atoned for" seems to suggest that both protases (i.e., "if clauses") contained in section 9 refer to a situation where an individual was, indeed, executed.

45   It is to be noted that the text printed here accepts the standard emendation of ἐπιγαμία⟨ι⟩ς (i.e., it does not accept ἐπιγαμίας which is inscribed on the stone). Frisch (1975: 77) does not accept that emendation and takes ἐπιγαμίας to be accusative plural and the subject of the infinitive μὴ καταλλάσ[σεσ]θαι. He thus translates, "Einen Mord sollen die Familien nicht versöhnend beilegen, auch nicht mit Geld." But it is easy to believe that the engraver made a simple mistake (as he did in lines 53–54, where he used accusatives where genitives are clearly required). And ἐπιγαμία in the plural means intermarriage (*LSJ* s.v. IIb). I thus conclude that both nouns were supposed to be datives of instrument and the infinitive is passive (*LSJ* s.v. καταλλάσσω II.2).

46   Compare the massacre of the Eleusinians during the time of the Thirty (Xen. *Hell.* 2.4.8–

included in this provision, however, might convince such individuals not to follow the lead of the more hardcore regime members. And that might prevent a cascade of votes in support of the execution.

SHAM ELECTIONS

Provision 11 addresses the possibility that someone, "during an oligarchy" (ἐν ὀλιγαρχίαι), might participate in a sham political processes (literally, misuse the laws) in order to make it look like he became a magistrate or councilmember "during a democracy" (ὡς ἐν δημοκρατίαι). Should someone do that, his selection is invalid and he may be treated as a leader of an oligarchy—that is, he may be assassinated. There appear to be two possible imagined scenarios, depending on what "during an oligarchy" means.

In perhaps the most likely scenario, Ilion is obviously ruled by an oligarchy when the fraud takes place: "during an oligarchy" is thus stating the acknowledged political reality. In this situation an individual might manipulate the laws to make it look like the regime is liberalizing or somehow becoming more democratic. To accomplish that, someone might remove other candidates' "names from the hat" (technically, remove their *pinakia* from the *kleroterion*—or the Ilian analog thereof); lie about the selection results; bribe or use force to convince other people not to seek the office. In any case, he is working to maintain the status quo, while apparently participating in a fully democratic process.

Another possible scenario is that Ilion is a democracy when the fraud takes place: "during an oligarchy" is thus stating the postfraud political reality.[47] In this situation an individual might manipulate the laws in order to disguise a silent oligarchic coup. For example, he might somehow convince the people to change the laws, thus allowing him to serve multiple terms in office.

The Ilians clearly crafted provision 10 in order to prevent anti-democrats from deceiving the population about the real nature of the ruling regime. This provision ensures that the people of Ilion will be aware of such tricks—that they will realize that "democracy in form" does not equal "democracy in substance." And they warn anybody who might engage in such deceptive practices that he very well might be assassinated.

PARTICIPATION IN A REVOLT IN ANY CAPACITY

Provision 12 addresses, very generally, anybody who participates in an anti-democratic coup in any capacity: a tyrant, a leader of an oligarchy, someone who sets up a tyrant, someone who joins in a revolt, or someone who over-

---

10). Kritias demanded that the vote—like that envisioned in this provision—be open. Thus everybody's hands would be bloody.

47   This basic interpretation is favored by Maffi (2005: 157–58).

throws the democracy. Such individuals will incur a "memory sanction" (often referred to as *damnatio memoriae*).[48] Specifically, the law states that their names must be chiseled off priest lists, votive offerings, and tombstones. No further directions are given for names engraved on a tombstone: they would simply be chiseled off, it seems. If an offender's name is on a priest list, that spot—after chiseling off the name—will be sold, presumably to the highest bidder. And the spot's new "owner" may engrave the name of anybody he wants, provided that that individual is (or was?) eligible to serve as priest. If an offender's name is on a votive offering, the nature of the sanction depends on the type of votive. There are two possibilities.

- It is a private votive offering—that is, one dedicated solely by the offender. In that case, the *dēmos* must ensure, first, that there will be no indication that it was, in fact, dedicated by the offender. It thus appears that the votive will still stand; perhaps the *dēmos* would rededicate it. The law also states that the *dēmos* must ensure that there is no *mnēmeion*. This is difficult to interpret since the word can mean "memory," "monument," and "record." I have chosen to translate the word as "record." Thus the people of Ilion must ensure not only that the offender's name is removed from the votive but also that there is no record of any kind that the offender made such a dedication.[49]
- It is a public votive offering that is also inscribed with the names of non-offenders. In this case the *dēmos* must ensure that only the offender's name is chiseled off. Thus, the votive offering itself will remain.

The most obvious function of the memory sanction was to ensure that the people of Ilion would permanently forget that the anti-democratic revolutionaries ever existed.[50] It is tempting to take that line of reasoning one step

48 I borrow the term "memory sanction" from Flower (2006). Memory sanctions appear to have been somewhat uncommon in the ancient Greek world. Well-known Athenian examples are these: against Hipparchos, sometime after his ostracism of 487 (Lykourg. *Leok.* 117–19); against Philip V in 200 (Livy 31.44.4); against Peisistratos, the son of Hippias, whereby the *dēmos* "effaced the inscription" (ἠφάνισε τοὐπίγραμμα: Thuc. 6.54.7) of the altar to the twelve gods; as indicted by his altar to Apollo, that altar would have contained his name. One might also note that the Amphipolitans, in 422, obliterated (ἀφανίσαντες) anything that reminded them of Hagnon (Thuc. 5.11.1). It is interesting to note that a local dynast's sarcophagus from Çan (midway between Ilion and Daskyleion) that dates to the first half of the fourth century might contain evidence of a memory sanction: the figure of an individual has been chiseled out. It is thus quite possible that the Ilians were drawing on a local Persian practice. For the sarcophagus, see Sevinç et al. (2001). That memory sanctions were a Persian practice: Sevinç et al. (2001: 395n50). The article does not mention the Ilian tyrant-killing law.

49 *IJG* (II: 33) translates *mnēmeion* as "monument." Friedel (1937: 93) translates it as "Erinnerungszeichen." Frisch (1975: 70) translates it as "Erinnerung." Dössel (2003: 204) translates it as "Gegenstand des Erinnerns."

50 Dössel (2003: 218) contrasts this with the Athenian pro-democrats' practice to publicly record the name of anti-democratic revolutionaries. She cites Andok. *Myst.* 78.

further and conclude that the implementation of the sanction would also facilitate the Ilians' collective effort both to "forget" about their troubled past and to forge a present as a unified, successful, democratically governed polis. But that is likely only half true. On the one hand, the people of Ilion would, over time, perhaps forget the exact identity of those who participated in an anti-democratic coup d'état. Yet, on the other hand, the chiseled-off names would be a constant reminder that there had been a coup and that one must be vigilant in order to prevent another one.

THIRD SECTION

The third extant section of the law (provisions 14–17)[51] addresses the dispensation of honors and financial compensation to those who "contributed or spent money" (εἰσενέγκας ἤ ἀναλώσας) in an effort to overthrow a non-democratic regime and reestablish the democracy.[52] It is clear, and was perhaps explicitly articulated in a lost (early) section of the law, that the magistrates, after the democracy is reestablished, were required both to return to such men the money they contributed and to ensure that (1) their generosity is announced in the Great Dionysia; (2) they received an honorary crown; (3) they are officially recorded as benefactors of Ilion. The extant provisions of this section focus on four contingencies that might arise in those matters.

Provision 14 addresses the possibility that the archons do not ensure that deserving individuals are correctly compensated and honored. Should that occur, there are, first, fines: each archon must pay a fine of thirty staters; each member of the boulē must pay a fine of ten staters; the treasurer must pay a fine of one hundred staters. In addition to fines, the archons, the members of the boulē, the treasurer, and the members of the special boards (τοῖς ἐνεστῶσιν ἀρχείοις) shall be without rights (atimoi) until such matters are settled.[53]

Provision 15 addresses the possibility that an individual is improperly compensated after the restoration of the democracy. The provision articu-

---

51 Nothing can be said about provision 13 other than that it is part of the law's second section (i.e., it addressed matters that occurred while the democracy is overthrown: thus the provision begins ἐάν τις ἐπὶ τυράννου ἤ ὀλ[ι]γαρχίας).

52 As Koch notes (1996: 61), the possibilities are endless: individuals could hire mercenaries, bribe people in the regime to act against the regime, etc. Recall the inscription from Erythrai (*I. Erythrai* 21), discussed in the section in chapter 5 titled "Erection of the Statue in Wake of Alexander's Conquest," that records honors for Phanes because he (line 7) χρήματά τε ἐσήν[ε]γκεν ἄτοκα. That money, as noted, was used both to help overthrow a nondemocratic regime and to ensure the permanence of the new, democratic regime.

53 It is unclear what these "special boards"—the translation provided by *LSJ* s.v. ἀρχεῖον II— were. Note that I take τὰ ἐπίτιμα ταὐτὰ εἶναι (line 148) to refer soley to the penalty of *atimia* articulated in lines 140–44, not both to the penalty of *atimia* and (somehow) to the fines articulated in lines 136–40.

lates three scenarios. First, someone is compensated despite the fact that he did not "contribute or spend money" to reestablish the democracy. Second, an individual "recovered what was not owed." Dittenberger (ad loc.) provided a plausible explanation for this perplexing scenario: somebody might make two successful claims for reimbursement—in which case he was "not owed" the second payment. Third, an individual recovers more than what is due. In all three cases, the guilty party must pay back twice the amount of money that he received, if he is convicted in court.

Provision 16 addresses the possibility that someone does not properly spend money that a contributor gave him. Specifically, the provision targets, first, those who do not spend the money to reestablish the democracy. And, second, it targets those who do not demonstrate that they spent the money in order to reestablish the democracy. In both cases, the guilty party must pay back double the amount he received, if convicted in court. It is quite likely, but not certain, that he would pay the fine to the individual who gave him the money initially.

Provision 17 addresses those guilty of breaking provisions 15. That is, it targets (1) anybody who is compensated although he did not contribute or spend money according to the law; (2) anybody who recovered what was not owed; (3) anybody who recovered more than what was owed. Those individuals shall not be crowned or inscribed as benefactors.

The third extant section seeks to accomplish three objectives. The first objective is to arrange for an orderly dispensation of rewards and honors after the refoundation of the democracy. The issue is potentially problematic. Without clear guidelines, for example, there can be confusion with regard to both which individuals deserve rewards and what those rewards should be. Also, people might try to become famous by falsely claiming to have participated in the liberation movement. The Athenians famously experienced both of those problems in the last decade of the fifth century: after the fall of the Four Hundred and after the fall of the Thirty.[54] The second objective is to ensure that the articulated rewards are perceived as credible—to ensure, that is, that everybody believes that, should he "contribute or spend money" to help overthrow a nondemocratic regime, he will be rewarded as promised. To accomplish that, the Ilians vowed to punish harshly both magistrates who do not provide the rewards and individuals who try to acquire rewards that they do not deserve. The third objective—and closely related to the second—

---

54 For the difficulties surrounding the honoring of those involved in the assassination of Phrynichos, see *ML* 85. For the difficulties surrounding the honoring of those involved in the overthrow of the Thirty, see the comments in *RO* 4. Friedel (1937: 97) concluded that the final provisions of the Ilian anti-tyranny law indicate that the Ilians had experienced a serious decline in civic morality. If that is the case, the Ilians nevertheless expected behavior like that found in late-fifth-century Athens.

is to assure potential contributors that any money that they might contribute would actually be spent to reestablish the democracy: if it were not, the person to whom they gave the money would have to pay back twice the money he received—likely to the initial contributor himself.

Historical Context

CIRCUMSTANCES WHEN PROMULGATED

It is difficult to construct the historical context within which the people of Ilion promulgated their tyrant-killing law. To begin with, the law does not refer to known people or historical events: it does not, for example, contain an archon date (vel sim.) like the law of Eukrates or refer to Alexander like the dossier from Eresos. Much more fundamentally problematic, however, is the fact that we know very little about Ilion's internal history during the Classical and early Hellenistic periods. Archaeologists have certainly shed important light on Ilion's domestic history through their analysis of the city's material culture. Work published in the journal *Studia Troica*, in particular, has laid the foundation for all subsequent historical analyses of Classical and Hellenistic Ilion. And the epigraphic and literary sources occasionally provide important information. But the gaps in our knowledge are still frustrating and, at times, paradoxical: there is no direct evidence for a tyranny at Ilion during the Hellenistic period, yet it is from Hellenistic Ilion that we have the most detailed tyrant-killing law.

Despite these difficulties, the comments presented in this section argue that the people of Ilion promulgated their tyrant-killing law circa 280, after having overthrown a nondemocratic regime that was in power sometime during the reign of Lysimachos. This is, admittedly, not an original thesis (although not every scholar agrees with it). But I defend it more thoroughly than it is defended elsewhere. I demonstrate, first, that internal evidence— evidence provided, that is, by the inscribed law itself—supports the thesis. I then demonstrate that external evidence also supports the thesis. Certainty is impossible. But the combined weight of both the internal and external evidence does make a reasonably solid case.

The law's language in lines 144–49 provides compelling internal evidence that, at the time of the law's promulgation, the people of Ilion had recently overthrown a nondemocratic regime. The law states, "and there shall be access always to the magistrates and the standing council—and this shall be [permissible] during the present year (ἔστω τοῦτο πρῶτον ἔτος)—and the penalty shall be the same for the members of the standing special boards." That stipulation, it will be recalled, addressed the possibility that the archons might not reward individuals who financially contributed to the successful overthrow of a nondemocratic regime. The relevant clause, of course, is "and this shall be [permissible] during the present year."[55] Funck (1994: 335) suggests that the Ilians inserted that clause in order to articulate the well-known legal principle that a law takes effect immediately after it is promulgated. But that just begs a question: why state a well-known principle? It is much more likely that the Ilians inserted the clause in order to ensure that people who contributed to the *recent* overthrow of a nondemocratic regime would be compensated.[56]

Additional internal evidence is provided by the inscription's letterforms. Brueckner noted in his editio princeps (1894: 468–69) that the inscription's lettering is similar to that found in *OGIS* 221, an inscription from Ilion that likely dates to the early 270s (or 280–260). This observation has found widespread acceptance.[57] But letterforms are not always a reliable indicator of an inscription's date. One might cite *OGIS* 219—a decree from Ilion honoring "King Antiochos, son of Seleukos"—as an example: it has been dated as early as circa 280 and as late as 197/6.[58] Thus the letterforms merely indicate that the Ilians *possibly* inscribed their tyrant-killing law circa 280.

Internal evidence thus suggests that the Ilians might have promulgated their tyrant-killing law circa 280, after having overthrown a nondemocratic regime. And that implies that the nondemocratic regime was in power sometime during the reign of Lysimachos. Several external points corroborate that preliminary finding.

---

55   Friedel (1937: 96): "und diese Bestimmungen sollen das erste Jahr lang gelten." Frisch (1975: 70): "und diese Regelung soll mit diesem Jahr in Kraft tretten." *IJG* (II: 35): "Il en sera ainsi dès la présente année." Dössel (2003: 205): "und es soll dies das erste Jahr sein."

56   It should be noted that Frisch concluded that lines 158–62 (i.e., provision 16) also indicate that the Ilians experienced a tyranny before they promulgated their anti-tyranny law: "And whoever receives [money] from them and does not spend it so that democracy is established, or whoever holding [money acquired] from them does not reveal the expenditures for those matters, he shall pay back double of what he received if convicted in court." Frisch (1975: 71) argues that it would be foolish to enact such a provision governing future efforts against a nondemocratic regime because doing so would practically force those who accepted money in good faith to spend it immediately, lest they still hold the money when the tyranny is overthrown. This is not an unreasonable suggestion. But it is perhaps more likely that Frisch has identified an unintended consequence. Also, Lund (1992: 121) suggests that the frequent use of imperatives in the law's final section might suggest that the Ilians had overthrown a nondemocratic regime.

Scholars who believe that there was a tyranny in Ilion before the promulgation of the Ilian anti-tyranny law: *IJG* (II: pp. 36–37), Friedel (1937: 83), Frisch (1975: 71–72), and Dössel (2003: 205–6). Scholars who have concluded that the Ilians might not have experienced a tyranny before they promulgated their anti-tyranny law: Dittenberger (*OGIS* 218); Magie (1950: 924–25n19); Funck (1994: 320). Koch (1996: 42–45) and Berve (1967: 422) are rather noncommittal. Maffi (2005: 141) suggests that the law was likely inspired by recent events in Ilion, but states that the nature of those events is unknowable.

57   See Dittenberger's description of the letterforms at the introduction to his commentary on the text. Berve (1967: 419), Friedel (1937: 83), *IJG* (II: 37), Funck (1994), and Koch (1996: 41) accept a post-Kouroupedion date.

58   For the arguments on the date of *OGIS* 219, see Ma (2000: 254–59).

Some corroboration is provided by the apparent fact that the people of Ilion did not enjoy Lysimachos's reign. One might note, first, the fact that the *dēmos* exuberantly honored Seleukos I after he defeated Lysimachos at Kouroupedion and subsequently took control of the Troad. The decree (*I. Ilion* 31) is fragmentary, but the apparent sentiment is fully evident: the *dēmos* decreed to build an altar inscribed with his name on it and placed in the agora; a month was named after him; and festivals and sacrifices were to be held in his honor. It is certainly possible, of course, that such honors did not reflect genuine enthusiasm for the Troad's new political order. And it is also possible that the people of Ilion were angry with Lysimachos not because he supported a tyrant but because he favored Alexandria Troas over their own polis.[59] To counter both of those objections, note that *I. Ilion* 1 (lines 24–26) refers to an embassy sent by the koinon of Athena Ilias to Antigonos "concerning the freedom and autonomy of the cities sharing in the temple and festal assembly" (ὑ[πὲρ]|τῆς ἐλευθερίας καὶ αὐτονομίας τῶν πόλεων τῶν κοινωνουσ[ῶν τοῦ]|ἱεροῦ καὶ τῆς πανηγύρεως). Billows has reasonably suggested (1990: 219) that this embassy was sent in 302, when Lysimachos and, later, his general Prepelaos ravaged various poleis in the Troad: Lysimachos besieged and subsequently garrisoned Sigeum; Prepelaos besieged Abydos, a polis in the Ilian koinon (Diod. Sic. 20.107). At that time (i.e., 302), the democrats of Ilion likely suspected that, were Lysimachos to gain control of the Troad, they would lose their freedom. And that is conceivably what happened.[60]

Additional corroboration is provided by the fact that a new democratic political order was established in Ilion after the battle of Kouroupedion. The evidence for that assertion is entirely epigraphic. There are only two extant, nonfragmentary inscriptions that carry public decrees from Ilion that antedate that battle (*I. Ilion* 23 [circa 359] and 24 [circa 300]). Both record honorary decrees and neither refers to the *dēmos*; they both refer, instead, to the "Ilians."[61] There are several extant inscriptions that date to the years immedi-

---

59   In a well-known passage, Strabo (13.1.26) appears to state that Lysimachos was Ilion's benefactor: he built a temple and extensive city walls, and transferred to it several of the surrounding towns. But Strabo was quite likely referring to Alexandria Troas, not to Ilion. See Rose (2003: 31–35).

60   Billow's suggestion is strengthened by the fact that Demetrios (the son of Antigonos) sent forces to relieve the people of Abydos (Diod. Sic. 20.107.3). It is also worth pointing out that the decree praising Seleukos (*I. Ilion* 31) is fragmentary and might have noted the liberation of Ilion. Note that *I. Ilion* 18, a decree of the Ilian koinon (ca. 300), refers (line 7) to a military context. It is possible that it could be tied to the difficulties of 302. On Prepelaos's campaign of 302, see Magie (1950: 89, 916–17nn2–3).

61   Note, however, that *I. Ilion* 66 (a fragment of an honorary decree) possibly dates circa 300 since its lettering is nearly identical to *I. Ilion* 24. The word *dēmos* is restored in the former (line 8). It is possible that both inscriptions date to the pre-Ipsos period. Perhaps they should be associated with the resistance to the ravaging of the Troad by Lysimachos and his general Prepelaos. Note, too,

ately after that battle, however. And all refer to the *dēmos*, and most include the motion formula "be it resolved by the *boulē* and *dēmos*" (δεδόχθαι τῆι βουλῆι καὶ τῶι δήμωι).[62]

A final corroborating point is that there were several anti-tyranny movements in and around Asia Minor after the battle of Kouroupedion. Such was the case in Erythrai, as chapter 5 demonstrated. Also, an interesting fragment of a plausibly contemporary inscription from Nisyros (*Syll.*[3] 1220) is possibly part of an anti-tyranny law. And, after the battle of Kouroupedion, the residents of Herakleia Pontica destroyed the citadel walls of the tyrant Klearchos, who had been installed in power by Lysimachos.[63] It thus appears that a wave of anti-tyranny activity swept through much of the region after Lysimachos's death. Seleukos might have promoted that.[64]

The previous comments support a brief historical reconstruction. A nondemocratic regime came to power in Ilion sometime during the reign of Lysimachos. During that time the people of Ilion watched Alexandria Troas prosper, while their own hopes for economic improvement were dashed; there are no known building projects in Ilion that date to this period. But the dynamic changed after the battle of Kouroupedion: the pro-democrats, perhaps with outside help, rallied and took control of the city, overthrowing the

---

that there are no extant inscriptions from Ilion that securely date to the reign of Lysimachos. *I. Ilion* 66 and 24 possibly do (if dated post-Ipsos). But the aforementioned pre-Ipsos scenario is more likely. Kent Rigsby (2007: 43–44) suggests that a newly found inscription that records an oath of synoecism between Ilion and Kokylion likely dates to the first half of the third century and might date to the reign of Lysimachos. Friedel (1937: 83n157) suggests that the lack of inscriptions dating to the period of Lysimachos's rule might be attributed to the "damnatio memoriae" provisions in the tyrant-killing law (i.e., provision 12).

62 There are four relevant inscriptions (numbers refer to *I. Ilion*): 31 (281, refers to the *dēmos*; it is very fragmentary and almost certainly contained the democratic motion formula); 32 (ca. 280, refers to *dēmos* and contains the motion formula, lines 19–20); 33 (ca. 274, refers to *dēmos* but, since it records letters written about and to Ilion, does not contain the motion formula); 34 (ca. 275–269, refers to the *dēmos* and contains the motion formula, lines 8–9). And one might also include *I. Ilion* 40. It records an honorary decree of the Ilion *dēmos* that contains the full motion formula (lines 6–7) and is dated to the third century, perhaps the first half of the century. The change of language in Ilian decrees after circa 280 is clearly demonstrated by a comparison between *I. Ilion* 23 (recording an honorary decree dated ca. 359) and *I. Ilion* 34 (an honorary decree dated 275–269). *I. Ilion* 23 reads, Ἰλιεῖς ἔδοσαν . . . προξενίαν καὶ εὐεργεσίαν. *I. Ilion* 34 reads, δεδόχθαι τῆι βουλῆι καὶ τῶι δήμωι . . . εἶναι δὲ αὐτὸν καὶ πρόξενον καὶ εὐεργέτην τῆς πόλεως.

63 Burstein (1976: 87). Note that *I. Ephesos* 1377 is likely an anti-tyranny law. It is dated to "4th/3rd c." Also, sometime during the first half of the third century, each citizen of Kalymna swore "I will establish neither oligarchy or tyranny nor any other regime other than democracy" (ὀλιγαρχίαν δὲ οὐδὲ τύραννον οὐδὲ ἄλλο πολίτευμα ἔξω δαμο|κρατίας οὐ καταστάσω) (Tit. Calymnii Test. XII, lines 21–22).

64 Funck (1994) argues that the Ilian tyrant-killing law was promulgated pursuant to Seleukid royal policy aimed at gaining the loyalty of Ilion ("ein Meisterstück seleukidischer Städtepolitik": p. 320). This is certainly possible but, because of the state of the evidence, speculative.

supporters of the nondemocratic regime. They then promulgated their tyrant-killing law in order to defend their own, reestablished regime.[65]

THE TYRANNICAL THREAT

In this section, I identify the nature of the tyrannical threat that confronted the people of Ilion. What, in particular, were the people of Ilion worried about? As noted above, we know very little about Ilion's domestic political history during the Hellenistic period. We do have, however, an elaborate tyrant-killing law that the people of Ilion promulgated in order to prevent anti-democrats from maintaining a nondemocratic regime. And a careful reading of that law provides at least a general answer to a couple of important questions. First, what is the basic profile of the expected tyrant or "leader of an oligarchy"? Second, how were such anti-democrats expected to maintain control of the polis?

WHO?

Two of the law's provisions suggest that the people of Ilion expected the would-be tyrant to be a wealthy local or regional military man. Provision 4 of the Ilion tyrant-killing law incentivized "fellow soldiers" (*sustratiōtai*) to kill the tyrant—the prefix *sun* [*sus* here] meaning "fellow." *Stratiōtai* can refer to both soldiers in general or hired mercenaries more particularly.[66] In the above analysis of the law, I suggested that this provision particularly addressed mercenary soldiers. Thus the Ilians possibly imagined the potential tyrant to be or to have been a mercenary and thus have "fellow mercenaries." (And it will be recalled from the opening of this chapter that Chares and Charidemos, two of Ilion's tyrants during the fourth century, were mercenary generals.) But it is also possible that the Ilian pro-democrats used the word *stratiōtai* in the law because it is more general and would thus include both run-of-the-mill mercenaries (commonly called μισθοφόροι) and more elite soldiers in the tyrant's inner circle (i.e., his *hetairoi*). In both cases, however, the Ilians imagined the tyrant to be a military man, as opposed, for example, to a banker (like Euboulos of Bithynia) or a philosopher (like Hermias, Euboulos's successor), both tyrants of nearby Atarneus, or a historian (like Douris, the tyrant of Samos).

The second relevant provision is number 12, the "memory sanction" provision. It required that the inscribed names of prominent members of an

---

65 Koch (1996: 43–44) suggests that the Ilian democrats might have crafted their tyrant-killing law while in exile. *IJG* (II: 37) refers to the law as a loi révolutionnaire (which accounts for its sloppiness and apparent lack of order).

66 Note the agreement between Eumenes I and his mercenaries (*OGIS* 266). In line 2, we learn that the mercenaries were called *stratiōtai* and were stationed at Philetaireia (base of Mount Ida—to protect the northern boarder) and Attaleia (near the source of the Kaïkos river—to protect the eastern boarder).

anti-democratic regime be erased from tombstones, the priest lists, and offerings in the temple of Athena. The people of Ilion thus imagined that a future tyrant might be (or have been) a priest and had likely dedicated offerings in the temple of Athena. A priest would have been a wealthy and prominent man: the tyrant-killing law itself indicates (line 123) that not all individuals were qualified to be priests and, as is well known, in Hellenistic Asia Minor priesthoods were often sold to the highest bidder.[67] Individuals from both Ilion and the wider Troad, however, dedicated offerings in Ilion's temple of Athena. Andrea Berlin (2002) has demonstrated that, beginning already in the mid fourth century, regional powers dedicated offerings in the temple of Athena in order to advance their political objectives.

The political history of the Troad and its immediate environs supports the basic profile derived from the law's provisions. As noted in the beginning of this chapter, regional strongmen, dynasts, dominated Ilion throughout much of the Classical period. And as evidenced by several examples, such was the case for the region in the late Classical and early Hellenistic periods. One might note, for example, the aforementioned Hermias, tyrant of Atarneus. An inscription (*RO* 68) repeatedly refers to his *hetairoi* ("companions," lines 1–2, 10–11, 13, 15, 20–21, 24): they likely commanded garrisons in the towns under his regional control.[68] The descendants of exiled Spartans and Eretrians who assisted the Persians at the time of the Persian Wars controlled small cities in the Kaïkos valley, even issuing coinage, into the mid fourth century.[69] The sarcophagus from Çan discussed above (note 48) quite likely belonged to a fourth century Anatolian dynast. In circa 275, Aristodikides of Assos (a "friend" of Antiochos I) was strong enough to successfully request that the king give him 8,000 plethra (2,000 hectares) of land—and, importantly, he added it to the city of Ilion (*I. Ilion* 33 = *RC* 10–13). And most famously, the Attalid Kingdom was essentially founded in 283, when Philetairos started ruling as a dynast—and allied with Seleukos—rather than as Lysimachos's subordinate.[70] Further examples could be cited.[71]

67 See *I. Erythrai* 201 (and commentary) for an elaborate example of this phenomenon: over fifty priesthoods are listed. It dates to the first half of the third century.

68 This was suggested at least as early as Hicks and Hill (1901: 266).

69 See Magie (1950: 725n2). King Demaratos and his descendants (the Demaratidae) controlled Teuthrania and Halisarna: Xen. *Hell.* 3.1.6; Xen. *Anab.* 2.1.3, 7.8.17; cf. Hdt. 6.67–70. The Eretrian Gongylos and his descendants (the Gongylidae) controlled Gambrion, Palaigambrion, Myrina, and Gryneion: Xen. *Hell.* 3.1.6; cf. Thuc. 1.128.6f and Diod. Sic. 11.44.3. It would appear that the Gongylidae controlled Pergamum in the early fourth century (Xen. *Anab.* 7.8.8), but it is not certain. See, too, McShane (1964: 16).

70 Paus. 1.10.4; Strabo 13.4.1; see McShane (1964: 30–31). The independence of Pergamum was solidified militarily, when Eumenes, shortly after inheriting control of Pergamum in 263/2, defeated Antiochos II in a battle near Sardeis. See Magie (1950: 733n16).

71 Although not explicitly referring to the Troad—but the Troad would no doubt have been included—Seleukos II "wrote to the kings, dynasts, cities, and leagues" requesting that they con-

Thus the tyrannical threat confronting the Ilians after the battle of Kouroupedion was similar in nature to that which confronted them for over a century: regional strongmen or dynasts. Such men likely sought to control as many communities as they could, perhaps with the acquiescence of larger powers—like, for example, the Dardanian dynasts under the Satrap of Phrygia or Philetairos under Lysimachos—perhaps not. And it is certainly possible that there were a greater number of opportunities for such men to make power grabs in the aftermath of Kouroupedion: the Seleukids needed to consolidate their control; the Gauls were causing havoc.[72] The region was at risk of splintering into a number of fiefdoms.

HOW MAINTAIN POWER?

Analysis of the tyrant-killing law suggests that the members of Ilion's nondemocratic regime were expected to implement a rather straightforward, yet comprehensive regime-preservation plan. The first part of the plan was to take money or property from the people of Ilion. Four of the law's seventeen extant provisions reflect this concern. The Ilians crafted provision 5, it will be recalled, to facilitate efforts to recoup property that had been confiscated by financial magistrates or taxing officials. Provisions 6 and 7 explicitly seek to prevent anti-democrats or their supporters from handling "the *dēmos's* money" (*chrēmata dēmosia*). And, as noted above, the clear implication behind provision 10 is that anti-democrats might force somebody to sell something, presumably at a low price.

The second part of the anticipated plan was to pay people—with, at least in part, the extracted money or property—to support the nondemocratic regime. Anti-democrats would be expected to purchase mercenary soldiers, of course. That is not stated in the tyrant-killing law. But it does refer to the tyrant's *stratiōtai* (lines 46–47). And, as noted above, that word simply means soldiers, but it can certainly mean mercenary soldiers. In addition, in Greek political culture, there was a strong connection between tyrants, mercenaries, and taxes.[73] The Spartan tyrant Nabis, for example, reportedly taxed his subjects harshly in order to pay for mercenaries, giving the pretext of an Achaean threat as justification (Polyb. 13.7). And, more generally, Xenophon's Hiero bemoans the fact that tyrants must extract money from the citizens to pay for mercenaries (*Hier.* 8.9–10).

---

sider the temple of Aphrodite Stratonikē to be inviolable (*asylon*) and Smyrna to be sacred and inviolable (*OGIS* 229 line 11). According to Thucydides (1.138.5–6), Themistocles ruled (ἦρχε) Magnesia on the Maiander, Lampsakos, and Myous. Themistocles issued personal coinage in Magnesia: Gardner (1913: 165).

72 According to Strabo (13.1.27), the Gauls briefly occupied Ilion.

73 For an interesting analysis of the codependency between mercenaries and tyrants, see Polyb. 11.13.3–8. See also Xen. *Hier.* 4.9 (and passim).

In addition to mercenaries, the Ilian democrats apparently expected the members of the nondemocratic regime to purchase political support with public money. Even the most oppressive regimes require some citizen support, people with a vested interest in maintaining the status quo. And regimes acquire that support, in large part, by offering money and status. Three of the law's provisions (5, 7, 10) thus represent attempts to prevent the creation of such an elite.

The final part of the anticipated regime-preservation plan was to induce an "anti-mobilization" threshold among the population through a combination of both intimidation and deception. The use of mercenary soldiers would be the most obvious element of the intimidation campaign. Their presence alone would send a clear message to democrats that the regime is well guarded and that any uprising will be forcefully repressed. If people thought that other people thought that, the average individual would require a prohibitively high percentage of the population to mobilize in defense of the democracy before he would do so too. In addition to such explicitly military functions, however, mercenary soldiers could serve (inter alia) as spies or assassins.[74] Nikokles, the tyrant of Sikyon, for example, reportedly sent hired agents to spy on Aratos while he was in exile in Argos (Plut. *Arat.* 6.4–5). And Nabis reportedly (Polyb. 13.6) sent mercenaries (μισθοφόροι) to hunt down and kill his political enemies.

Provision 8 suggests that anti-democrats might also use the law courts (*dikasteria*) to intimidate the population. The feared dynamic might have been similar to what Aristophanes parodied of later-fifth-century Athens: demagogues, in an effort to both ingratiate themselves with the members of the regime and make financial gain, recklessly indict individuals for purportedly "treasonous" behavior.[75] And because tyrants are notoriously and understandably paranoid, that dynamic might have been quite pronounced in a tyrannical regime.[76] An informal and self-sustaining spy system would emerge.

The use of special tribunals to issue death sentences is the final element of an intimidation campaign reflected in the law. This is similar to the use of the courts. But there is an important difference: with special tribunals, regime members both issue the indictment and render the verdict. There is no need

---

74   It is also worth noting that Thrasyboulos (tyrant of Miletos) apparently advised Periandros (tyrant of Korinth) to assassinate the city's best men in order to maintain power. For the famous story, see Hdt. 5.92.

75   Aristophanes's comedies *Wasps* and *Knights* reveal this phenomenon. On the dynamic here noted, see Henderson (2003) and Ostwald (1986: 199–229).

76   The paranoia of tyrants was proverbial: "there is nothing more timorous than a tyrant" (Plut. *Arat.* 6.5). Writers of the Athenian dissent community also stressed that point: e.g., Xen. *Hier.* 5; Pl. *Resp.* 579 B–C.

for a lay accuser (who might not materialize). It is quite possible, then, that tribunals would be used (inter alia) to intimidate regime members—people whom "ordinary" citizens would be afraid to accuse. Also, this would ensure that dissenters would be punished even if no lay accuser came forward.

Provision 11 provides the evidence for a campaign of large-scale deception. That provision focused on the possibility that anti-democrats might disguise the nature of their regime, making it look like a democracy when it is, in fact, an oligarchy. The law specifically notes rigging the process of selection to the *boulē* or other magistracies as a means toward that end.[77] And we can assume that the anti-democrats would engage, at the same time, in pro-democracy lip service, such as what happened in Athens and Eretria.[78] If such machinations were conducted successfully, democrats might conclude, or think that others have concluded, that the ruling regime is democratic and thus legitimate. And since the democracy was new, the populace might have been somewhat naïve and thus more susceptible to sophisticated acts of deception.

It thus appears as though the people of Ilion were concerned that the anti-democratic regime would complete what might be called the "triad of non-democratic regime maintenance." First, take money. Second, use that money to purchase support. Third, atomize the population through intimidation and deception. Once all three parts are operative, the resulting dynamic reinforces itself in a vicious spiral: anti-democrats are better able to take more money; they purchase more and better support; they more effectively intimidate, deceive, and thus atomize the population. The people of Ilion likely had experience with that and sought to prevent it by promulgating their tyrant-killing law.

Effectiveness

I argue in this section that the promulgation of their tyrant-killing law actually helped the Ilian pro-democrats maintain their newly founded democratic regime. The argument is somewhat involved and is not—indeed cannot be—ironclad. But the validity of two subtheses makes a fairly strong case.

The first subthesis is that anti-democrats apparently were deterred from staging a coup after the promulgation of the tyrant-killing law. Support for that claim is provided, to begin with, by the likelihood that pro-democrats

---

77 Note that the rule of the Thirty was preceded by the rigging of the selection to the *boulē*; see Munn (2000: 207–9).

78 For such deceptive rhetoric in late-fifth-century Athens, see the section in chapter 1 titled "Coordination Problem." For concern over the use of deceptive rhetoric in Eretria, see the section in chapter 2 titled "First Particular Layer of Defense."

would have had a difficult time responding to a coup d'état, were nothing done to assist their efforts. As noted in the beginning of this chapter, various regional strongmen, Persians, and tyrants dominated Ilion from (at least) the end of the fifth century until Alexander's conquest. Ilion was apparently democratically governed from the late 330s until shortly after the battle of Ipsos in 301. But, as argued above, it fell to a tyrant sometime during the reign of Lysimachos. Thus, when the tyrant-killing law was promulgated, the Ilians had, for all intents and purposes, only about thirty years of experience with democracy; and, quite importantly, that period ended with a successful anti-democracy coup d'état. Consequently, pro-democrats lacked the trust and the experience needed to maintain a pro-mobilization threshold sequence. They were vulnerable.

Second, there likely were anti-democrats, local or regional, who wanted to overthrow Ilion's democracy after the promulgation of the tyrant-killing law. The fact that the Ilians promulgated their lengthy law is powerful evidence for the existence of such a threat: they thought that they were confronting a very serious and well-orchestrated opponent. And one must not forget that the Troad was still a very dangerous, volatile region in the early to mid-third century. In a letter to Meleagros (*I. Ilion* 33 = *RC* 10–13—dated 277), for example, Antiochos I decreed (lines 46–49) that the royal peasants (*basilikoi laoi*) be allowed to live on the land near Petra (a stronghold near Ilion) "because of the safety" that that stronghold provided. Anti-democrats, assuming they existed, might be expected to take advantage of such a dynamic.

Finally, democracy was Ilion's "normal" regime type after the promulgation of the tyrant-killing law. All extant inscriptions that date to the years after the battle of Kouroupedion and give some indication of regime type suggest that the *dēmos* controlled the polis.[79] There is, in addition, no literary evidence that suggests that a nondemocratic regime governed the polis. And it is worth pointing out that the Ilians modeled their important temple of Athena, built after the promulgation of the law, on the Athenian Parthenon: (1) it has carved figural metopes on all four sides—the only other such example in the eastern Mediterranean is the Parthenon; (2) one of the themes represented in the metopes is the Ilioupersis, a theme also represented on the

---

79 There are at least twenty-one relevant inscriptions that are more or less securely dated to the third century, yet after the tyrant-killing law: *I. Ilion* 31, 32, 33, 34, 35, 36, 40, 51, 61, 67 (third/second century), 38, 44, 202, 203, 204, 205 (third/second century), 207 (third/second century), 201 (early Hellenistic); Rigsby (2002), (2004), (2007). Eleven of those inscriptions suggest that the *dēmos* controlled the city: *I. Ilion* 31, 32, 33, 34, 35 (*dēmos* restored), 36, 40, 51, 61, 67; Rigsby (2002). Nine of the remaining ten are quite fragmentary and give no indication of the ruling regime: *I. Ilion* 38, 202, 203, 204, 205, 207, 201; Rigsby (2004), (2007). That leaves *I. Ilion* 44. But it is a private dedication of a woman from Pergamum, dated 209–205, to the gods in Samothrace on behalf of Ptolemy IV and his family; it would not be expected to indicate the nature of Ilion's regime.

Parthenon.[80] One might suppose, then, that the Ilians imitated the Athenian democratic *politeia* too.[81]

Although not directly relevant to the argument, one should note that the Ilians' material conditions improved in the decades following the promulgation of their tyrant-killing law. Improvement began under the early Seleukids, to which period we have evidence for an increase in trade and, for the first time, house building in the lower city.[82] And starting circa 250 the people of Ilion commenced a large-scale building program: fortification walls, a temple of Athena, a temnos portico with adjoining propylaia, a bouleuterion, restoration of the south side of the mound.[83] That might reflect a more dynamic, democratic political culture.[84]

The second subthesis is that the promulgation of the tyrant-killing law likely would have deterred anti-democrats from staging a coup. That is impossible to prove, of course. But I can demonstrate that, by promulgating the law, pro-democrats increased the likelihood that they would both successfully mobilize in defense of their regime and punish all who participated in the anti-democratic coup. And the greater the likelihood they could do that, the more likely anti-democrats would be deterred from staging a coup. As a consequence of promulgating their tyrant-killing law, the Ilian democrats significantly increased the probability that, should there be a coup d'état, they could mobilize in the defense of their regime. The spark plus bandwagon dynamic, as would be expected, is particularly significant. All members of the Ilian society, citizens, free foreigners, and slaves, were explicitly incentivized to commit tyrannicide. And, as noted in the discussion of the law's first section, by increasing the number of opportunities for assassination, Ilian pro-democrats increased the likelihood that there would

---

80   Also, the tribute of the Lokrian maidens was revived in the middle of the third century. That practice, as suggested by Rose (2003: 57), "functionally . . . parallels the office of the *arrhephoroi* on the Athenian acropolis." On Athens as the architectural model for Ilion, see Rose (2003).

81   Aylward and Wallrodt (2003: 96) also suggest that the people of Ilion followed the Athenian model in making the Acropolis the backdrop for their theater. And the koinon of Athena Ilias, founded, perhaps, in 310, appears to have looked to democratic Athens as its model: the festival of the Panathenaia was likely similar to the Athenian festival and the theater perhaps inspired by the Lykourgan-era example. See Rose (1992).

82   Lawall (1999: 215), Aylward (1999). Also, Antiochos II minted silver tetradrachms in Ilion (Magie [1950: 933n27]).

83   See Aylward (2005). Heirax held the Troad from 241 to 228. After he was defeated by Attalos, Ilion apparently entered into alliance with Attalos (Magie: 1950: 9).

84   The economic improvement is likely due to a better political equilibrium. Ober (2008: 13) writes: "because social cooperation produces economic value (as well as being valuable in nonmaterial ways), more cooperative and (in changing environments) more dynamically adaptive equilibria perform relatively well in economic terms." Compare this to Herodotos's famous explanation for the Athenians' prosperity after the overthrow of the Peisistratids (5.78). A similar dynamic might have been operative in Ilion after the overthrow of their nondemocratic regime circa 280.

be an assassination. Equally important, however, is the fact that, after the promulgation of the law, it would have been common knowledge that there was widespread commitment to defend the democracy. Promulgation of the law would have generated such knowledge, of course: the Ilians had a theater by 306 (*I. Ilion.* 1 line 10), and in a polis of Ilion's size, discussion and ratification of a law in such a setting would have generated deep common knowledge among the citizenry.[85] But it is also important to remember that the Ilians likely overthrew a tyranny shortly before they promulgated their law. Thus the credibility of their commitment to defend the democracy would have been virtually beyond doubt. As a result, individuals would lower their personal revolutionary thresholds and particularly brave individuals would lower theirs to 0. The Ilians thus would be defined by a pro-mobilization threshold sequence.

In addition to the all-important spark plus bandwagon dynamic, the promulgation of the law increased the likelihood that individuals would participate in a large-scale resistance movement, should that become necessary. There are two contributing factors. First, the tyrant-killing law explicitly incentivized wealthy individuals to contribute to such a movement and sought to ensure that those incentives were seen as credible (provisions 14–17).[86] Second, after the promulgation of the law, there was common knowledge of widespread credible commitment to defend the democracy. Thus wealthy individuals would be more likely to contribute because the movement likely would succeed; and other individuals—almost certainly including citizens of the poleis of the koinon[87]—would be even more likely to join because the movement would be adequately supplied or funded. And it is also worth pointing out that there are several examples of successful resistance movements in Greek history: the movement against the Thirty Tyrants succeeded

---

85   Ilion was a small polis: the city walls were 3.6 kilometers in length. For a discussion of the walls (built circa 250–220), see Aylward and Wallrodt (2003). On the population of Ilion in the first years of third century, Cook (1973: 100) suggests "about 5,000"—but the population soon increased significantly. The Ilians celebrated the Panathenaia by at least the end of the fourth century (*I. Ilion* 24 line 18; *I. Ilion* 1 lines 50–51). That festival would have performed the function of a "rational ritual." And it is important to note that many of Ilion's inscriptions—including the one engraved with the tyrant-killing law—were likely placed in the temple of Athena; thus attendees were encouraged to discuss politics. On the placement of inscriptions in the temple of Athena, see Rose (2003: 60–63).

86   In their resistance to the tyrant Hiero, the exiles of Priene sent *psephismata* to King Demetrios, Lysimachos, and the citizens of Rhodes (*I. Priene* 37 lines 73–77); that likely implies the sending of ambassadors to read them (cf. the fifth text in the dossier from Eresos). Lysias (in exile at Megara) provided funds and two hundred shields to help the democrats reclaim Athens during the reign of the Thirty Tyrants: Plut. *Mor.* 835f. Aratos hired mercenaries to help reclaim Sikyon (Plut. *Arat.* 6).

87   The citizens of other cities in the koinon would presumably be among the first foreigners to help the citizens of Ilion since all of the cities were quite closely bound. See the brief remarks about the koinon in Frisch (1975: xv).

(chapter 1); Eretrians, led by (the future tyrant) Kleitarchos, reclaimed their city (chapter 2); democrats of Priene reclaimed their city from the tyrant Hiero (*I. Priene* 37, 111–12); and Aratos led a successful movement to take back Sikyon from the tyrant Nikokles (Plut. *Arat.* 4–9).

In addition to increasing the likelihood that the democrats would reclaim control of the polis in the event of a coup, the promulgation of the tyrant-killing law made it clear that the pro-democrats, once they assume control of the polis, will punish anybody who benefited from or cooperated with the nondemocratic regime. If somebody benefited economically, he would lose more than he gained: thus provisions 5, 6, 7, and 10. If somebody used the courts (or participated in a special tribunal), he, too, would lose more than he gained: thus provisions 8 and 9. And anyone who participated in the coup in any way would be punished with a memory sanction: thus provision 12. In short, the democrats publically ruled out any possibility of an amnesty.

One might thus conclude that, by promulgating their tyrant-killing law, the Ilians deterred anti-democrats from staging a coup. First, the democrats will likely retake control of the polis and, in the process, kill many of those defending the nondemocratic regime. Second, once the democrats take control, they will punish everybody who was involved with or otherwise benefited from the nondemocratic regime. Anti-democrats would therefore conclude that, should they stage a coup, an insufficient number of people would follow them; they thus would choose not to defect. The result would be a stable democracy. And in the years after the promulgation of their law, the Ilian democracy was, in fact, stable and prosperous.

Conclusion

In the conclusion to chapter 4, I demonstrated that Alexander the Great heavily promoted anti-tyranny or tyrant-killing ideology during his conquest of western Asia Minor: he publicly referred to prominent members of cities' pro-Persian faction as "tyrants"; he issued an anti-tyranny proclamation after the battle of Gaugamela; he made known his intention to return to Athens the original statues of Harmodios and Aristogeiton. I now defend this much bolder thesis: the promulgation of anti-tyranny or tyrant-killing laws and decrees contributed significantly to the success of democracy in Hellenistic western Asia Minor. As would be expected, the argument in defense of that thesis is complex, consisting of several parts.

First, the citizens of several different poleis, dispersed widely in and around western Asia Minor, promulgated anti-tyranny or tyrant-killing laws or decrees during the first two generations of the Hellenistic period. The final three chapters of this book studied significant examples in Eresos, Erythrai, and Ilion. And, as noted in the introduction to this book, we must add a few more (mostly fragments) to that list.

- Ephesos (*I. Ephesos* 1377). This is a small fragment likely dated to the fourth or third century BCE—thus an early Hellenistic date is quite likely. That it is an anti-tyranny law is suggested by (1) ἤν τις ("if someone") in line 3; (2) ἢ τύραννον ("or a tyrant") in line 6.
- Priene (*I. Priene* 11). This is a decree of the *dēmos* establishing a Soteria festival after having overthrown a tyrant. The reference to the tyrant is restored by Robert (1944: 7–8) in line 11 (τ[ὸν τύραννον καὶ τοὺς στρατιώ|τ]ας [ἐκ]πεσεῖν [ἐ]κ τῆς πόλεως). The reference is almost certainly correct, in light of the fact that the people of Priene did suffer through the tyranny of Hiero. And Hiero is repeatedly referred to as ὁ τύραννος in a later decree of Priene (*I. Priene* 37).
- Mylasa (*I. Labraunda* 41). This is a very fragmentary decree (dated to the second half of the fourth century) that quite possibly concerns a democratic constitution. Line 2 reads [-]. τυρα[νν? .c.3.] ("tyra[nt" vel sim.). And line 4 reads [-δ]ικαζε[.c.5.] ("a]djudica[te").
- Olbia (Lebedev [1996], pp. 263–68). This inscription copies part of the epigram engraved on Harmodios and Aristogeiton's Athenian tomb. Lebedev noted that the lettering is virtually identical to *IOSPE* I² 160—a dedication of a statue to Zeus Eleutherius that dates to the first half of the third century. Lebedev prefers to date the inscribing of the tyrannicide epigram in Olbia, however, to the last third of the fourth century. The final two lines of the inscription read: [o]ἳ κτάνο[ν] ἄνδρα τύρα[ννον ἐλευεθερίην τ᾽ ἐσάωσαν]|πατρίδι καὶ λαοὺς αὀτ[ονόμους ἔθεσαν (vel ἐθέτην)] ("who killed the tyrant, preserved freedom for the fatherland, and made the people autonomous").
- Kalymna (Tit. Calymnii Test. XII). This inscription, dated to the first half of the third century, records a mass public oath to defend the democracy. They swore (lines 21–22) ὀλγαρχίαν δὲ οὐδὲ τύραννον οὐδὲ ἄλλο πολίτευμα ἔξω δαμο|κρατίας οὐ καταστάσω ("I will not establish an oligarchy and not a tyranny nor any other regime except democracy").
- Nisyros (*Syll.*³ 1220). This fragment, dated to the third century, forbids burials or the erection of any type of grave monuments for certain individuals. It is quite likely, as noted by Dittenberger, that this fragment is part of a tyrant-killing law.

Thus, if we include the enactments studied in the last three chapters of this book (i.e., from Eresos, Erythrai, and Ilion), there is evidence for anti-tyranny or tyrant-killing enactments promulgated in six different geographic regions during the early Hellenistic period: the northern Black Sea Area (Olbia), the eastern Aegean (Nisyros, Kalymna), Troas (Ilion), Lesbos (Eresos), Ionia (Erythrai, Priene, Ephesos), and Karia (Mylasa).[88] Such a distribution, by it-

88 One should also recall (from chapter 4) that the people of Nasos (an Aeolian city) promulgated a law against overthrowing the *damos* (τῷ νόμ[ω π]ερὶ τῶ καλλ[ύο]ντος τὸν δᾶ[μον]. The law

self, suggests that inscribed anti-tyranny proclamations were very popular in and around Asia Minor at that time. And when we include the fact that Alexander widely promoted anti-tyranny and tyrant-killing ideology during his conquest of Asia Minor, there can be little doubt about it.

Second, tyrant-killing legislation was effective in the three Asia Minor cases that we can fully analyze. I made the argument for Eresos, Erythrai, and Ilion in chapters 4, 5, and 6, respectively. In each case, it appears that, subsequent to the law's promulgation, anti-democrats were deterred from staging a coup d'état. There thus is no reason to suppose that tyrant-killing legislation, for some reason, would be ineffective in Asia Minor poleis.

Third, it is unlikely that tyrant-killing legislation would spread so widely in Asia Minor unless it was effective. This is just common sense: people and states adopt new technologies if they actually solve problems. The more effective the technology, the more likely it will spread, assuming, of course, that it is suitable and sufficiently publicized. The diffusion of hoplite warfare and the spread of coinage throughout the Greek world are prominent examples of this dynamic.

Finally, it appears that Ilian pro-democrats expected their tyrant-killing law to work. The key point here is that the law focuses so extensively—provisions 5 through 13—on punishing various activities that would take place while the democracy is overthrown. It is true that the law from Eretria articulates a punishment for anyone who does not help the *dēmos* regain control of the polis after a successful anti-democratic coup (new fragment, line 30 to end). But the law from Ilion goes much further, for example, by outlawing different types of financial transactions and prescribing different punishments for those who use the law court, depending on the trial's outcome. The detailed articulation in the law of what will be done once pro-democrats regain control of the polis strongly suggests that the Ilian pro-democrats believed that the promulgation of the law would facilitate their efforts to respond to a coup. Perhaps they knew that tyrant-killing legislation had been effective in other cities in Asia Minor.

Many factors contributed to the success of democracy in Hellenistic western Asia Minor. The ability of pro-democrats to mobilize in defense of their regime, however, was virtually a necessary condition for its survival. And the argument presented above demonstrated that Athenian-invented tyrant-killing law was both popular and effective in Asia Minor from the time of Alexander's conquest through the early years of the Hellenistic period. Any accounting for the success of what might be called Asia Minor's

is referred to in *OGIS* 4 (lines 106–10), an inscription dated 319–317. Also, an epigram celebrating Harmodios and Aristogeiton (and commemorating the Athenians' decision to build a grave monument for them) has been found in Chios. Trypanis (1960:70) suggests an inscribing date of late third or early second century, admittedly not during the "early" Hellenistic period.

"Hellenistic democratic revolution" must thus include the important role played by tyrant-killing law.

Finally, I would like to return to the conclusion of chapter 2, where I suggested that there might be a link between the success of the Eretrian tyrant-killing law and the subsequent popularity of tyrant-killing legislation in the early Hellenistic period. That connection can now be made more explicit. Simply put, Alexander likely observed that both the Athenians and the Eretrians, by promulgating tyrant-killing law, successfully countered his father's attempt to subvert their democracy. Alexander thus promoted that law type and its underlying ideology in order to prevent his opponents from subverting the democracies that he established in and around Asia Minor. That explains how and why the technology of tyrant-killing law "jumped" from the Greek mainland to Asia Minor.

Conclusion

The persistence of democracy within the ancient Greek world during the Classical and early Hellenistic periods was an achievement of profound historical significance. In scores of cities, from Attika to Euboia, from the Troad to Karia and beyond, the nonelite masses controlled their state; the elites were forced to share political power. It was the first time in history that democracy became a normal regime type within an international system of independent states. And it would be well over two millennia until anything even remotely like that would happen again. How were Greek pro-democrats able to maintain such a historical anomaly for so long?

I have argued in this book that the promulgation of tyrant-killing law contributed significantly to the persistence of democracy in the ancient Greek world. The previous six chapters demonstrated that that law type was effective in five different states in different times. And I also have demonstrated that those examples represent just the tip of the iceberg. In the conclusion to chapter 6, for example, I argued that tyrant-killing law contributed significantly to the successful democratization of Hellenistic western Asia Minor. And, as noted in the introduction to this book, literary sources indicate that, by the second quarter of the fourth century, tyrant killing became a widely accepted and celebrated means to overthrow nondemocratic regimes and usher in democracy.

In these concluding remarks, I provide a simple conceptual framework within which we might interpret the long and complex history of tyrant-killing legislation. The framework has two parts. The first focuses on the dynamics of learning and innovation in Athens. The second briefly explores the likely dynamics of learning and adoption outside Athens.

Learning and Innovation in Athens

The origin of ancient Greek tyrant-killing legislation is directly tied to the Athenians' failure to respond to the coup of the Four Hundred. In the years before that coup, pro-democrats had some reason to be confident in the long-term durability of their regime: they had already controlled the city for generations, and even anti-democrats concluded that it could not be overthrown.[1] It seemed invulnerable. But that confidence was shattered in the summer of 411, when a small number of committed anti-democrats overthrew the democracy and established a narrow oligarchy. The loss of power was no doubt a psychological blow to Athens's pro-democrats. But it did force them to seriously identify the foundations of their democracy and how they might defend their regime against future tyrannical threats. The coup, that is, was a learning experience.

The fundamental lesson that the Athenian pro-democrats learned from their experience in the coup of the Four Hundred is that the survival of their democracy ultimately depended on whether or not they could mobilize en masse even if their democracy was overthrown. It is not enough, that is, simply to have institutions that help individuals prevent a coup: people can be manipulated, and those institutions can thus fail. That lesson became clear when the pro-democrats, intimidated and misinformed by the anti-democrats' policies, annulled the *graphē paranomōn*, an institution specifically designed to prevent a coup d'état.[2] Again, Athenian pro-democrats realized that they must have the ability to draw upon their collective strength *after* a successful coup—when established institutions are no longer functioning. If they do not have that ability, their numerical superiority is meaningless.

In an effort to facilitate the pro-democrats' ability to mobilize even if their regime is overthrown, Demophantos invented and the Athenians then promulgated the first-ever tyrant-killing law. Passage of the law—especially the swearing of the oath that it mandated—accomplished that crucial objective by inducing what I have called a pro-mobilization threshold sequence. First, it generated common knowledge of widespread credible commitment to defend the democracy in the event of a coup. Second, it incentivized brave individuals to commit the first public act in defense of the democracy—to "kill a tyrant." In the event of a coup, therefore, it would be more likely that someone would commit a conspicuous act in defense of the democracy and that that act would trigger an ever-growing cascade of pro-democracy resistance. Pro-democrats would thus be able to mobilize in the absence of a functioning democracy

The successful mobilization against the Thirty Tyrants demonstrated that the promulgation of the decree of Demophantos did, in fact, facilitate revolutionary mobilization and thus secured the foundation of the Athenians'

1 This is the conclusion of the author known as "the Old Oligarch." See Ober (1998: 14–27) on this author and his assessment of the Athenian democracy's apparent invulnerability.

2 Thus Demosthenes (58.34) equates the annulment of the *graphē paranomōn* with the overthrow (*katalusis*) of the *dēmos*. On the *graphē paranomōn* see also Lanni and Vermeule (2013), Schwartzberg (2013), and Teegarden (2013).

democracy. Despite the fact that the democracy was overthrown and the Thirty sought to atomize the pro-democrats, Thrasyboulos and his men set out from Thebes reasonably expecting that they would attract a sufficient number of supporters—that is, they believed that the Athenian population was defined by a pro-mobilization threshold sequence because of the oath and decree of Demophantos. They were right. The pro-democrats mobilized and soon overwhelmed the Thirty.

Thus the most powerful and influential democratic polis in the Greek world had invented an institution that gave pro-democrats a credible threat—second strike capability—against their anti-democrat opponents. Henceforth, anti-democrats knew that if they staged a coup, the pro-democrats would nonetheless be able to mobilize in sufficient numbers. Staging a coup would now be irrational. Pro-democrats thus proceeded into the fourth century with confidence, knowing that their domestic opponents were deterred: the *dēmos* had the *kratos* to impose their will on the state.

Learning and Adoption Outside of Athens

Despite originating in Athens and being deeply imbued with Athenian democratic ideology, the citizens of several poleis subsequently promulgated their own tyrant-killing law. How did this happen? What significant dynamics were involved? What, if anything, were the larger effects? In order to explore those questions, I present a diffusion model that is based on inter-polis social learning. It is admittedly hypothetical. But, as I will demonstrate below, it is quite plausible; and it does provide an efficient and effective means to explore what we might call the Nachleben of the decree of Demophantos.

At its most basic level, the dynamic of diffusion likely consisted of two steps. First, the citizens of city x learned from the citizens of city w that the promulgation of tyrant-killing law helps defend a democracy by inducing (what I, certainly not they, call) a pro-mobilization threshold sequence among the population. This implies, of course, a broader awareness: namely, that the pro-democrats' capability to mobilize is at the heart of the struggle for control of the polis. They (i.e., the citizens of city x) came to understand that if anti-democrats successfully implement practices of widespread disinformation and intimidation, pro-democrats would be unable to draw upon their collective strength, despite the fact that they all would like to do so. They learned, that is, that the revolutionary coordination problem constitutes perhaps the most serious threat to the viability of their democracy. But they also learned (from city w) that if they are able to generate and maintain common knowledge of widespread credible commitment to defend the democracy and if they properly incentivize brave individuals to take the all-important first steps in their defense, pro-democrats will be able to draw upon their collective strength and mobilize in defense of their regime, no matter how thorough the anti-democrats' "anti-mobilization" practices might be. In brief, the citizens of city x would have learned from city w what the Athenians themselves learned in the late fifth century.

Second, the citizens of city x decided to promulgate their own tyrant-killing law.[3] This was their "Demophantos moment." After having considered what they were doing and why they were doing it, the citizens generated common knowledge of their pledge to resist tyranny and to reward tyrant killers. They now were defined by a pro-mobilization threshold sequence: henceforth, individuals believed that, if they acted in defense of their democracy, a sufficient number of individuals would follow them. The foundation of their democracy was thus secure. The promulgation of the tyrant-killing law also made the citizens of city x more like the citizens of democratic Athenians, the paradigmatic tyrant killers: they too had fully adopted the ideology of tyrannicide—the call to act "just like" Harmodios and Aristogeiton—as a means to defend their democracy. Thus not only did the citizens of city x learn from city w what the Athenians learned in the late fifth century, they became what the Athenians then became.

As the number of cities that adopted tyrant-killing law increased (i.e., as city x learned form city w, and so on), cities that had not yet adopted would become more likely to do so. That would be due to a number of reasons. First, the citizens of a greater number of cities simply became aware of the law type; word spread, that is, thus making promulgation conceivable. Second, it would be easier for a citizen of city x to convince his fellow citizens to promulgate such a law if he could cite examples of such activity in other cities. The logic here, too, is simple: if tyrant-killing law were known to work in many poleis, it likely would work in polis x too; it would thus be worth the effort to craft and promulgate such a law in city x. And finally, as tyrant-killing law became more normal, individuals in city x likely would want to become part of the movement—to have their own tyrant-killing law and thus become committed tyrant killers themselves.

The inter-polis cascade of learning and adopting would have increased the credibility of pro-democrats' commitment to mobilize pursuant to the promulgation of their own tyrant-killing law. The single most important dynamic here is that people would have known that tyrant-killing law actually worked. If it were common knowledge in city x that the promulgation of tyrant-killing law helped the citizens of cities v and w defend their democracy, the credibility of the commitment of the citizens in city x would be increased: since everybody knows that tyrant-killing law works, people would be even more

---

3 The emphasis here is on the word "decided." I do not here describe a "contagion model" like that used to assess the spread (for example) of influenza. The diffusion of institutions is the result of an individual or individuals' conscious decision to adopt after having considered why it would be advantageous to do so.

convinced that, should they act in defense of their democracy, a sufficient number of individuals will follow them. Thus the citizens of polis *x*—both pro-democrats and, just as important, anti-democrats—would know that their population is in fact defined by a pro-mobilization sequence. It is important to note, however, that the increased credibility would not just flow to new adopters (like from city *x* to city *y*, to city *z*, and so on): as more and more cities adopted tyrant-killing legislation, the credibility of earlier adopters to enforce their law would also increase—they, too, would be emboldened by the success of others and thereby maintain their own pro-mobilization threshold sequence.

The logical consequence of the cascading dynamic I just described would be the gradual creation of a common, Panhellenic, democratic culture that celebrates tyrant killing in defense of democracy, and thereby worked to lower the revolutionary thresholds among democracy supporters in the various cities. A level of cultural standardization or homogenization, that is, would emerge: tyrant killing and the use of public law (vel sim.) to make it a rational act becoming a common part of Greek democratic political culture. Thus, although the ideology and law type might have originated in Athens, it would become the property of Greek democrats everywhere. It would become the standard solution to the "defense of democracy" problem.

As noted above, my diffusion model and the effects thereof are by necessity hypothetical. But the following two points give it considerable support.

First, for well over two centuries following the promulgation of the decree of Demophantos, we find evidence for tyrant-killing ideology and/or tyrant-killing law when the survival of democracy is at stake. I have pointed out in this book significant examples: in Asia Minor shortly after the Peloponnesian War; on the mainland during the second and third quarters of the fourth century; on the mainland in response to Philip II's imperialism; in early Hellenistic Asia Minor. And there are other examples too. Timoleon's campaigns for "democracy" in Sicily during the third quarter of the fourth century, for example, were clearly configured as anti-tyranny or tyrant-killing campaigns.[4] And the leaders of the Achaean League from the mid-third to the early second century considered their enemies to be tyrants and were themselves prominent tyrant killers.[5] We thus have evidence for the type of Pan-

4 See, for example, Plut. *Tim.* 24.1, 32.1. Plutarch also writes (*Tim.* 39) that the people of Syracuse buried Timoleon at public expense and conducted annual music and athletic contests in his honor "because he overthrew the tyrants."

5 Margos of Karuneia killed the tyrant of Bura in 275/4 (Polyb. 2.41.14) and in 255 became the first sole holder of the office of *strategos* (Polyb. 2.43.2). Aratos of Sikyon was famous for his anti-tyranny policy and campaigns (e.g., Polyb. 2.44; Plut. *Arat.* 10.1). The people of Sikyon erected a bronze statue of him after he liberated them in 251 from the tyrant Nikokles. After Aratos died, they buried his body in the agora and conducted annual sacrifices to him on the day that he liberated their city (Plut. *Arat.* 53.3–4). Philopoimen, the last great leader of the league, personally killed

hellenic cultural standardization or homogenization that was predicted by my simple model.

Second, the "diffusion of institutions" dynamic I outlined with respect to tyrant-killing law is consistent with other episodes in ancient Greek history. This is particularly clear in the Archaic period, when institutions such as the alphabet, the hoplite phalanx, and coinage diffused through various areas of the Greek world, creating a certain decree of standardization in important domains of Greek culture.[6] And this dynamic is also evident in the Hellenistic period, when peer polity interactions—that is, the transmission of information between the citizens of the various states—contributed to the standardization of a large set of diplomatic formulae and protocols (e.g., those involved with *asylia*, *syngeneia*, and traveling judges), of dialect (i.e., *koinē*), and practices such as euergetism and the epigraphic habit—to name just a few of the obvious examples.[7] Simply put, good ideas spread throughout the ancient Greek world and contributed to a common Greek culture. The invention and diffusion of tyrant-killing law and ideology was part of that characteristic phenomenon.

———————

Tyrants, ancient as well as modern, fear the collective power of their people perhaps more than anything else. They have accordingly devised and implemented sophisticated practices that work to atomize the population—to prevent the people from doing what they actually want to do. And most often they succeed: thus the rarity of democracy in world history. Over 2,400 years ago, however, the Athenians invented a tool—tyrant-killing law—that enabled pro-democrats to draw upon their collective strength and mobilize against nondemocratic regimes despite whatever anti-mobilization practices they might have implemented. And like great technological innovations throughout history, it spread as the citizens of other poleis adopted it in order to gain control of their own political destiny. That helped secure the world's first democratic age.

the Spartan "tyrant" Machanidas in 207 at the battle of Mantinea (Polyb. 11.18.4). The Achaeans subsequently erected in Delphi a bronze statue of him in the act of killing the tyrant (Plut. *Phil.* 10.7–8, *Syll.*[3] 625; Plut. *Phil.* 21.5, *Syll.*[3] 624).

6   For general comments on the innovation and diffusion through the Greek world of the alphabet, hoplite phalanx warfare, and coinage, see Snodgrass (1980: 78–84, 99–107, 134–36).

7   On peer polity interactions in the Hellenistic period, see Ma (2003).

The Number and Geographic Distribution of Different Regime
Types from the Archaic to the Early Hellenistic Periods

In the introduction I made significant assertions about the success of democracy within the larger ancient Greek world during the Archaic, Classical, and early Hellenistic periods. I here provide the data to support those assertions. In order to present the data within a more useful and compelling context, however, I also provide data on the success of other regime types during those same periods.

The data are culled exclusively from Hansen and Nielsen's *Inventory of Archaic and Classical Poleis* (2004), in particular from its appendix 11. I entered the data into a database that allows simple yet fundamental queries relating, most importantly, to the total number of cities for which we have regime-type information and the percentage of those cities that experienced the different regime-types in a particular period of time. The result, I believe, is a fairly compelling rough sketch of the relative success of the major regime types over several centuries.

I have not examined the evidential basis for all of the data that I included. Acknowledged experts wrote the entries for each of the poleis contained in the *Inventory*. If they suggest that city *x* experienced a democracy (or another regime type) in time *y*, I took their word at face value.

I have divided the data into periods of a half century. Using shorter units of time is unfortunately not practicable. There is one problem, however, in dividing the data even into periods of a half century. One of Hansen and Nielsen's temporal categories refers to the "middle" of a century, which corresponds to the forth to sixth decades of that century. For example, C7m ("middle of seventh century") refers to the years 660–640, C4m refers to the years 360–340. Yet Hansen and Nielsen also have temporal categories that refer to the first or second half of a century. For example, C7f ("first half of seventh century") refers to 699–650, while C7 ("second half of seventh century) refers to 649–600. Likewise C4f refers to 399–350, while C4 refers to 349–300. The difficulty (for this appendix) arises when there is evidence for a particular regime type in a city during the "middle" of the century, since that city could have experienced that regime during the first or the second half of the century, or both. I have decided to have it refer to both halves of the century. Thus, for example, if there is evidence for democracy in city x in C4m, I mark it as experiencing democracy in both the first half and the second half of the fourth century.

I must also comment on what I mean by a city having "experienced" a particular regime type. First, that experience need not have been long in duration: if a democracy controlled city x for a month in, for example, C4f, that city experienced democracy in the first half of the fourth century. Second, a polis can experience several different regimes types in one half century. Thus the combined number of regime types experienced by all cities in a particular half century will be greater than the number of poleis for which we have regime type information for that half century; likewise, the sum of the percentages of cities experiencing all of the various regime types in a given half century will be greater than one hundred. For example, in a particular half century we might have regime-type information for ten cities, each of which experienced democracy, oligarchy, and tyranny. In that case there would thirty different regimes experienced by ten poleis, and the sum of the percentages of cities experiencing the various regime types for that half century would be 300: 100 percent experienced democracy, tyranny, and oligarchy.

I here present two charts that efficiently capture the data. Figure A1 indicates both how many cities are known to have experienced a particular regime type in a given half century and the percentage of cities known to have experienced that particular regime type during that half century (out of all cities for which we have regime-type information for that half century). Figure A2 indicates the percentage of geographic regions known to have contained at least one city that experienced a particular regime type in a given half century. The two charts thus provide a decent basis to quickly gauge the success of a particular regime type over time. The more successful a regime type is, the greater the percentage of both cities and regions that experienced it.

I also include the raw data, organized by half century. The reader can thus assess for himself or herself the accuracy of my conclusions.

Numbers of Cities for Which Regime Type Data Are Available

FIRST HALF OF THE SEVENTH CENTURY

There is regime-type information for 28 different cities: Amathous, Argos, Athenai, Axos, Epidauros, Idalion, Istros, Kolophon, Korinthos, Kourion, Kroton, Kyme (in Italia), Lampsakos, Lapethos, Lokroi, Marion, Metapontion, Paphos, Paros, Rhegion, Salamis, Samos, Sikyon, Soloi, Sparta, Sybaris, Syrakousai, Taras. There is regime-type information for ten (out of thirty-

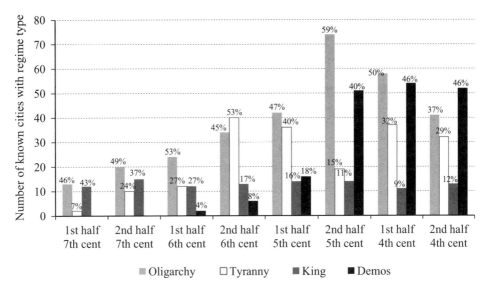

Figure A1. Regime type occurances over time.

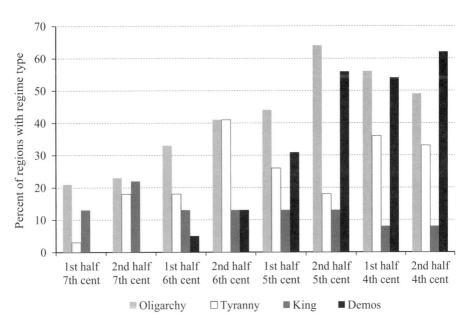

Figure A2. Regime type distributions over time.

nine)[1] different regions: Cyprus, Argolis, Attica, Crete, Black Sea Area, Ionia, Megaris-Korinthia-Sikyonia, Italia and Kampania, the Aegean, Propontic Coast of Asia Minor.

OLIGARCHY

Thirteen cities are known to have experienced oligarchy: Athenai, Epidauros, Istros, Kolophon, Korinthos, Kroton, Kyme (in Italia), Lokroi, Metapontion, Paros, Rhegion, Sybaris, Syrakousai. Thus 46 percent of the cities for which there is regime-type information experienced an oligarchy.

Eight different regions contained at least one city governed by an oligarchy: Attika, Argolis, Black Sea Area, Ionia, Megaris-Korinthia-Sikyonia, Italia and Kampania, the Aegean, Sikelia. Thus 21 percent of the regions contained at least one city that was governed by an oligarchy.

TYRANNY

Two cities are known to have experienced a tyranny: Korinthos, Sikyon. Thus 7 percent of the cites for which there is regime-type information experienced a tyranny.

One region contained at least one city governed by a tyranny: Megaris-Korinthia-Sikyonia. Thus 3 percent of the regions contained at least one city governed by a tyranny.

KINGSHIP

Twelve cities are known to have been governed by a king: Amathous, Argos, Axos, Idalion, Kourion, Lampsakos, Lapethos, Marion, Paphos, Samamis, Samos, Soloi. Thus 43 percent of the cities for which there is regime-type information were governed by a king.

Five regions contained at least one city governed by a king: Cyprus, Argolis, Crete, Propontic Coast of Asia Minor, Ionia. Thus 13 percent of the regions contained at least one city governed by a king.

DEMOCRACY

There is no evidence for democracy in a Greek polis during the first half of the seventh century.

1 The thirty-nine regions: Achaia, the Adriatic, the Aegean, Aiolis and Southwestern Mysia, Akarnania, Argolis, Arkadia, South Coast of Asia Minor, Attika, Black Sea Area, Boiotia, Crete, Cyprus, Elis, Euboia, Ionia, Italia and Kampania, Karia, Lakedaimon, Lesbos, East Lokris, West Lokris, Makedonia, Megaris-Korinthia-Sikyonia, Messenia, Phokis, Propontic Coast of Asia Minor, Rhodos, the Saronic Gulf, Sikelia, Spain and France, Syria to the Pillars of Herakles, Thessalia, Thrace (Axios to Strymon), Thrace (Nestos to Hebron), Thrace (Strymon to Nestos), Propontic Thrace, Thracian Chersonesos, Troas.

SECOND HALF OF THE SEVENTH CENTURY

There is regime-type information for forty-one different cities: Amathous, Apollonia, Argos, Athenai, Epidamnos/Dyrrhachion, Epidauros, Erythrai, Idalion, Istros, Kolophon, Korinthos, Korkyra, Kourion, Kroton, Kyme (in Italia), Kyrene, Lampsakos, Lampthos, Leontinoi, Leukas, Lokroi, Marion, Megara, Metapontion, Miletos, Mytilene, Olbia/Borysthenes, Paphos, Paros, Rhegion, Salamis, Samos, Sigeion, Sikyon, Soloi, Sparta, Sybaris, Syrakousai, Taras, Tenedos, Thera.

There is regime-type information for sixteen (out of thirty-nine) different regions: Cyprus, Black Sea Area, Argolis, Attika, the Adriatic, Ionia, Megaris-Korinthia-Sikyonia, Akarnania, Italia and Kampania, Syria to the Pillars of Herakles, Propontic Coast of Asia Minor, Sikelia, Lesbos, the Aegean, Troas, Lakedaimon.

OLIGARCHY

Twenty cities are known to have experienced oligarchy: Apollonia, Athenai, Epidamnos/Dyrrhachion, Epidauros, Erythrai, Istros, Kolophon, Korinthos, Kroton, Kyme (in Italia), Leontinoi, Lokroi, Megara, Metapontion, Olbia/Borysthenes, Paros, Rhegion, Samos, Sybaris, Syrakousai. Thus 49 percent of the cities for which there is regime-type information experienced an oligarchy.

Nine different regions contained at least one city governed by an oligarchy: Black Sea Area, Attika, the Adriatic, Argolis, Ionia, Megaris-Korinthia-Sikyonia, Italia and Kampania, Sikelia, the Aegean. Thus 23 percent of the regions contained at least one city that was governed by an oligarchy.

TYRANNY

Ten cities are known to have experienced tyranny: Epidauros, Korinthos, Korkyra, Leontinoi, Leukas, Megara, Miletos, Mytilene, Sigeion, Sikyon. Thus 24 percent of the cites for which there is regime-type information experienced a tyranny.

Seven different regions contained at least one city governed by a tyranny: Argolis, Megaris-Korinthia-Sikyonia, Akarnania, Sikelia, Ionia, Lesbos, Troas. Thus 18 percent of the regions contained at least one city governed by a tyranny.

KINGSHIP

Fifteen cities are known to have been governed by a king: Amathous, Argos, Idalion, Kourion, Kyrene, Lampsakos, Lapethos, Marion, Mytilene, Paphos, Salamis, Samos, Soloi, Tenedos, Thera. Thus 37 percent of the cities for which there is regime-type information were governed by a king.

Eight regions contained at least one city governed by a king: Cyprus, Argolis, Syria to the Pillars of Herakles, Propontic Coast of Asia Minor, Lesbos, Ionia, Troas, the Aegean. Thus 22 percent of the regions contained at least one city governed by a king.

DEMOCRACY

There is no evidence for democracy in a Greek polis during the second half of the seventh century.

FIRST HALF OF THE SIXTH CENTURY

There is regime-type information for forty-five different cities: Akragas, Amathous, Ambrakia, Apollonia, Argos, Athenai, Epidamnos/Dyrrhachion, Erythrai, Herakleia (Pontica), Idalion, Istros, Kolophon, Korinthos, Korkyra, Kourion, Kroton, Kyme (in Aiolis), Kyme (in Italia), Kyrene, Lampsakos, Lapethos, Leontinoi, Leukas, Lokroi, Marion, Massalia, Megara, Metapontion, Miletos, Mytilene, Olbia/Borysthenes, Paphos, Paros, Rhegion, Salamis, Samos, Selinous, Sikyon, Soloi, Sparta, Sybaris, Syrakousai, Taras, Tenedos, Thebai.

There is regime-type information for nineteen (out of thirty-nine) different regions: Sikelia, Cyprus, Akarnania, Black Sea Area, Argolis, Attika, the Adriatic, Ionia, Megaris-Korinthia-Sikyonia, Italia and Kampania, Aiolis and Southwestern Mysia, Syria to the Pillars of Herakles, Propontic Coast of Asia Minor, Spain and France, Lesbos, the Aegean, Ladedaimon, Troas, Boiotia.

OLIGARCHY

Twenty-four different cities are known to have experienced oligarchy: Ambrakia, Apollonia, Argos, Athenai, Epidamnos/Dyrrhachion, Erythrai, Istros, Kolophon, Korinthos, Kroton, Kyme (in Italia), Lokroi, Massalia, Megara, Metapontion, Mytilene, Olbia/Borysthenes, Paros, Rhegion, Samos, Sikyon, Sybaris, Syrakousai, Thebai. Thus 53 percent of the cities for which there is regime-type information experienced an oligarchy.

Thirteen different regions contained at least one city governed by an oligarchy: Akarnania, Black Sea Area, Argolis, Attika, the Adriatic, Ionia, Megaris-Korinthia-Sikyonia, Italia and Kampania, Spain and France, Lesbos, the Aegean, Sikelia, Boiotia. Thus 33 percent of the regions contained at least one city that was governed by an oligarchy.

TYRANNY

Twelve cities are known to have experienced tyranny: Akragas, Athenai, Korinthos, Korkyra, Kyme (in Aiolis), Leontinoi, Leukas, Miletos, Mytilene, Samos, Selinous, Sikyon. Thus 27 percent of the cities for which there is regime-type information experienced a tyranny.

Seven different regions contained at least one city governed by a tyranny: Sikelia, Attika, Megaris-Korinthia-Sikyonia, Akarnania, Aiolis and South-western Mysia, Ionia, Lesbos. Thus 18 percent of the regions contained at least one city governed by a tyranny.

KINGSHIP

Twelve cities are known to have been governed by a king: Amathous, Argos, Idalion, Kourion, Kyrene, Lampsakos, Lapethos, Marion, Paphos, Salamis, Soloi, Tenedos. Thus 27 percent of the cities for which there is regime-type information were governed by a king.

Five regions contained at least one city governed by a king: Cyprus, Argo-lis, Syria to the Pillars of Herakles, Propontic Coast of Asia Minor, Troas. Thus 13 percent of the regions contained at least one city governed by a king.

DEMOCRACY

Two different cities are known to have experienced democracy: Herakleia (Pontica), Megara. Thus 4 percent of the cities for which there is regime-type information experienced a democracy.

Two different regions contained at least one city governed by a democ-racy: Black Sea Area, Megaris-Korinthia-Sikyonia. Thus 5 percent of the re-gions contained at least one city that was governed by an oligarchy.

SECOND HALF OF THE SIXTH CENTURY

There is regime-type information for seventy-six different cities: Abydos, Aiane, Akragas, Alopekonnesos, Amathous, Ambrakia, Apollonia, Argos, Athenai, Barke, Byzantion, Chalkis, Chersonesos/Agora, Chios, Elaious, Elis, Ephesos, Epidamnos/Dyrrhachion, Eretria, Erythrai, Gela, Halikarnassos, Herakleia (Pontica), Idalion, Istros, Kardia, Kaulonia, Kentoripa, Kolophon, Korinthos, Korkyra, Kourion, Krannon, Krithote, Kroton, Kyme (in Italia), Kyme (in Aiolis), Kyrene, Kyzikos, Lampsakos, Lapethos, Leontinoi, Leukas, Limnai, Lokroi, Madytos, Magnesia, Matinea, Marion, Massalia, Megara, Metapontion, Miletos, Myrkinos, Mytilene, Olbia/Borysthenes, Paktye, Pa-phos, Parion, Paros, Phleious, Prokonnesos, Rhegion, Salamis, Samos, Seli-nous, Sestos, Sigeion, Sikyon, Soloi, Sparta, Sybaris, Syrakousai, Taras, Tene-dos, Thebai.

There is regime-type information for twenty-eight (out of thirty-nine) dif-ferent regions: Troas, Makedonia, Sikelia, Thracian Chersonesos, Cyprus, Akarnania, Black Sea Area, Argolis, Attika, Syria to the Pillars of Herakles, Propontic Thrace, Euboia, Ionia, Elis, the Adriatic, Karia, Italia and Kampa-nia, Megaris-Korinthia-Sikyonia, Thessalia, Aiolis and Southwestern Mysia, Propontic Coast of Asia Minor, Arkadia, Spain and France, Thrace (Strymon-to-Nestos), Lesbos, the Aegean, Lakedaimon, Boiotia.

OLIGARCHY

Thirty four different cities are known to have experienced oligarchy: Ambrakia, Apollonia, Argos, Barke, Chalkis, Elis, Epidamnos/Dyrrhachion, Eretria, Erythrai, Herakleia (Pontica), Istros, Kaulonia, Kolophon, Korinthos, Korkyra, Krannon, Kroton, Kyme (in Italia), Leontinoi, Leukas, Lokroi, Magnesia, Massalia, Megara, Metapontion, Miletos, Mytilene, Olbia/Borysthenes, Paros, Rhegion, Sikyon, Sybaris, Syrakousai, Thebai. Thus 45 percent of the cities for which there is regime-type information experienced an oligarchy.

Sixteen different regions contained at least one city governed by an oligarchy: Akarnania, Black Sea Area, Argolis, Syria to the Pillars of Herakles, Euboia, Elis, the Adriatic, Ionia, Italia and Kampania, Megaris-Korinthia-Sikyonia, Thessalia, Sikelia, Spain and France, Lesbos, the Aegean, Boiotia. Thus 41 percent of the regions contained at least one city that was governed by an oligarchy.

TYRANNY

Forty cities are known to have experienced tyranny: Abydos, Akragas, Alopekonnesos, Ambrakia, Athenai, Byzantion, Chalkis, Chersonesos/Agora, Chios, Elaious, Ephesos, Gela, Halikarnassos, Herakleia (Pontica), Kardia, Kentoripa, Korkyra, Krithote, Kroton, Kyme (in Aiolis), Kyme (in Italia), Kyzikos, Lampsakos, Limnai, Madytos, Miletos, Myrkinos, Mytilene, Paktye, Parion, Phleious, Prokonnesos, Samos, Selinous, Sestos, Sigeion, Sikyon, Sybaris, Syrakousai, Taras. Thus 53 percent of the cites for which there is regime-type information experienced a tyranny.

Sixteen different regions contained at least one city governed by a tyranny: Troas, Sikelia, Thracian Chersonesos, Akarnania, Attika, Propontic Thrace, Euboia, Ionia, Karia, Black Sea Area, Aiolis and Southwestern Mysia, Propontic Coast of Asia Minor, Thrace (Strymon-to-Nestos), Lesbos, Argolis, Italia and Kampania. Thus 41 percent of the regions contained at least one city governed by a tyranny.

KINGSHIP

Thirteen cities are known to have been governed by a king: Aiane, Amathous, Barke, Idalion, Kourion, Kyrene, Lampsakos, Lapethos, Marion, Paphos, Salamis, Soloi, Tenedos. Thus 17 percent of the cities for which there is regime-type information were governed by a king.

Five regions contained at least one city governed by a king: Makedonia, Cyprus, Syria to the Pillars of Herakles, Propontic Coast of Asia Minor, Troas. Thus 13 percent of the regions contained at least one city governed by a king.

DEMOCRACY

Six cities are known to have experienced democracy: Athenai, Chalkis, Eretria, Herakleia (Pontica), Kroton, Matinea. Thus 8 percent of the cities for which there is regime-type information experienced a democracy.

Five different regions contained at least one democratically governed city: Attika, Euboia, Black Sea Area, Italia and Kampania, Arkadia. Thus 13 percent of the regions contained at least one city that was governed by a democracy.

FIRST HALF OF THE FIFTH CENTURY

There is regime-type information for 89 cities: Aiane, Aitna, Akragas, Akraiphia, Alabanda, Alopekonnesos, Amathous, Ambrakia, Apollonia, Argos, Athenai, Barke, Chaironeia, Chaleion, Chalkis, Chersonesos/Agora, Chios, Elaious, Elis, Ephesos, Epidamnos/Dyrrhachion, Eretria, Erythrai, Gela, Haliartos, Halikarnassos, Halissarna, Herbita, Himera, Histiaia/Oreos, Hyele/Elea, Hyettos, Idalion, Istros, Kamarina, Kardia, Kaulonia, Kolophon, Kopai, Korinthos, Korkyra, Koroneia, Kourion, Krithote, Kroton, Kyme (in Aiolis), Kyme (in Italia), Kyrene, Kyzikos, Lampsakos, Lapethos, Lappa, Leukas, Limnai, Lokroi, Madytos, Mantinea, Marion, Massalia, Megara, Metapontion, Miletos, Mytilene, Oianthea, Olbia/Borysthenes, Opous, Orchomenos, Paktye, Pantikapaion/Bosporos, Paphos, Paros, Pergamon, Pharsalos, Plataiai, Rhegion, Salamis, Samos, Sestos, Sikyon, Sinope, Soloi, Sparta, Syrakousai, Tanagra, Taras, Teuthrania, Thebai, Thespiai, Zankle/Messana.

There is regime-type information for twenty-eight (out of thirty-nine) different regions: Makedonia, Sikelia, Boiotia, Karia, Thracian Chersonesos, Cyprus, Akarnania, the Adriatic, Argolis, Attika, Syria to the Pillars of Herakles, West Lokris, Euboia, Ionia, Elis, Aiolis and Southwestern Mysia, Italia and Kampania, Black Sea Area, Megaris-Korinthia-Sikyonia, Propontic Coast of Asia Minor, Crete, Arkadia, Spain and France, Lesbos, East Lokris, the Aegean, Thessalia, Ladedaimon.

OLIGARCHY

Forty-two different cities are known to have experienced oligarchy: Akragas, Akraiphia, Ambrakia, Argos, Barke, Chaironeia, Chaleion, Chalkis, Elis, Epidamnos/Dyrrhachion, Eretria, Erythrai, Haliartos, Histiaia/Oreos, Hyettos, Istros, Kaulonia, Kolophon, Kopai, Korinthos, Korkyra, Koroneia, Kroton, Kyme (in Italia), Leukas, Lokroi, Massalia, Megara, Metapontion, Miletos, Oianthea, Olbia/Borysthenes, Opous, Orchomenos, Paros, Pharsalos, Rhegion, Samos, Sikyon, Tanagra, Thebai, Thespiai. Thus 47 percent of the cities for which there is regime-type information experienced an oligarchy.

Seventeen different regions contained at least one city governed by an oligarchy: Sikelia, Boiotia, Akarnania, Argolis, Syria to the Pillars of Herakles, West Lokris, Euboia, Elis, the Adriatic, Ionia, Black Sea Area, Italia and Kampania, Megaris-Korinthis-Sikyonia, Spain and France, East Lokris, the Aegean, Thessalia. Thus 44 percent of the regions contained at least one city that was governed by an oligarchy.

TYRANNY

Thirty-six cities are known to have experienced tyranny: Aitna, Akragas, Alabanda, Alopekonnesos, Ambrakia, Chersonesos/Agora, Chios, Elaious, Ephesos, Gela, Halikarnassos, Halisarna, Herbita, Himera, Hyele/Elea, Kamarina, Kardia, Korkyra, Krithote, Kroton, Kyme (in Aiolia), Kyme (in Italia), Lampsakos, Limnai, Madytos, Mytilene, Olbia/Borysthenes, Paktye, Pantikapaion/Bosporos, Pergamon, Rhegion, Samos, Sestos, Sinope, Syrakousai, Teuthrania. Thus 40 percent of the cites for which there is regime-type information experienced a tyranny.

Ten different regions contained at least one city governed by a tyranny: Sikelia, Karia, Thracian Chersonesos, Akarnania, Ionia, Aiolis and Southwestern Mysia, Italia and Kampania, Propontic Coast of Asia Minor, Lesbos, Black Sea Area. Thus 26 percent of the regions contained at least one city governed by a tyranny.

KINGSHIP

Fourteen cities are known to have been governed by a king: Aiane, Aitna, Amathous, Herbita, Idalion, Kourion, Kyrene, Lapethos, Lappa, Marion, Paphos, Salamis, Soloi, Zankle/Messana. Thus 16 percent of the cities for which there is regime-type information were governed by a king.

Five regions contained at least one city governed by a king: Makedonia, Sikelia, Cyprus, Syria to the Pillars of Herakles, Crete. Thus 13 percent of the regions contained at least one city governed by a king.

DEMOCRACY

Sixteen cities are known to have experienced democracy: Akragas, Apollonia, Argos, Athenai, Elis, Ephesos, Erythrai, Kyrene, Kyzikos, Leukas, Mantinea, Miletos, Plataiai, Samos, Syrakousai, Taras. Thus 18 percent of the cities for which there is regime-type information experienced a democracy.

Twelve different regions contained at least one democratically governed city: Sikelia, the Adriatic, Argolis, Attika, Elis, Ionia, Syria to the Pillars of Herakles, Propontic Coast of Asia Minor, Akarnania, Arkadia, Boiotia, Italia and Kampania. Thus 31 percent of the regions contained at least one city that experienced democracy.

SECOND HALF OF THE FIFTH CENTURY

There is regime-type information for 126 cities: Abdera, Abydos, Aiane, Aigai, Aigeira, Aigina, Aigion, Akanthos, Akragas, Akraiphia, Amathous, Ambrakia, Amisos/Peiraieus, Andros, Amphipolis, Apollonia, Argos, Ascheion, Astakos, Athenai, Barke, Beroia, Byzantion, Chaironeia, Chaleion, Chalkis, Chersonesos, Chios, Dyme, Eleusis, Elis, Ephesos, Epidamnos/Dyrrachion, Eretria, Erythrai, Euhesperides, Gambrion, Gela, Gergis, Gryneion/

Gryneia, Haliartos, Halikarnassos, Halisarna, Henna, Herakleia (Pontica), Herbita, Histiaia/Oreos, Hyettos, Ialysos, Idalion, Istros, Kamiros, Karystos, Keryneia, Kindye, Klazomenai, Kolophon, Kopai, Korinthos, Korkyra, Koroneia, Kourion, Kroton, Kyllandos, Kyme (in Aiolis), Kyrene, Kyzikos, Lapethos, Larisa, Leontinoi, Leontion, Leukas, Lokroi, Lindos, Mantinea, Marion, Massila, Megara, Mende, Metapontion, Methymna, Miletos, Myrina, Mytilene, Neapolis (Thrace: Strymon to Nexos), Nymphaion, Oianthea, Olenos, Orchomenos, Palaigambrion, Pantikapaion/Bosporos, Paphos, Paros, Patrai, Pellene, Pergamon, Pharai, Pharsalos, Phelloe, Pherai, Plataiai, Rhodos, Rhypes, Salamis, Samos, Sikyon, Sinope, Siphai, Siphnos, Soloi, Sparta, Syangela, Syrakousai, Tanagra, Taras, Tenos, Teos, Teuthrania, Thasos, Thebai, Thespiai, Thourioi, Torone, Tritaia, Tyritake, Zakynthos.

There is regime-type information for thirty-three (out of thirty-nine) different regions: Thrace (Nestos to Hebros), Troas, Makedonia, Achaia, Saronic Gulf, Thrace (Axios to Strymon), Thrace (Strymon to Nestos), Sikelia, Boiotia, Cyprus, Akarnania, Black Sea Area, the Aegean, the Adriatic, Argolis, Attika, Syria to the Pillars of Herakles, Propontic Thrace, West Lokris, Euboia, Ionia, Elis, Aiolis and Southwestern Mysia, Karia, Rhodos, Megaris-Korinthia-Sikyonia, Italia and Kampania, Propontic Coast of Asia Minor, Thessalia, Arkadia, Spain and France, Lesbos, Lakedaimon.

OLIGARCHY

Seventy-four different cities are known to have experienced oligarchy: Abydos, Aigai, Aigeira, Aigina, Aigion, Akragas, Akraiphia, Ambrakia, Andros, Argos, Ascheion, Athenai, Barke, Beroia, Byzantion, Chaironeia, Chaleion, Chios, Dyme, Eleusis, Epidamnos/Dyrrhachion, Eretria, Erythrai, Euhesperides, Gela, Haliartos, Histiaia/Oreos, Hyettos, Ialysos, Istros, Kamiros, Karystos, Keryneia, Kolophon, Kopai, Korinthos, Korkyra, Koroneia, Kroton, Kyme (Aiolia), Larisa, Leontinoi, Leontion, Lokroi, Massalia, Megara, Mende, Metapontion, Miletos, Mytilene, Oianthea, Olenos, Orchomenos, Paros, Patrai, Pellene, Pharai, Pharsalos, Phelloe, Rhodos, Rhypes, Samos, Sikyon, Siphai, Siphnos, Tanagra, Tenos, Thasos, Thebai, Thespiai, Thourioi, Torone, Tritaia, Zakynthos. Thus 59 percent of the cities for which there is regime-type information experienced an oligarchy.

Twenty-five different regions contained at least one city governed by an oligarchy: Troas, Achaia, Saronic Gulf, Sikelia, Boiotia, Akarnania, the Aegean, Argolis, Attika, Syria to the Pillars of Herakles, Makedonia, Propontic Thrace, West Lokris, Ionia, the Adriatic, Euboia, Black Sea Area, Rhodos, Megaris-Korinthia-Sikyonia, Italia and Kampania, Aiolis and Southwestern Mysia, Thessalia, Spain and France, Thrace (Axios to Strymon), Lesbos. Thus 64 percent of the regions contained at least one city that was governed by an oligarchy.

TYRANNY

Nineteen cities are known to have experienced tyranny: Astakos, Gambrion, Gryneion/Gryneia, Halikarnassos, Halisarna, Henna, Herbita, Kindye, Kroton, Kyllandos, Myrina, Palaigambrion, Pantikapaion/Bosporos, Pergamon, Pherai, Sinope, Syangela, Syrakousai, Teuthrania. Thus 15 percent of the cities for which there is regime-type information experienced a tyranny.

Seven different regions contained at least one city governed by a tyranny: Akarnania, Aiolis and Southwestern Mysia, Karia, Sikelia, Italia and Kampania, Black Sea Area, Thessalia. Thus 18 percent of the regions contained at least one city governed by a tyranny.

KINGSHIP

Fourteen cities are known to have been governed by a king: Aiane, Amathous, Herbita, Idalion, Kourion, Kyrene, Lapethos, Marion, Nymphaion, Pantikapaion/Bosporos, Paphos, Salamis, Soloi, Tyritake. Thus 11 percent of the cities for which there is regime-type information were governed by a king.

Five regions contained at least one city governed by a king: Makedonia, Cyprus, Sikelia, Syria to the Pillars of Herakles, Black Sea Area. Thus 13 percent of the regions contained at least one city governed by a king.

DEMOCRACY

Fifty-one cities are known to have experienced democracy: Abdera, Akanthos, Amisos/Peiraieus, Andros, Amphipolis, Apollonia, Argos, Athenai, Chalkis, Chersonesos, Elis, Ephesos, Epidamnos/Dyrrhachion, Eretria, Erythrai, Herakleia (Pontica), Histiaia/Oreos, Ialysos, Istros, Kamiros, Karystos, Klazomenai, Kolophon, Korkyra, Kyme (in Aiolis), Kyrene, Kyzikos, Leontinoi, Leukas, Lindos, Mantinea, Megara, Mende, Mentapontion, Methymna, Miletos, Mytilene, Neapolis (Thrace: Strymon to Nexos), Paros, Plataiai, Samos, Sinope, Siphnos, Syrakousai, Taras, Tenos, Teos, Thasos, Thourioi, Torone, Zakynthos. Thus 40 percent of the cities for which we have regime-type information experienced a democracy.

Twenty-two different regions contained at least one democratically governed city: Thrace (Nestos-to-Hebros), Thrace (Axios to Strymon), Black Sea Area, the Aegean, the Adriatic, Argolis, Attika, Euboia, Elis, Ionia, Rhodos, Akarnania, Aiolis and Southwestern Mysia, Syria to the Pillars of Herakles, Propontic Coast of Asia Minor, Sikelia, Arkadia, Megaris-Korinthia-Sikyonia, Italia and Kampania, Lesbos, Boiotia. Thus 56 percent of the regions had at least one city that experienced a democracy.

FIRST HALF OF THE FOURTH CENTURY

There is regime-type information for 117 cities: Abydos, Agyrion, Aiane, Aigai, Aigeira, Aigina, Aigion, Akraiphia, Amathous, Ambrakia, Andros,

Amphipolis, Apollonia, Argos, Ascheion, Assos, Atarneus, Athenai, Barke, Beroia, Byzantion, Chaironeia, Chalkis, Chersonesos, Chios, Dyme, Elis, Engyon, Ephesos, Epidamnos/Dyrrhachion, Eretria, Erythrai, Euhesperides, Gambrion, Gergis, Gryneion/Gryneia, Haliartos, Halikarnassos, Halisarna, Helisson, Heraia, Herakleia (Pontica), Histiaia/Oreos, Hyettos, Idalion, Kalchedon, Katane, Kentoripa, Keryneia, Kindye, Klazomenai, Kolophon, Kopai, Korinthos, Korkyra, Koroneia, Kos, Kourion, Kyme (in Aiolis), Kyrene, Lampsakos, Lapethos, Larisa, Leontion, Lokroi, Mantinea, Marion, Massalia, Megale Polis, Megara, Messene/Ithome, Methymna, Miletos, Mylasa, Myrina, Mytilene, Oianthea, Olbia/Borysthenes, Olenos, Orchomenos, Pagasai, Palaigambrion, Pantikapaion/Bosporos, Paphos, Paros, Patrai, Pellene, Pergamon, Pharai, Pharsalos, Phelloe, Pherai, Phigaleia, Philippoi, Phleious, Rhodos, Rhypes, Salamis, Samos, Sigeion, Sikyon, Siphnos, Soloi, Sparta, Syrakousai, Tanagra, Taras, Tauromenion, Tegea, Teuthrania, Thasos, Thebai, Thespiai, Tritaia, Tyritake, Zakynthos, Zankle/Messana.

There is regime-type information for thirty-three (out of thirty-nine) different regions: Troas, Sikelia, Makedonia, Achaia, Saronic Gulf, Boiotia, Cyprus, Akarnania, the Aegean, Thrace (Axios to Strymon), the Adriatic, Argolis, Aiolis and Southwestern Mysia, Attika, Syria to the Pillars of Herakles, Propontic Thrace, Euboia, Black Sea Area, Ionia, Elis, Karia, Arkadia, Propontic Coast of Asia Minor, Megaris-Korinthis-Sikyonia, Thessalia, Italia and Kampania, Spain and France, Messenia, Lesbos, West Lokris, Thrace (Strymon to Nestos), Rhodos, Lakedaimon.

OLIGARCHY

Fifty-eight different cities are known to have experienced oligarchy: Abydos, Aigai, Aigeira, Aigina, Aigion, Akraiphia, Andros, Ascheion, Barke, Beroia, Byzantion, Chaironeia, Chios, Dyme, Elis, Epidamnos/Dyrrhachion, Erythrai, Euhesperides, Haliartos, Histiaia/Oreos, Hyettos, Keryneia, Kolophon, Kopai, Korinthos, Korkyra, Koroneia, Kos, Kyme (in Aiolis), Larisa, Leontion, Lokroi, Mantinea, Massalia, Megara, Miletos, Mytilene, Olenos, Orchomenos, Paros, Patrai, Pellene, Pharai, Pharsalos, Phelloe, Phleious, Rhodos, Rhypes, Samos, Sikyon, Siphnos, Tanagra, Tegea, Thasos, Thebai, Thespiai, Tritaia, Zakynthos. Thus 50 percent of the cities for which there is regime-type information experienced an oligarchy.

Twenty-two different regions contained at least one city governed by an oligarchy: Troas, Achaia, Saronic Gulf, Boiotia, the Aegean, Syria to the Pillars of Herakles, Makedonia, Propontic Thrace, Ionia, Elis, the Adriatic, Euboia, Megaris-Korinthia-Sikyonia, Akarnania, Aiolis and Southwestern Mysia, Thessalia, Italia and Kampania, Arkadia, Spain and France, Lesbos, Argolis, Rhodos. Thus 56 percent of the regions contained at least one city that was governed by an oligarchy.

TYRANNY

Thirty-seven cities are known to have experienced tyranny: Abydos, Agyrion, Apollonia, Assos, Atarneus, Engyon, Eretria, Gambrion, Gryneion/Gryneia, Halikarnassos, Halisarna, Herakleia (Pontica), Histiaia/Oreos, Katane, Kentoripa, Kindye, Klazomenai, Korinthos, Lampsakos, Lokroi, Methymna, Miletos, Mylasa, Myrina, Mytilene, Oianthea, Pagasai, Palaigambrion, Paros, Pergamon, Pherai, Sigeion, Sikyon, Syrakousai, Tauromenion, Teuthrania, Zankle/Messana. Thus 32 percent of the cites for which there is regime-type information experienced a tyranny.

Fourteen different regions contained at least one city governed by a tyranny: Troas, Sikelia, Aiolis and Southwestern Mysia, Euboia, Karia, Black Sea Area, Ionia, Megaris-Korinthia-Sikyonia, Propontic Coast of Asia Minor, Italia and Kampania, Lesbos, West Lokris, Thessalia, the Aegean. Thus 36 percent of the regions contained at least one city governed by a tyranny.

KINGSHIP

Eleven cities are known to have been governed by a king: Aiane, Amathous, Idalion, Kourion, Lapethos, Marion, Pantikapaion/Bosporos, Paphos, Salamis, Soloi, Tyritake. Thus 9 percent of the cities for which there is regime-type information were governed by a king.

Three regions contained at least one city governed by a king: Makedonia, Cyprus, Black Sea Area. Thus 8 percent of the regions contained at least one city governed by a king.

DEMOCRACY

Fifty-four cities are known to have experienced democracy: Aigai, Aigeira, Aigion, Ambrakia, Andros, Amphipolis, Apollonia, Argos, Ascheion, Athenai, Byzantion, Chalkis, Chersonesos, Dyme, Elis, Ephesos, Eretria, Erythrai, Helisson, Heraia, Herakleia (Pontica), Histiaia/Oreos, Kalchedon, Keryneia, Klazomenai, Korinthos, Korkyra, Kos, Kyrene, Leontion, Mantinea, Megale Polis, Megara, Messene/Ithome, Miletos, Mytilene, Olbia/Borysthenes, Olenos, Paros, Patrai, Pellene, Pharai, Phelloe, Phigaleia, Phleious, Rhodos, Rhypes, Siphnos, Taras, Tegea, Thasos, Thebai, Tritaia, Zakynthos. Thus 46 percent of the cities for which we have regime-type information experienced a democracy

Twenty-one different regions contained at least one democratically governed city: Achaia, Akarnania, the Aegean, Thrace (Axios-to-Strymon), the Adriatic, Argolis, Attika, Thrace (Propontic), Euboia, Black Sea area, Elis, Ionia, Arkadia, Propontic Coast of Asia Minor, Megaris-Korinthia-Sikyonia, Syria to the Pillars of Herakles, Messenia, Lesbos, Rhodos, Italia and Kampania, Boiotia. Thus 54 percent of the regions had at least one city that experienced a democracy.

SECOND HALF OF THE FOURTH CENTURY

There is regime-type information for 112 cities: Abydos, Agyrion, Aiane, Aigai, Aigeira, Aigion, Amathous, Ambrakia, Amphipolis, Antissa, Aphytis, Apollonia, Argos, Ascheion, Assos, Atarneus, Athenai, Barke, Beroia, Byzantion, Chalkis, Chersonesos, Chios, Delphoi, Dyme, Elis, Engyon, Ephesos, Epidamnos/Dyrrhachion, Epidauros, Eresos, Eretria, Erythrai, Euhesperides, Gergis, Halikarnassos, Herakleia (Pontica), Histiaia/Oreos, Iasos, Idalion, Ilion, Kalchedon, Kardia, Katane, Kentoripa, Keryneia, Kindye, Kios, Klazomenai, Knidos, Kolophon, Korinthos, Korkyra, Kos, Kourion, Krannon, Kyme (in Aiolis), Kyrene, Kyzikos, Lampsakos, Lapethos, Larisa, Leontion, Lokroi, Magnesia, Marion, Massalia, Megara, Messene/Ithome, Methymna, Miletos, Mylasa, Myrleia, Mytilene, Nasos, Neapolis (in Italia), Olbia/Borysthenes, Olenos, Pantikapaion/Bosporos, Paphos, Paros, Patrai, Pellene, Phanagoria, Pharai, Pharsalos, Phelloe, Pherai, Phillippoi, Phleious, Priene, Rhodos, Rhypes, Salamis, Samos, Sigeion, Sikyon, Sinope, Siphnos, Soloi, Sparta, Syrakousai, Taras, Taourmenion, Thebai, Theodosia, Thourioi, Tritaia, Tyritake, Zakynthos, Zankle/Messana, Zeleia.

There is regime-type information for thirty-two (out of thirty-nine) different regions: Troas, Sikelia, Makedonia, Achaia, Cyprus, Akarnania, Thrace (Axios to Strymon), Lesbos, the Adriatic, Argolis, Aiolis and Southwestern Mysia, Attika, Syria to the Pillars of Herakles, Propontic Thrace, Euboia, Black Sea Area, Ionia, Phokis, Elis, Karia, Propontic Coast of Asia Minor, Thracian Chersonesos, Megaris-Korinthia-Sikyonia, the Aegean, Thessalia, Italia and Kampania, Spain and France, Messenia, Thrace (Strymon to Nestos), Rhodos, South Coast of Asia Minor, Lakedaimon.

OLIGARCHY

Forty-one different cities are known to have experienced oligarchy: Aigai, Aigeira, Aigion, Ambrakia, Ascheion, Barke, Beroia, Chios, Delphoi, Dyme, Elis, Ephesos, Epidamnos/Dyrrhachion, Erythrai, Euhesperides, Keryneia, Knidos, Kolophon, Korinthos, Korkyra, Kos, Kyme (in Aiolis), Larisa, Leontion, Lokroi, Massalia, Mytilene, Olenos, Patrai, Pellene, Pharai, Pharsalos, Phelloe, Phleious, Rhodos, Rhypes, Samos, Sikyon, Syrakousai, Tritaia, Zakynthos. Thus 37 percent of the cities for which there is regime-type information experienced an oligarchy.

Nineteen different regions contained at least one city governed by an oligarchy: Achaia, Akarnania, Syria to the Pillars of Herakles, Makedonia, Ionia, Phokis, Elis, the Adriatic, Karia, Megaris-Korinthia-Sikyonia, the Aegean, Aiolis and Southwestern Mysia, Thessalia, Italia and Kampania, Spain and France, Lesbos, Argolis, Rhodos, Sikelia. Thus 49 percent of the regions contained at least one city that was governed by an oligarchy.

TYRANNY

Thirty-two cities are known to have experienced tyranny: Abydos, Agyrion, Antissa, Apollonia, Assos, Atarneus, Engyon, Eresos, Eretria, Halikarnassos, Herakleia (Pontica), Histiaia/Oreos, Kardia, Katane, Kentoripa, Kindye, Kios, Klazomenai, Krannon, Lampsakos, Lokroi, Methymna, Miletos, Mylasa, Myrleia, Mytilene, Pellene, Pherai, Sigeion, Syrakousai, Tauromenion, Zankle/Messana. Thus 29 percent of the cites for which there is regime-type information experienced a tyranny.

Thirteen different regions contained at least one city governed by a tyranny: Troas, Sikelia, Lesbos, Aiolis and Southwestern Mysia, Karia, Black Sea Area, Euboia, Thracian Chersonesos, Propontic Coast of Asia Minor, Ionia, Thessalia, Italia and Kampania, Achaia. Thus 33 percent of the regions contained at least one city governed by a tyranny.

KINGSHIP

Thirteen cities are known to have been governed by a king: Aiane, Amathous, Idalion, Kourion, Lapethos, Marion, Pantikapaion/Bosporos, Paphos, Phanagoria, Salamis, Soloi, Theodosia, Tyritake. Thus 12 percent of the cities for which there is regime-type information were governed by a king.

Three regions contained at least one city governed by a king: Makedonia, Cyprus, Black Sea Area. Thus 8 percent of the regions contained at least one city governed by a king.

DEMOCRACY

Fifty-two cities are known to have experienced democracy: Ambrakia, Amphipolis, Antissa, Aphytis, Apollonia, Argos, Athenai, Byzantion, Chalkis, Chersonesos, Chios, Ephesos, Epidauros, Eresos, Eretria, Erythrai, Histiaia/Oreos, Iasos, Ilion, Kalchedon, Kios, Klazomenai, Knidos, Kolophon, Kos, Kyme, Kyrene, Kyzikos, Lampsakos, Lokroi, Magnesia, Megara, Messene/Ithome, Methymna, Miletos, Mylasa, Mytilene, Nasos, Neapolis (in Italia), Olbia/Borysthenes, Paros, Pellene, Priene, Rhodos, Sinope, Siphnos, Soloi, Syrakousai, Taras, Thebai, Thourioi, Zeleia. Thus 46 percent of the cities for which we have regime-type information experienced a democracy.

Twenty-four different regions contained at least one democratically governed city: Akarnania, Thrace (Axios-to-Strymon), Lesbos, the Adriatic, Argolis, Attika, Propontic Thrace, Euboia, the Black Sea Area, Ionia, Karia, Troas, the Propontic Coast of Asia Minor, the Aegean, Aiolis and Southwestern Mysia, Syria to the Pillars of Herakles, Italia and Kampania, Megaris-Korinthia-Sikyonia, Messenia, Achaia, Rhodos, South Coast of Asia Minor, Sikelia, Boiotia. Thus 62 percent of the regions had at least one city that experienced democracy.

Bibliography

Allen, Danielle S. 2000. *The World of Prometheus: Politics of Punishing in Democratic Athens*. Princeton, N.J.: Princeton University Press.

Arnaoutoglou, Ilias. 1998. *Ancient Greek Laws: A Sourcebook*. New York: Routledge.

Aslan, Carolyn Chabot. 2009. "New Evidence for a Destruction at Troia in the Mid 7th Century B.C." *Studia Troica* 18: 33–58.

Atkinson, K.M.T. 1968. "The Seleucids and Greek Cities of Western Asia Minor." *Antichthon* 2: 32–57.

Austin, J. L. [1962] 1975. *How to Do Things with Words*. Cambridge, Mass.: Harvard University Press.

Austin, M. M. (Ed.). 1981. *The Hellenistic World from Alexander to the Roman Conquest*. Cambridge: Cambridge University Press.

Aylward, William. 1999. "Studies in Hellenistic Ilion: The Houses in the Lower City." *Studia Troica* 9: 159–86.

———. 2005. "The Portico and Propylaia of the Sanctuary of Athena Ilias at Ilion." *Studia Troica* 15: 127–75.

Aylward, William, and John Wallrodt. 2003. "The Other Walls of Troia: A Revised Trace for Ilion's Hellenistic Fortification." *Studia Troica* 13: 89–112.

Badian, E. 1966. "Alexander the Great and the Greeks of Asia." Pp. 37–69 in *Ancient Society and Institutions: Studies Presented to Victor Ehrenberg*. Oxford: Basil Blackwell.

Bagnall, Roger S., and Peter Derow (Eds.). 2004. *The Hellenistic Period*. Oxford: Blackwell.

Bakewell, Geoffrey W., and James P. Sickinger (Eds.). 2002. *Gestures: Essays in Ancient History, Literature, and Philosophy Presented to Alan L. Boegehold*. Oxford: Oxbow Books.

Bates, Robert H., Avner Greif, Margaret Levi, Jean-Laurent Rosenthal, and Barry R. Weingast. 1998. *Analytic Narratives*. Princeton, N.J.: Princeton University Press.

Beazley, J. D. 1963. *Attic Red-Figure Vase-Painters*. 2nd ed. Oxford: Clarendon.

Beazley, L. D. [1951] 1986. *The Development of Attic Black-Figure*. Berkeley: University of California Press.

Bengtson, H. and H. H. Schmitt. 1962–69. *Die Staatsverträge des Altertums*. 2 vols. Munich: C. H. Beck.

Berlin, Andrea M. 2002. "Ilion Before Alexander: A Fourth-Century B.C. Ritual Deposit." *Studia Troica* 12: 131–65.

Berve, Helmut. 1967. *Die Tyrannis bei den Griechen*. 2 vols. Munich: C. H. Beck.

Bikhchandani, Sushil, David Hirshleifer, and Ivo Welch. 1992. "A Theory of Fads, Fashion, Custom, and Cultural Change as Informational Cascades." *Journal of Political Economy* 100: 992–1026.

Billows, R. A. 1990. *Antigonos the One-Eyed and the Creation of the Hellenistic State*. Berkeley: University of California Press.

———. 2005. "Cities." Pp. 196–215 in *A Companion to the Hellenistic World*, edited by Andrew Erskine. Malden, Mass.: Blackwell.

Blanshard, A.J.L. 2004. "Depicting Democracy." *Journal of Hellenic Studies* 124: 1–15.

Boeckh, A. [1828–77]. 1977. *Corpus Inscriptionum Graecarum*. 4 vols. Berlin, repr., Hildesheim: Subsidia Epigraphica.

Bolmarcich, S. 2007. "Oaths in Greek International Relations." Pp. 26–38 in *Horkos: The Oath in Greek Society*, edited by A. H. Sommerstein and J. Fletcher. Bristol, U.K.: Bristol Phoenix Press.

Bosworth, A. B. 1980–95. *A Historical Commentary on Arrian's History of Alexander*. 2 vols. Oxford: Clarendon.

———. 1988. *Conquest and Empire: The Reign of Alexander the Great*. Cambridge: Cambridge University Press.

Brock, Roger. 2009. "Did the Athenian Empire Promote Democracy?" Pp. 149–66 in *Interpreting the Athenian Empire*, edited by John Ma, Nikolaos Papazarkadas, and Robert Parker. London: Duckworth.

Bruce, I.A.F. 1967. *An Historical Commentary on the Hellenica Oxyrhynchia*. Cambridge: Cambridge University Press.

Brueckner, A. 1894. "Ein Gesetz der Ilienser gegen Tyrannis und Oligarchie." *Sitzungsberichte der Königlich Preussischen Akademie der Wissenschaften zu Berlin*: 461–78.

Brunnsåker, Sture. 1971. *The Tyrant-slayers of Kritios and Nesiotes*. Stockholm: Svenska Institutet i Athen.

Brunt, P. A. 1969. "Euboea in the Time of Philip II." *Classical Quarterly* 19: 245–65.

Buck, Robert J. 1998. *Thrasybulus and the Athenian Democracy: The Life of an Athenian Statesman*. Stuttgart: F. Steiner Verlag.

Burstein, S. M. 1976. *Outpost of Hellenism: The Emergence of Heraclea on the Black Sea*. Berkeley: University of California, Classical Studies 14.

——— (Ed.). 1985. *The Hellenistic Age from the Battle of Ipsos to the Death of Kleopatra VII*. Cambridge: Cambridge University Press.

Camp, John M. 2001. *The Archaeology of Athens*. New Haven: Yale University Press.

Caravan, Edwin. 2002. "The Athenian Amnesty and the 'Scrutiny of the Laws.'" *Journal of Hellenic Studies* 122: 1–23.

Cargill, Jack. 1981. *The Second Athenian League: Empire or Free Alliance?* Berkeley: University of California Press.

Carlsson, Susanne. 2010. *Hellenistic Democracies: Freedom, Independence and Political Procedure in Some East Greek States*. Stuttgart: F. Steiner Verlag.

Carter, J. M. 1971. "Athens, Euboea, and Olynthus." *Historia* 20: 418–29.

Cartledge, Paul, and Antony Spawforth. 2002. *Hellenistic and Roman Sparta: A Tale of Two Cities*. 2nd ed. London: Routledge.

Cataldi, Silvio (Ed.). 2004. *Poleis e politeiai: esperienze politiche, tradizioni letterarie, progetti costituzionali: atti del convegno internazionale di storia greca, Torino, 29–31, Maggio 2002*. Alessandria: Edizioni dell'Orso.

Cawkwell, George L. 1961. "A Note on Ps. Demosthenes 17.20." *Phoenix* 15: 74–78.

———. 1962. "The Defence of Olynthus." *Classical Quarterly* 12: 122–40.

———. 1978a. "Euboea in the Late 340's." *Phoenix* 32: 42–67.

———. 1978b. *Philip of Macedon*. London: Faber and Faber.

Chwe, Michael Suk-Young. 2001. *Rational Ritual: Culture, Coordination, and Common Knowledge*. Princeton, N.J.: Princeton University Press.

Cole, Susan G. 1996. "Oath Ritual and Male Community at Athens." Pp. 227–48 in *Dēmokratia: A Conversation on Democracies, Ancient and Modern*, edited by Josiah Ober and Charles W. Hedrick. Princeton, N.J.: Princeton University Press.

Connor, Robert W. 1989. "City Dionysia and Athenian Democracy." *Classica et Mediaevalia* 40: 7–32.

Cook, J. M. 1973. *The Troad: An Archaeological and Topographical Study*. Oxford: Clarendon.

Crampa, J. 1969–72. *Greek Inscriptions*. In *Labraunda: Swedish Excavations and Researches*. 2 vols. Lund: Gleerup.

Dareste, R., B. Haussoullier, and T. Reinach. [1894–1904] 1965. *Recueil des inscriptions juridiques grecques: Texte, traduction, commentaire*. 2 vols. Paris, repr., Rome: Studia juridica 6.

Detienne, Marcel. 1996. *The Masters of Truth in Archaic Greece*. New York: Zone Books.

Diels, H., and W. Kranz. 1951–52. *Die Fragmente der Vorsokratiker*. 3 vols., 6th ed. Berlin: Weidmann.

Dittenberger, W. [1903–5] 2001. *Orientis Graeci Inscriptiones Selectae*. 2 vols. Leipzig, repr., Chicago: Ares.

———. [1915–24] 1999. *Sylloge Inscriptionum Graecarum*. 4 vols., 3rd ed. Leipzig, repr., Chicago: Ares.

Dössel, Astrid. 2003. *Die Beilegung innerstaatlicher Konflikte in den griechischen Poleis vom 5.-3. Jahrhundert v. Chr*. Frankfurt: Peter Lang.

———. 2007. "Einige Bemerkungen zum 'Gesetz gegen Tyrannis und Oligarchie' aus Eretria, 4. Jahrhundert v. Chr." *Zeitschrift für Papyrologie und Epigraphik* 161: 115–24.

Droysen, Joannes. 1873. *De Demophanti Patroclidis Tisameni Populiscitis Quae Inserta Sunt Andocidis Orationi* ΠΕΡΙ ΜΥΣΤΕΡΙΩΝ. Berlin.

Dunbar, Nan. 1995. *Aristophanes*, Birds: *Edited with Introduction and Commentary*. Oxford: Clarendon.

Ellis, J. R. 1976. *Philip II and Macedonian Imperialism*. London: Thames and Hudson.

Ellis-Evans, Aneurin. 2012. "The Tyrants Dossier from Eresos." *Chiron* 42: 183–212.

Engelmann, Helmut, and Reinhold Merkelbach. 1972–73. *Die Inschriften von Erythrai und Klazomenai*. 2 vols. Bonn: Habelt.

Flower, Harriet I. 2006. *Disgrace and Oblivion in Roman Political Culture*. Chapel Hill: University of North Carolina Press.

Fornara, C. W. 1970. "The Cult of Harmodius and Aristogeiton." *Philologus* 114: 155–80.

——— (Ed.) 1983. *Archaic Times to the End of the Peloponnesian War*. Cambridge: Cambridge University Press.

Friedel, H. 1937. *Der Tyrannenmord in Gesetzgebung und Volksmeinung der Griechen*. Stuttgart: W. Kohlhammer.

Frisch, Peter. 1975. *Die Inschriften von Ilion*. Bonn: Rudolf Habelt Verlag.

Funck, Bernd. 1994. "Seleukos Nikator und Ilion: Einige Beobachtungen zum Verhältnis von König und Staat im frühen Hellenismus." *Historische Zeitschrift* 258: 317–37.

Gaertringen, F. Hiller von. 1906. *Die Inschriften von Priene*. Berlin: Reimer.

Gagarin, Michael. 1981. "The Thesmothetai and the Earliest Athenian Tyranny Law." *Transactions of the American Philological Association* 111: 71–77.

Gagarin, Michael, and David Cohen (Eds.). 2005. *The Cambridge Companion to Ancient Greek Law*. Cambridge: Cambridge University Press.

Gardner, P. 1913. "Coinage of the Athenian Empire." *Journal of Hellenic Studies* 33: 147–188.

Gauthier, Philippe. 1982. "Notes sur trois décrets honorant des citoyens bienfaiteurs." *Revue de philology, de literature et d'histoire anciennes* 56: 215–31.

———. 1993. "Les cites hellénistiques." Pp. 211–31 in *The Ancient Greek City-State*, edited by Mogens Herman Hansen. Copenhagen: Munksgaard.

———. 2004. "Eubée." Bulletin épigraphique. *Revue des études grecques* 117 (nos. 251–22): 641–44.

Gehrke, Hans-Joachim. 1985. *Stasis: Untersuchungen zu den inneren Kriegen in den griechischen Staaten des 5. und 4. jarhhunderts v. Chr*. Munich: C. H. Beck.

Gladwell, Malcolm. 2000. *The Tipping Point: How Little Things Can Make a Big Difference*. Boston: Little, Brown.

Goldstone, Jack A. 2001. "Toward a Fourth Generation of Revolutionary Theory." *American Review of Political Science* 4: 139–87.

Gomme, A. W., A. Andrewes, and K. J. Dover. 1948–81. *A Historical Commentary on Thucydides*. 5 vols. Oxford: Clarendon.

Grainger, John D. 2010. *The Syrian Wars*. Mnemosyne Supplements 320. Leiden: Brill.

Granovetter, Mark S. 1978. "Threshold Models of Collective Behavior." *American Journal of Sociology* 83: 1420–43.

A Greek-English Lexicon. 1968. Compiled by Henry George Liddell and Robert Scott, revised and augmented by Sir Henry Stuart Jones. 9th ed., with supplement. Oxford: Clarendon.

Grieb, Volker. 2008. *Hellenistische Demokratie: Politische Organisation und Struktur in freien griechischen Poleis nach Alexander dem Grossen*. Stuttgart: F. Steiner Verlag.

Griffith, G. T. 1979. *A History of Macedonia, vol. 2, 550–336 B.C.* In N.G.L. Hammond and G. T. Griffith, *The Macedonian State: Origins, Institutions and History*. Oxford: Clarendon.

Gruen, E. S. 1986. "The Polis in the Hellenistic World." Pp. 339–54 in *Nomodeiktes: Greek Studies in Honor of Martin Ostwald*, edited by R. M. Rosen and J. Farrell. Ann Arbor: University of Michigan Press.

Günzler, Eduard. 1907. "Das Psephisma des Demophantos." *Schulnachrichten des Königlichen Gymnasiums zu Schwäbisch Hall* 1906–7: 3–14.

Habicht, Christian. 1997. *Athens from Alexander to Antony*, translated by Deborah Lucas Schneider. Cambridge, Mass.: Harvard University Press.

Hammond, N.G.L. 1989. *The Macedonian State: Origins, Institutions and History*. Oxford: Clarendon.

Hammond, N.G.L., and G. T. Griffith. 1979. *A History of Macedonia*. Vol. 2. Oxford: Clarendon.

Hansen, Mogens Herman. 1975. *Eisangelia: The Sovereignty of the People's Court in Athens in the Fourth Century B.C. and the Impeachment of Generals and Politicians*. Odense, Denmark: Odense University Press.

———. 1976. *Apagoge, Endeixis and Ephegesis against Kakourgoi, Atimoi and Pheugontes*. Odense, Denmark: Odense University Press.

———. 1985. "Athenian Nomothesia." *Greek, Roman, and Byzantine Studies* 26: 345–71.

———. 1998. *Polis and City-State: An Ancient Concept and Its Modern Equivalent*. Acts of the Copenhagen Polis Centre 5. Copenhagen: Royal Danish Academy of Science and Letters.

———. 1999. *The Athenian Democracy in the Age of Demosthenes: Structure, Principles, and Ideology*. Norman: University of Oklahoma Press.

———. 2006a. *The Shotgun Method: The Demography of the Ancient Greek City-State Culture*. Columbia: University of Missouri Press.

———. 2006b. *Studies in the Population of Aigina, Athens and Eretria*. Copenhagen: Royal Danish Academy.

Hansen, Mogens Herman, and Thomas Heine Nielsen (Eds.). 2004. *An Inventory of Archaic and Classical Poleis*. Oxford: Oxford University Press.

Hansen, Mogens Herman, Nigel Spencer, and Hector Williams. 2004. "Lesbos." Pp. 1018–32 in *An Inventory of Archaic and Classical Poleis*, edited by Mogens Herman Hansen and Thomas Heine Nielsen. Oxford: Oxford University Press.

Harding, Phillip (Ed.). 1985. *From the End of the Peloponnesian War to the Battle of Ipsus*. Cambridge: Cambridge University Press.

Hedrick, Charles W., Jr. 1999. "Democracy and the Athenian Epigraphic Habit." *Hesperia* 68: 387–439.

Heisserer, A. J. 1979. "The Philites Stele." *Hesperia* 48: 281–93.

———. 1980. *Alexander the Great and the Greeks: The Epigraphic Evidence.* Norman: University of Oklahoma Press.

Henderson, Jeffrey. 2003. "Demos, Demagogue, Tyrant in Attic Old Comedy." Pp. 155–80 in *Popular Tyranny: Sovereignty and Its Discontents in Ancient Greece*, edited by Kathryn Morgan. Austin: University of Texas Press.

Herman, Gabriel. 2006. *Morality and Behaviour in Democratic Athens: A Social History (508–322 B.C.).* Cambridge: Cambridge University Press.

Hicks, E. L., and G. F. Hill. 1901. *A Manual of Greek Historical Inscriptions.* Oxford: Clarendon.

Highby, Leo Ingemann. 1936. *The Erythrae Decree: Contributions to the Early History of the Delian League and the Peloponnesian Confederacy.* Klio, Beiheft XXXVI. Leipzig: Dieterich'sche Verlagsbuchhandlung.

Hornblower, Simon. 1991–2008. *A Commentary on Thucydides.* 3 vols. Oxford: Oxford University Press.

Inscriptiones Graecae. 1873–. Berlin: De Gruyter.

Jacoby, F. 1923–58. *Die Fragmente der griechischen Historiker.* 15 vols. Berlin: Weidmann and Brill.

Joyce, Christopher J. 2008. "The Athenian Amnesty and Scrutiny of 403." *Classical Quarterly* 58: 507–18.

Kagan, Donald. 1987. *The Fall of the Athenian Empire.* Ithaca, N.Y.: Cornell University Press.

Kirchhoff, A. 1863. Untitled contribution. *Monatsberichte der Berliner Akademie*, June 25: 265–68.

Knoepfler, Denis. 1972. "Carystos et les Artemisia d'Amarynthos." *Bulletin de Correspondance Hellénique* 96: 283–301.

———. 1995. "Une paix de cent ans et un conflit en permanence: étude sur les relations diplomatiques d'Athèns avec Érétrie et les autres cités de l'Eubée au IVe siècle av. J.-C." Pp. 309–64 in *Les Relations Internationales: Actes de colloque de Strasbourg 15–17 juin 1993*, edited by Ed. Frézouls and A. Jacquemin. Paris: De Boccard.

———. 1997. "Le territoirie d'Érétrie et l'organisation politique de la cité." Pp. 352–449 in *The Polis as an Urban Centre and as a Political Community*, Acts of the Copenhagen Polis Centre, vol. 4, edited by Mogens Herman Hansen. Copenhagen: Royal Danish Academy of Sciences and Letters.

———. 2001a. *Décrets érétriens de proxénie et de citoyenneté, in Eretria: Fouilles et recherches XI.* Lausanne: Nadir.

———. 2001b. "Loi d'Eretrie contre la tyrannie et l'oligarchie (première partie)." *Bulletin de Correspondance Hellénique* 125: 195–238.

———. 2002. "Loi d'Eretrie contre la tyrannie et l'oligarchie (seconde partie)." *Bulletin de Correspondance Hellénique* 126: 149–204.

———. 2004. "'Pauvres et malheureux Érétriens': Démosthène et la nouvelle loi d'Érétrie contre la tyrannie." Pp. 403–19 in *Poleis e politeiai: Esperienze politiche, tradizioni letterarie, progetti costituzionali*, edited by Silvio Cataldi. Alessandria: Edizioni dell'Orso.

Koch, Christian. 1996. "Die Wiederherstellung der Demokratie in Ilion." *Zeitschrift der Savigny-Stiftung für Rechtsgeschichte* 113: 32–63.

Kourouniotes, K., and H. A. Thompson. 1932. "The Pnyx in Athens." *Hesperia* 1: 90–217.

Krentz, Peter. 1982. *The Thirty at Athens.* Ithaca, N.Y.: Cornell University Press.

Kuran, Timur. 1989. "Sparks and Prairie Fires: A Theory of Unanticipated Political Revolution." *Public Choice* 61: 41–74.

————. 1991. "Now Out of Never: The Element of Surprise in the East European Revolution of 1989." *World Politics* 44: 7–48.

Kuran, Timur, and C. R. Sunstein. 1999. "Availability Cascades and Risk Regulation." *Stanford Law Review* 51: 683–768.

Lanni, Adriaan, and Adrian Vermeule. 2013. "Precautionary Constitutionalism in Ancient Athens." *Cardozo Law Review* 34: 893–915.

Latyšev, B. [1885–1901] 1965. *Inscriptiones Antiquae Orae Septentrionalis Ponti Euxini Graecae et Latinae.* 3 vols. St. Petersburg, repr., Hildesheim: Olms.

Lawall, Mark L. 1999. "Studies in Hellenistic Ilion: Transport Amphoras from the Lower City." *Studia Troica* 9: 187–224.

————. 2002. "Ilion Before Alexander: Amphoras and Economic Archaeology." *Studia Troica* 12: 197–244.

Lawton, Carol L. 1995. *Attic Document Reliefs: Art and Politics in Ancient Athens.* Oxford: Clarendon Press.

Lebedev, A. 1996. "A New Epigram for Harmodios and Aristogeiton." *Zeitschrift für Papyrologie und Epigraphik* 112: 263–68.

Lintott, A. W. 1982. *Violence, Civil Strife, and Revolution in the Classical City, 750–330 B.C.* London: Croom Helm.

Loening, Thomas Clark. 1987. *The Reconciliation Agreement of 403/402 B.C. in Athens: Its Content and Application.* Stuttgart: F. Steiner Verlag.

Lohmann, Susanne. 1994. "The Dynamics of Informational Cascades: The Monday Demonstrations in Leipzig, East Germany, 1989–91." *World Politics* 47: 42–101.

Loraux, Nicole. 2002. *The Divided City: On Memory and Forgetting in Ancient Athens,* translated by Corinne Pache. New York: Zone Books.

Lott, J. Bert. 1996. "Philip II, Alexander, and the Two Tyrannies of Eresos of IG XII. 2.526." *Phoenix* 50: 26–40.

Lund, H. S. 1992. *Lysimachus: A Study in Early Hellenistic Kingship.* London: Routledge.

Ma, John. 2000. *Antiochos III and the Cities of Western Asia Minor.* Oxford: Oxford University Press. (Paperback ed., 2002, contains an extra chapter and addenda.)

————. 2003. "Peer Polity Interaction in the Hellenistic Age." *Past & Present* 180: 9–39.

Ma, John, Nikolaos Papazarkadas, and Robert Parker (Eds.). 2009. *Interpreting the Athenian Empire.* London: Duckworth.

MacDowell, Douglas M. 1962. *Andokides on the Mysteries.* Oxford: Clarendon.

————. 1975. "Law-Making at Athens in the Fourth Century B.C." *Journal of Hellenic Studies* 95: 62–74.

Maffi, Alberto. 2005. "De la loi de Solon à la loi d'Ilion ou comment défendre la démocratie." Pp. 137–61 in *La violence dans les monds grec et romain: Actes du colloque international* (Paris, 2–4 mai 2002). Paris: Sorbonne.

Magie, David. 1950. *Roman Rule in Asia Minor to the End of the Third Century after Christ.* 2 vols. Princeton, N.J.: Princeton University Press.

Manning, Joseph Gilbert, and Ian Morris (Eds.). 2005. *The Ancient Economy: Evidence and Models.* Stanford, Calif.: Stanford University Press.

Marsden, E. W. 1969. *Greek and Roman Artillery: Historical Development.* Oxford: Clarendon.

Mattingly, Harold B. 1996. *The Athenian Empire Restored: Epigraphic and Historical Studies.* Ann Arbor: University of Michigan Press.

McCabe, D. F., and J. V. Brownson. 1986. *Erythrai Inscriptions: Texts and Lists.* Princeton, N.J.: Institute for Advanced Study.

McGlew, James F. 1993. *Tyranny and Political Culture in Ancient Greece.* Ithaca, N.Y.: Cornell University Press.

McShane, Roger B. 1964. *The Foreign Policy of the Attalids of Pergamum*. Urbana: University of Illinois Press.

Meiggs, Russell. 1972. *The Athenian Empire*. Oxford: Oxford University Press.

Meiggs, Russell, and David M. Lewis. 1988. *A Selection of Greek Historical Inscriptions to the End of the Fifth Century B.C.* Oxford: Clarendon.

Meritt, B. D. 1952. "Athenian Inscriptions." *Hesperia* 21: 340–80.

Meritt, B. D., H. T. Wade-Gery, and M. F. McGregor. 1939–53. *Documents on the Athenian Tribute Lists*. 4 vols. Cambridge, Mass.: Harvard University Press.

Meyer, E. 1925. Die Grenzen der hellenistischen Staaten in Kleinasien. Zurich: O. Füssli.

Michel, C. 1900. *Recueil d'inscriptions grecques*. Brussels: Lamertin.

Morgan, Kathryn A. (Ed.). 2003. *Popular Tyranny: Sovereignty and Its Discontents in Ancient Greece*. Austin: University of Texas Press.

Mørkholm, O. 1969. "Some Seleucid Coins of the Mint of Sardes." *Nordisk Numismatisk Arsskrift* 1969: 5–20.

——. 1991. *Early Hellenistic Coinage from the Accession of Alexander to the Peace of Apamea (336–188 B.C.)*. Cambridge: Cambridge University Press.

Morris, Ian. 2005. "The Athenian Empire (478–404 B.C.)." Princeton/Stanford Working Papers in Classics 120508.

Mossé, Claude. 1970. "A propos de la loi d'Eukrates sur la tyrannie." *Eirene* 8: 71–78.

——. 1973. *Athens in Decline, 404–86 B.C.*, translated by J. Stewart. London: Routledge and Kegan Paul.

Munn, Mark Henderson. 2000. *The School of History: Athens in the Age of Socrates*. Berkeley: University of California Press.

Murray, Oswyn, and Simon Price (Eds.). 1991. *The Greek City: From Homer to Alexander*. Oxford: Clarendon.

Neer, Richard T. 2002. *Style and Politics in Athenian Vase-Painting: The Craft of Democracy, ca. 530–460 B.C.E.* Cambridge: Cambridge University Press.

Ober, Josiah. 1989. *Mass and Elite in Democratic Athens: Rhetoric, Ideology, and the Power of the People*. Princeton, N.J.: Princeton University Press.

——. 1996. *The Athenian Revolution: Essays on Ancient Greek Democracy and Political Theory*. Princeton, N.J.: Princeton University Press.

——. 1998. *Political Dissent in Democratic Athens: Intellectual Critics of Popular Rule*. Princeton, N.J.: Princeton University Press.

——. 2005a. *Athenian Legacies: Essays in the Politics of Going on Together*. Princeton, N.J.: Princeton University Press.

——. 2005b. "Historical Legacies: Moral Authority and the Useable Past." Pp. 43–68 in *Athenian Legacies: Essays in the Politics of Going on Together*. Princeton, N.J.: Princeton University Press.

——. 2005c. "Tyrant-Killing as Therapeutic Conflict: A Political Debate in Images and Texts." Pp. 212–47 in *Athenian Legacies: Essays in the Politics of Going on Together*. Princeton, N.J.: Princeton University Press.

——. 2006. "The Original Meaning of Democracy: Capacity to Do Things, Not Majority Rule." Princeton/Stanford Working Papers in Classics 090704

——. 2008. *Democracy and Knowledge: Innovation and Learning in Classical Athens*. Princeton, N.J.: Princeton University Press.

Ober, Josiah, and Charles W. Hedrick (Eds.). 1996. *Dēmokratia: A Conversation on Democracies, Ancient and Modern*. Princeton, N.J.: Princeton University Press.

Ogden, Daniel. 1996. *Greek Bastardy in the Classical and Hellenistic Period*. New York: Oxford University Press.

Olson, Mancur. 1965. *The Logic of Collective Action: Public Goods and the Theory of Groups*. Cambridge, Mass.: Harvard University Press.

Ostwald, Martin. 1955. "The Athenian Legislation Against Tyranny and Subversion." *Transactions of the American Philological Association* 86: 103–28.

———. 1986. *From Popular Sovereignty to the Sovereignty of Law: Law, Society, and Politics in Fifth-Century Athens.* Berkeley: University of California Press.

Özyiğit, Ömer. 2003. "Recent Work at Phokaia in the Light of Akurgal's Excavations." *Anadolu* (Anatolia) 25: 109–27.

Paga, Jessica. 2010. "Deme Theaters in Attica and the Trittys System." *Hesperia* 79: 351–84.

Parke, W. H. 1929. "Athens and Euboea, 349–8 B.C." *Journal of Hellenic Studies* 49: 246–52.

Parker, Robert. 2005. "Τέκνων ὄνησις." *Zeitschrift für Papyrologie und Epigraphik* 152: 152–54.

Picard, Olivier. 1979. *Chalcis et la Confédération Eubéenne: Étude de numismatique et d'histoire (IVe-Ier siècle).* Paris: Boccard.

Piérart, Marcel. 2000. "Argos: Un autre démocratie." Pp. 297–314 in *Polis and Politics: (Festschrift Hansen),* edited by P. Flensted-Jensen, T. H. Nielsen, and L. Rubinstein. Copenhagen: Museum Tusculanum Press.

Pistorius, Hans. 1913. *Beiträge zur Geschichte von Lesbos im vierten Jahrhundert v. Chr.* Bonn: A. Marcus & E. Weber.

Plescia, Joseph. 1970. *The Oath and Perjury in Ancient Greece.* Tallahassee: Florida State University Press.

Podlecki, W. H. 1966. "The Political Significance of the Athenian 'Tyrannicide'-Cult." *Historia* 15: 129–41.

Pouilloux, J. 1960. *Choix d'inscriptions grecques.* Paris: Les Belles Lettres.

Quillen, James. 2002. "Achieving Amnesty: The Role of Events, Institutions, and Ideas." *Transactions of the American Philological Association* 132: 71–107.

Raaflaub, Kurt A. 2003. "Stick and Glue: The Function of Tyranny in Fifth-Century Athenian Democracy." Pp. 59–94 in *Popular Tyranny: Sovereignty and Its Discontents in Ancient Greece,* edited by Kathryn Morgan. Austin: University of Texas Press.

Raubitschek, A. E. 1941. "The Heroes of Phyle." *Hesperia* 10: 284–95.

———. 1962. "Demokratia." *Hesperia* 31: 238–43.

Reber, Karl, Mogens Herman Hansen, and Pierre Ducrey. 2004. "Euboia." Pp. 643–63 in *An Inventory of Archaic and Classical Poleis,* edited by Mogens Herman Hansen and Thomas Heine Nielsen. Oxford: Oxford University Press.

Rhodes, P. J. 1985a. *The Athenian Boule.* Rev. ed. Oxford: Clarendon.

———. 1985b. "*Nomothesia* in Fourth-Century Athens." *Classical Quarterly* 35: 55–60.

———. 1993. *A Commentary on the Aristotelian Athenaion Politeia.* Rev. ed. Oxford: Clarendon.

———. 2007. "Oaths in Political Life." Pp. 11–25 in *Horkos: The Oath in Greek Society,* edited by Alan H. Sommerstein and J. Fletcher. Bristol, U.K.: Bristol Phoenix Press.

———. 2008. "After the Three-Bar *Sigma* Controversy: The History of Athenian Imperialism Reassessed." *Classical Quarterly* 58: 501–6.

Rhodes, P. J., and David M. Lewis. 1997. *The Decrees of the Greek States.* Oxford: Clarendon.

Rhodes, P. J., and Robin Osborne. 2003. *Greek Historical Inscriptions: 404–323 B.C.* Oxford: Oxford University Press.

Rigsby, Kent J. 2002. "A Greek Inscription from Troia, 2001." *Studia Troica* 12: 275–77.

———. 2004. "A Greek Inscription from Troia, 2003." *Studia Troica* 14: 117–18.

———. 2007. "A New Greek Inscription from Troia." *Studia Troica* 17: 43–44.

Robert, L. 1944. "Hellenica." *Revue de Philologie, de Littérature et d'Histoire Anciennes* 18: 3–56.

Robinson, Eric W. 1997. *The First Democracies: Early Popular Government Outside Athens.* Stuttgart: F. Steiner.

———. 2000. "Democracy in Syracuse, 466–412 B.C." *Harvard Studies in Classical Philology* 100: 189–205.

———. 2011. *Democracy Beyond Athens: Popular Government in the Greek Classical Age.* Cambridge: Cambridge University Press.

Roebuck, Carl. 1948. "The Settlements of Philip II with the Greek States in 338 B.C." *Classical Philology* 43: 73–92.

Rose, Charles Brian. 1992. "Post-Bronze Age Excavations 1991." *Studia Troica* 2: 43–60.

———. 1999. "The 1998 Post-Bronze Age Excavations at Troia." *Studia Troica* 9: 35–71.

———. 2003. "The Temple of Athena at Ilion." *Studia Troica* 13: 27–88.

Rosivach, Vincent J. 1994. *The System of Public Sacrifice in Fourth-Century Athens.* Atlanta: Scholars Press.

Rossetto, P. C., and G. P. Sartorio. 1994. *Teatri greci e romani: alle origini del linguaggio rappresentato.* Rome: Edizione SEAT.

Rubinstein, Lene. 2004. "Ionia." Pp. 1053–1107 in *An Inventory of Archaic and Classical Poleis*, edited by Mogens Herman Hansen and Thomas Heine Nielsen. Oxford: Oxford University Press.

Ruschenbusch, E. 1985. "Die Zahl der griechischen Staaten und Arealgrösse und Bürgerzahl der Normalpolis." *Zeitschrift für Papyrologie und Epigraphik* 59: 253–63.

Rutter, N. K. 2000. "Syracusan Democracy: 'Most Like the Athenian.'" Pp. 137–51 in *Alternatives to Athens: Varieties of Political Organization and Community in Ancient Greece*, edited by Roger Brock and Stephen Hodkinson. Oxford: Oxford University Press.

Ryder, T.T.B. 1965. *Koine Eirene: General Peace and Local Independence in Ancient Greece.* London: Oxford University Press.

Schanck, Richard. 1932. *A Study of a Community and Its Groups and Institutions Conceived of as Behavior of Individuals.* Psychological Monographs 43.2. Princeton, N.J.: The Psychological Review Company.

Schwartzberg, Melissa. 2013. "Was the *Graphe Paranomon* a Form of Judicial Review?" *Cardozo Law Review* 34: 1049–62.

Schwenk, Cynthia J. 1985. *Athens in the Age of Alexander: The Dated Laws and Decrees of "the Lykourgan Era" 338–322 B.C.* Chicago: Ares.

Sealey, Raphael. 1958. "On Penalizing Areopagites." *American Journal of Philology* 79: 71–73.

———. 1993. *Demosthenes and His Time: A Study in Defeat.* Oxford: Oxford University Press.

Segre, M. 1952. *Tituli Calymnii.* Bergamo: Instituto italiano d'arti grafiche.

Sevinç, Nurten, Reyhan Körpe, Musa Tombul, Charles Brian Rose, Donna Strahan, Henrike Kiesewetter, and John Wallrodt. 2001. "A New Painted Graeco-Persian Sarcophagus from Çan." *Studia Troica* 11: 383–420.

Shear, Julia L. 2007. "The Oath of Demophantos and the Politics of Athenian Identity." Pp. 148–60 in *Horkos: The Oath in Greek Society*, edited by A. H. Sommerstein and J. Fletcher. Bristol, U.K.: Bristol Phoenix Press.

———. 2011. *Polis and Revolution: Responding to Oligarchy in Classical Athens.* Cambridge: Cambridge University Press.

Shear, T. L., Jr. 1978. *Kallias of Sphettos and the Revolt of Athens in 286 B.C.* Hesperia Supplement XVII. Princeton, N.J.: American School of Classical Studies at Athens.

Shefton, B. B. 1960. "Some Iconographic Remarks on the Tyrannicides." *American Journal of Archaeology* 64: 173–79.

Sherwin-White, S. M. 1985. "Ancient Archives: The Edict of Alexander at Priene, a Reappraisal." *Journal of Hellenic Studies* 105: 69–89.

Simmons, Beth A., and Zachary Elkins. 2004. "The Globalization of Liberalization: Policy Diffusion in the International Political Economy." *American Political Science Review* 98: 171–89.

Smyth, H. W. [1920] 1956. *Greek Grammar*. Cambridge, Mass.: Harvard University Press.

Snodgrass, Anthony. 1980. *Archaic Greece: The Age of Experiment*. Berkeley: University of California Press.

Sommerstein, Alan H., and Judith Fletcher (Eds.). 2007. *Horkos: The Oath in Greek Society*. Bristol, U.K.: Bristol Phoenix Press.

Strauss, Barry S. 1986. *Athens after the Peloponnesian War: Class, Faction and Policy 403–386 B.C.* London: Croom Helm.

Stroud, R. S. 1971. "Greek Inscription: Theozotides and the Athenian Orphans." *Hesperia* 40: 280–301.

Taylor, M. C. 2002a. "Implicating the Demos: A Reading of Thucydides on the Rise of the Four Hundred." *Journal of Hellenic Studies* 122: 91–108.

———. 2002b. "One Hundred Heroes of Phyle?" *Hesperia* 71: 377–97.

Taylor, Michael W. 1981. *The Tyrant Slayers: The Heroic Image in Fifth Century B.C. Athenian Art and Politics*. Salem, N.H.: Ayers.

Teegarden, David A. 2012. "The Oath of Demophantos, Revolutionary Mobilization, and the Preservation of the Athenian Democracy." *Hesperia* 81: 433–65.

———. 2013. "Tyrant-Killing Legislation and the Political Foundation of Ancient Greek Democracy." *Cardozo Law Review* 34: 965–82.

Thompson, Margaret. 1968. "The Mints of Lysimmachus." Pp. 163–82 in *Essays in Greek Coinage Presented to Stanley Robinson*, edited by C. M. Kraay and G. K. Jenkins. Oxford: Clarendon.

Tod, M. N. 1933–48. *A Selection of Greek Historical Inscriptions*. 2 vols. Oxford: Clarendon.

Trypanis, C. A. 1960. "A New Collection of Epigrams from Chios." *Hermes* 88: 69–74.

Vischer, Wilhelm. 1857. "Erinnerungen und Eindrücke aus Griechenland." *Neue Jahrbücher für Philologie und Paedagogik* 75: 341–53.

Walbank, F. W. 1957–79. *A Historical Commentary on Polybius*. 3 vols. Oxford: Clarendon.

Wallace, Robert W. 1989. *The Areopagos Council, to 307 B.C.* Baltimore: Johns Hopkins University Press.

Wankel, H., C. Börker, R. Merkelbach, H. Engelmann, D. Knibe, J. Nollé, R. Meriç, and S. Sahin. 1979–84. *Die Inschriften von Ephesos*. 8 vols. Bonn: Habelt.

Weingast, Barry R. 1997. "The Political Foundations of Democracy and the Rule of Law." *American Political Science Review* 91: 245–63.

Welles, C. B. [1934] 1974. *Royal Correspondence in the Hellenistic Period: A Study in Greek Epigraphy*. New Haven, repr., Chicago: Ares.

Whitehead, David. 1986. *The Demes of Attica, 508/7–ca. 250 B.C.: A Political and Social Study*. Princeton, N.J.: Princeton University Press.

———. 1990. *Aineias the Tactician: How to Survive Under Siege*. Oxford: Clarendon.

Wilhelm, Adolf. 1905. "Zwei Denkmäler des eretrischen Dialekts." *Jahresheft des österreichischen archäologischen Instituts in Wien* 8: 6–17.

———. 1915. "Ein Verschleppter Beschluss der Klazomenier?" *Neue Beiträge* 4: 30–38.

Wilson, Peter. 2009. "Tragic Honours and Democracy: Neglected Evidence for the Politics of the Athenian Dionysia." *Classical Quarterly* 59: 8–29.

Wolpert, Andrew. 2002. *Remembering Defeat: Civil War and Civic Memory in Ancient Athens*. Baltimore: Johns Hopkins University Press.

Worthington, Ian. 1992. *A Historical Commentary on Dinarchus: Rhetoric and Conspiracy in Later Fourth-Century Athens*. Ann Arbor: University of Michigan Press.

———. 2008. *Philip II of Macedonia*. New Haven: Yale University Press.

Zagare, Frank C., and D. Marc Kilgour. 2000. *Perfect Deterrence*. Cambridge: Cambridge University Press.

Index

Persians: Asia Minor, Macedonian conquest of, 122–27, 124–25*t*, 140–41, 142, 145n5, 153, 154, 157–58, 163n55, 174, 211, 213; coup of the Four Hundred and, 18–19, 20, 24; Ilion as part of Persian empire, 173. *See also specific Persian rulers*
Petra, 208
Petrakos, V., 61
Phanes, 157, 197n52
Philetaereia, 203n66
Philetairos, 204, 205
Philip II of Macedon: Asia Minor, Macedonian conquest of, 122; assassination of, 90, 122, 124*t*; *dēmos* personified as king on law of Eukrates stele and, 106, 108; invasion of Euboia, 57–58; Korinthian League, founding of, 85n2; Krenidean mining communities (Philippoi) and, 83–84n61; letter to the Euboians, 60n10; threat to Greek democracy posed by, 7, 67, 83–84; typical pro-Macedonian coup instigated by, 68–70; tyrannical threat from Athenian dependency on Macedonian goodwill and, 89–90. *See also* Chaironeia, battle of
Philip III Arrhidaios, 115, 132, 137
Philip V, 168n69, 196n48
Philippoi (Krenidean mining communities), 83–84n61
Philippides, Hypereides' speech against, 53n75, 89–90, 92, 109
Philistides, 57
Philites statue and stele, Erythrai, 6, 142–72; Alexandrian conquest of Asia Minor and, 142, 145n5, 153, 154, 157–58, 163n55; common knowledge generated by, 171–72; dating issues, 7, 153–54; erection of statue, 158; Eretrian tyrant-killing law compared to, 78n52; historical context, 142, 144–47; Ipsos, oligarchic control of city after battle of, 159–61; Kouroupedion, democratic control of city after battle of, 161–63; maintenance and crowning of statue, 144, 145, 146, 151, 152, 161–64; political status quo in Erythrai after reestablishment of democracy, 164–71; pre-Alexandrian scenarios for, 153–57; reasons for oligarchic/democratic manipulation of statue, 147–53; rewards for tyrant-killers and, 73n41, 152; sword, removal and replacement of, 144–46, 150, 152, 159–61; text on stele and translation, 143–44

Philochoros fragment, 59n5
Philopoimen, 8, 219–20n5
Philostratos, 44
Philoxenos, 82n57
Phleious, 59
Phoenicia, 165n60
Phokaia, 157, 167, 168
Phokion, 59, 101, 102
Phokis, 68
Phrygia, 125*t*, 173n2, 205
Phrynichos (archon), 87, 88n8, 89
Phrynichos (Four Hundred member), 17, 25n21, 26–30, 36n43, 37n45, 39–40, 42, 95–96, 105n44, 198n54
Phyle, 15, 16n4, 44
the Piraeus, 16, 25n21, 26–28, 42, 72n39, 87, 88n7, 91, 100, 111, 170n78
Pistorius, Hans, 123n17
Pitane, 125*t*na, 168n70
Plato: *Leges,* 47n63, 152n23; *Respublica,* 108n50, 209n76
Platonic *Seventh Letter,* 48
Pliny the Elder, *Natural History,* 34n35, 140
Ploutarchos, 58n4, 60, 66, 67nn29–30, 79
pluralistic ignorance, 23, 24, 28, 40, 151
Plutarch
  Moralia, 16n3, 210n86
  Vitae decem oratum, 30n29, 105n44
  Vitae Parallelae: Alexander, 140, 158, 174n4; *Aratos,* 8, 44, 153n24, 190n35, 206, 210n86, 211, 219n5; *Demetrios,* 160n48; *Demosthenes,* 89n12, 90, 100n34; *Philopoimen,* 8n20, 220n5; *Phokion,* 58n4, 101, 111n56; *Timoleon,* 8, 128, 219n4
Pnyx, Athens, 20, 27, 92n18, 110
Politics (Aristotle), 3, 8, 10n22, 92n19, 106, 108n48, 164n56, 188
Polyainos, 124*t*
Polybios, 8, 128, 166, 167, 168, 170n80, 171, 205, 205n73, 206, 219–20n5
Pontos, 124*t*
Porthmos, 57, 61n16, 74n46
Prepelaos, 157n37, 160, 201
Priapos, 166n64
Priene, 7, 124*t*, 125*t*ne, 126, 153, 160, 166, 170n77, 210n86, 211, 212
private and public preferences regarding regime in power, 22–24
prize amphoras depicting Harmodios and Aristogeiton, 45, *46*